MADAGASCAR

COUNTRY STUDY GUIDE

International Business Publications, USA
Washington, DC, USA - Myanmar

MADAGASCAR
COUNTRY STUDY GUIDE

Editorial content: International Business Publications, USA
Editor-in-Chief: Dr. Igor S. Oleynik
Editor: Natasha Alexander
Managing Editor: Karl Cherepanya

Published by: International Business Publications, USA
P.O.Box 15343, Washington, DC 20003
Phone: (202) 546-2103, Fax: (202) 546-3275, E-mail: rusric@erols.com

UPDATED ANNUALLY

Databases & Information: Global Investment Center, USA
Cover Design: International Business Publications, USA

We express our sincere appreciation to all government agencies and international organizations which provided information and other materials for this guide

2006 Updated Reprint International Business Publications, USA
ISBN 0-7397-1500-3

This guide provides basic information for starting or/and conducting business in the country. The extraordinary volume of materials covering the topic, prevents us from placing all these materials in this guide. For more detailed information on issues related to any specific investment and business activity in the country, please contact Global Investment Center, USA
Please acquire the list of our business intelligence and marketing reports and other business publications. We constantly update and expand our business intelligence and marketing materials. Please contact the center for the updated list of reports on over 200 countries.

in the USA: **Global Investment Center, USA.**
P.O.Box 15343, Washington, DC 20003
Phone: (202) 546-2103, Fax: (202) 546-3275, E-mail: rusric@erols.com

**For additional analytical, marketing and other information please contact
Global Investment Center, USA**

Printed in the USA

For additional analytical, business and investment opportunities information,
please contact Global Investment & Business Center, USA
at (202) 546-2103. Fax: (202) 546-3275. E-mail: rusric@erols.com

MADAGASCAR

COUNTRY STUDY GUIDE

TABLE OF CONTENTS

**For additional analytical, business and investment opportunities information,
please contact Global Investment & Business Center, USA
at (202) 546-2103. Fax: (202) 546-3275. E-mail: rusric@erols.com**

**For additional analytical, business and investment opportunities information,
please contact Global Investment & Business Center, USA
at (202) 546-2103. Fax: (202) 546-3275. E-mail: rusric@erols.com**

For additional analytical, business and investment opportunities information, please contact Global Investment & Business Center, USA at (202) 546-2103. Fax: (202) 546-3275. E-mail: rusric@erols.com

**For additional analytical, business and investment opportunities information,
please contact Global Investment & Business Center, USA
at (202) 546-2103. Fax: (202) 546-3275. E-mail: rusric@erols.com**

STRATEGIC & DEVELOPMENT PROFILES

STRATEGIC PROFILE

Formerly an independent kingdom, Madagascar became a French colony in 1886, but regained its independence in 1960. During 1992-93, free presidential and National Assembly elections were held, ending 17 years of single-party rule. In 1997, in the second presidential race, Didier RATSIRAKA, the leader during the 1970s and 1980s, was returned to the presidency. The 2001 presidential election was contested between the followers of Didier RATSIRAKA and Marc RAVALOMANANA, nearly causing secession of half of the country. In April 2002, the High Constitutional Court announced RAVALOMANANA the winner.

GEOGRAPHY

Location:	Southern Africa, island in the Indian Ocean, east of Mozambique
Geographic coordinates:	20 00 S, 47 00 E
Map references:	Africa
Area:	total: 587,040 sq km water: 5,500 sq km land: 581,540 sq km
Area - comparative:	slightly less than twice the size of Arizona
Land boundaries:	0 km
Coastline:	4,828 km
Maritime claims:	contiguous zone: 24 NM territorial sea: 12 NM exclusive economic zone: 200 NM continental shelf: 200 NM or 100 NM from the 2,500-m deep isobath
Climate:	tropical along coast, temperate inland, arid in south
Terrain:	narrow coastal plain, high plateau and mountains in center
Elevation extremes:	lowest point: Indian Ocean 0 m highest point: Maromokotro 2,876 m

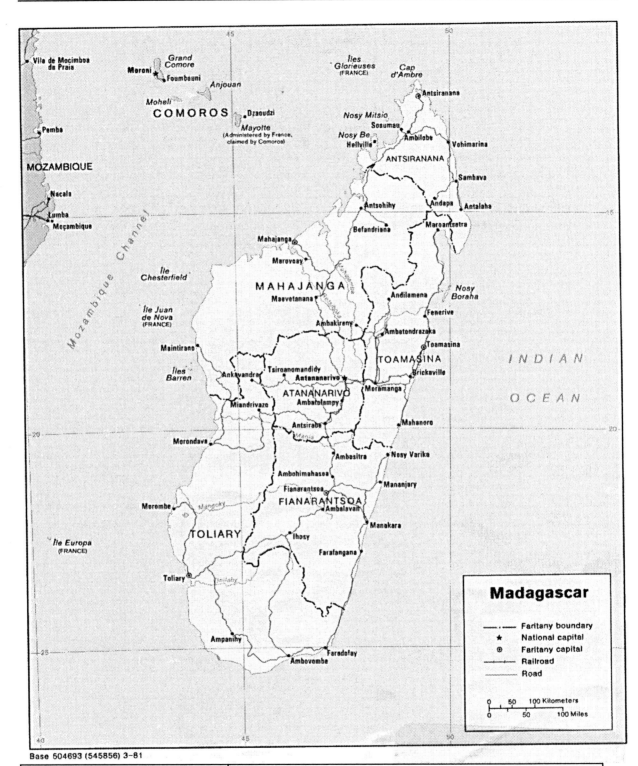

Natural resources:	graphite, chromite, coal, bauxite, salt, quartz, tar sands, semiprecious stones, mica, fish, hydropower

For additional analytical, business and investment opportunities information, please contact Global Investment & Business Center, USA at (202) 546-2103. Fax: (202) 546-3275. E-mail: rusric@erols.com

Land use:	arable land: 4.41% permanent crops: 0.93% other: 94.66%
Irrigated land:	10,900 sq km
Natural hazards:	periodic cyclones
Environment - current issues:	soil erosion results from deforestation and overgrazing; desertification; surface water contaminated with raw sewage and other organic wastes; several species of flora and fauna unique to the island are endangered
Environment - international agreements:	party to: Biodiversity, Climate Change, Desertification, Endangered Species, Hazardous Wastes, Law of the Sea, Marine Life Conservation, Nuclear Test Ban, Ozone Layer Protection, Wetlands signed, but not ratified: none of the selected agreements
Geography - note:	world's fourth-largest island; strategic location along Mozambique Channel

PEOPLE

Population:	16,979,744
Age structure:	0-14 years: 45% (male 3,822,823; female 3,807,958) 15-64 years: 51.9% (male 4,366,748; female 4,452,686) 65 years and over: 3.1% (male 243,411; female 286,118)
Median age:	total: 17.4 years male: 17.2 years female: 17.6 years
Population growth rate:	3.03%
Birth rate:	42.16 births/1,000 population
Death rate:	11.88 deaths/1,000 population
Net migration rate:	0 migrant(s)/1,000 population
Sex ratio:	at birth: 1.03 male(s)/female under 15 years: 1 male(s)/female 15-64 years: 0.98 male(s)/female 65 years and over: 0.85 male(s)/female total population: 0.99 male(s)/female
Infant mortality rate:	total: 80.21 deaths/1,000 live births female: 71.53 deaths/1,000 live births male: 88.63 deaths/1,000 live births
Life expectancy at birth:	total population: 56.14 years

For additional analytical, business and investment opportunities information,
please contact Global Investment & Business Center, USA
at (202) 546-2103. Fax: (202) 546-3275. E-mail: rusric@erols.com

	male: 53.82 years female: 58.53 years
Total fertility rate:	5.73 children born/woman
HIV/AIDS - adult prevalence rate:	0.3%
HIV/AIDS - people living with HIV/AIDS:	22,000
HIV/AIDS - deaths:	870
Nationality:	noun: Malagasy (singular and plural) adjective: Malagasy
Ethnic groups:	Malayo-Indonesian (Merina and related Betsileo), Cotiers (mixed African, Malayo-Indonesian, and Arab ancestry - Betsimisaraka, Tsimihety, Antaisaka, Sakalava), French, Indian, Creole, Comoran
Religions:	indigenous beliefs 52%, Christian 41%, Muslim 7%
Languages:	French (official), Malagasy (official)
Literacy:	definition: age 15 and over can read and write total population: 68.9% male: 75.5% female: 62.5%

GOVERNMENT

Country name:	conventional long form: Republic of Madagascar conventional short form: Madagascar local short form: Madagascar former: Malagasy Republic local long form: Republique de Madagascar
Government type:	republic
Capital:	Antananarivo
Administrative divisions:	6 provinces (faritany); Antananarivo, Antsiranana, Fianarantsoa, Mahajanga, Toamasina, Toliara
Independence:	26 June 1960 (from France)
National holiday:	Independence Day, 26 June (1960)
Constitution:	19 August 1992 by national referendum
Legal system:	based on French civil law system and traditional Malagasy law; has not accepted compulsory ICJ jurisdiction
Suffrage:	18 years of age; universal

Executive branch:	chief of state: President Marc RAVALOMANANA (since 6 May 2002) head of government: Prime Minister Jacques SYLLA (27 May 2002) cabinet: Council of Ministers appointed by the prime minister elections: president elected by popular vote for a five-year term; election last held 16 December 2001 (next to be held NA November 2006); prime minister appointed by the president from a list of candidates nominated by the National Assembly election results: percent of vote - Didier RATSIRAKA (AREMA) 40.89%, Marc RAVALOMANANA 46.21%; note - on 29 April 2002, the High Constitutional Court announced RAVALOMANANA the winner by 51.5% after a recount; RATSIRIKA's prime minister was put under house arrest on 27 May 2002, and SYLLA was appointed the new prime minister by President RAVALOMANANA
Legislative branch:	unicameral National Assembly or Assemblee Nationale (160 seats; members are directly elected by popular vote to serve four-year terms); note - the legislature is scheduled to become a bicameral Parliament with the establishment of a Senate; two-thirds of the seats of this Senate will be filled by regional assemblies whose members will be elected by popular vote; the remaining one-third of the seats will be appointed by the president; the total number of seats will be determined by the National Assembly; all members will serve four-year terms elections: National Assembly - last held 15 December 2002 (next to be held NA 2006) election results: National Assembly - percent of vote by party - NA%; seats by party - TIM 103, FP 22, AREMA 3, LEADER/Fanilo 2, RPSD 5, others 3, independents 22
Judicial branch:	Supreme Court or Cour Supreme; High Constitutional Court or Haute Cour Constitutionnelle
Political parties and leaders:	Association for the Rebirth of Madagascar or AREMA [leader vacant]; Economic Liberalism and Democratic Action for National Recovery or LEADER/Fanilo [Herizo RAZAFIMAHALEO]; I Love Madagascar or TIM [leader NA]; National Union or FP [leader NA]; Renewal of the Social Democratic Party or RPSD [Evariste MARSON]
Political pressure groups and leaders:	Federalist Movement; National Council of Christian Churches or FFKM
International organization participation:	ACCT, ACP, AfDB, ECA, FAO, G-77, IAEA, IBRD, ICAO, ICCt (signatory), ICFTU, ICRM, IDA, IFAD, IFC, IFRCS,

	ILO, IMF, IMO, InOC, Interpol, IOC, IOM, ISO (correspondent), ITU, NAM, OAU, UN, UNCTAD, UNESCO, UNHCR, UNIDO, UPU, WCL, WCO, WFTU, WHO, WIPO, WMO, WToO, WTrO
Diplomatic representation in the US:	chief of mission: Ambassador Narisoa RAJAONARIVONY consulate(s) general: New York FAX: [1] (202) 483-7603 telephone: [1] (202) 265-5525, 5526 chancery: 2374 Massachusetts Avenue NW, Washington, DC 20008
Diplomatic representation from the US:	chief of mission: Ambassador Wanda L. NESBITT embassy: 14-16 Rue Rainitovo, Antsahavola, Antananarivo 101 mailing address: B. P. 620, Antsahavola, Antananarivo telephone: [261] (20) 22-212-57, 22-212-73, 22-209-56 FAX: [261] (20) 22-345-39
Flag description:	two equal horizontal bands of red (top) and green with a vertical white band of the same width on hoist side

ECONOMY

Economy - overview:	Having discarded past socialist economic policies, Madagascar has since the mid 1990s followed a World Bank and IMF led policy of privatization and liberalization, which has placed the country on a slow and steady growth path. Agriculture, including fishing and forestry, is a mainstay of the economy, accounting for one-fourth of GDP and employing four-fifths of the population. Export earnings primarily are earned in the small industrial sector, which features textile manufacturing and agriculture processing. Deforestation and erosion, aggravated by the use of firewood as the primary source of fuel are serious concerns. The separatist political crisis of 2002 undermined macroeconomic stability, with the estimated drop in output being subject to a wide margin of error. Poverty reduction will be the centerpiece of economic policy for the next few years.
GDP:	purchasing power parity - $12.6 billion
GDP - real growth rate:	-11.9%
GDP - per capita:	purchasing power parity - $760
GDP - composition by sector:	agriculture: 25% industry: 12% services: 63%
Population below	71%

poverty line:	
Household income or consumption by percentage share:	lowest 10%: 3% highest 10%: 29%
Distribution of family income - Gini index:	38.1
Inflation rate (consumer prices):	7.4%
Labor force:	7.3 million
Unemployment rate:	5.9%
Budget:	revenues: $553 million expenditures: $735 million, including capital expenditures of $NA
Industries:	meat processing, soap, breweries, tanneries, sugar, textiles, glassware, cement, automobile assembly plant, paper, petroleum, tourism
Industrial production growth rate:	3%
Electricity - production:	830.2 million kWh
Electricity - production by source:	fossil fuel: 36.1% hydro: 63.9% other: 0% nuclear: 0%
Electricity - consumption:	772.1 million kWh
Electricity - exports:	0 kWh
Electricity - imports:	0 kWh
Oil - production:	0 bbl/day
Oil - consumption:	13,000 bbl/day
Oil - proved reserves:	0 bbl
Natural gas - proved reserves:	0 cu m
Agriculture - products:	coffee, vanilla, sugarcane, cloves, cocoa, rice, cassava (tapioca), beans, bananas, peanuts; livestock products
Exports:	$700 million f.o.b.
Exports -	coffee, vanilla, shellfish, sugar; cotton cloth, chromite, petroleum

For additional analytical, business and investment opportunities information,
please contact Global Investment & Business Center, USA
at (202) 546-2103. Fax: (202) 546-3275. E-mail: rusric@erols.com

commodities:	products
Exports - partners:	France 29.9%, US 27.6%, Germany 6.4%, UK 3.5%, Japan 3.0%
Imports:	$985 million f.o.b.
Imports - commodities:	capital goods, petroleum, consumer goods, food
Imports - partners:	France 24.1%, Hong Kong 7.0%, China 6.6%, Singapore 3.5%, Germany 2.9%, Japan
Debt - external:	$4.6 billion
Economic aid - recipient:	$838 million
Currency:	Malagasy franc (MGF)
Currency code:	MGF
Exchange rates:	Malagasy francs per US dollar - 6,831.96 (2002), 6,588.49 (2001), 6,767.48 (2000), 6,283.77 (1999), 5,441.4
Fiscal year:	calendar year

COMMUNICATIONS

Telephones - main lines in use:	55,000
Telephones - mobile cellular:	63,100
Telephone system:	general assessment: system is above average for the region domestic: open-wire lines, coaxial cables, microwave radio relay, and tropospheric scatter links connect regions international: submarine cable to Bahrain; satellite earth stations - 1 Intelsat (Indian Ocean) and 1 Intersputnik (Atlantic Ocean region)
Radio broadcast stations:	AM 2 (plus a number of repeater stations), FM 9, shortwave 6
Television broadcast stations:	1 (plus 36 repeaters)
Internet country code:	.mg
Internet Service Providers (ISPs):	2
Internet users:	35,000

For additional analytical, business and investment opportunities information,
please contact Global Investment & Business Center, USA
at (202) 546-2103. Fax: (202) 546-3275. E-mail: rusric@erols.com

TRANSPORTATION

Railways:	total: 732 km narrow gauge: 732 km 1.000-m gauge
Highways:	total: 49,837 km paved: 5,781 km unpaved: 44,056 km (1996)
Waterways:	of local importance only
Ports and harbors:	Antsiranana, Antsohimbondrona, Mahajanga, Toamasina, Toliara
Merchant marine:	total: 11 ships (1,000 GRT or over) 14,865 GRT/17,936 DWT ships by type: cargo 8, chemical tanker 1, roll on/roll off 2
Airports:	121
Airports - with paved runways:	total: 29 over 3,047 m: 1 2,438 to 3,047 m: 2 1,524 to 2,437 m: 4 914 to 1,523 m: 20 under 914 m: 2
Airports - with unpaved runways:	total: 92 1,524 to 2,437 m: 2 914 to 1,523 m: 46 under 914 m: 44

MILITARY

Military branches:	People's Armed Forces (comprising Intervention Force, Development Force, Aeronaval [Navy and Air] Force), Gendarmerie, Presidential Security Regiment
Military manpower - military age:	20 years of age
Military manpower - availability:	males age 15-49: 3,880,332
Military manpower - fit for military service:	males age 15-49: 2,300,587
Military manpower - reaching military age annually:	males: 163,864
Military expenditures - dollar figure:	$52.3 million (FY02)
Military expenditures - percent of GDP:	1.2%

TRANSNATIONAL ISSUES

Disputes - international:	claims Bassas da India, Europa Island, Glorioso Islands, and Juan de Nova Island (all administered by France)
Illicit drugs:	illicit producer of cannabis (cultivated and wild varieties) used mostly for domestic consumption; transshipment point for heroin

NARCOTICS

Madagascar is not a major producer, supplier or exporter of drugs or precursor chemicals. Cannabis is the main narcotic cultivated in Madagascar and it is produced in the northern and far southern provinces of the island. In 1998 Madagascar established an inter-ministerial commission, the CICLD ("the Commission"), headed by the Prime Minister, to address narcotics control. The Commission's first objective is to develop a national plan to address all aspects of narcotics control. The Commission says the national plan, which it hopes to present to the cabinet in early 2003, will provide both a complete overview of the drug problem in Madagascar and an integrated approach for dealing with it. Narcotics control as an issue may have assumed new relevance as the promised national plan is supposed to link narcotics control to overall development questions.

STATUS OF COUNTRY

Available statistics (which the GOM acknowledges are inadequate) indicate that production, cultivation and trafficking in illicit drugs in Madagascar are chiefly limited to cannabis. Conditions in the northern provinces of Mahajanga and Antsiranana in particular favor rapid, plentiful growth of this crop. Significant cultivation also occurs in the southern provinces of Tulear and Fianarantsoa. A portion of this production may be finding its way to illicit markets on neighboring islands and the African continent, but the majority is intended for domestic consumption. Production, cultivation and traffic of cannabis are directly linked to overall economic conditions in Madagascar. Over 80 percent of the Malagasy people live in rural areas in severe poverty, and cannabis provides rural populations with vital additional income as well as a widely used folk remedy for many ailments.

Greater deployment of military and law enforcement assets in rural areas, and the appearance of roadblocks along all the major arteries of the island during the 2002 political crisis, may have had the unintended positive result of interdicting increased quantities of harvested cannabis in 2002. GOM figures indicate that in 2001, 693 metric tons of cannabis were seized, while in 2002 seizures rose to 1,744 metric tons.

Small seizures of heroin and cocaine at Madagascar's international airport suggest at least some trafficking in these drugs. However, neither of these seizures occurred within the last two years. The draft national plan also mentions that morphine priced at 300,000 Malagasy Francs per dose (about U.S. $55) is sometimes available in a small number of big city nightclubs. Since this sum is more than a month's salary for the average Malagasy, the consumers are assumed to be primarily foreigners. Malagasy law enforcement conducts frequent checks on main highways and at main ports and, in concert with regular army units, is engaged in several interdiction operations in cannabis producing regions. While law enforcement certainly takes the threat of narcotics trafficking seriously, traditional high-profile crimes, such as cattle rustling, continue to absorb a significant share of law enforcement resources.

COUNTRY ACTIONS AGAINST DRUGS IN 2002

On the international level, Madagascar is a party to the 1988 UN Drug Convention, the 1961 Single Convention on Narcotic Drugs and its 1972 Protocol and the 1971 Vienna Convention on Psychotropic Substances. On a regional level, Madagascar has been a party since 1990 to a bilateral agreement with Mauritius aimed at preventing illicit traffic in narcotics. There are also plans for increased bilateral cooperation between Madagascar and the Comoros on this issue. Since 1997, Madagascar has been working on both its legal system and administrative practices to comply fully with international standards embodied in the UN agreements to which it is party. In 1998, the GOM created the "Commission Interministerielle de Coordination de la Lutte Contre la Drogue" or CICLD, which, although officially headed by the Prime Minister, is managed on a day-to-day basis by its own Secretary General, the Malagasy equivalent of a "drug czar". As noted above, the Commission promises an overall counternarcotics strategy linked to Madagascar's overall development strategy for 2003.

The draft national plan reflects important requirements of the 1988 UN Drug Convention by aiming at three distinct results: 1) to reduce the supply of narcotics by disrupting its traffic; 2) to reduce demand for narcotics by implementing programs reflecting traditional Malagasy values and targeting the most vulnerable segments of the Malagasy population; and 3) to streamline gathering and analysis of relevant statistics. However, many aspects of the program remain mere aspirations without concrete, realistic implementation strategies. As an example of the draft plan's questionable realism, an overall program to eradicate cannabis cultivation is scheduled entirely for the first trimester of 2004. There is a component of the plan that calls for an ongoing study into possible medicinal uses of cannabis. It also calls for studies, planned for the second half of 2003, on the links between narcotics trafficking and corruption of public officials and political party financing, but there currently is no plan for funding and carrying out these studies.

U.S. POLICY INITIATIVES AND PROGRAMS

In November 2002, the U.S. Embassy in Madagascar provided funding for DEA training in Mauritius for two field grade level law enforcement officers. The USG is also in the process of transferring to the Malagasy Navy seven motor lifeboats, scheduled for deployment in early 2003. These motorized lifeboats will significantly increase Madagascar's ability to monitor its 5,000 kilometers of coastline and enhance the overall security of its borders.

The Road Ahead. The U.S. will work closely with Madagascar to improve the interdiction capacity of law enforcement personnel.

For additional analytical, business and investment opportunities information, please contact Global Investment & Business Center, USA at (202) 546-2103. Fax: (202) 546-3275. E-mail: rusric@erols.com

IMPORTANT INFORMATION FOR UNDERSTANDING THE COUNTRY

OFFICIAL NAME: **Republic of Madagascar**

GEOGRAPHY

Area: 592,800 sq. km. (228,880 sq. mi.).
Cities: *Capital*--Antananarivo (pop. about 1,300,000). *Other cities*--Antsirabe (about 500,000), Mahajanga (about 400,000), Toamasina (about 450,000).
Terrain: Mountainous central plateau, coastal plain.
Climate: Moderate interior, tropical coasts.

Madagascar can be divided into five geographical regions: the east coast, the Tsaratanana Massif, the central highlands, the west coast, and the southwest. The highest elevations parallel the east coast, whereas the land slopes more gradually to the west coast (see fig. 3).

The east coast consists of a narrow band of lowlands, about fifty kilometers wide, formed from the sedimentation of alluvial soils, and an intermediate zone, composed of steep bluffs alternating with ravines bordering an escarpment of about 500 meters in elevation, which gives access to the central highlands. The coastal region extends roughly from north of Baie d'Antongil, the most prominent feature on the east coast of the island formed by the Masoala Peninsula, to the far south of the island. The coastline is straight, with the exception of the bay, offering less in the way of natural harbors than the west coast. The Canal des Pangalanes (Lakandranon' Ampalangalana), an 800-kilometerlong lagoon formed naturally by the washing of sand up on the island by the Indian Ocean currents and by the silting of rivers, is a feature of the coast; it has been used both as a means of transportation up and down the coast and as a fishing area. The beach slopes steeply into deep water. The east coast is considered dangerous for swimmers and sailors because of the large number of sharks that frequent the shoreline.

The Tsaratanana Massif region at the north end of the island contains, at 2,880 meters, the highest point on the island and, north of this, the Montagne d'Ambre (Ambohitra), which is of volcanic origin. The coastline is deeply indented; two prominent features are the excellent natural harbor at Antsiranana (Diégo Suarez), just south of the Cap d'Ambre (Tanjon' i Bobaomby), and the large island of Nosy-Be to the west. The mountainous topography to the south, however, limits the potential of the port at Antsiranana by impeding the flow of traffic from other parts of the island.

The central highlands, which range from 800 to 1,800 meters in altitude, contain a wide variety of topographies: rounded and eroded hills, massive granite outcrops, extinct volcanoes, eroded peneplains, and alluvial plains and marshes, which have been converted into irrigated rice fields. The central highlands extend from the Tsaratanana Massif in the north to the Ivakoany Massif in the south. They are defined rather clearly by the escarpments along the east coast, and they slope gently to the west coast. The central highlands include the Anjafy High Plateaux; the volcanic formations of Itasy (Lake Itasy itself is found in a volcanic crater) and the Ankaratra Massif, reaching a height of 2,666 meters; and the Ivakoany Massif in the south. The Isalo Roiniforme Massif lies between the central highlands and the west coast. Antananarivo, the national capital, is located in the northern portion of the central highlands at 1,468 meters above sea level. A prominent feature of the central highlands is a rift valley running north to south, located east of Antananarivo and including Lac Alaotra, the largest body of water on the island, having a length of forty kilometers. The lake is located 761 meters above sea level and is bordered by two cliffs, rising 701 meters to the west and 488 meters to the east, which form the walls of a valley resembling the rift valleys of East Africa. This region has experienced geological subsidence, and earth tremors are frequent here.

The west coast, composed of sedimentary formations deposited in several layers over time, is more indented than the east coast, especially in the northwest, thus offering a number of fine harbors sheltered from cyclones, such as the harbor at Mahajanga. Deep bays and well-protected harbors have attracted explorers, traders, and pirates from Europe, Africa, and the Middle East since ancient times; thus, the area has served as an important bridge between Madagascar and the outside world. Yet the broad alluvial plains found on the coast between Mahajanga and Toliara, which are believed to have great agricultural potential, are thinly inhabited and remain largely unexploited.

The southwest is bordered on the east by the Ivakoany Massif and on the north by the Isala Roiniforme Massif. It includes two regions along the south coast, the Mahafaly Plateau and the desert region occupied by the Antandroy people.

The Mananara and Mangoro rivers flow from the central highlands to the east coast, as does the Maningory, which flows from Lake Alaotra. Other rivers flowing east into the Indian Ocean include the Bemarivo, the Ivondro, and the Mananjary. These rivers tend to be short because the watershed is located close to the east coast. Owing to the steep elevations, they flow rapidly, often over spectacular waterfalls. The rivers flowing to the west coast and emptying into the Mozambique Channel tend to be longer and slower, because of the more gradual slope of the land. The major rivers on the west coast are the Sambirano, the Mahajamba, the Betsiboka (the port of Mahajanga is located at the mouth), the Mania, the North and South Mahavavy, the Mangoky, and the Onilahy. The Ikopa, which flows past Antananarivo, is a tributary of the Betsiboka. The Mangoky River has a basin area of some 50,000 square kilometers; the Ikopa River and the Betsiboka River have basin areas of 18,550 and 11,800 square kilometers, respectively. The principal river in the south, the Mandrare, has a basin area of some 12,435 square kilometers, but it runs dry during certain months in this desert region. Important lakes, aside from Alaotra, include Lake Kinkony in the northwest and Lake Ihotry in the southwest.

Madagascar has been called the "Great Red Island" because of the supposed preponderance of red lateritic soils. The red soils predominate in the central highlands, although there are much richer soils in the regions of former volcanic activity--Itasy and Ankaratra, and Tsaratamana to the north. A narrow band of alluvial soils is found all along the east coast and at the mouths of the major rivers on the west coast; clay, sand, and limestone mixtures are found in the west; and shallow or skeletal laterite and limestone are located in the south.

CLIMATE

The climate is dominated by the southeastern trade winds that originate in the Indian Ocean anticyclone, a center of high atmospheric pressure that seasonally changes its position over the ocean. Madagascar has two seasons: a hot, rainy season from November to April; and a cooler, dry season from May to October. There is, however, great variation in climate owing to elevation and position relative to dominant winds. The east coast has a subequatorial climate and, being most directly exposed to the trade winds, has the heaviest rainfall, averaging as much as 3.5 meters annually. This region is notorious not only for a hot, humid climate in which tropical fevers are endemic but also for the destructive cyclones that occur during the rainy season, coming in principally from the direction of the Mascarene Islands. Because rain clouds discharge much of their moisture east of the highest elevations on the island, the central highlands are appreciably drier and, owing to the altitude, also cooler. Thunderstorms are common during the rainy season in the central highlands, and lightning is a serious hazard.

Antananarivo receives practically all of its average annual 1.4 meters of rainfall between November and April. The dry season is pleasant and sunny, although somewhat chilly, especially in the mornings. Although frosts are rare in Antananarivo, they are common at higher elevations. During this time, the blue skies of the central highlands around Antananarivo are considered by many to be among the clearest and most beautiful in the world.

The west coast is drier than either the east coast or the central highlands because the trade winds lose their humidity by the time they reach this region. The southwest and the extreme south are semidesert; as little as one-third of a meter of rain falls annually at Toliara. Overall, surface water is most abundant along the east coast and in the far north (with the exception of the area around Cap d'Ambre, which has relatively little surface water). Amounts diminish to the west and south, and the driest regions are in the extreme south.

Madagascar suffers the impact of cyclones from time to time. From February 2-4, 1994, Madagascar was struck by Cyclone Geralda, the worst cyclone to come ashore on the island since 1927. The cyclone killed seventy people and destroyed enough property to leave approximately 500,000 homeless, including 30,000 in Antananarivo and 80,000 in Toamasina. The cyclone also significantly damaged the country's infrastructure, most notably coastal roads, railroads, and telecommunications, as well as agriculture. Damage has been estimated at US$45 million, and the World Bank's (see Glossary) International Development Association and various European organizations are engaged in financing the reconstruction. The Madagascar government will contribute US$6 million toward the infrastructure rehabilitation.

PEOPLE AND HISTORY

Nationality: *Noun and adjective*--Malagasy.
Population : 15,467,300.
Annual growth rate : 4.7%.
Ethnic groups: 18 Malagasy tribes; small groups of Comorians, French, Indians, and

For additional analytical, business and investment opportunities information,
please contact Global Investment & Business Center, USA
at (202) 546-2103. Fax: (202) 546-3275. E-mail: rusric@erols.com

Chinese.
Religions: Traditional beliefs 47%, Christian 45%, Muslim 7%.
Languages: Malagasy (official), French.
Education: *Years compulsory--5. Attendance--65%. Literacy--53%.*
Health: *Infant mortality rate--90/1,000. Life expectancy--55 yrs.*
Work force (2000): 8 million. *Agriculture--80%; industry--7%.*

Madagascar's population is predominantly of mixed Asian and African origin. Recent research suggests that the island was uninhabited until Indonesian seafarers arrived in roughly the first century A.D., probably by way of southern India and East Africa, where they acquired African wives and slaves. Subsequent migrations from both the Pacific and Africa further consolidated this original mixture, and 18 separate tribal groups emerged. Asian features are most predominant in the central highlands people, the Merina (3 million) and the Betsileo (2 million); the coastal people are of African origin.

The largest coastal groups are the Betsimisaraka (1.5 million) and the Tsimihety and Sakalava (700,000 each).

The Malagasy language is of Malayo-Polynesian origin and is generally spoken throughout the island. French also is spoken among the educated population of this former French colony.

Most people practice traditional religions, which tend to emphasize links between the living and the dead. They believe that the dead join their ancestors in the ranks of divinity and that ancestors are intensely concerned with the fate of their living descendants. This spiritual communion is celebrated by the Merina and Betsileo reburial practice of famadihana, or "turning over the dead." In this ritual, relatives' remains are removed from the family tomb, rewrapped in new silk shrouds, and returned to the tomb following festive ceremonies in their honor.

About 45% of the Malagasy are Christian, divided almost evenly between Roman Catholic and Protestant. Many incorporate the cult of the dead with their religious beliefs and bless their dead at church before proceeding with the traditional burial rites. They also may invite a pastor to attend a famadihana.

A historical rivalry exists between the predominantly Catholic masses, considered to be underprivileged, and the predominantly Protestant Merina aristocrats, who tend to prevail in the civil service, business, and professions. A new policy of decentralizing resources and authority is intended to enhance the development potential of all Madagascar's provinces. Provincial Council members were elected by popular vote in December 2000. In March 2001, the new Provincial Council members joined mayors and communal council members in each province in electing Senators to represent them in the national parliament. Governors were elected by Electoral College in June 2001. Transfer of duties and establishments of budgets are in progress.

The written history of Madagascar began in the seventh century A.D., when Arabs established trading posts along the northwest coast. European contact began in the 1500s, when Portuguese sea captain Diego Dias sighted the island after his ship became separated from a fleet bound for India. In the late 17th century, the French established trading posts along the east coast. From about 1774 to 1824, it was a favorite haunt for pirates, including Americans, one of whom brought Malagasy rice to South Carolina.

Beginning in the 1790s, Merina rulers succeeded in establishing hegemony over the major part of the island, including the coast. In 1817, the Merina ruler and the British governor of Mauritius concluded a treaty abolishing the slave trade, which had been important in Madagascar's economy. In return, the island received British military and financial assistance. British influence remained strong for several decades, during which the Merina court was converted to Presbyterianism, Congregationalism, and Anglicanism.

The British accepted the imposition of a French protectorate over Madagascar in 1885 in return for eventual control over Zanzibar (now part of Tanzania) and as part of an overall definition of spheres of influence in the area. Absolute French control over Madagascar was established by military force in 1895-96, and the Merina monarchy was abolished.

Malagasy troops fought in France, Morocco, and Syria during World War I. After France fell to the Germans, Madagascar was administered first by the Vichy government and then in 1942 by the British, whose troops occupied the strategic island to preclude its seizure by the Japanese. The Free French received the island from the United Kingdom in 1943.

In 1947, with French prestige at low ebb, a nationalist uprising was suppressed only after several months of bitter fighting. The French subsequently established reformed institutions in 1956 under the Loi Cadre (Overseas Reform Act), and Madagascar moved peacefully toward independence. The Malagasy Republic was proclaimed on October 14, 1958, as an autonomous state within the French Community. A period of provisional government ended with the adoption of a constitution in 1959 and full independence on June 26, 1960.

Madagascar has experienced steady population growth throughout the twentieth century. Since the first systematic census was undertaken by colonial authorities at the turn of the twentieth century, the population has grown from 2.2 million in 1900 to 7.6 million in 1975 (the last year that a census was undertaken) and to a population estimated by the IMF in mid-1993 at 11.86 million. It is expected that the population will approach 17 million by the end of the twentieth century, underscoring a more than fivefold increase in less than a hundred years. Moreover, the average rate of population growth itself has increased from 2.3 percent in 1975 to 3.1 percent over the 1980 to 1990 decade. This rate has made Madagascar one of the most rapidly growing countries in Africa, with a large youthful population--in 1992 nearly 55 percent of the population was under twenty years of age.

The increase in population is significantly influenced by Madagascar's increasingly healthy and youthful population. As a result of more extensive and accessible health care services, for example, Madagascar has witnessed a 36 percent decline in infant mortality from 177 per 1,000 live births in 1981 to 114 per 1,000 in 1991--the average for sub-Saharan Africa was 103. Moreover, as of 1991 a significant portion of the population (estimates range from 40 to 50 percent) was below fourteen years of age, and population density (per square kilometer) had risen to twenty (from roughly fourteen in 1981).

The urban population percentage has doubled since 1975, rising from 13 percent of the population to 26 percent in 1992. The annual urban population growth rate in the 1980s was 6.4 percent. Figures for Madagascar's foreign population in the early 1990s are lacking, but in 1988, such persons were estimated to include 25,000 Comorans, 18,000 French, 17,000 Indians, and 9,000 Chinese.

A unique blend of African and Asian landscapes and cultures is usually one of the first things recognized by first-time travelers to Madagascar. In the zebu cattle-raising regions of the south and west, for example, the savannas resemble those of East Africa. In the central highlands, however, irrigated and terraced rice fields evoke images of Southeast Asia. These contrasting images lie at the heart of an ongoing debate over the origins of the Malagasy people.

According to one theory, peoples from the Indonesian archipelago migrated along the coast of south Asia, across the Arabian Peninsula into the east coast of Africa and, finally, across the Mozambique Channel into present-day Madagascar. This movement occurred over several generations and, because of the gradual interaction between Asian and African populations, led to the arrival and eventual implantation of a distinct Malagasy people and culture. A second theory emphasizes the diversity of the peoples inhabiting Madagascar. Simply put, proponents argue that the Malagasy resulted from a series of migrations by different peoples over time. According to this theory, migrants from the Indonesian archipelago arrived first and eventually settled in the central highlands, followed by the arrival of African peoples as a result of normal migrational trends and the rise of the slave trade. Recent scholarship has suggested that perhaps the theories are complementary, with greater emphasis being placed on the first.

Scholars traditionally have described Madagascar as being divided into eighteen or twenty ethnic groups, each with its own distinct territory; political developments in the contemporary period are often described in terms of ethnic conflict. Yet ethnicity is potentially misleading in the Malagasy context because it connotes a more or less self-sufficient and unique cultural, socioeconomic, and historically united group that perceives itself as being different from other groups.

The population of Madagascar, however, is remarkably homogeneous in terms of language. Unlike most African countries, the vast majority speak the indigenous national Malagasy language. Moreover, despite significant variations, important cultural elements unify the Malagasy people and give them a "panislandic " identity. These include a system of kinship in which descent can be traced through either the paternal or the maternal line. The same kinship terms are used by all Malagasy. A second important element is the centrality of respect for the dead (*razana*) to the social, moral, and religious life of the people. Tombs and the ceremonies related to them are prominent features of both the Malagasy landscape and the way of life of the people. A third important feature is the division of Malagasy societies into three relatively rigid strata:

nobles, commoners, and slaves (or descendants of slaves). Other common elements include the circumcision of children, the practice of astrology and divination, and certain concepts associated with authority, such as *hasina* (sacred, or life-giving, power), which legitimate the position of political and familial authorities.

Another potentially valuable method of analyzing Malagasy society is to differentiate between the so-called *côtiers*, or peoples living in coastal areas, and those who live in the central highlands. Indeed, scholars have noted in recent years that the salience of ethnic group identity has declined, while the division between the central highlands peoples and the *côtiers* continues to be of great importance in understanding social and political competition. Although many observers equate the term central highlander with the Merina ethnic group (once again suggesting the importance of ethnicity), it is important to note that the Betsileo people also live within this region, and the Merina themselves have settled in other regions of the country. Equally important, many *côtiers* do not live anywhere near the coast. In this sense, the central highlands/*côtier* split is best understood as the historical outcome of the domination of the Merina empire, the original center of which was Imerina (around the city of Antananarivo) and was located in the central highlands.

A true understanding of the character of Madagascar's population and historical development requires an appreciation of the inhabitants' shared characteristics, including language and kinship structure, as well as the central highlands/*côtier* split and other divisions based on geographical regions. These latter divisions coincide with the major geographical divisions of the island: east coast, west coast, central highlands, southwest, and the Tsaratamana Massif. Within these regions, the people have certain cultural similarities accentuated by the natural environment.

PEOPLES OF THE EAST COAST

The Betsimisaraka constitute the second largest (14.9 percent) group of Madagascar's population and clearly are the most numerous on the east coast. They are divided into three subgroups: the northern Betsimisaraka, the Betanimena, and the southern Betsimisaraka. Their territory extends along the coast in a narrow band from the Bemarivo River in the north to the Mananjary River in the south, a distance of some 640 kilometers. The Betsimisaraka, whose name means "numerous and inseparable," have traditionally been traders, seafarers, and fishers, as well as cultivators of the tropical lowland areas. They trace their origins to the confederacy established by Ratsimilaho, allegedly the son of a British pirate and a Malagasy princess, who unified several small coastal states in the eighteenth century. The confederation continued after Ratsimilaho died in 1751, but it was much weakened by internal conflict and external pressure. The Betsimisaraka territory has included the important port city of Toamasina, as well as Fenerive and Maroansetra at the head of the Baie d'Antongil.

South of the Betsimisaraka are ethnic groups who trace their origins to Islamic traders of mixed Arab, African, and MalayoIndonesian origin who settled on the coasts after the fourteenth century, and are known as Antalaotra ("people of the sea"). The Antambahoaka, whose name is translated as "the people," make up 0.4 percent of the population and live around the Mananjary River just south of the Betsimisaraka territory.

They claim as their ancestor Raminia, a king who came from Mecca around the early fourteenth century, and are part of a larger group known as the Zafi-Raminia, or "descendants of Raminia;" some of this group migrated from the Mananjary region to become rulers of peoples to the south. Some scholars have speculated that the Zafi-Raminia may have formed part of the ruling class of the Merina, who came to dominate Madagascar in the nineteenth century. Their power and prestige derived from their willingness to use their knowledge of astrology, medicine, and divination to serve the courts of kings throughout Madagascar.

Another people descended from the Antalaotra, the Antaimoro ("people of the shore") constitute 3.4 percent of the population and also live south of the Betsimisaraka. The Antaimoro were apparently the last significant arrivals, appearing around the end of the fifteenth century, possibly from the Arabian Peninsula with a sojourn in Ethiopia or Somalia, just before the coming of the Europeans in the sixteenth century. They are the only Malagasy people before the nineteenth century to possess a system of writing, based on Arabic script. Their books, the *sorabe* (from the Arabic *sura*, meaning "writing," and the Malagasy *be*, meaning "big" or "great"), which were inscribed in ink on special paper made from beaten wood bark, dealt with astrology, divination, medicine, and historical chronicles. Like the Antambahoaka, the Antaimoro are noted throughout Madagascar for their knowledge of the supernatural and medicine.

Among a number of other groups around Farafangana, at the southern end of the Canal des Pangalanes, the most important are the Antaifasy ("people of the sands"), who constitute 1.2 percent of the population. To the south, the Antaisaka (5.3 percent of the population) are found in large numbers around the alluvial valley of the Mananara River. The Antanosy ("people of the island"), who live in the extreme southeastern part of the island around Faradofay, make up 2.3 percent of the population.

The peoples of the eastern escarpment separating the east coast from the central highlands are the Sihanaka ("people of the lake"), who represent 2.4 percent of the population; the Bezanozano (0.8 percent), living south of the Sihanaka; and the Tanala (3.8 percent). The Sihanaka live around Lake Alaotra and practice wet-rice cultivation in a manner similar to that of the Merina. The Bezanozano ("many little braids," referring to their hair style), the Tanala ("people of the forest"), and the inland Betsimisaraka practice slash-and-burn agriculture in the forests, cultivating dry rice, corn, yams, and other crops. Although the Merina conquered the Sihanaka, the Bezanozano, and the inland Betsimisaraka in the early nineteenth century, the southern Tanala remained independent up to the French occupation.

PEOPLES OF THE WEST COAST

The peoples of the west coast, known as the Sakalava ("people of the long valley"), constitute 6.2 percent of the population. Their large territory of some 128,000 square kilometers extends in a broad band up the coast from the Onilahy River in the south to Nosy-Be in the north. The Sakalava were among the most dynamic and expansionist of the Malagasy peoples from the sixteenth to the early nineteenth centuries, when the Merina conquered them. During this period, Sakalava territory was divided into a number of kingdoms ruled by branches of the royal Maroserana clan. In the early eighteenth

For additional analytical, business and investment opportunities information, please contact Global Investment & Business Center, USA at (202) 546-2103. Fax: (202) 546-3275. E-mail: rusric@erols.com

century, the kings of Menabe in the south and Boina in the north united these divisions into confederations.

The Sakalava, along with the Bara people of the southwest, are considered the most "African" of the Malagasy peoples. Specifically, several elements in Sakalava culture bear a strong resemblance to those of Africa, including the keeping of relics (such as pieces of bone) considered to have magical powers and the practice of spirit possession, in which a medium transmits the wishes of dead kings to the living. The Sakalava are also a pastoral people, and those who live in the hinterland keep large herds of zebu cattle that outnumber the human population.

The Sakalava are perhaps best known for the seafaring skills they developed throughout history. In the seventeenth century, they were potentially the first to receive firearms from Europeans in exchange for cattle and slaves and, thus, were in a position to force many of the other peoples of the island to pay them tribute. During the late eighteenth and early nineteenth centuries, large fleets of Sakalava outrigger canoes went on seasonal raids to capture slaves in the Comoro Islands and on the East African coast, causing much devastation. They also sought slaves in the central highlands of Madagascar. Because of the Merina conquest and subsequent French occupation at the end of the century, Sakalava fortunes declined somewhat. They have not increased in number as rapidly as many of the other Malagasy peoples, and their territories, still the largest of all the ethnic groups, have been encroached upon, particularly by the Tsimihety people to the east. A people known as the Makoa, the descendants of slaves brought from Africa by slave raiders, also live along the northwest coast and constitute about 1.1 percent of the population.

PEOPLES OF THE CENTRAL HIGHLANDS

The Merina, whose name means "those from the country where one can see far" (an eloquent yet important reference to their control of the central highlands) are not only the most numerous of the Malagasy peoples, representing more than one-quarter of the total population (26.2 percent), but since the early nineteenth century have been the most organized in terms of social, economic, and political structure. During the nineteenth century, the Merina almost succeeded in unifying the entire island under a centralized administration. Although their influence declined somewhat during the French colonial period, especially after the unsuccessful Revolt of 1947, they are heavily represented among the country's socioeconomic and political elite. Merina territory originally consisted only of the lands encircling the current capital of Antananarivo, but as they expanded in the eighteenth and nineteenth centuries, it came to include most of the northern central highlands, now the province of Antananarivo. Many Merina have settled in other parts of the island as government officials, professionals, and traders, and all the major cities have sizable Merina populations.

The Merina are considered the most "Asian" of the Malagasy ethnic groups in terms of their physical characteristics and culture. Having relatively light complexions and straight black hair, as well as a way of life based on wet-rice cultivation, they are strongly reminiscent of the peoples of Southeast Asia. It has been suggested that the ancestors of the Merina may have preserved their Malayo-Indonesian characteristics through the practice of endogamy or intermarriage. Such a practice would have discouraged their marrying with African peoples even during their hypothesized sojourn on the East African coast, which may have lasted centuries. The plausibility of this thesis is supported by the fact that the Merina continue to practice endogamy, although it is also plausible that Merina ancestors may simply have migrated directly to Madagascar without settling first in Africa. The Merina are sensitive to physical differences and distinguish between people who are *fotsy* (white), with relatively light complexions and descended from the freeborn of the nineteenth-century Merina kingdom, and those who are *mainty* (black), descendants of slaves or captives from other parts of the island who are described as being more "African" in physical appearance. *Fotsy* and *mainty* are not always clearly distinguishable, even to the Merina themselves, but this racial distinction nonetheless divides Merina society into two distinct groups and contributes to its highly unequal nature.

The Betsileo, who constitute 12.1 percent of the population and live in the central highlands south of the Merina in a region of about 40,000 square kilometers, have a culture similar to that of their northern neighbors. They are reputedly the best farmers in Madagascar, building rice terraces on the slopes of steep hills similar to those of Indonesia or the Philippines. They were united in the late eighteenth century by King Andriamanalimbetany of Isandra, one of the four Betsileo royal principalities, but were incorporated into the Merina kingdom in 1830. The Betsileo share something of the privileged position of the Merina, constituting a significant portion of Madagascar's official, professional, and skilled artisan classes.

South of the Betsileo live the Bara (3.3 percent of the population), who are divided into five clans in the dry regions at the southern end of the central highlands. They keep large herds of zebu cattle and are the most pastoral people in Madagascar; they also have a reputation of being valiant warriors.

The Tsimihety (7.3 percent of the population), whose lands are located north of Imerina, illustrate rather strikingly the birth and development of a Malagasy people. Their name, "those who do not cut their hair," refers to the refusal of their forebears in the early eighteenth century to submit to the Sakalava custom of cutting their hair when the king died; rather, they migrated to the unsettled north-central region of the island. The Tsimihety are noted for the rapid expansion of their population and for their penchant for migration, expanding the boundaries of their territory and encroaching on the lands of neighboring peoples. Primarily raisers of cattle, they are divided into a large number of traditional clans with little political organization. They are described as the individualists of the island, desiring to live a life free of government control in the

PEOPLES OF THE TSARATAMANA MASSIF AND THE SOUTHWEST

The Antakarana, living on the Tsaratamana Massif and the northern tip of the island, make up 0.6 percent of the population. The topography of the region isolates them from the other Malagasy peoples. They are both cattle herders and tropical horticulturalists.

The major peoples of the arid southwest region are the Mahafaly and the Antandroy, making up 1.6 and 5.4 percent of the population, respectively. The Mahafaly occupy a

For additional analytical, business and investment opportunities information, please contact Global Investment & Business Center, USA at (202) 546-2103. Fax: (202) 546-3275. E-mail: rusric@erols.com

region between the Onilahy River to the north and the Menarandra River to the south, encompassing an area of some 45,000 square kilometers. The Antandroy territory lies to the east, a desert area full of cacti and thorn bushes. Its terrain makes their name, translated as "people of the thorns," especially apt. Both peoples depend upon the raising of cattle. Limited cultivation is also practiced. The Antandroy region is especially poor, causing workers to migrate to other parts of the island to make a living. Along with cattle, the prickly pear cactus is vital to the people's livelihood. Its spiny growths have served as a source of water and nourishment and as a means of defense against outside invaders.

MINORITIES

Madagascar is also inhabited by nonindigenous minorities who constitute roughly 1.7 percent of the population. Because of the status of France as the former colonial power, Madagascar is home to many former French colonial administrators and military officers. The country is also home to French professionals, businesspersons, managers of large plantations, and colons (small farmers) working their own holdings. Approximately 18,000 French citizens lived and worked in Madagascar in the early 1990s.

The Comorans (currently numbering 25,000) historically have constituted a second important nonindigenous population group, but their numbers decreased after racial riots in Mahajanga in December 1976 resulted in nearly 1,400 killed; in addition, some 20,000 were repatriated to the islands in the ensuing months. They have been concentrated in the northern part of Madagascar, along the coast, and prior to 1976 formed more than one-tenth of the populations of the port cities of Mahajanga and Antsiranana. Most of the Comorans, who adhere to the Muslim faith, have migrated from the island of Njazidja (Grande Comore); they typically work as unskilled laborers in the fields or on the docks of the ports.

Indo-Pakistanis (roughly numbering 17,000) represent a third nonindigenous minority group, and trace their origins to the regions of Gujerat or Bombay on the Indian subcontinent. Like the Comorans, they are for the most part Muslim. Despite living on the island for several generations (or even several centuries), the Indo-Pakistanis still maintain contact with their home areas in northwestern India and Pakistan. Historically, they have worked as merchants and small entrepreneurs and in the past have monopolized the wholesale and retail trade in textiles. They tend to be concentrated in the cities along the west coast.

The Chinese (numbering approximately 9,000) constitute a fourth major nonindigenous population group. Like the IndoPakistanis , they are engaged primarily in commerce but are found mostly along the east coast and around Antananarivo. They are more commonly found in the rural areas than the Indo-Pakistanis. They work as small traders and often marry Malagasy.

LANGUAGE

The Malagasy language--spoken throughout Madagascar by the entire population--is the only one in the African region that belongs to the Malayo-Polynesian language family.

For additional analytical, business and investment opportunities information, please contact Global Investment & Business Center, USA at (202) 546-2103. Fax: (202) 546-3275. E-mail: rusric@erols.com

Linguists believe that it shares a common origin with, and is most closely related to Maanyan, a language spoken in southeast Borneo. Both Malagasy and Maanyan bear a close affinity with the languages of the western Indonesian archipelago, such as Malay, Javanese, Balinese, and the Minangkabau language of Sumatra.

The origins of the Malagasy language in southeast Asia are clearly demonstrated by common words and meanings shared with several of the Indonesian languages. For example, the Malagasy term *antalaotra* (people of the sea) echoes the Malay *laut* (sea). Even more geographically widespread and interesting affinities have been discovered. *Vahiny* means "stranger" in Malagasy, while *vahini* means "girl" in Tahitian Polynesian. Scholars suggest that the two words (assuming they share a common origin) reveal that the first Malayo-Indonesian settlers along the African coast, or Madagascar itself, were male and that women came later as guests or strangers to settlements already established.

Although different regional dialects of Malagasy exist, these are mutually intelligible, and the language is a significant basis of cultural unity. Words are formed from roots with basic meanings, which are combined with prefixes or suffixes to create derivatives. Many Malagasy words, particularly names (such as that of the Merina king, Andrianampoinimerina), are very long, but certain syllables, particularly the last, are lightly accented or not at all.

A number of foreign words are found in the Malagasy vocabulary. The names of the days of the week and the months of the year are taken from Arabic, and the names of animals are taken from a Swahili dialect of East Africa. A number of English and French words also entered the language in the nineteenth and twentieth centuries.

Before the nineteenth century, the only Malagasy people with a written language were the Antaimoro, keepers of the *sorabe*. By 1824-25, a written form of Malagasy using Roman characters was developed by members of the London Missionary Society working under the patronage of Merina King Radama I. The result was an almost perfectly consistent phonetic language that continues to be used throughout the country; the consonants are pronounced as in English and the vowels as in French, a compromise apparently promoted by Radama I. The completion of the alphabet enabled the missionaries to publish a Malagasy Bible and other books for their schools, and the possession of a written language was to prove decisive to the development of the Merinadominated portion of Madagascar.

The colonial period witnessed the emergence of French as the dominant language of the island, and Malagasy was relegated to an inferior position, particularly in official and academic circles. Although the First Republic adopted an official policy of bilingualism (French and Malagasy), French continued to dominate until the inauguration of Ratsiraka and his promulgation of an official policy of Malagachization. Originally conceived by nationalists as the promotion of education in the national language, Malagachization also ultimately included the more radical denunciation of French culture and influence over the national economy and political system. Malagachization further entailed the creation of a common Malagasy language that partook of dialects from all the regions and peoples of the island rather than being primarily a Merina dialect, as remains the case

For additional analytical, business and investment opportunities information,
please contact Global Investment & Business Center, USA
at (202) 546-2103. Fax: (202) 546-3275. E-mail: rusric@erols.com

with official Malagasy today. After 1982 the drive toward Malagachization increasingly faltered in favor of a continuing trend toward reembracing the concept of Madagascar's inclusion in the international francophone community. Indeed, French remains important, largely because of its international status and the fact that most of the leadership has been educated in French. Both Malagasy and French are used in official government publications.

TRADITIONAL BELIEFS AND RELIGION

A firm belief in the existence of close ties between the living and the dead constitutes the most basic of all traditional beliefs and the foundation for Malagasy religious and social values. All the Malagasy peoples have traditionally accepted the existence of a supreme God, known commonly as Zanahary (Creator) or Andriamanitra (Sweet, or Fragrant, Lord). The dead have been conceived as playing the role of intermediary between this supreme God and humankind and are viewed as having the power to affect the fortunes of the living for good or evil. The dead are sometimes described as "gods on earth," who are considered the most important and authoritative members of the family, intimately involved in the daily life of the living members. At the same time, the *razana* (best defined as "ancestors") are the sources from which the life force flows and the creators of Malagasy customs and ways of life. The living are merely temporary extensions of the dead. Great hardship or trouble can result if the dead are offended or neglected.

The burial tomb, a prominent part of the island landscape in all regions, is the primary link between the living and the dead among the Malagasy. It is built with great care and expense, reflecting the privileged position of the dead, and is often more costly and substantial than the houses of the living. The land upon which a family tomb is situated-- *tanindrazana* (land of the ancestors)--is inalienable, and social and economic practices are designed to guarantee that tomb lands are kept within the family. Anthropologists have described the Merina as living, in effect, in two localities: the place where one happens to work and keep one's household, and the *tanindrazana*, a locality of much deeper sentimental significance, the spiritual center where the family tomb is located. The two are usually separated by a considerable distance. Among some groups, whether one decides to be buried in the tombs of the father's or mother's family determines individual descent-group allegiance.

The tombs of the various peoples around the island differ somewhat in form. Merina tombs tend to be solid, stone structures, built partially underground, with a chamber in which the bodies of ancestors are kept on shelves, wrapped in silk shrouds. The traditional tombs of the Mahafaly in the southwest were built of stone but surmounted by intricately carved wooden posts depicting human and animal figures. More recent Mahafaly tombs, particularly those built by rich families, are often made of concrete, with glass windows, brightly painted designs and often remarkable depictions of airplanes, taxicabs, or other modern paraphernalia mounted on the roof. At one time, it was the custom of the Sakalava people living around the Morondava River on the west coast to decorate their tombs with carvings showing explicit sexual activity. These were meant to illustrate the life-giving force, or fertility, of the ancestors.

For additional analytical, business and investment opportunities information, please contact Global Investment & Business Center, USA at (202) 546-2103. Fax: (202) 546-3275. E-mail: rusric@erols.com

Among the Merina and Betsileo peoples of the central highlands, the custom of *famadihana* ("placing" or the "turning" of the dead) reaffirms the link between the living and the dead. This occurs when a person is taken from a temporary to a permanent tomb in the *tanindrazana*, and the remains are taken out of the tomb to be wrapped in new shrouds, or when a body is moved from one tomb to another. These ceremonies are costly, mainly because of the expense of providing food for a large number of relatives and guests. They represent for the peoples of the central highlands a time of communion with the *razana* and a means of avoiding or reducing guilt or blame. It is considered a serious transgression not to hold a *famadihana* when one is financially able to do so. The ceremony is presided over by an astrologer, but the chief participants are the close relatives of those persons whose remains are being moved or rewrapped. In this regard, the *famadihana* resembles in spirit a family reunion or the more austere ancestral ceremonies of China and Korea, where the spirits of ancestors are invited to a feast given by members of a family or lineage, rather than the funerals of the West, which are "final endings."

Although the *famadihana* does not occur outside the central highlands and the attitudes of the Merina and Betsileo toward the dead differ in certain significant respects, the idea of the dead as beings to be respected is universal in Madagascar. A number of different "souls" are recognized by the Malagasy. Among the Merina, these include the *fanahy*, a kind of essence which determines individual character and behavior; thus, an individual can have a good or a bad *fanahy*. Another is the soul of the person after death, the *ambiroa*, which is called to the tomb for the celebration of the *famadihana*, but which, over time, is believed to blend with the collective spirit of other ancestors. The *ambiroa* is believed to permeate the tomb building, the family household, and the hills and valleys of the *tanindrazana*, being in a sense omnipresent. Other concepts include the soul of a recently deceased person, the *lolo*, which is said to be harmless but feels homesick for its old surroundings and often appears in the form of a moth or a butterfly. The *angatra*, ghosts of the unknown dead, are often malevolent and frighten people at night. The emphases in the minds of the people, however, are not on the afterlife or on the experiences of the dead souls either as ghosts or in heaven or hell, but on the relationship of the dead with the living and the role of the former as bearers of power and authority.

The *ombiasy* and the *mpanandro* combine the functions of diviners, traditional healers, and astrologers. They originated among the Antaimoro and the Antambahoaka of the southwest coast, who were influenced by the Antalaotra. Among the Antandroy, it is the *ombiasy* who are often asked to eradicate a mistake made by neglecting a taboo. The Bara consult the *ombiasy* to look after the sick and dying. Family heads ask them when to begin certain agricultural tasks or when to marry or circumcise those entering adulthood. Merina families have their personal diviners who consult the stars; their advice is requested on all enterprises that are thought to involve dangers. They are paid a regular salary and additional fees for extra services. They set the auspicious day for a *famadihana*. Even a highly educated Merina would not think of building a house without consulting the *ombiasy* or the *mpanandro* for the favorable day to begin work. When a marriage is contemplated, both sets of parents will ask the *ombiasy* and the *mpanandro* whether the partners will be compatible.

The science of the *ombiasy* and the *mpanandro* is tied to the concept of *vintana*, which means fate ordained by the position of moon, sun, and stars. Accordingly, different values and different forces, either active or passive, are attributed to each fraction of time. Space, too, is thought to be affected by these forces, east being superior to west, and north being superior to south. Northeast therefore is believed to be the most favorable direction. People build their houses on the north-south axis and reserve the northeastern corner for prayers. Guests are seated on the northern side, and chickens are kept in the southwestern corner.

Fate is impersonal and cannot be changed, but certain aspects can be foretold and avoided. For divination the *ombiasy* use a system of Arabic origin in which fruit seeds or grains of corn are put into rows of eight. Various figure combinations indicate the future and what to do regarding sickness, love, business, and other enterprises. The *ombiasy* also sell talismans made of such objects as dried or powdered vegetables, glass beads, or animal teeth.

Fady are taboos on the use of certain substances, particularly foods, or on the performance, including the timing, of certain acts. They continue to regulate much of Malagasy life. Many are connected with *vintana*, while others express certain social values. For example, to deny hospitality to a stranger is *fady*, as is the act of refusing this hospitality. The concept of *fady* often also expresses a well-developed metaphorical sense. According to one *fady*, it is wrong to sit in the doorway of a house while the rice is sprouting, since the door of the house is compared to the "gateway" of birth and by blocking it, one might impede the "birth" of the rice. It is important to remember, however, that *fady*, particularly dietary prohibitions, vary widely among different ethnic groups, and from village to village within the same ethnic group. To be at home in a different locality, travelers must acquaint themselves with a large number of local variations.

Traditional beliefs are augmented by imported organized religions. Although exact figures on religious affiliations do not exist, it is estimated that approximately 55 percent of the total population adhere to traditional beliefs, and 40 percent are Christian, about evenly divided between Roman Catholics and Protestants, the remaining 5 percent being Muslim. Indeed, Protestant and Roman Catholic churches have found themselves competing for new adherents, most notably underscored by the fact that villages in the central highlands often have two churches, one Protestant and one Roman Catholic, that face each other at opposite ends of the village. The Roman Catholic church enjoys its largest support among the Betsileo people in the southern portion of the central highlands, and is also associated with former slaves and the *côtiers*. Protestantism enjoys its largest support among the Merina of the central highlands and, therefore, historically has been perceived as the Christian affiliation of the upper classes. Despite the minority status of Christians, the Council of Christian Churches in Madagascar played a major role in arbitrating a resolution to the conflict resulting from the violence and general strikes in May and August 1991 (see The Second Republic, 1975-92 , this ch.).

The nineteenth century witnessed a confrontation between Christianity and traditional religious beliefs, as Queen Ranavalona I expelled foreign missionaries and persecuted Christians, putting many of them to death. The tide reversed at her death, and at the

For additional analytical, business and investment opportunities information,
please contact Global Investment & Business Center, USA
at (202) 546-2103. Fax: (202) 546-3275. E-mail: rusric@erols.com

beginning of the reign of Ranavalona II, the old *sampy*--idols or talismans endowed with supernatural powers to protect the kingdom--were destroyed, and Protestantism became the religion of the royal family. Yet opposition has given way in many cases to a kind of mutual assimilation. Christian missionaries were able to build on the Malagasy concept of a supreme God by using the term, "Andriamanitra," to refer to the biblical God and by choosing one of the traditional terms for soul, *fanahy*, to define its Christian counterpart. Although the supremacy of Christianity in the central highlands led to the demise of idol worship, Malagasy pastors have not challenged the strength of traditional beliefs in the power and authority of the *razana*. Christians have their dead blessed at a church before burying them according to the old ceremonies, and may invite the pastor to attend a *famadihana* and place a cross on top of the tomb. Christian belief in the power of a transcendent and somewhat distant God has blended with older beliefs in the closeness and intimacy of the dead as spiritual beings. Some Malagasy Christians will even say that the dead have become Christians themselves and continue to be the arbiters of right and wrong.

Exact figures are not available, but followers of the Sunni (see Glossary) and Shia (see Glossary) variants of Islam together constitute somewhere around 5 percent of the total population. Most are Comorans or Indo-Pakistanis; a small number are converted Malagasy. The majority are located in Mahajanga Province. A small minority of the Indian community practices Hinduism.

SOCIAL STRUCTURE AND FAMILY

Traditional society is hierarchical in structure. Kinship groups are ranked precisely along a superior/inferior continuum, and individuals within these groups are ranked according to age, descent, and gender. This pervasive ranking reflects the perceived power of ancestors as the source of *hasina* (life-giving power), which is distributed unequally among individuals and family groups. Royal or noble persons are supposed to possess a greater level of *hasina* than others, so that their descendants enjoy superior social status. Within families of any rank, elders possess greater *hasina* than the young not only by virtue of their maturity and experience but also because they are perceived as closer to the dead and thus share in part of their power. Rulers do not rule alone but share their offices in effect with their ancestors, who are, in fact, more powerful and influential than the rulers themselves. Among the Sakalava, it is believed that the soul or spirit of a royal ancestor can take possession of a person in order to make known its commands to the living.

Social values are highly conservative, demonstrating an awareness of hierarchy and place that permeates the daily life of the people. Observers have noted, for example, that in Merina households each member of the family is expected to eat a meal in turn according to age; the youngest is served last. Family members are seated around the table in an arrangement that reflects age-rank, the father or grandfather occupying the "noble corner" (the northeast). Failure to honor the rank is considered a serious violation of *fady*. Children who eat before their elders can be severely punished. Within the village, the local notables and respected elders of kin groups, who are usually male, have preponderant influence in village affairs.

For additional analytical, business and investment opportunities information, please contact Global Investment & Business Center, USA at (202) 546-2103. Fax: (202) 546-3275. E-mail: rusric@erols.com

The society as a whole remains divided into a number of unequal social groups based entirely on descent. Among the Merina, Madagascar's dominant ethnic group, these are referred to as the *andriana* (nobles), the *hova* (commoners), and the *andevo* (slaves or, more properly, the descendants of slaves). The distinction between *andriana* and *hova* on the one hand and *andevo* on the other hand corresponds to the distinction between "whites" and "blacks" in Merina society. Among the Sakalava, royal clans descended from the Maroserana occupy the highest social position, followed by noble and commoner clans; the descendants of slaves again occupy the lowest status. Noble and commoner clans possess histories that define their relations to the king and their different social roles. The social hierarchy of the Malagasy people, however, is actually far more differentiated than this system might suggest, because within each "caste" constituent clans or kin groups are also arranged in a precise hierarchy of superior and inferior that is well known to all individuals.

Among the Merina, the Malagasy people most thoroughly studied by anthropologists, the population is divided into a number of *karazana* (large kin groups) that are defined in terms of the common land upon which the family tomb is located. They are hierarchically ranked and usually named after a single ancestor. Members of the same *karazana* are described as being "of one womb." The general practice is for individuals to marry within the *karazana* or even within the same subunit to which they belong. Although endogamy carries with it the taint of incest, intermarriage is preferred because, in this way, land (especially tomb land) can be kept within the kin unit rather than being inherited by outsiders. Preserving the boundaries of the kinship unit through intermarriage preserves the integrity of the all-important link between the living and the dead.

Below the level of the *karazana*, the Merina are divided into *fianakaviana* (family), which includes close relatives by blood and affiliation. The family is less defined by territory than by its role as the locus of feelings of loyalty and affection. Members of the same *fianakaviana* are *havana* (relatives) but with a strong emotional connotation. The ideal of *fihavanana* (amity, solidarity) is that *havana* should love and trust one another, rendering mutual aid and sharing each other's possessions. When a man moves to new lands, his relatives will often come after him to claim parcels of land to cultivate. Persons who are not *havana* are often considered untrustworthy. However, fictive kinship, described as "those who are kin because they are loved," is a widespread Malagasy institution drawing individuals into an intermediate status between strangers and kin. This system can be very useful in daily life, particularly outside the *tanindrazana*.

Descent among the Merina is neither strictly patrilineal nor matrilineal. Instead, the practice of endogamy enables the two families involved in a marriage to define the situation as one in which they each receive a new child. The husband and wife are equally deferential to both sets of in-laws. Although women have occupied social roles inferior to those of men in traditional society, they are not completely subject to the will of their husbands or parents-in-law, as has been the case in strictly patrilineal societies.

There is some choice of which tomb group an individual will join and, thus, in which tomb he or she will be buried. Tomb groups consist of closely related *fianakaviana* members who own and maintain a tomb in common. The heads of tomb groups are local notables or government officials, and each member contributes to the tomb's upkeep, often a heavy financial burden because the tomb buildings are large and in frequent need of repair. New tombs are built, and new tomb groups are formed with the passing of generations. Both social identity and relationship with the dead are determined by one's tomb group. The most unfortunate persons are those who, because they are strangers or because of some other disqualification, cannot be interred within a tomb.

The difference between former free persons and former slaves remains particularly significant, despite the formal abolition of slavery by the French in 1897. Persons of slave origin are generally poorer than other Merina and are expected to perform the most menial tasks and to be particularly deferential to others. One observer noticed among the Betsileo in a rural household that during a meal to which a number of men had been invited, two persons of slave origin had to use a common plate, while free persons had their own plates. Former slaves are also often stereotypically described as rude, uncultured, and ugly. Marriages between persons of slave origin and other Merina are rare. When they do occur, the offspring are considered part of the slave group and are denied a place in the tomb of the free parent's family. In fact, the parent of the offspring may also be denied entrance. Former slaves do not possess links to a *tanindrazana* and, thus, are apt to be more mobile than the descendants of free persons, because migration offers the possibility of escaping from the stigma of slave descent. It is estimated that as much as 50 percent of the population of Imerina is of slave origin, whereas the percentage for the Betsileo territory is much lower.

Although the Merina social and kinship pattern is to a great degree common to all the peoples of Madagascar, there are important variations based in part on different histories and on ecological variations between the rice-growing and pastoral regions of the country. The pastoral Bara and the Tsimihety, who are agriculturalists but place great cultural and sentimental significance on herds of zebu, base descent and inheritance on patrilineality more strictly than the Merina.

GOVERNMENT

In March 1998, Malagasy voters approved a revised constitution. The principal institutions of the Republic of Madagascar are a presidency, a parliament (National Assembly and Senate), a prime ministry and cabinet, and an independent judiciary. The president is elected by direct universal suffrage for a 5-year term, renewable twice.

The National Assembly consists of 150 representatives elected by direct vote every 5 years. The Senate consists of 90 senators, two-thirds elected by local legislators and one-third appointed by the president, all for 6-year terms. A Prime Minister and council of ministers carries out day-to-day management of government. The President appoints the Prime Minister.

The Prime Minister and members of Parliament initiate legislation and the government executes it. The President can dissolve the National Assembly. For its part, the National Assembly can pass a motion of censure and require the Prime Minister and council of ministers to step down. The Constitutional Court approves the constitutionality of new laws.

For additional analytical, business and investment opportunities information, please contact Global Investment & Business Center, USA at (202) 546-2103. Fax: (202) 546-3275. E-mail: rusric@erols.com

Territorial administration is to be determined by legislation. In an effort to decentralize administration, the constitution calls for the six provinces (faritany) to become autonomous.

PRINCIPAL GOVERNMENT OFFICIALS

President-- Marc Ravalomanana
Prime Minister, Minister of Finance--Tantely Andrianarivo
Minister of Foreign Affairs--Lila Ratsifandrihamanana
Ambassador to the U.S.--Zina Andrianarivelo-Razafy
Ambassador to the UN--Jean de la Croix Bakoniarivo

Madagascar maintains an embassy in the United States at 2374 Massachusetts Avenue NW., Washington, DC 20008 (tel. 202-265-5525).

POLITICAL CONDITIONS

GOVERNMENT

Type: Republic.
Independence: June 26, 1960.
Constitution: Entered into force in March 1998
Branches: *Executive*--president, prime minister, cabinet. *Legislative*--National Assembly and Senate. *Judicial*--Supreme Court, High Court of Justice, Constitutional High Court.
Subdivisions: Six autonomous provinces (faritany).
Political parties: There are more than 130 with a dozen major ones, including Pillar and Podium for the Development of Madagascar (AREMA), Militants for the Development of Madagascar (MFM), Be Judged by your Work (AVI), Work, Truth and Harmonized Development (AFFA), National Union for Development and Democracy (UNDD), Social Democrat Party (PSD), Reflection and Action Group for Development in Madagascar (GRAD-Iloafo), Rally for Social Democracy (RPSD), Economic Liberalism and Democratic Action for Reconstruction Party (LEADER-Fanilo), Independence and Renewal Party of Madagascar (AKFM-Fanavoazana).
Suffrage: Universal at 18.
National holiday: June 26.

Flag:

Madagascar's first President, Philibert Tsiranana, was elected when his Social Democratic Party gained power at independence in 1960 and was reelected without opposition in March 1972. However, he resigned only 2 months later in response to massive antigovernment demonstrations. The unrest continued, and Tsiranana's

For additional analytical, business and investment opportunities information, please contact Global Investment & Business Center, USA at (202) 546-2103. Fax: (202) 546-3275. E-mail: rusric@erols.com

successor, Gen. Gabriel Ramanantsoa, resigned on February 5, 1975, handing over executive power to Lt. Col. Richard Ratsimandrava, who was assassinated 6 days later. A provisional military directorate then ruled until a new government was formed in June 1975, under Admiral Didier Ratsiraka.

During the 16 subsequent years of President Ratsiraka's rule, Madagascar continued under a government committed to revolutionary socialism based on the 1975 constitution establishing a highly centralized state. National elections in 1982 and 1989 returned Ratsiraka for a second and third 7-year presidential term. For much of this period, only limited and restrained political opposition was tolerated, with no direct criticism of the president permitted in the press.

With an easing of restrictions on political expression, beginning in the late 1980s, the Ratsiraka regime came under increasing pressure for fundamental change. In response to a deteriorating economy, Ratsiraka had begun relaxing socialist dogma to institute some liberal, private-sector reforms. But these and other political reforms--like the elimination of press censorship in 1989 and the formation of more political parties in 1990--were insufficient to placate a growing opposition force known as Hery Velona or "Active Forces," centered in the capital city and the surrounding high plateau.

In response to largely peaceful mass demonstrations and crippling general strikes, Ratsiraka replaced his prime minister in August 1991 but suffered an irreparable setback soon thereafter when his troops fired on peaceful demonstrators marching on his suburban palace, killing more than 30.

In an increasingly weakened position, Ratsiraka acceded to negotiations on the formation of a transitional government. The resulting "Panorama Convention" of October 31, 1991, stripped Ratsiraka of nearly all of his powers, created interim institutions, and set an 18-month timetable for completing a transition to a new form of constitutional government. The High Constitutional Court was retained as the ultimate judicial arbiter of the process.

In March 1992, a new constitution was drafted by a widely representative National Forum organized by the Malagasy Christian Council of Churches (FFKM). Troops guarding the proceedings clashed with pro-Ratsiraka "federalists" who tried to disrupt the forum in protest of draft constitutional provisions preventing the incumbent president from running again. The text of the new constitution was put to a nationwide referendum in August 1992 and approved by a wide margin, despite efforts by federalists to disrupt balloting in several coastal areas.

Presidential elections were held on November 25, 1992, after the High Constitutional Court had ruled, over Active Forces objections, that Ratsiraka could become a candidate. A runoff election was held in February 1993, and active forces leader Albert Zafy defeated Ratsiraka. He was sworn in as President on March 27, 1993.

A nationwide legislative election was held in June 1993 to elect a new National Assembly, which, under the new constitution, exercises legislative initiative along with the Prime Minister, whom it elects.

For additional analytical, business and investment opportunities information, please contact Global Investment & Business Center, USA at (202) 546-2103. Fax: (202) 546-3275. E-mail: rusric@erols.com

The proportional representation system for the election of legislators contributed to a significant increase in the number of political parties and special interest groups. These and a free press promote open and lively discussion of political issues in Madagascar.

ECONOMY

GDP (U.S.$million): $3,877. GDP per capita: $269. Unemployment: 23%. Natural resources: Graphite, chrome, coal, bauxite, ilmenite, gold, tar sands, semiprecious stones, hardwoods.
Agriculture (29% of GDP): *Products*--rice, livestock, seafood, coffee, vanilla, sugar, cloves, cotton, sisal, peanuts, tobacco.
Industry (14% of GDP): *Types*--processed food, clothing, textiles, mining, paper, refined petroleum products, glassware, construction, soap, cement, tanning.
Trade (2000): Exports--$1,061 million: apparel, shrimp, vanilla, coffee, sugar, cloves, graphite, essential oils, industrial and gemstones. Major export markets--France, U.S., Germany, Japan, Singapore, Italy, EU. Imports (2000)--$1,464 million: consumer goods, foodstuffs, crude oil, machinery and vehicles, iron and steel, electronics, computers and accessories. Major suppliers--EU, France, Iran, Japan.

In 2000, Madagascar embarked on the preparation of a Poverty Reduction Strategy Paper (PRSP) under the Heavily Indebted Poor countries (HIPC) Initiative. The boards of the IMF and of the World Bank concurred in December 2000 that the country is eligible under the HIPC Initiative, and Madagascar has reached the decision point for debt relief. On March 1, 2001, the IMF Board granted the country $103 million for 2001-03 under the Poverty Reduction and Growth Facility (PRGR). Resources freed up from HIPC will be directed toward improving access to health, education, rural roads, water, and direct support to communities. In addition, on March 7, 2001, the Paris Club approved a debt cancellation of $161 million. On February 28, 2001, the African Development Bank (ADB) approved under the HIPC a debt cancellation of $71.46 million and granted in June 2001 an additional credit of $20 million to fight against AIDS and poverty.

Partly as a result of these credits but also as a result of previous reforms, average GDP growth exceeded the population growth rate of 2.8% in 1997 (3.5%), 1998 (3.9%), 1999 (4.7%) and 2000 (4.8%). Madagascar's appeal to investors stems from its competitive, trainable work force. More than 200 investors, particularly garment manufacturers, have organized under the country's Export Processing Zone (EPZ) system since it was established in 1989. The absence of quota limits on textile imports to the European market under the Lome Convention has helped stimulate this growth. In addition, there is evidence that Madagascar's recent eligibility for AGOA is significantly increasing Malagasy exports and foreign investment.

In the short and medium terms, considerable economic growth can arise from greater efficiency in the allocation and use of resources. Since the mid-1980s, Madagascar has run sizeable balance-of-payment deficits. The current account deficit as a percentage of GDP averaged in excess of 6% during the last 6 years and registered nearly 4% in 1999. Madagascar's debt ratio, which had reached 46% in 1996, is estimated at 15.4% in 2000. Within an overall framework of poverty reduction, the HIPC Initiative would enable the country to reduce its debt service ratio to 5.5% in 2003, and remain at around 5% throughout the projection period 2000-19.

An optimistic high-growth scenario is predicated on recovery of private investor interest and a continuing drop in inflation. From more than 60 % in 1994, the inflation rate dropped to 6.4% in 1998, before rising again to 14.4% in 1999 and 8.7% in 2000. The government hopes to bring this down to 5.8% by the end of 2001. In 2000, real GDP growth reached 4.8% and was forecast to accelerate to 6% in 2001. Tax revenues increased to more than 11% of GDP in 2000 and in 2001, the government forecasts a rate approaching 12%.

FOREIGN RELATIONS

Madagascar historically has remained outside the mainstream of African affairs, although it is an active member of the Organization of African Unity and the Non-Aligned Movement. From 1978 until 1991, then-President Ratsiraka emphasized independence and nonalignment and followed an "all points" policy stressing ties with socialist and radical regimes, including North Korea, Cuba, Libya, and Iran. Taking office in 1993, President Albert Zafy expressed his desire for diplomatic relations with all countries. Early in his tenure, he established formal ties with South Korea and sent emissaries to Morocco.

Globalization has encouraged the government and President Ratsiraka since 1997 to adhere to market-oriented policies and to engage world markets. External relations reflect this trend although Madagascar's physical isolation and strong traditional insular orientation have limited its activity in regional economic organizations and relations with its East African neighbors. It enjoys closer and generally good relations with its Indian Ocean neighbors--Mauritius, Réunion, and the Comoros Islands. Active relationships with Europe, especially France, Germany, and Switzerland, as well as with Russia, Japan, India, and China have been strong since independence.

U.S.-MALAGASY RELATIONS

Relations with the United States date to the early 1800s. The two countries concluded a commercial convention in 1867 and a treaty of peace, friendship, and commerce in 1881. These traditionally warm relations suffered considerably during the 1970s, when Madagascar expelled the U.S. ambassador, closed a NASA tracking station, and nationalized two U.S. oil companies. In 1980, relations at the ambassadorial level were restored.

Throughout the troubled period, commercial and cultural relations remained active. In 1990, Madagascar was designated as a priority aid recipient, and assistance increased from $15 million in 1989 to $40 million in 1993. Recent U.S. assistance has contributed to a population census and family planning programs, conservation of Madagascar's remarkable biodiversity, private sector development, agriculture, democracy and governance initiatives, and media training.

U.S. EMBASSY OFFICIALS

Ambassador-- **WANDA L. NESBITT**
Deputy Chief of Mission/Chargé--Phillip Carter III
USAID Director--Karen Poe
Defense Attache--Daniel Lafferty
Public Affairs Officer--Roy Whitaker
Consular Officer--Robert Ruehle
Political/Economic/Commercial Officer--Eric Rueter
Administrative Officer--Chanh Nguyen
Peace Corps Director--KathleenTilford

The U.S. Embassy in Madagascar is at 14, rue Rainitovo, Antsahavola, Antananarivo (tel. 261-20-22-212-57, 22-209-56; fax 261-20-345-39. The postal address is Ambassade Americaine, B.P. 620, Antananarivo, Madagascar.

WANDA L. NESBITT U.S. AMBASSADOR TO THE REPUBLIC OF MADAGASCAR

President Bush nominated Ms. Wanda Nesbitt, a career member of the Senior Foreign Service, to be the United States Ambassador to the Republic of Madagascar on

For additional analytical, business and investment opportunities information,
please contact Global Investment & Business Center, USA
at (202) 546-2103. Fax: (202) 546-3275. E-mail: rusric@erols.com

September 25, 2001. She was confirmed by the Senate on October 30, 2001 and took up her assignment in January 2002.

Prior to becoming Ambassador to Madagascar, Ms. Nesbitt was the Deputy Chief of Mission at the U.S. Embassy in Dar es Salaam, Tanzania where she worked extensively on Great Lakes issues and on helping to restore at atmosphere of normalcy to the American Mission, in the wake of the 1998 terrorist bombing. She was Chargé d'Affaires for ten months in Tanzania, including during the critical period following the September 11 attacks on the World Trade Center and the Pentagon.

Ms. Nesbitt was the Deputy Chief of Mission in Kigali, Rwanda from 1997 to 1999 and during her twenty-year Foreign Service career also served as the Regional Consular Officer in Kinshasa, Zaire (1990-1992); as a Vice-Consul in Paris, France (1983-85) and also in Port-au-Prince, Haiti (1982-1983). Ms. Nesbitt also has extensive experience with the domestic side of the State Department having served as the Officer in Charge of Immigration and Refugee Issues for the Bureau of Legislative Affairs (1995-97); Chief of the Europe and Africa Division of Citizens Emergency Center (1992-93); and Deputy Director of the Department's Executive Secretariat (1994-95).

Ms. Nesbitt is the recipient of numerous awards, including four Superior Honor Awards. She completed the National War College's prestigious National Security Strategy program (academic year 1996-1997), where she won an award rarely given to civilian officers for a paper entitled "Military Strategy in Ethnic Conflicts." She is a graduate of the University of Pennsylvania and holds a B.A. in International Relations and French.

Ms. Nesbitt was born December 7, 1956 in Philadelphia, Pennsylvania, the third of five children. She is married to Mr. James Stejskal, a retired Special Forces Warrant Officer. Their favorite pastimes include gardening, tennis, and music of all kinds. Mr. Stejskal is an avid photographer who enjoys compiling albums of the couple's posts of assignment.

TRAVEL AND BUSINESS INFORMATION

The U.S. Department of State's Consular Information Program provides Consular Information Sheets, Travel Warnings, and Public Announcements.

Consular Information Sheets exist for all countries and include information on entry requirements, currency regulations, health conditions, areas of instability, crime and security, political disturbances, and the addresses of the U.S. posts in the country.

Travel Warnings are issued when the State Department recommends that Americans avoid travel to a certain country.

Public Announcements are issued as a means to disseminate information quickly about terrorist threats and other relatively short-term conditions overseas which pose significant risks to the security of American travelers. Free copies of this information are available by calling the Bureau of Consular Affairs at 202-647-5225 or via the fax-on-demand system: 202-647-3000. Consular

Information Sheets and Travel Warnings also are available on the Consular Affairs Internet home page: http://travel.state.gov. Consular Affairs Tips for Travelers publication series, which contain information on obtaining passports and planning a safe trip abroad are on the internet and hard copies can be purchased from the Superintendent of Documents, U.S. Government Printing Office, telephone: 202-512-1800; fax 202-512-2250.

Emergency information concerning Americans traveling abroad may be obtained from the Office of Overseas Citizens Services at (202) 647-5225. For after-hours emergencies, Sundays and holidays, call 202-647-4000.

Passport information can be obtained by calling the National Passport Information Center's automated system ($.35 per minute) or live operators 8 a.m. to 8 p.m. (EST) Monday-Friday ($1.05 per minute). The number is 1-900-225-5674 (TDD: 1-900-225-7778). Major credit card users (for a flat rate of $4.95) may call 1-888-362-8668 (TDD: 1-888-498-3648). It also is available on the internet.

Travelers can check the latest health information with the U.S. Centers for Disease Control and Prevention in Atlanta, Georgia. A hotline at 877-FYI-TRIP (877-394-8747) and a web site at http://www.cdc.gov/travel/index.htm give the most recent health advisories, immunization recommendations or requirements, and advice on food and drinking water safety for regions and countries. A booklet entitled Health Information for International Travel (HHS publication number CDC-95-8280) is available from the U.S. Government Printing Office, Washington, DC 20402, tel. (202) 512-1800.

Information on travel conditions, visa requirements, currency and customs regulations, legal holidays, and other items of interest to travelers also may be obtained before your departure from a country's embassy and/or consulates in the U.S. (for this country, see "Principal Government Officials" listing in this publication).

U.S. citizens who are long-term visitors or traveling in dangerous areas are encouraged to register at the U.S. embassy upon arrival in a country (see "Principal U.S. Embassy Officials" listing in this publication). This may help family members contact you in case of an emergency.

HISTORY & POLITICAL DEVELOPMENTS

THE REPUBLIC OF MADAGASCAR, formerly known as the Malagasy Republic and the Democratic Republic of Madagascar, has undergone significant socioeconomic and political changes during the nineteenth and twentieth centuries. Occupying a strategic location off the southeast coast of Africa, the island historically became the target of British and French imperial ambitions. Ultimately, the competition resulted in French colonization at the end of the nineteenth century. The country gained full independence from colonial rule on June 26, 1960. Philibert Tsiranana headed the conservative regime of the First Republic, which was superseded in 1975 by a Marxist-oriented military regime under Lieutenant Commander Didier Ratsiraka.

In the face of rising political dissent and socioeconomic decline that reached its height at the beginning of the 1990s, the Second Republic succumbed to the wave of democratization spreading throughout the African continent. On March 27, 1993, the inauguration of Albert Zafy as the third elected president of Madagascar since independence marked the beginning of the Third Republic.

PRECOLONIAL ERA, PRIOR TO 1894

The ruins of fortifications built by Arab traders as far back as the ninth century underscore Madagascar's historical role as a destination for travelers from the Middle East, Asia, and Africa. Not until the beginning of the sixteenth century, however, did European ships flying Portuguese, Dutch, English, and French flags explore Madagascar's shoreline. Beginning in 1643, several French settlements emerged; the best known of these, Tolagnaro (formerly Faradofay) on the southeast coast, lasted for more than thirty years. The settlement survived in part because the colonists had taken pains to establish cordial relations with the Antanosy, the ethnic group inhabiting the area. Relations deteriorated later, however, and in 1674 a massacre of nearly all the inhabitants ended French colonization endeavors for more than a century; survivors fled by sea to the neighboring territory of Reunion.

This early checking of French imperial designs coincided with the spread of piracy into the Indian Ocean. In the absence of a significant naval power in waters remote from Europe, privateer vessels attacked ships of many nations for nearly forty years. The favorite hunting grounds were in the north in the Arabian Sea and Red Sea areas, but Madagascar was a popular hiding place where crews could recuperate and replenish supplies for another attack. By this time, the institution of slavery also had been implanted on the island. Madagascar became a source of slaves, not only for the neighboring islands of Mauritius and Rodrigues, but also for more distant points, including the Western Hemisphere.

Madagascar's social and political structure facilitated the slave trade. Within several small coastal kingdoms, stratified societies of nobles, commoners, and slaves gave allegiance to a single king or queen. For example, the Sakalava ethnic group dominated the western and northern portions of Madagascar in two separate kingdoms. Menabe, on the barren western grasslands, had its first capital at Toliara; Boina, in the northwest, included the port of Mahajanga. The towns became centers of trade where cattle and slaves, taken in war, were exchanged with European merchants for guns and other manufactured goods. These political domains were complemented by the Betsimisaraka kingdom along the east coast, and the southern coastal kingdoms dominated by the Mahafaly and the Antandroy ethnic groups.

The most powerful of Madagascar's kingdoms--the one that eventually established hegemony over a great portion of the island--was that developed by the Merina ethnic group. Before the Merina emerged as the dominant political power on the island in the nineteenth century, they alternated between periods of political unity and periods in which the kingdom separated into smaller political units. The location of the Merina in the central highlands afforded them some protection from the ravages of warfare that recurred among the coastal kingdoms. The distinction, recognized both locally and internationally, between the central highlanders (the Merina) and the *côtiers* (inhabitants of the coastal areas) would soon exert a major impact on Madagascar's political system (see Population and Ethnicity , this ch.). Organized like the coastal kingdoms in a hierarchy of nobles, commoners, and slaves, the Merina developed a unique political institution known as the *fokonolona* (village council). Through the *fokonolona*, village elders and other local notables were able to enact regulations and exert a measure of local control in such matters as public works and security.

Two monarchs played key roles in establishing Merina political dominance over Madagascar. The first, who ruled under the name of Andrianampoinimerina (r. 1797-1810), seized the throne of one of the Merina kingdoms in 1787. By 1806 he had conquered the remaining three kingdoms and united them within the former boundaries of Imerina, the capital established at the fortified city of Antananarivo. Radama I (r. 1816-28), an able and forward-looking monarch, succeeded to the throne in 1810 upon the death of his father. By adroitly playing off competing British and French interests in the island, he was able to extend Merina authority over nearly the entire island of Madagascar. Radama I first conquered the Betsileo ethnic group in the southern part of the central highlands and subsequently overpowered the Sakalava, an ethnic group that also sought at times to assert its hegemony over other groups. With the help of the British, who wanted a strong kingdom to offset French influence, Radama I modernized the armed forces. In 1817 the peoples of the east coast, facing an army of 35,000 soldiers, submitted with little or no protest; Radama then conquered the entire southeast as far as Tolagnaro. Particularly barren or impenetrable parts of the island escaped conquest, especially in the extreme south, but before his death Radama I succeeded in bringing the major and more hospitable portions of the country under Merina rule.

Radama I's interest in modernization along Western lines extended to social and political matters. He organized a cabinet and encouraged the Protestant London Missionary Society to establish schools and churches and to introduce the printing press--a move that was to have far-reaching implications for the country. The society made nearly half a million converts, and its teachers devised a written form of the local language, Malagasy, using the Latin alphabet. By 1828 several thousand persons, primarily Merina, had become literate, and a few young persons were being sent to Britain for schooling. Later the Merina dialect of Malagasy became the official language. Malagasylanguage publications were established and circulated among the Merina-educated elite; by 1896 some 164,000 children, mainly Merina and Betsileo, another ethnic group, attended the mission's primary schools. Along with new ideas came some development of local

**For additional analytical, business and investment opportunities information,
please contact Global Investment & Business Center, USA
at (202) 546-2103. Fax: (202) 546-3275. E-mail: rusric@erols.com**

manufacturing. Much productive time was spent, however, in military campaigns to expand territory and acquire slaves for trade.

The reign of Radama I's wife and successor, Queen Ranavalona I (r. 1828-61), was essentially reactionary, reflecting her distrust of foreign influence. Under the oligarchy that ruled in her name, rivals were slain, numerous Protestant converts were persecuted and killed, and many Europeans fled the island. The ruling elite held all the land and monopolized commerce, except for the handful of Europeans allowed to deal in cattle, rice, and other commodities. Remunerations to the queen provided the French traders a supply of slaves and a monopoly in the slave trade. Enjoying particular favor owing to his remarkable accomplishments was French artisan Jean Laborde, who established at Mantasoa, near Antananarivo, a manufacturing complex and agricultural research station where he manufactured commodities ranging from silk and soap to guns, tools, and cement.

During the reign of Radama II (r. 1861-63), the pendulum once again swung toward modernization and cordial relations with Western nations, particularly France. Radama II made a treaty of perpetual friendship with France, but his brief rule ended with his assassination by a group of nobles alarmed by his pro-French stance. He was succeeded by his widow, who ruled until 1868, during which time she annulled the treaty with France and the charter of Laborde's company.

After 1868 a Merina leader, Rainilaiarivony, ruled the monarchy. To avoid giving either the French or the British a pretext for intervention, Rainilaiarivony emphasized modernization of the society and tried to curry British favor without giving offense to the French. He made concessions to both countries, signing a commercial treaty with France in 1868 and with Britain in 1877. Important social developments under his leadership included the outlawing of polygamy and the slave trade; promulgation of new legal codes; the spread of education, especially among the Merina; and the conversion of the monarchy in 1869 to Protestantism.

COLONIAL ERA, 1894-1960

The French largely ended the attempts of Malagasy rulers to stymie foreign influence by declaring a protectorate over the entire island in 1894. A protectorate over northwest Madagascar, based on treaties signed with the Sakalava during the 1840s, had existed since 1882. But Queen Ranavalona III refused to recognize the 1894 effort to subordinate her kingdom to French rule. As a result, a French expeditionary force occupied Antananarivo in September 1895. A wave of antiforeign, anti-Christian rioting ensued. In 1896 France declared Madagascar a French colony and deported the queen and the prime minister--first to Reunion, then to Algeria.

Nationalist sentiment against French colonial rule eventually emerged among a small group of Merina intellectuals who had been educated by Europeans and exposed to Western intellectual thought. The group, based in Antananarivo, was led by a Malagasy Protestant clergyman, Pastor Ravelojoana, who was especially inspired by the Japanese model of modernization. A secret society dedicated to affirming Malagasy cultural identity was formed in 1913, calling itself Iron and Stone Ramification (Vy Vato Sakelika-

For additional analytical, business and investment opportunities information,
please contact Global Investment & Business Center, USA
at (202) 546-2103. Fax: (202) 546-3275. E-mail: rusric@erols.com

-VVS). Although the VVS was brutally suppressed, its actions eventually led French authorities to provide the Malagasy with their first representative voice in government.

Malagasy veterans of military service in France during World War I bolstered the embryonic nationalist movement. Throughout the 1920s, the nationalists stressed labor reform and equality of civil and political status for the Malagasy, stopping short of advocating independence. For example, the French League for Madagascar under the leadership of Anatole France demanded French citizenship for all Malagasy people in recognition of their country's wartime contribution of soldiers and resources. A number of veterans who remained in France were exposed to French political thought, most notably the anticolonial and proindependence platforms of French socialist parties. Jean Ralaimongo, for example, returned to Madagascar in 1924 and became embroiled in labor questions that were causing considerable tension throughout the island.

Among the first concessions to Malagasy equality was the formation in 1924 of two economic and financial delegations. One was composed of French settlers, the other of twenty-four Malagasy representatives elected by the Council of Notables in each of twenty-four districts. The two sections never met together, and neither had real decision-making authority.

Only in the aftermath of World War II was France willing to accept a form of Malagasy self-rule under French tutelage. In the fall of 1945, separate French and Malagasy electoral colleges voted to elect representatives from Madagascar to the Constituent Assembly of the Fourth Republic in Paris. The two delegates chosen by the Malagasy, Joseph Raseta and Joseph Ravoahangy, both campaigned to implement the ideal of the self-determination of peoples affirmed by the Atlantic Charter of 1941 and by the historic Brazzaville Conference of 1944.

Raseta and Ravoahangy, together with Jacques Rabemananjara, a writer long resident in Paris, had organized the Democratic Movement for Malagasy Restoration (Mouvement Démocratique de la Rénovation Malgache--MDRM), the foremost among several political parties formed in Madagascar by early 1946. Although Protestant Merina were well represented in MDRM's higher echelons, the party's 300,000 members were drawn from a broad political base reaching across the entire island and crosscutting ethnic and social divisions. Several smaller MDRM rivals included the Party of the Malagasy Disinherited (Parti des Déshérités Malgaches), whose members were mainly côtiers or descendants of slaves from the central highlands.

The 1946 constitution of the French Fourth Republic made Madagascar a territoire d'outre-mer (overseas territory) within the French Union. It accorded full citizenship to all Malagasy parallel with that enjoyed by citizens in France. But the assimilationist policy inherent in its framework was incongruent with the MDRM goal of full independence for Madagascar, so Ravoahangy and Raseta abstained from voting. The two delegates also objected to the separate French and Malagasy electoral colleges, even though Madagascar was represented in the French National Assembly. The constitution divided Madagascar administratively into a number of provinces, each of which was to have a locally elected provincial assembly. Not long after, a National Representative Assembly was constituted at Antananarivo. In the first elections for the provincial assemblies, the MDRM won all seats or a majority of seats, except in Mahajanga Province.

Despite these reforms, the political scene in Madagascar remained unstable. Economic and social concerns, including food shortages, black-market scandals, labor conscription, renewed ethnic tensions, and the return of soldiers from France, strained an already volatile situation. Many of the veterans felt they had been less well treated by France than had veterans from metropolitan France; others had been politically radicalized by their wartime experiences. The blend of fear, respect, and emulation on which Franco-Malagasy relations had been based seemed at an end.

On March 29, 1947, Malagasy nationalists revolted against the French. Although the uprising eventually spread over one-third of the island, the French were able to restore order after reinforcements arrived from France. Casualties among the Malagasy were estimated in the 60,000 to 80,000 range (later reports estimated 11,000 casualties, of whom 180 were non-Malagasy). The group of leaders responsible for the uprising, which came to be referred to as the Revolt of 1947, never has been identified conclusively. Although the MDRM leadership consistently maintained its innocence, the French outlawed the party. French military courts tried the military leaders of the revolt and executed twenty of them. Other trials produced, by one report, some 5,000 to 6,000 convictions, and penalties ranged from brief imprisonment to death.

In 1956 France's socialist government renewed the French commitment to greater autonomy in Madagascar and other colonial possessions by enacting the *loi-cadre* (enabling law). The *loi-cadre* provided for universal suffrage and was the basis for parliamentary government in each colony. In the case of Madagascar, the law established executive councils to function alongside provincial and national assemblies, and dissolved the separate electoral colleges for the French and Malagasy groups. The provision for universal suffrage had significant implications in Madagascar because of the basic ethnopolitical split between the Merina and the *côtiers*, reinforced by the divisions between Protestants and Roman Catholics. Superior armed strength and educational and cultural advantages had given the Merina a dominant influence on the political process during much of the country's history. The Merina were heavily represented in the Malagasy component of the small elite to whom suffrage had been restricted in the earlier years of French rule. Now the *côtiers*, who outnumbered the Merina, would be a majority.

The end of the 1950s was marked by growing debate over the future of Madagascar's relationship with France. Two major political parties emerged. The newly created Democratic Social Party of Madagascar (Parti Social Démocrate de Madagascar--PSD) favored self-rule while maintaining close ties with France. The PSD was led by Philibert Tsiranana, a well-educated Tsimihety from the northern coastal region who was one of three Malagasy deputies elected in 1956 to the National Assembly in Paris. The PSD built upon Tsiranana's traditional political stronghold of Mahajanga in northwest Madagascar and rapidly extended its sources of support by absorbing most of the smaller parties that had been organized by the *côtiers*. In sharp contrast, those advocating complete independence from France came together under the auspices of the Congress Party for the Independence of Madagascar (Antokon'ny Kongresy Fanafahana an'i Madagasikara-- AKFM). Primarily based in Antananarivo and

For additional analytical, business and investment opportunities information, please contact Global Investment & Business Center, USA at (202) 546-2103. Fax: (202) 546-3275. E-mail: rusric@erols.com

Antsiranana, party support centered among the Merina under the leadership of Richard Andriamanjato, himself a Merina and a member of the Protestant clergy. To the consternation of French policy makers, the AKFM platform called for nationalization of foreign-owned industries, collectivization of land, the "Malagachization" of society away from French values and customs (most notably use of the French language), international nonalignment, and exit from the Franc Zone (see Glossary).

INDEPENDENCE, THE FIRST REPUBLIC, AND THE MILITARY TRANSITION, 1960-75

After France adopted the Constitution of the Fifth Republic under the leadership of General Charles de Gaulle, on September 28, 1958, Madagascar held a referendum to determine whether the country should become a self-governing republic within the French community. The AKFM and other nationalists opposed to the concept of limited self-rule mustered about 25 percent of votes cast. The vast majority of the population at the urging of the PSD leadership voted in favor of the referendum. The vote led to the election of Tsiranana as the country's first president on April 27, 1959. After a year of negotiations between Tsiranana and his French counterparts, Madagascar's status as a self-governing republic officially was altered on June 26, 1960, to that of a fully independent and sovereign state. The cornerstone of Tsiranana's government was the signing with France of fourteen agreements and conventions designed to maintain and strengthen Franco-Malagasy ties. These agreements were to provide the basis for increasing opposition from Tsiranana's critics.

A spirit of political reconciliation prevailed in the early 1960s. By achieving independence and obtaining the release of the MDRM leaders detained since the Revolt of 1947, Tsiranana had coopted the chief issues on which the more aggressively nationalist elements had built much of their support. Consistent with Tsiranana's firm commitment to remain attached to Western civilization, the new regime made plain its intent to maintain strong ties to France and the West in the economic, defense, and cultural spheres. Not entirely sanguine about this prospect, the opposition initially concurred in the interest of consolidating the gains of the previous decade, and most ethnic and regional interests supported Tsiranana.

Similar to other African leaders during the immediate independence era, Tsiranana oversaw the consolidation of his own party's power at the expense of other parties. A political system that strongly favored the incumbent complemented these actions. For example, although the political process allowed minority parties to participate, the constitution mandated a winner-take-all system that effectively denied the opposition a voice in governance. Tsiranana's position was further strengthened by the broad, multiethnic popular base of the PSD among the *côtiers*, whereas the opposition was severely disorganized. The AKFM continued to experience intraparty rifts between leftist and ultranationalist, more orthodox Marxist factions; it was unable to capitalize on increasingly active but relatively less privileged Malagasy youth because the party's base was the Merina middle class.

A new force on the political scene provided the first serious challenge to the Tsiranana government in April 1971. The National Movement for the Independence of Madagascar

For additional analytical, business and investment opportunities information, please contact Global Investment & Business Center, USA at (202) 546-2103. Fax: (202) 546-3275. E-mail: rusric@erols.com

(Mouvement National pour l'Indépendance de Madagascar--Monima) led a peasant uprising in Toliara Province. The creator and leader of Monima was Monja Jaona, a *côtier* from the south who also participated in the Revolt of 1947. The main issue was government pressure for tax collection at a time when local cattle herds were being ravaged by disease. The protesters attacked military and administrative centers in the area, apparently hoping for support in the form of weapons and reinforcements from China. Such help never arrived, and the revolt was harshly and quickly suppressed. An estimated fifty to 1,000 persons died, Monima was dissolved, and Monima leaders, including Jaona and several hundred protesters, were arrested and deported to the island of Nosy Lava.

Another movement came on the scene in early 1972, in the form of student protests in Antananarivo. A general strike involving the nation's roughly 100,000 secondary-level students focused on three principal issues: ending the cultural cooperation agreements with France; replacing educational programs designed for schools in France and taught by French teachers with programs emphasizing Malagasy life and culture and taught by Malagasy instructors; and increasing access for economically underprivileged youth to secondary-level institutions. By early May, the PSD sought to end the student strike at any cost; on May 12 and 13, the government arrested several hundred student leaders and sent them to Nosy-Lava. Authorities also closed the schools and banned demonstrations.

Mounting economic stagnation--as revealed in scarcities of investment capital, a general decline in living standards, and the failure to meet even modest development goals--further undermined the government's position. Forces unleashed by the growing economic crisis combined with student unrest to create an opposition alliance. Workers, public servants, peasants, and many unemployed urban youth of Antananarivo joined the student strike, which spread to the provinces. Protesters set fire to the town hall and to the offices of a French-language newspaper in the capital.

The turning point occurred on May 13 when the Republican Security Force (Force Républicaine de Sécurité--FRS) opened fire on the rioters; in the ensuing melee between fifteen and forty persons were killed and about 150 injured. Tsiranana declared a state of national emergency and on May 18 dissolved his government, effectively ending the First Republic. He then turned over full power to the National Army under the command of General Gabriel Ramanantsoa, a politically conservative Merina and former career officer in the French army. The National Army had maintained strict political neutrality in the crisis, and its intervention to restore order was welcomed by protesters and opposition elements.

The Ramanantsoa military regime could not resolve rising economic and ethnic problems, and narrowly survived an attempted coup d'état on December 31, 1974. The fact that the coup was led by several *côtier* officers against a Merina military leader underscored the growing Merina/*côtier* polarization in the military. In an attempt at restoring unity, Ramanantsoa, on February 5, 1975, turned over power to Colonel Richard Ratsimandrava (a Merina with a less "aristocratic" background). Five days later, Ratsimandrava was assassinated, and a National Military Directorate was formed to restore order by declaring martial law, strictly censoring political expression, and suspending all political parties.

For additional analytical, business and investment opportunities information, please contact Global Investment & Business Center, USA at (202) 546-2103. Fax: (202) 546-3275. E-mail: rusric@erols.com

The political transition crisis was resolved on June 15, 1975, when the National Military Directorate selected Lieutenant Commander Didier Ratsiraka as head of state and president of a new ruling body, the Supreme Revolutionary Council (SRC). The choice of Ratsiraka allayed ethnic concerns because he was a *côtier* belonging to the Betsimisaraka ethnic group. In addition, Ratsiraka--a dedicated socialist--was perceived by his military peers as a consensus candidate capable of forging unity among the various leftist political parties (such as AKFM and Monima), students, urban workers, the peasantry, and the armed forces.

THE SECOND REPUBLIC, 1975-92

Ratsiraka was elected to a seven-year term as president in a national referendum on December 21, 1975, confirming the mandate for consensus and inaugurating Madagascar's Second Republic. The guiding principle of Ratsiraka's administration was the need for a socialist "revolution from above." Specifically, he sought to radically change Malagasy society in accordance with programs and principles incorporated into the *Charter of the Malagasy Socialist Revolution*, popularly referred to as the "Red Book" (Boky Mena). According to this document, the primary goal of the newly renamed Democratic Republic of Madagascar was to build a "new society" founded on socialist principles and guided by the actions of the "five pillars of the revolution": the SRC, peasants and workers, young intellectuals, women, and the Popular Armed Forces. "The socialist revolution," explains the Red Book, "is the only choice possible for us in order to achieve rapid economic and cultural development in an autonomous, humane, and harmonious manner." The Red Book advocated a new foreign policy based on the principle of nonalignment, and domestic policies focused on renovating the *fokonolona*, decentralizing the administration, and fomenting economic development through rigorous planning and popular input.

Several early policies collectively decided by Ratsiraka and other members of the SRC set the tone of the revolution from above. The first major SRC decision was to bring the French-held sectors of the economy under government control. This "economic decolonization" was welcomed by nationalists, who long had clamored for economic and cultural independence from France. The government also lifted martial law but retained rigid press censorship. Finally, the SRC ordered the closure of an earth satellite tracking station operated by the United States as part of its commitment to nonaligned foreign relations.

Political consolidation proceeded apace following the addition of ten civilians to the SRC in January 1976. This act constituted the beginning of a civil-military partnership in that the SRC became more representative of the country's major political tendencies and ethnic communities. In March the Vanguard of the Malagasy Revolution (Antokin'ny Revolisiona Malagasy--Arema) was founded as the government party, and Ratsiraka became its secretary general. In sharp contrast to the single-party states created by other African Marxist leaders, Arema served as simply one (albeit the most powerful) member of a coalition of six parties united under the umbrella of the National Front for the Defense of the Revolution (Front National pour la Défense de la Révolution--FNDR). Membership in the FNDR, necessary for participation in the electoral process, was preconditioned on party endorsement of the revolutionary principles and programs contained in the Red Book.

For additional analytical, business and investment opportunities information, please contact Global Investment & Business Center, USA at (202) 546-2103. Fax: (202) 546-3275. E-mail: rusric@erols.com

Ratsiraka and Arema clearly dominated the political system. In the *fokonolona* elections held in March 1977, for example, Arema captured 90 percent of 73,000 contested seats in 11,400 assemblies. In June 1977, Arema won 220 out of a total of 232 seats in elections for six provincial general assemblies, and 112 out of a total of 137 seats in the Popular National Assembly. This trend toward consolidation was most vividly demonstrated by Rasiraka's announcement of his 1977 cabinet in which Arema members held sixteen of eighteen ministerial posts.

Yet, less than three years after taking power, Ratsiraka's regime was confronted with growing popular disenchantment. As early as September 1977, antigovernment demonstrations erupted in Antananarivo because of severe shortages in foodstuffs and essential commodities. This trend intensified as the economy worsened under the weight of ill-conceived economic policies that gradually centralized government control over the key sectors of the economy, including banking and agriculture. Ratsiraka defiantly adopted authoritarian tactics in response to the evolving opposition, sending in the armed forces to stifle dissent and maintain order during student riots in May 1978. In the economic realm, however, Ratsiraka accepted the free-market reforms demanded by the International Monetary Fund (IMF--see Glossary) in order to ensure an infusion of foreign assistance vital to keeping the economy functioning. Whereas Ratsiraka's drift toward authoritarianism provided his enemies with political cannon fodder, his economic reforms led them to charge him with abandoning "scientific socialism" and alienated his traditional base of political supporters, as well.

The results of presidential elections within the de facto single-party framework that prevailed throughout the Second Republic clearly demonstrated Ratsiraka's declining political fortunes. Widespread initial enthusiasm for his socialist revolution from above secured him nearly 95 percent of the popular vote in the 1975 presidential elections, but support declined to 80 percent in 1982 and to only 63 percent in 1989. The year of 1989 marked a special turning point in that the fall of the Berlin Wall heralded the intellectual death of singleparty rule in Eastern Europe and the former Soviet Union and similarly transformed electoral politics in Africa. In the case of Madagascar, increasingly vocal opposition parties denounced what they and international observers considered massive fraud in the 1989 presidential election, including Ratsiraka's refusal to update outdated voting lists that excluded the anti-Ratsiraka youth vote and the stuffing of ballot boxes at unmonitored rural polling stations. Massive demonstrations against Ratsiraka's inauguration led to violent clashes in Antananarivo that, according to official figures, left seventy-five dead and wounded.

Popular discontent with the Ratsiraka regime heightened on August 10, 1991, when more than 400,000 citizens marched peacefully on the President's Palace in order to oust the Ratsiraka government and create a new multiparty political system. Ratsiraka already faced an economy crippled by a general strike that had begun in May, as well as a divided and restless military whose loyalty no longer could be assumed. When the Presidential Guard opened fire on the marchers and killed and wounded hundreds, a crisis of leadership occurred.

The net result of these events was Ratsiraka's agreement on October 31, 1991 to support a process of democratic transition, complete with the formulation of a new constitution and the holding of free and fair multiparty elections. Albert Zafy, the central leader of the opposition forces and a *côtier* of the Tsimihety ethnic group, played a critical role in this transition process and ultimately emerged as the first president of Madagascar's Third Republic. The leader of the Comité des Forces Vives (Vital Forces Committee, known as Forces Vives), an umbrella opposition group composed of sixteen political parties that spearheaded the 1991 demonstrations, Zafy also emerged as the head of what became known as the High State Authority, a transitional government that shared power with the Ratsiraka regime during the democratization process.

A new draft constitution was approved by 75 percent of those voting in a national referendum on August 19, 1992. The first round of presidential elections followed on November 25. Frontrunner Zafy won 46 percent of the popular vote as the Forces Vives candidate, and Ratsiraka, as leader of his own newly created progovernment front, the Militant Movement for Malagasy Socialism (Mouvement Militant pour le Socialisme Malgache--MMSM), won approximately 29 percent of the vote. The remaining votes were split among a variety of other candidates. Because neither candidate obtained a majority of the votes cast, a second round of elections between the two frontrunners was held on February 10, 1993. Zafy emerged victorious with nearly 67 percent of the popular vote.

THE THIRD REPUBLIC, 1993-

The Third Republic officially was inaugurated on March 27, 1993, when Zafy was sworn in as president. The victory of the Forces Vives was further consolidated in elections held on June 13, 1993, for 138 seats in the newly created National Assembly. Voters turned out in low numbers (roughly 30 to 40 percent abstained) because they were being called upon to vote for the fourth time in less than a year. The Forces Vives and other allied parties won seventy-five seats. This coalition gave Zafy a clear majority and enabled him to chose Francisque Ravony of the Forces Vives as prime minister.

By the latter half of 1994, the heady optimism that accompanied this dramatic transition process had declined somewhat as the newly elected democratic government found itself confronted with numerous economic and political obstacles. Adding to these woes was the relatively minor but nonetheless embarrassing political problem of Ratsiraka's refusal to vacate the President's Palace. The Zafy regime has found itself under increasing economic pressure from the IMF and foreign donors to implement market reforms, such as cutting budget deficits and a bloated civil service, that do little to respond to the economic problems facing the majority of Madagascar's population. Zafy also confronts growing divisions within his ruling coalition, as well as opposition groups commonly referred to as "federalists" seeking greater power for the provinces (known as "faritany") under a more decentralized government (see fig. 2). Although recently spurred by the desire of anti-Zafy forces to gain greater control over local affairs, historically Madagascar has witnessed a tension between domination by the central highlanders and pressures from residents of outlying areas to manage their own affairs. In short, the Zafy regime faces the dilemma of using relatively untested political structures and "rules of the game" to resolve numerous issues of governance.

For additional analytical, business and investment opportunities information, please contact Global Investment & Business Center, USA at (202) 546-2103. Fax: (202) 546-3275. E-mail: rusric@erols.com

GOVERNMENT AND POLITICS

NATURE OF POLITICAL RELATIONSHIP WITH THE UNITED STATES

The Government and the people of Madagascar are favorably disposed towards the United States and relations are friendly. The United States provides significant bilateral assistance, mainly in the environment, health, population, and governance sectors. The United States also contributes resources indirectly, through multilateral development institutions such as the United Nations Development Program, the United Nations Environment Program, the World Bank, the International Monetary Fund and the African Development Bank.

Madagascar is historically linked to its former colonial power, France. Its government, legislature and judicial system emulate the French model in many ways. Madagascar is a member of the Indian Ocean Commission (and currently holds the rotating presidency), COMESA, the Indian Ocean Rim, the Non-Aligned Movement, and the Organization of African Unity. Its non-alignment is reflected in its "all points" diplomatic and commercial relations, which include Israel, North and South Korea, Taiwan, and China, as well as Libya and Iran.

MAJOR POLITICAL ISSUES AFFECTING BUSINESS CLIMATE

After years of failed socialist economic policies, Madagascar has taken important steps towards economic reform by beginning to reduce the government's presence in the productive sectors of the economy.

Most political groupings do not overtly take issue with the need for structural adjustment. As in other countries, including the United States, vested interests reportedly provide campaign financing to political parties and individual politicians in an effort to influence policy outcomes.

CIVIL SOCIETY INCLUDING BUSINESS-TO-GOVERNMENT AND BUSINESS-TO-BUSINESS DIALOGUE

The civil society, through many business associations, is very active in the country. A special body called CRC (Competitiveness Committee), supported by the World Bank, was created in 1998 to establish a permanent dialogue between the Government and the private sector.

POLITICAL SYSTEM, SCHEDULE FOR ELECTIONS AND ORIENTATION OF MAJOR POLITICAL PARTIES

Madagascar's political system was changed by the adoption of a new Constitution, approved by referendum in March 1998. The new Constitution strengthens the role of the President of the Republic and promises more autonomy to the provinces. In May 1998, the Malagasy people elected a new National Assembly. The Constitution provides for a Senate, but this second chamber has yet to be put in place. The President is elected by direct, universal suffrage for a five-year term. The Prime Minister, appointed by the President, and his cabinet are part of the executive branch. They cannot be members of the legislature. Matters of national sovereignty--foreign affairs and national defense --belong to the President. The executive and the legislature share legislative initiative. In addition to the executive (President and Government) and the legislative (National Assembly and Senate), the Constitution provides for an independent judiciary.

With the new Constitution, there are few checks and balances to temper executive authority. Only the National Assembly, with the Senate's agreement, can impeach the President. On the other hand, the President and the Council of Government (the Prime Minister and his Cabinet) can by decree dissolve the National Assembly. The Constitutional Court must approve the constitutionality of every law before it is promulgated.

GOVERNEMNT STRUCTURE

MARC RAVELOMANANA, PRESIDENT

CABINET

Jacques SYLLA
Premier Ministre

For additional analytical, business and investment opportunities information, please contact Global Investment & Business Center, USA at (202) 546-2103. Fax: (202) 546-3275. E-mail: rusric@erols.com

RAMANDIMBIARISON Zaza Manitranja

Vice-Premier Ministre chargé des Programmes Economiques, Ministre des Transports, des Travaux Publics et de l'Aménagement du Territoire

RAJAONAH Alice

Garde des Sceaux, Ministre de la Justice

RAMBELOALIJAONA Jean Seth

Ministre de l'Intérieur et de la Réforme Administrative

RANJIVASON Jean Théodore

Ministre de l'Enseignement Supérieur et de la Recherche Scientifique

AMADY Augustin

Ministre de la Sécurité Publique

RANJEVA Marcel

Ministre des Affaires Etrangères

RABOTOARISON Charles Sylvain

Ministre de l'Environnement, des Eaux et Forêts

For additional analytical, business and investment opportunities information, please contact Global Investment & Business Center, USA at (202) 546-2103. Fax: (202) 546-3275. E-mail: rusric@erols.com

MAMIZARA Jules

Ministre de la
Défense Nationale

**RAZAFINDRALAMBO Vola
Dieudonné**

Ministre de la Fonction Publique

**RASAMINDRAKOTROKA
Andry**

Ministre de la Santé

**ANDRIAMPANJAVA
Jacob Félicien**

Ministre de la
Population

**Monique ANDREAS
ESOAVELOMANDROSO**

Ministre auprès de la Présidence
de la République chargé de la
Décentralisation de du
Développement des Provinces
Autonomes et des Communes

RAHAINGOSOA Odette

Ministre de la Culture

NDALANA René

Ministre de la
Jeunesse et des

**RAZAFINDRANDRIANTSIMANIRY
Michel**

Ministre de l'Enseignement
Secondaire et de l'Education de
Base

RAZAFINJATOVO Haja

Ministre
Télécommunications, des
Postes et de la

Jeunesse et des
Sports et des Loisirs

Ministre de l'Enseignement
Secondaire et de l'Education de
Base

Télécommunications, des
Postes et de la
Communication

**RADAVIDSON
Andriamparany
Benjamin**

Ministre de
l'Economie, des
Finances et du
Budget

**RANDRIASANDRANTRINIONY
Yvan**

Ministre de l'Agriculture, de
l'Elevage et de la Pêche

**RAZAFIMIHARY
Mejamirado**

Ministre de
l'Industrialisation, du
Commerce et du
Développement du
Secteur Privé

**RABARISON
Jacquis H.**

Ministre de l'Energie
et des Mines

MAHAZOASY Roger F.
Ministre du Tourisme

**RABENIRINA Jean
Jacques**

Ministre du travail et des
Lois Sociales

CONSTITUTION AND INSTITUTIONS OF GOVERNANCE

The Third Republic received its first expression of popular support and legitimacy on August 19, 1992, when the constitutional framework constructed by the National Conference was approved by more than 75 percent of those voting in a popular referendum (the constitution took effect on September 12). On this date, the people overwhelmingly approved a new constitution consisting of 149 articles that provided for the separation of powers among the executive, legislative, and judicial branches of government; the creation of a multiparty political system; and the protection of individual human rights and freedom of speech.

The power of the executive branch is divided between a president who is elected by universal suffrage and a prime minister from the parliament who is nominated by his/her peers but who must be approved by the president. If the nominee for prime minister does not achieve an absolute majority of support within the parliament, the president may choose a candidate from the parliament who will serve for one year. As captured in the Malagasy concept *ray aman-dreny* (father and mother of the nation), enshrined in Article 44 of the constitution, the president serves as the symbol of national unity. The president also is the recognized leader of foreign policy and constitutes by far the single most powerful political person within the country. All presidential decrees must be countersigned, however, and the president is bound by the constitutional reality that the prime minister is responsible for the functioning of the government.

The president is elected for a five-year period and is limited to two terms in office. In the event that no candidate wins a simple majority of the popular vote, a run-off election is held between the two leading candidates within a period of two months. The most important unwritten law regarding the executive branch revolves around the *côtier*/central highlands distinction. If a *côtier* is elected president, it is understood that a Merina will fill the position of prime minister, and vice versa. In the case of the first national elections held under the Third Republic, for example, the elected president-- Zafy--who is a *côtier*, chose a prime minister-- Francisque Ravony--from the ranks of the Merina (although several of the Merina elite were not entirely happy with the choice because Ravony is only half Merina).

The constitution provides for a bicameral parliament composed of a Senate and a National Assembly (Assembleé Nationale). The Senate represents territorial groups and serves as the consultative chamber on social and economic issues. Two-thirds of its members are chosen by an Electoral College and the remaining one-third are chosen by the president. Envisioned elections for 1994 had not been held as of June 1994. The National Assembly consists of 138 deputies elected by universal suffrage using a proportional representation list-system. Both senators and deputies serve for four years. The June 16, 1993 elections resulted in about half the deputies elected being members of the Forces Vives. The remainder belonged to six parties of which the largest had fifteen deputies and the smallest nine deputies. The parliament as a whole operates with a variety of classic parliamentary measures, such as a vote of no confidence, that enable it to serve as a check on the power of the executive.

A new system of local governance under the constitution is known as the Decentralized Territorial Authorities (Collectivités Territoriales Décentralisées). According to the decentralization law adopted by the National Assembly in March 1994, twenty-eight regions (*faritra*), more than 100 departments (*fileovana*), and a little less than 1,000 communes (*faribohitra*) have been created. Certain urban communes, such as the cities of Antananarivo, Nosy-Be, and Sainte Marie will function as departments. Envisioned as regional vehicles for popular input in which members are elected by universal suffrage, these authorities have yet to be implemented; their exact role in the policy-making process remains ill-defined, but it is contemplated that the national government will handle such areas as foreign affairs, defense, public security, justice, currency, and broad economic planning and policy, leaving economic implementation to the decentralized bodies. However, the Zafy regime is confident that, once functioning, these regional boards will take the political initiative away from the so-called federalist opposition, which has been seeking to shift power away from the central government to the regions.

A strong, independent judiciary is also enshrined in the 1992 constitution. An eleven-member Supreme Court serves as the highest arbiter of the laws of the land. Other judicial bodies include the Administrative and Financial Constitutional Court, the Appeals Courts, tribunals, and the High Court of Justice. The creation of this complex system indicates the desire of the constitutional framers for a society built upon the rule of law. Indeed, the constitution explicitly outlines the fundamental rights of individual citizens and groups (most notably freedom of speech) and guarantees the existence of an independent press free from government control or censorship.

The creation of a truly free and fair multiparty system is the centerpiece of the new constitutional order. In sharp contrast to the Ratsiraka era, when political parties could only exist under the ideological umbrella of the FNDR, democratization of the political system has led to the proliferation of political parties of all ideological stripes. In the first legislative elections held under the Third Republic in 1993, for example, more than 120 political parties fielded at least 4,000 candidates for a total of 138 legislative seats. Despite constitutional guarantees concerning the rights of citizens to form political parties without fear of government retribution, parties that call for ethnic or religious segregation or demonstrably endanger national unity are subject to being banned.

The electoral system is designed to promote and facilitate widespread popular participation. In fact, it is argued that the proportional representation list-system (including the rule of the largest remainder) for electing deputies actually encourages large numbers of candidates to take part. All resident citizens eighteen years of age or older can vote in elections, but candidates must be at least twenty-one years of age to participate. Electoral registers are usually revised during a two-month period beginning in December, and the country is divided into sixty-eight constituencies for electoral purposes. Although there was a four-month gap between the end of the first presidential elections and the first legislative elections held under the Third Republic in 1993, legislative elections are supposed to be held no less than two months after the end of presidential elections. The next presidential elections are scheduled for 1998.

THE FOKONOLONA AND TRADITIONAL GOVERNANCE

Madagascar has a tradition of limited village self-rule associated with the institution of the *fokonolona*--a village council composed of village elders and other local notables. After having been alternately suppressed and encouraged by the French colonial authorities, authorities officially revived the *fokonolona* in 1962 in an attempt to involve local communities in plans for rural economic and social development. The perceived usefulness of the *fokonolona* derived from its traditional role of maintaining order in the village and providing social and economic assistance.

In 1973 the Ramanantsoa military regime furthered the selfrule concept by establishing self-governing bodies at the local level. Government functionaries who were formerly appointed were to be replaced by elected officials. Yet it was not until 1975, under the leadership of Ratsiraka, that the *fokonolona* was given constitutional recognition as the "decentralized collective of the state" responsible for economic, social, cultural, and municipal development at the local level. Despite his best intentions, during Ratsiraka's rule the *fokonolona* was still far from an idealized self-governing institution. Its governing bodies were dominated, as in the past, by conservative elders, and participation by youth was either minimal or not encouraged by elders. Under the Zafy regime the *fokonolona* will continue to offer policy guidance at the local level, but it has been superseded by the Decentralized Territorial Collectives.

The *fokonolona* often is characterized as one of the most characteristic Malagasy social institutions. It is, in fact, not a "pan-Malagasy" cultural element but an institution that evolved among the Merina and was implanted in other parts of the country by both the Merina and the French. Even among the neighboring Betsileo, it is considered something of a foreign implantation. Nonetheless, the *fokonolona* offers aid to members in need (such as when a child is born or a funeral is held), undertakes village projects (such as the repair of rice fields or village buildings after a cyclone), coordinates mutual aid at planting and harvest time, and occasionally chastises--or ostracizes--those considered wrongdoers.

The *fokonolona* ties individuals together in a network of mutual obligations. Its meetings bring together in a cooperative setting people of different kinship groups within a village, and the common use of fictive kinship terms promotes the creation of an atmosphere of amity and solidarity (*fihavanana*), necessary for sincere cooperation. The *fokonolona*, however, traditionally has not been a democratic institution despite its town-meeting character, because its meetings tend to be dominated by influential local notables. Local political power remains a function of age and membership in a high-status kinship group; in some cases, the descendants of slaves (*andevo*) attend *fokonolona* meetings, but their influence is marginal.

At *fokonolona* meetings, it is possible to see one of Madagascar's most striking cultural expressions, the *kabary* (discourse), a lengthy speech in which a speaker uses flowery and poetic language to make a critical point in a most indirect fashion. The people will listen silently from beginning to end. Those who disagree will not express their opinion but will counter with a speech that at first seems to support the first speaker but that actually contains a hidden counterproposal. Speakers may express their views by telling jokes. If people laugh or if they simply act according to the second speaker's proposal, the first has lost. Rarely if ever does an open confrontation between speakers occur.

THE MALAGASY NATIONAL ASSEMBLY

"Solombavambahoaka", is the malagasy name of the deputy; freely translated it means: "those who speak in the name of the people". This is then its represent, its lawyer in some way, to take the people defense in front of all other governmental instances.

POLITICAL STRUCTURE

Speaker :
Permanent Bureau :
6- Vice Presidents

02- Questeurs (one for Administration and Budgetthe second for Public Relations and Legislation).

National Assembly Commissions (or committees : 12 subject areas)

1. **Finance.**
2. **Foreign affairs and International Relations.**
3. **National defense and security.**
4. **Rural Development : Agricultural, Fishing, Breeding.**
5. **Infrastructure, Communication, Transport, Post Telecommunication-Lands & housing.**
6. **Social Affairs, Health, Population.**
7. **Education and Cultural Affairs, Research, Youth and Sports.**
8. **Juridical & Legislation.**
9. **Interior & Decentralization.**
10. **Industry, Mines, Trading, Crafts.**
11. **Public Works.**
12. **Environment, Forests, Tourism.**

Administrative structure

The Administrative staff was created to help Deputies in their work and responsabilities. Over 100 employees deal with every day issues such as administration, secretarial work, security, and housing. Five directorates have been set up to oversee these different tasks, under the supervision of a General Secretary. They are :

1. **Administration and Staffing**
2. **Finances.**
3. **Public Relations.**
4. **Legislation.**
5. **Security.**

External Relations Division

The External Relations Division was established during the first legislature of the Third Republic. According to the flow chart of the National Assembly, the External Relations Service (SRE) provides administrative and technical support in relations between the National Assembly and foreign entities such as embassies ministries and national and international organizations. The SRE also deals with interparlementary relations and the preparation of Malagasy parliamantary delegation documents. Furthemore this service is available for the translation of reccords, such as the development projects of the Deputies' districts and mail from other countries. For further information, embassies, ministries, cultural centers, and national and international organizations are invited to get in touch with this service, and we'll do our best to satisfy your requests.

THE HISTORY OF THE MALAGASY NATIONAL ASSEMBLY

It is difficult to separate the history of the National Assembly from that of the whole Malagasy Nation. The legislative organ always evolved together with the political system. The legislation have always been a tool for each regime to set its general policy in order to better lead to the type of society they intended to build.
The last years of the colonial period (between 1945 and 1960) where marked by the accession of many formerly colonized countries to political independence. A period particularly rich in events lead to the leadership of the colonized people.

Thus, the adoption of "la loi cadre" in 1956 and the establishment of the "communauté" in 1958 have been decisive in the progression to political independence in respect to France.

In the mean time, several pressure where made to lead France in this inevitable, "image de la loi Lamine Guye (to equal work, equal wage) and the foundation of the UNO which consecrated in its fundamental text the Right of People to dispose of themselves. The Law No 56-615 of June 23rd 1956 called "Loi Cadre" or "Loi Deffere" was then applied to Madagascar among the French community. This text enforces a "closer involvement of outer-seas populations to the management of their own interests by administrative decentralization".

After 1958 events in France, and the accession of General de Gaule as President, events will move faster, the "loi cadre" is replaced by the "French Community". This is where the malagasy legislative history starts. October 14 th 1958, indeed, the Malagasy Republic was proclaimed by High Commissar Soucadaux.

A CONSTITUTIVE ASSEMBLY

On October 15 th 1958, a Constitutive Assembly was lead by Norbert Zafimahova in order to elaborate the new Constitution of Madagascar. Norbert Zafimahova pronounced a historical speech at the opening of this Assembly in which he invited its members to overcome their political and ethnical divisions to better erect the malagasy nation.

On April 29 th 1959, the Constitution of the Malagasy Republic was adopted and on June 26 th 1960, Madagascar proclaimed its independence. The first legislative elections took place and lead to a majority of Social Democrates (PSD) of President Philibert Tsiranana at the Assembly. "I am glad that their exist an opposition in this country" he declared at the opening of the first parliamentary session on October 2 nd 1963. Only a few seats had been taken by this opposition.

At this time, the National Assembly had a president, Alfred Nany, 5 vice-president and 3 questeurs. Only the President possessed a cabinet made of a cabinet director, a cabinet head and a secretary as for the Primer Minister's. Questeurs had their own secretaries.

At first, the Assembly staff members where all public functionaries detached by decision of the permanent office to later permanently become part of the parliament functionaries.

Staff members of the permanent board where housed in the building inside the National Assembly walls. Fdf

THE LEGISLATIVE FUNCTION OF THE PARLIAMENT OF THE FIRST REPUBLIC

The legislative function was then taken by the National Assembly and the Senat. While there function could be withdrawn for a time, they both controlled the action of the Government through, for example, the reading of the annual report at the "Chambre des Comptes".

If on the constitutional level all democratic mechanisms have been set up to exercise control on the State leadership, these did never truly work because of the supremacy of the PSD which in fact ruled the country until 1972 leaving true legislative power in the hands of the President.

After the bloodshed of may 1972 which obliged President Tsiranana to get dismissed in favor of General Ramanantsoa and after the referendum of October 8 th 1927, the first National Assembly and the Senat where replaced by a Popular National Council for Development (CNPD) lead by priest Fety Michel.

This CNPD is not a true legislative organ. It is a legal frame for dialog between the people and its government. It is mainly used for social and development matters. At this time, the government in fact possessed all legislative and executive authorities. The CNPD will disappear with Ramanantsoa leadership.

Indeed, on January 1975, Ramanantsoa dissolves his government and, 10 days after confers all rights to Colonel Ratsimandrava who is assassinated on February 11 th. General Gilles Andriamahazo declares the martial law and constitute a military regime which rules through decrees. During this period of exceptions, the Assembly functions where ceased.

After a few months, the regime elected a young captain, Didier Ratsiraka to lead the country back to a normal situation.

After having erected, with the help of closely related, the Charter of the Malagasy Socialist Revolution, where all objectives and means where put forward, Ratsiraka prepares a new Constitution which, with December 21 st 1975 referendum will lead to the Second Republic in which the legislative organ is called the Popular National Assembly (ANP).

THE POPULAR NATIONAL ASSEMBLY

Elected for 5 years through direct votes, the ANP is the state organ to which all legislative rights are delegated as mention in article 56 of the new Constitution. The ANP votes laws but this function was much reduced by the normative rôle of the President. He was indeed authorized to rule through decrees. Some of the decrees where even immediately applied without ratification by the ANP. The rare occasions where the ANP exercised some weight where in controlling the state budget for example.

As the First Republic Assembly, the ANP was dominated by the Presidential party, AREMA which was represented by 112 congressmen out of 137 during the first legislation (1977-1982). The ANP was presided by Lucien Xavier Michel Andrianarahinjaka from the beginning to the end of the Second Republic in 1991. At that time, the National Assembly staff was composed of 1 President, 5 vice-presidents and 2 questeurs. Only the president had its own cabinet.

The existence of the AREMA as a major political force have considerably reduced the role of the ANP as a place for discussion on political ideas which were given at the executive level.

The ANP was then said to be only a formal organ with no real power. The 31 st October 1991 convention replaced the ANP by a consultative organ, the Committee for the Economical and Social Development (CRES). During the transition period to the 3 rd Republic, the Government was again authorized to rule thourgh decrees which ought to be ratified by the High Authority of the State.

The CRES was composed of 130 members originating from diverse groups. Its board was lead by priest Richard Andriamanjato and Manandafy Rakotonirina.
The CRES had to be consulted on every financial aspects and the elaboration of any development plans. In other domains, its role was limited to recommendations until the setup of the National Assembly of the 3 rd Republic in 1993.

THE NATIONAL ASSEMBLY OF THE III RD REPUBLIC

Unlike in previous times, no one party presently dominates the National Assembly. There is instead a proliferation of political parties or and party causes. Thus it is not easy to kow where the majority is, as it moves and adapts to changing political realities, as do the Deputies, this situation has been termed *une majorite à géométrie variable* by the National Assembly Speaker, Reverend Richard Andriamanjato. The present speaker was one of the youngest deputies in the First Republic, and skillfully dealt with Malagasy politics in the Second Republic. With 35 yeras of political experience behind him, he has led the new Assembly proficientely and professionally as its first speaker, working with the remaining 137 deputies. This is brief, the history of legislatures in Madagascar. According to the constitution of the Third Republic, the executive, legislative and judicial powers must work together to govern Madagascar.

For additional analytical, business and investment opportunities information,
please contact Global Investment & Business Center, USA
at (202) 546-2103. Fax: (202) 546-3275. E-mail: rusric@erols.com

According to set rules and legislation, the National Assembly's 138 membres work within the following administrative and political structures to carry out their work.

Political structure

Speaker : Professor Andrianarisoa Ange Christophe Félix

Permanent Bureau : 12 Vice-Présidents, 02 Questeurs.

National Assembly Commissions (or Committees : 12 Subject areas)

1. Finance.
2. Foreign Affairs and International Relations.
3. National defense and Security.
4. Rural Development : Agriculture, Fisheries, Livestock
5. Infrastructure, Communication, Transport, Post telecommunication - Lands & housign.
6. Social Affairs, Health, Population.
7. Education and Cultural Affairs, Research, Youth and Sports.
8. Juridical & Legislation.
9. Interior & Decentralization.
10. Industry, Mines, Tradring, Drafts
11. Public works
12. Environment, Forests, Tourism

Administrative structure

The Administrative staff was created to help Deputies in their work and responsabilities. Over 100 employees deal with everydayissues susch as administration, secretarial work, security, and housing. Five directorates have been set up to oversee thes different tasks, under the supervision of a General Secretary. They are :

- Administration and Staffing
- Finances
- Public Relations
- Legislation
- Security

External Relations Division

The External Relations Division was established during the first legislature of the Third Republic. According to the flow chart of the National Assembly, the External Relations Service (SRE) provides administrative and technical support in relations between the National Assembly and foreign entities such as embassies ministries and national and international organisations. The SRE also deals with interpalementary relations and the preparation of malagasy parliamentary delagation documents. Furthemore this service is available for the translation of records, such as the development projects of the deputies districts ans mail from other countries. For further information, embassies, ministries, cultural centers, and national and international organisations are invited to get in touch with this Service, and we'll do our best to satidfy your requests.

NATIONAL ASSEMBLY/COMMITTEE

- **National Defense & Security Commitee**
- **Foreign Affairs Committee**
- **Rural Development Committee**
- **Substructure Communication Committee : Publics works, Telecommunication & Transport**
- **Social wellfare Committee : Health, Population**
- **Education & Cultural Affairs Committee**
- **Juridical & Legislation**
- **Interior, Decentralization & Territory Administration**
- **Industry, Manual Trade, Commerce, Mine & Energy**
- **Public Office & Private works**
- **Environment**

NATIONAL ASSEMBLY BY POLITICAL ALLIANCES

TIM

ANDRIANTSILAVO Christian Joseph , Antananarivo IV , Antananarivo

FANJAVA Refeno , Miarinarivo , Antananarivo

MANANJARA Arthur , Manjakandriana , Antananarivo

RABEMANANJARA Michel , Fenoarivobe , Antananarivo

RAHARINAIVO Andrianatoandro , Ambohidratrimo , Antananarivo

RAHARIVELO Jean Marie , Antananarivo Avaradrano , Antananarivo

RAJAONARIVELO , Tsiroanomandidy , Antananarivo

RAKOTOARIVELO Mamy , Antananarivo III , Antananarivo

RAKOTOMANDIMBINDRAIBE Mamisoa , Ambatolampy , Antananarivo

RAKOTONDRAJAONA Aimé , Antananarivo II , Antananarivo

RAKOTONDRAMARY Eugène , Antanifotsy , Antananarivo

RAMAROMANANA Harinirina Haingoarisoa , Arivonimamo , Antananarivo

RANAIVOMANANTSOA William Joseph , Antsirabe II , Antananarivo

RANAIVOSOA Andriamiadamanana Désiré , Antananarivo I , Antananarivo

RANDRIAMAMPIANINA Ramilison , Antanifotsy , Antananarivo

RANDRIAMAMPIANINA Vincent de Paul , Antananarivo V , Antananarivo

RANDRIANANTENAINA Olivier Antonny José , Antsirabe II , Antananarivo

RANDRIANJANAHARY Soloniaina Olivier , Ambatolampy , Antananarivo

RANDRIANJARIVO Matio , Antananarivo VI , Antananarivo

RANDRIASANDRATRINIONY Yvon , Antananarivo Atsimondrano , Antananarivo

RASAMINDRAKOTROKA Andriamiliharison Jean , Faratsiho , Antananarivo

RASOANAIVO Jean de Dieu , Betafo , Antananarivo

RATOLOJANAHARY De Sales Hygin Marius , Antsirabe I , Antananarivo

RATSIMANDRESY Solofo , Antananarivo IV , Antananarivo

RAVELOARSON Rahelimalala Wellinat , Ankazobe , Antananarivo

RAZAKA Elisé Alitera , Antananarivo Avaradrano , Antananarivo

RAZAKANIARIVO Maurice Emie , Tsiroanomandidy , Antananarivo

RAZANOELISON Julien , Arivonimamo , Antananarivo

ALI , Ambanja , Antsiranana

AMAD , Antsiranana , Antsiranana

INDRAY Grégoire Arson , Andapa , Antsiranana

JAOMIFIDY Clovis , Sambava , Antsiranana

JAOSOA Jean Pascal , Sambava , Antsiranana

JEAN Adolphe , Antsiranana , Antsiranana

RAMAROMISY Auguste , Vohémar , Antsiranana

RANDRIANAIVOARIVONY Jeannot , Antalaha , Antsiranana

VOLO Alain , Ambilobe , Antsiranana

ZAFINDRAPAOLY , Antalaha , Antsiranana

ZARA Roger , Nosy-Be , Antsiranana

ANDRIAMADIOZAFY Hery Francquis , Iakora , Fianarantsoa

ANDRIANASOLO Calixte Léong , Manakara , Fianarantsoa

ANDRIATSIFERANIAINA Iréné , Nosy Varika , Fianarantsoa

LALANIRINA Brigitte , Ikongo , Fianarantsoa

LECHAT RAMAMPY Marie Zénaïde , Ambalavao , Fianarantsoa

PARAINA Auguste Richard , Farafangana , Fianarantsoa

PHILIPPISON Gérard Aimé , Fianarantsoa I , Fianarantsoa

RAKA Noël Georgial , Nosy Varika , Fianarantsoa

RAKOTONANDRASANA Samuel , Manakara , Fianarantsoa

RAMAROSAONA Edmond , Ambositra , Fianarantsoa

RAMBOLAZAFY Cyriaque Alexandre , Ivohibe , Fianarantsoa

RANDRIAMBOAVONJY Jean de Dieu , Fianarantsoa I , Fianarantsoa

RANDRIANIRINA Emmanuël , Ambatofinandrahana , Fianarantsoa

RANOELISON Roche , Vangaindrano , Fianarantsoa

RASOLOFONIRINA Louis , Manandriana , Fianarantsoa

RATSIMARISON Richard , Fianarantsoa II , Fianarantsoa

RAZAFINDRANDRIANTSIMANIRY Dieudonné Michel , Fianarantsoa II , Fianarantsoa

RAZAFY Jean Simon Victor , Ambohimahasoa , Fianarantsoa

TATAGERA Jeannot Célestin , Vondrozo , Fianarantsoa
JEAN CLEMENT , Befandriana Nord , Mahajanga
MOHAMADY SAKRA , Besalampy , Mahajanga
RAFATROLAZA Bary Emmanuel , Kandreho , Mahajanga
RAHAINGOSOA Louise Odette , Bealanana , Mahajanga
RAJIMISON Jean Paul , Mandritsara , Mahajanga
RAKOTORALAHY Jean de la Croix , Mahajanga II , Mahajanga
RAMINOSOA FALIARIVO Luc , Mitsinjo , Mahajanga
RANDIMBIMANANTSOA Zafy Miakadaza , Ambatomainty , Mahajanga
RANDRIAMITOMBO Marcellin David , Mandritsara , Mahajanga
RANDRIANARIVO Louis , Mahajanga I , Mahajanga
RANDRIANJAFININDRINA Jean Roger , Tsaratanana , Mahajanga
RAVOKATRA TIANA ANDRIANAIVO , Maevatanana , Mahajanga
RAZAFIPIERA RAKOTOMAVO Mihamintso , Ambato-Boeni , Mahajanga
SOALAHY , Mahajanga I , Mahajanga
SOUNDARDJEE IBRAHIM FERID , Analalava , Mahajanga
NDALANA René , Vatomandry , Toamasina
RAHARISON Francis Tamisy , Anosibean'ala , Toamasina
RANAIVOSON Jeannot Fils , Moramanga , Toamasina
RANDRIAMAHARO Jacobson Maxime , Andilamena , Toamasina
RASOANIRINA Méline , Amparafaravola , Toamasina
RAZAFINDRAKOTOASIMBOLA , Amparafaravola , Toamasina
RAZOARIMIHAJA Solofonantenaina , Ambatondrazaka , Toamasina
SYLLA Jacques Hugues , Sainte Marie , Toamasina
ZAFILAHY Rakotomandimby Stanislas , Vavatenina , Toamasina
BENARIA François , Toliara I , Toliara
BETKOU Aimé François , Sakaraha , Toliara
JEAN MICHEL Henri , Ambovombe , Toliara
JEANTRI Gatera , Morondava , Toliara
LAHINIRIKO Jean , Betioky Sud , Toliara
LAMARRE Roger Claude , Toliara I , Toliara
LELAHY , Manja , Toliara
RAKOTOARISON Faraniaina Yves Aimé , Faradofay , Toliara
RAKOTONIAINA ADRIEN MARIE , Miandrivazo , Toliara
RAMIANDRISOA Ezekiela , Faradofay , Toliara
RANDRIAMANGA Théodore Léonard , Ampanihy , Toliara
RANDRIANARIJAONA Albert José , Betroka , Toliara
RAZAFINDRAKOTOHARIFANJA Francette , Beroroha , Toliara
RAZAKANIRINA Mahafaritsy Samuel , Toliara II , Toliara
ROLLAND , Morombe , Toliara
ROSTAND André , Mahabo , Toliara
THRIMOSON Jean Gualbert , Bekily , Toliara
ZAFISOLO Louis , Ambovombe , Toliara

FP

RABEMANOELA Solomon , Betafo , Antananarivo
RABENANDRIANINA Louis , Antananarivo VI , Antananarivo
RAHARISON Liva Solonirina , Antananarivo Atsimondrano ,
Antananarivo
RAKOTOMIARANA Solofomandimbisoa Aimé , Manjakandriana ,
Antananarivo
RAKOTONDRANDRIA Joseph Constant , Ambohidratrimo ,
Antananarivo
RAKOTONDRATOANDRO René , Andramasina , Antananarivo
RAMAROSON Laurent Pulchéri , Antananarivo V , Antananarivo
RANDRIANALIFERA Hery Luc Mario , Antsirabe I , Antananarivo
RANDRIANARIVONY Edmond , Antananarivo III , Antananarivo
RANDRIATOLOJANAHARY Roger , Soavinandriana ,
Antananarivo
RATSIRAHONANA Lala Harijaona , Antananarivo II ,
Antananarivo
RAVELONAHINA , Anjozorobe , Antananarivo
RAZAFINJATOVO Haja Nirina , Antananarivo I , Antananarivo
ANDRIAMAMPANDRY Joseph Désiré , Mananjary , Fianarantsoa
MARSON Evariste , Vohipeno , Fianarantsoa
RABESAIKY Guillaume Marie , Ambohimahasoa , Fianarantsoa
RAZAFINIARIVO Jean Pierre , Ambositra , Fianarantsoa
SOAMANEVA , Mampikony , Mahajanga
NDAHIMANANJARA née Randrianarison , Toamasina I ,
Toamasina
RAZAFINDRALETOAVINA Pierrot , Antanambao , Toamasina
VOTSIBOY Marcel , Ambatondrazaka , Toamasina
REBOZA Razafindrevalo , Amboasary Sud , Toliara

Partis minoritaires et indépendants

JEAN NOEL , Midongy du Sud , RPSD , Fianarantsoa
MALAZAMANA Jean Noël , Befotaka Sud , RPSD , Fianarantsoa
PELOPS ARIANE , Morafenobe , RPSD , Mahajanga
REMI dit Jao Jean , Antsohihy , RPSD , Mahajanga
RAVONISON Bien-Aimé Roger , Maroantsetra , AREMA ,
Toamasina
RAZAFIARIVELONA Médard Daniel , Soanierana Ivongo ,
AREMA , Toamasina
VELO Alexandre , Toamasina II , AREMA , Toamasina
LAINIRINA Max , Toamasina II , TOAMASINA TONGA SAINA ,
Toamasina
MASO José Michel , Toamasina I , TOAMASINA TONGA SAINA ,

For additional analytical, business and investment opportunities information,
please contact Global Investment & Business Center, USA
at (202) 546-2103. Fax: (202) 546-3275. E-mail: rusric@erols.com

Toamasina
RANDRIANIRINA Herihajaina , Ikalamavony , MFM , Fianarantsoa
RAMAROLAHY Maurice , Antsalova , MFM , Mahajanga
RANDRIANAMBININA Alphonse , Vangaindrano , LEADER
FANILO , Fianarantsoa
LERIVA Manahirana , Brickaville , LALA-SOA , Toamasina
NASSER Ahmed , Antsiranana II , ZDS , Antsiranana
MEKTOUB Omar El Camille , Mananjary , GRAAM , Fianarantsoa
RADAOROZANDRY Jacques , Ifanadiana , HBM , Fianarantsoa
RANDRIAMAHEFA Henri Charles , Moramanga , Indép. ,
Toamasina
RANDRIANANDRASANA Auguste , Farafangana , Indép. 3FA
GISTA , Fianarantsoa
RAKOTONANDRASANA Fabrice , Ikongo , Indép. BIBISY ,
Fianarantsoa
MAOLIDY , Soalala , Indép. BOENI MANDROSO , Mahajanga
RAJAONSON BRUNO dit BRUN-LY , Marovoay , Indép. BRUN-
LY , Mahajanga
DRAMSY NIZAR , Port-Bergé , Indép. DRAMSY Nizar ,
Mahajanga
LAHIMARINA Benoît , Marolambo , Indép. LAHIMARINA ,
Toamasina
RABOTOMONINA Lala Bertrand , Fénérive-Est , Indép. LALA-
SOA , Toamasina
MARA Niarisy , Ankazoabo Sud , Indép. MARA Niarisy , Toliara
RADAVID Marie Esther , Fandriana , Indép. RADAVID Marie ,
Fianarantsoa
IMBININA André , Mahanoro , Indép. TIAKO , Toamasina
MANASOA Donnat Tang , Mahanoro , Indép. TOAMASINA ,
Toamasina
SAINA Michel Désiré , Fénérive-Est , Indép. Toamasina ,
Toamasina
ANDRIANJAKA Samson Goulzar , Ampanihy , Indép. TSARA
MAGNITSE , Toliara
FAHARO Ratsimbalson , Belo/Tsiribihina , Indép. Tsiribihina ,
Toliara
ZAKAHELY Boniface Berthin , Mananara Nord , Indép.
ZAKAHELY , Toamasina
REVONJEA Jonah , Tsihombe , , Toliara

NATIONAL ASSEMBLY BY PROVINCE

Antananarivo

ANDRIANTSILAVO Christian Joseph , Antananarivo IV , TIM
FANJAVA Refeno , Miarinarivo , TIM
MANANJARA Arthur , Manjakandriana , TIM
RABEMANANJARA Michel , Fenoarivobe , TIM
RABEMANOELA Solomon , Betafo , FP

RABENANDRIANINA Louis , Antananarivo VI , FP
RAHARINAIVO Andrianatoandro , Ambohidratrimo , TIM
RAHARISON Liva Solonirina , Antananarivo Atsimondrano , FP
RAHARIVELO Jean Marie , Antananarivo Avaradrano , TIM
RAJAONARIVELO , Tsiroanomandidy , TIM
RAKOTOARIVELO Mamy , Antananarivo III , TIM
RAKOTOMANDIMBINDRAIBE Mamisoa , Ambatolampy , TIM
RAKOTOMIARANA Solofomandimbisoa Aimé , Manjakandriana , FP
RAKOTONDRAJAONA Aimé , Antananarivo II , TIM
RAKOTONDRAMARY Eugène , Antanifotsy , TIM
RAKOTONDRANDRIA Joseph Constant , Ambohidratrimo , FP
RAKOTONDRATOANDRO René , Andramasina , FP
RAMAROMANANA Harinirina Haingoarisoa , Arivonimamo , TIM
RAMAROSON Laurent Pulchéri , Antananarivo V , FP
RANAIVOMANANTSOA William Joseph , Antsirabe II , TIM
RANAIVOSOA Andriamiadamanana Désiré , Antananarivo I , TIM
RANDRIAMAMPIANINA Ramilison , Antanifotsy , TIM
RANDRIAMAMPIANINA Vincent de Paul , Antananarivo V , TIM
RANDRIANALIFERA Hery Luc Mario , Antsirabe I , FP
RANDRIANANTENAINA Olivier Antonny José , Antsirabe II , TIM
RANDRIANARIVONY Edmond , Antananarivo III , FP
RANDRIANJANAHARY Soloniaina Olivier , Ambatolampy , TIM
RANDRIANJARIVO Matio , Antananarivo VI , TIM
RANDRIASANDRATRINIONY Yvon , Antananarivo Atsimondrano , TIM
RANDRIATOLOJANAHARY Roger , Soavinandriana , FP
RASAMINDRAKOTROKA Andriamiliharison Jean , Faratsiho , TIM
RASOANAIVO Jean de Dieu , Betafo , TIM
RATOLOJANAHARY De Sales Hygin Marius , Antsirabe I , TIM
RATSIMANDRESY Solofo , Antananarivo IV , TIM
RATSIRAHONANA Lala Harijaona , Antananarivo II , FP
RAVELOARSON Rahelimalala Wellinat , Ankazobe , TIM
RAVELONAHINA , Anjozorobe , FP
RAZAFINJATOVO Haja Nirina , Antananarivo I , FP
RAZAKA Elisé Alitera , Antananarivo Avaradrano , TIM
RAZAKANIARIVO Maurice Emie , Tsiroanomandidy , TIM
RAZANOELISON Julien , Arivonimamo , TIM

Antsiranana

ALI , Ambanja , TIM
AMAD , Antsiranana , TIM
INDRAY Grégoire Arson , Andapa , TIM
JAOMIFIDY Clovis , Sambava , TIM
JAOSOA Jean Pascal , Sambava , TIM
JEAN Adolphe , Antsiranana , TIM
NASSER Ahmed , Antsiranana II , ZDS
RAMAROMISY Auguste , Vohémar , TIM
RANDRIANAIVOARIVONY Jeannot , Antalaha , TIM
VOLO Alain , Ambilobe , TIM

ZAFINDRAPAOLY , Antalaha , TIM
ZARA Roger , Nosy-Be , TIM

Fianarantsoa

ANDRIAMADIOZAFY Hery Francquis , Iakora , TIM
ANDRIAMAMPANDRY Joseph Désiré , Mananjary , FP
ANDRIANASOLO Calixte Léong , Manakara , TIM
ANDRIATSIFERANIAINA Iréné , Nosy Varika , TIM
JEAN NOEL , Midongy du Sud , RPSD
LALANIRINA Brigitte , Ikongo , TIM
LECHAT RAMAMPY Marie Zénaïde , Ambalavao , TIM
MALAZAMANA Jean Noël , Befotaka Sud , RPSD
MARSON Evariste , Vohipeno , FP
MEKTOUB Omar El Camille , Mananjary , GRAAM
PARAINA Auguste Richard , Farafangana , TIM
PHILIPPISON Gérard Aimé , Fianarantsoa I , TIM
RABESAIKY Guillaume Marie , Ambohimahasoa , FP
RADAOROZANDRY Jacques , Ifanadiana , HBM
RADAVID Marie Esther , Fandriana , Indép. RADAVID Marie
RAKA Noël Georgial , Nosy Varika , TIM
RAKOTONANDRASANA Fabrice , Ikongo , Indép. BIBISY
RAKOTONANDRASANA Samuel , Manakara , TIM
RAMAROSAONA Edmond , Ambositra , TIM
RAMBOLAZAFY Cyriaque Alexandre , Ivohibe , TIM
RANDRIAMBOAVONJY Jean de Dieu , Fianarantsoa I , TIM
RANDRIANAMBININA Alphonse , Vangaindrano , LEADER FANILO
RANDRIANANDRASANA Auguste , Farafangana , Indép. 3FA GISTA
RANDRIANIRINA Emmanuël , Ambatofinandrahana , TIM
RANDRIANIRINA Herihajaina , Ikalamavony , MFM
RANOELISON Roche , Vangaindrano , TIM
RASOLOFONIRINA Louis , Manandriana , TIM
RATSIMARISON Richard , Fianarantsoa II , TIM
RAZAFINDRANDRIANTSIMANIRY Dieudonné Michel , Fianarantsoa II , TIM
RAZAFINIARIVO Jean Pierre , Ambositra , FP
RAZAFY Jean Simon Victor , Ambohimahasoa , TIM
TATAGERA Jeannot Célestin , Vondrozo , TIM

Mahajanga

DRAMSY NIZAR , Port-Bergé , Indép. DRAMSY Nizar
JEAN CLEMENT , Befandriana Nord , TIM
MAOLIDY , Soalala , Indép. BOENI MANDROSO
MOHAMADY SAKRA , Besalampy , TIM
PELOPS ARIANE , Morafenobe , RPSD
RAFATROLAZA Bary Emmanuel , Kandreho , TIM
RAHAINGOSOA Louise Odette , Bealanana , TIM
RAJAONSON BRUNO dit BRUN-LY , Marovoay , Indép. BRUN-LY
RAJIMISON Jean Paul , Mandritsara , TIM
RAKOTORALAHY Jean de la Croix , Mahajanga II , TIM
RAMAROLAHY Maurice , Antsalova , MFM

RAMINOSOA FALIARIVO Luc , Mitsinjo , TIM
RANDIMBIMANANTSOA Zafy Miakadaza , Ambatomainty , TIM
RANDRIAMITOMBO Marcellin David , Mandritsara , TIM
RANDRIANARIVO Louis , Mahajanga I , TIM
RANDRIANJAFININDRINA Jean Roger , Tsaratanana , TIM
RAVOKATRA TIANA ANDRIANAIVO , Maevatanana , TIM
RAZAFIPIERA RAKOTOMAVO Mihamintso , Ambato-Boeni , TIM
REMI dit Jao Jean , Antsohihy , RPSD
SOALAHY , Mahajanga I , TIM
SOAMANEVA , Mampikony , FP
SOUNDARDJEE IBRAHIM FERID , Analalava , TIM

Toamasina

IMBININA André , Mahanoro , Indép. TIAKO
LAHIMARINA Benoît , Marolambo , Indép. LAHIMARINA
LAINIRINA Max , Toamasina II , TOAMASINA TONGA SAINA
LERIVA Manahirana , Brickaville , LALA-SOA
MANASOA Donnat Tang , Mahanoro , Indép. TOAMASINA
MASO José Michel , Toamasina I , TOAMASINA TONGA SAINA
NDAHIMANANJARA née Randrianarison , Toamasina I , FP
NDALANA René , Vatomandry , TIM
RABOTOMONINA Lala Bertrand , Fénérive-Est , Indép. LALA-SOA
RAHARISON Francis Tamisy , Anosibean'ala , TIM
RANAIVOSON Jeannot Fils , Moramanga , TIM
RANDRIAMAHARO Jacobson Maxime , Andilamena , TIM
RANDRIAMAHEFA Henri Charles , Moramanga , Indép.
RASOANIRINA Méline , Amparafaravola , TIM
RAVONISON Bien-Aimé Roger , Maroantsetra , AREMA
RAZAFIARIVELONA Médard Daniel , Soanierana Ivongo , AREMA
RAZAFINDRAKOTOASIMBOLA , Amparafaravola , TIM
RAZAFINDRALETOAVINA Pierrot , Antanambao , FP
RAZOARIMIHAJA Solofonantenaina , Ambatondrazaka , TIM
SAINA Michel Désiré , Fénérive-Est , Indép. Toamasina
SYLLA Jacques Hugues , Sainte Marie , TIM
VELO Alexandre , Toamasina II , AREMA
VOTSIBOY Marcel , Ambatondrazaka , FP
ZAFILAHY Rakotomandimby Stanislas , Vavatenina , TIM
ZAKAHELY Boniface Berthin , Mananara Nord , Indép. ZAKAHELY

Toliara

ANDRIANJAKA Samson Goulzar , Ampanihy , Indép. TSARA
MAGNITSE
BENARIA François , Toliara I , TIM
BETKOU Aimé François , Sakaraha , TIM
FAHARO Ratsimbalson , Belo/Tsiribihina , Indép. Tsiribihina
JEAN MICHEL Henri , Ambovombe , TIM
JEANTRI Gatera , Morondava , TIM
LAHINIRIKO Jean , Betioky Sud , TIM
LAMARRE Roger Claude , Toliara I , TIM

For additional analytical, business and investment opportunities information,
please contact Global Investment & Business Center, USA
at (202) 546-2103. Fax: (202) 546-3275. E-mail: rusric@erols.com

LELAHY , Manja , TIM
MARA Niarisy , Ankazoabo Sud , Indép. MARA Niarisy
RAKOTOARISON Faraniaina Yves Aimé , Faradofay , TIM
RAKOTONIAINA ADRIEN MARIE , Miandrivazo , TIM
RAMIANDRISOA Ezekiela , Faradofay , TIM
RANDRIAMANGA Théodore Léonard , Ampanihy , TIM
RANDRIANARIJAONA Albert José , Betroka , TIM
RAZAFINDRAKOTOHARIFANJA Francette , Beroroha , TIM
RAZAKANIRINA Mahafaritsy Samuel , Toliara II , TIM
REBOZA Razafindrevalo , Amboasary Sud , FP
REVONJEA Jonah , Tsihombe ,
ROLLAND , Morombe , TIM
ROSTAND André , Mahabo , TIM
THRIMOSON Jean Gualbert , Bekily , TIM

- ZAFISOLO Louis , Ambovombe , TIM

ARMY AND NATIONAL SECURITY

HISTORICALLY, the western Indian Ocean has played a vital role in international politics. In ancient times, maritime commerce attracted numerous nations to the region, including Egypt, Persia (Iran), Ceylon (Sri Lanka), India, Indonesia, and China. During the period of European colonial empires, Portugal, the Netherlands, Britain, and France sought to protect their respective strategic and commercial interests by protecting the lines of communications and providing external defense and internal security to Madagascar, Mauritius, Comoros, Seychelles, and Maldives. After 1945, Cold War considerations provoked competition between the United States and the former Soviet Union for access to strategically important air and naval bases in the western Indian Ocean and for the loyalties of the area's indigenous governments. Britain and France also maintained a military and political presence in the region throughout much of the Cold War. After the collapse of communism in the Soviet Union, Moscow ended its military presence in the western Indian Ocean. However, the United States has continued to maintain an interest in the region. The post-Cold War era also has provided traditional powers such as France and emerging regional states such as India, South Africa, and Australia with an opportunity to increase their activities in the western Indian Ocean.

In addition to the presence of foreign military powers in the region, Madagascar, Mauritius, Comoros, Seychelles, and Maldives have pursued their own national security objectives. Apart from providing internal stability, indigenous security forces have sought to protect the Exclusive Economic Zones (EEZs) claimed by all five countries and to prevent the use of the western Indian Ocean as a transshipment point for illegal drugs.

SECURITY CONCERNS

Madagascar faces no external threat. However, during the 1980s, Madagascar experienced periods of tension with South Africa. Although it had the capabilities to launch an air or amphibious attack, South Africa never threatened Madagascar, largely because it feared international condemnation. After Frederik Willem de Klerk became South Africa's president in 1989, relations between the two countries gradually improved.

Since independence, there have been several internal threats against the Malagasy government. This domestic instability reflected the growing restiveness of opposition elements and popular frustration with the government's inability to resolve the political, economic, and social problems confronting the island. Also, the Malagasy armed forces repeatedly have acted against the government for failing to preserve law and order.

The first serious challenge to the government occurred on April 1-2, 1971, when more than 1,000 armed members of the left wing National Movement for the Independence of Madagascar (Mouvement National pour l'Indépendance de Madagascar--Monima) attacked five military posts in Tuléar Province. Government forces quickly restored order and imprisoned Monima's leader, Monja Jaona. According to a government communiqué, Monima casualties included forty-five killed, nine wounded, and 847 held for questioning while security forces suffered one killed and eleven wounded. According to Jaona, the revolt had been directed against the local administration, which had failed to provide disaster relief to the province after it had experienced a drought, followed by floods caused by cyclones. Also at issue were government pressures for tax collection at a time when local cattle herds were being ravaged by disease.

In early 1972, what began as a student protest against French cultural domination of the island's schools quickly spread to a call for a general strike to protest poor economic conditions. Within days antigovernment protests were occurring in the capital and throughout the provinces. On May 13, 1972, elements from the Republican Security Forces (Forces Républicaines de Sécurité-- FRS) opened fire on a group of rioters in Antananarivo, killing between fifteen and forty and injuring about 150. Additionally, the government declared a state of national emergency. On May 18, 1972, President Philibert Tsiranana dissolved his government and turned over power to the army, under the command of General Gabriel Ramanantsoa. The army, which had remained neutral throughout the general strike, quickly restored order by placing military officers in control of the six provinces and establishing a new, multiethnic cabinet. In November 1972, after a national referendum, Ramanantsoa became the new head of state.

Continued political and economic instability doomed the Ramanantsoa regime. On December 31, 1974, the armed forces launched an unsuccessful coup attempt. On February 5, 1975, Ramanantsoa, hoping to promote political unity, handed over the government to the former minister of interior, Colonel Richard Ratsimandrava. On February 11, 1975, several members of the Mobile Police Group (Groupe Mobile de Police--GMP) assassinated Ratsimandrava. The government responded by declaring martial law, imposing censorship, and suspending political parties. Also, General Gilles Andriamahazo formed the National Military Directorate, consisting of nineteen military officers from all branches of service and from all over the island. On June 15, 1975, Didier Ratsiraka, who had a seat on the National Military Directorate, became head of state and president of the new ruling body, the Supreme Revolutionary Council.

The next major internal threat surfaced in the mid-1980s, when about 6,000 members of various Chinese martial arts Kung-Fu associations battled the Tanora Tonga Saina (TTS), which acted as Ratsiraka's private presidential security force. Problems started in September 1984, after Ratsiraka banned the practice of martial arts, which led to several clashes between Kung-Fu adherents and the TTS. On December 4, 1984, a larger confrontation occurred when Kung-Fu groups attacked TTS headquarters in Behorika, and killed more than 100 TTS members. Kung-Fu demonstrations continued for the next few years. Finally, on July 31, 1986, army units supported by twelve armored cars and helicopters demolished Kung-Fu headquarters in Antananarivo, and killed the movement's leader and about 200 of his followers.

In the early 1990s, cycles of escalating political unrest and increased governmental repression led to at least three failed coup attempts (1989, 1990, and 1992). Additionally, general strike demonstrations organized by a pro-democracy opposition coalition called Forces Vives (Active Forces) occurred in Antananarivo, and several other Malagasy towns. Following the near paralysis of the economy and demonstrations at the presidential palace during which government forces opened fire on civilians, opposition leaders announced the formation of a transitional government of national unity. Eventually, presidential elections, held between November 1992 and February 1993, resulted in a victory for Forces Vives leader Albert Zafy over Ratsiraka.

ARMED FORCES IN NATIONAL LIFE

Madagascar has a rich military history. During the early nineteenth century, the Merina kings relied on the army to extend their control through most of Madagascar. A small permanent force of career soldiers formed the backbone of the royal army. Periodic levies of freemen augmented these core units. Theoretically, military service was obligatory for all males. However, conscription laws excused sons of members of the ruling class and barred slaves from serving in the army. All soldiers shared in the spoils of war as the Merina expanded and consolidated their control over the island.

During the 1820s, the army's size increased to about 14,000 professional soldiers. Britain, hoping to counter French influence in Madagascar, furnished new weapons, ammunition, uniforms, and technical assistance to the army. The British also helped reorganize and train the army.

Increasing French interest in Madagascar prompted numerous clashes with the island's indigenous forces. Between 1883 and 1885, France launched several attacks on Madagascar. To end hostilities, the Merina recognized French control over Diego Suarez, agreed to pay an indemnity, and allowed a French resident at Antananarivo to control the country's foreign relations. In 1894 France declared a protectorate over the island but the Malagasy refused to recognize French authority. As a result, in September 1895 a French expeditionary force occupied the capital and obtained recognition of the protectorate from Queen Ranavalona III.

A Menalamba (red cloth) revolt broke out, however, among Merina conservatives against the institutions and agents of a repressive state-church society. Some observers also have suggested that the revolt was an attempt to overthrow the newly established

For additional analytical, business and investment opportunities information,
please contact Global Investment & Business Center, USA
at (202) 546-2103. Fax: (202) 546-3275. E-mail: rusric@erols.com

colonial government. France reacted to this unrest by exiling the queen and the former prime minister to Algeria and by declaring Madagascar a French colony. The new French governor, General Joseph Gallieni, eventually pacified the country and carried out many reforms, including the abolition of slavery.

During the French period, which lasted from 1896 to 1960, the Malagasy could be conscripted into the colonial forces. During World War I and World War II, several thousand Malagasy served in France, North Africa, and other combat zones. After 1945 many Malagasy started agitating for independence. In March 1947, the Merina, who regarded themselves as Madagascar's genuine rulers, and some *côtiers*, members of another ethnic group, staged an uprising against the French. The island's colonial governor responded by unleashing a reign of terror against the rebels. Estimates of the numbers of Malagasy who perished in the revolt ranged from 11,000 to 80,000 (relatively few French soldiers died during the fighting). Notwithstanding these losses, France retained its influence in Madagascar, even after the island gained its independence.

During the postcolonial period, the Malagasy armed forces reflected the French heritage. Military personnel continued to receive training in France and to use French-manufactured weapons. Moreover, with the exception of a brief period in the late 1970s, French military advisers continued to serve in Madagascar.

THE MILITARY AND THE GOVERNMENT

After he came to power in 1975, Ratsiraka promised to bring about a "socialist revolution." As part of this policy, Ratsiraka enlarged and reorganized the security forces to make them appropriate for a "people's army" in a "socialist revolutionary" state. In 1975 he renamed the National Army the People'a Armed Forces (Forces Armées Populaires--FAP) and expanded its mission. Henceforth, the FAP engaged in civic-action programs and spread ideological education in the countryside. Between 1975 and 1980, the FAP doubled in size.

This reorganization diluted the power of the former National Army, which owed little loyalty to Ratsiraka. To prevent the FAP from challenging his authority, Ratsiraka started transferring able and experienced officers from troop command responsibilities to more senior, but less powerful, positions. Invariably, the new posts were in the inspector general's section of the Office of the President and in various Ministry of Defense committees that studied how the FAP could best facilitate national development.

Despite these changes, the FAP contributed little to the country's "socialist revolution" and remained a potentially important political player. Nevertheless, Ratsiraka, relying on manipulation and intimidation, retained almost absolute control of the armed forces until the growth of the pro-democracy movement in the early 1990s. Pro- and anti-democracy factions emerged in the FAP and many other state security services. Clashes among these factions added to the political turmoil sweeping through Madagascar, which eventually doomed the Ratsiraka regime.

Under the Ratsiraka regime, the FAP, in conjunction with the Ministry of Defense, annually assessed the military's needs. The Ministry of Defense then sent budget recommendations to Ratsiraka, who made final budget decisions. With the formation of the FAP in 1975, the cost of maintaining the military establishment became a greater burden on the national budget. However, after the Cold War ended and foreign military assistance declined, the Malagasy defense budget also decreased from more than US$101 million in 1979 to about US$36 million in 1991.

FORCES ARMÉES POPULAIRES

In 1993 the FAP numbered about 21,000. Madagascar's president is commander in chief of the FAP. There is no reserve force. Males aged eighteen to fifty are subject to conscription for eighteen months of military or civil service. The majority of conscripts belonged to the relatively poor *côtiers* because exceptions to the conscription law allow influential or prosperous persons to avoid military service. The officer corps remains a promising career for most Malagasy. The FAP is divided into two operational services, the army and the aeronaval forces. The former is responsible for land operations and ground-based air defense; however, its primary role has been to defend state institutions and the president from armed opposition. The latter conducts air, naval, and amphibious operations.

The 20,000-member army, which is deployed as a coastal and internal security force, consists of two battalion groups, one engineer regiment, one signals regiment, one service regiment, and seven construction regiments. There is no reserve force. Because Madagascar lacks an indigenous arms production industry, the army imports all its equipment. The army weapons system includes twelve PT-76 light tanks; eight M-8, twenty M-3A1, ten FV-701 Ferret, and 35 BRDM-2 reconnaissance vehicles; and thirty M-3A1 half-track armored personnel carriers. Additionally, the army possesses fifty 14.5-mm ZPU-4 and twenty 37-mm Type 55 air defence guns; and twelve 76-mm ZIS-3, twelve 122-mm, and an unknown number of 105-mm artillery pieces. The mortar inventory consists of eight 120-mm M-43, twenty-four 82-mm M-43, and some 81-mm M-29s. There also are an unknown number of 89-mm rocket launchers and 106-mm M-40A1 recoilless launchers.

The mission of the aeronaval forces' 500-personnel air component includes combat, transport, and maritime patrol duties. The air force maintains its headquarters at Ivato, near Antananarivo, and operates from bases at Antalaha, Antsohiky, Arivoniamamo, Diego Suarez, Fianarantsoa, Fort Dauphin, Majunga, Nosy Be, Tamatave, and Tuléar. The air force consists of one fighter squadron with ten MiG-21 Fishbed and four MiG-17 Fresco aircraft; a transport squadron that includes four An-26 Curl, two Yak-40 Codling, three BN-2 Defender, two C-47 Dakotas, and two C212 Aviocar aircraft; and a helicopter squadron with six Mi-8 Hip transport helicopters. Additionally, the air force possesses one Cessna 310, three Cessna 337, one PA-23 Aztec utility/communications aircraft, and four Cessna 172 trainer aircraft.

The 500-member Malagasy navy, which lacks a sea-going capability, performs a coastal patrol mission from bases at Diego Suarez, Tamatave, Fort Dauphin, Tuléar, and Majunga. The naval inventory consists of one Malaika (French type PR48-meter design) patrol boat; and one Toky (French BATRAM design), one LCT (French EDIC design), one LCA, and three LCVP amphibious craft.

For additional analytical, business and investment opportunities information, please contact Global Investment & Business Center, USA at (202) 546-2103. Fax: (202) 546-3275. E-mail: rusric@erols.com

STATE SECURITY SERVICES

Apart from the FAP, there are five state security services in Madagascar: the National Gendarmerie, the Republican Security Force (Force Républicaine de Sécurité--FRS), the Civil Police, the Civil Service, and the Antigang Brigade. With the exception of the National Gendarmerie, all these units are outside the FAP chain of command.

A 7,500-member National Gendarmerie operates within the Ministry of Defense. This organization maintains public order, preserves security at the village level, protects government facilities, pursues criminals, and prevents cattle rustling. National Gendarmerie units are stationed throughout the island. The organization's equipment inventory includes automatic weapons, armored cars, and aircraft. The National Gendarmerie also operates a maritime police contingent that possesses five Philiberi Isiranana-class patrol craft (German Bayerische Schiffbau design).

Shortly after becoming president, Tsiranana created the 700- member FRS to safeguard his personal security and to act as an antiriot unit. By 1972 the FRS, which eventually became the GMP, included about 1,000 personnel. In late 1981 Ratsiraka established and commanded a similar organization called the Presidential Security Regiment (Regiment de Sécurité Présidentielle--Reser), or simply the Presidential Guard. Initially, North Korean instructors trained this 1,200-member unit, whose personnel belonged to Ratsiraka's Betsimisaraka ethnic group. The Reser possesses a bunker at Iavoloha near Antananarivo, and the Mahajamba Regiment, which specializes in riot control. In the late 1980s, the French assumed responsibility for training the Presidential Guard.

A 3,000-member Civil Police force is attached to the Ministry of Interior. Most Civil Police personnel serve in the island's cities. The head of each prefecture has at least a small contingent under his control. Like the National Gendarmerie, the Civil Police often overreact during times of civil strife, thus earning the enmity of protesters and dissidents alike. Since the late 1980s, however, both organizations have attempted to improve their image.

The Civil Service is a paramilitary force that serves as a reserve element of the defense forces. Its operations are nonmilitary in nature and often involve working in rural and social development programs. Potential draftees serve in the Civil Service as an alternative to regular military duty.

During his early days as president, Ratsiraka created a 300- member intelligence and political investigation unit known as the General Directorate of Information and Documentation Internal and External (Direction Générale de l'Information et de la Documentation, Intérieure et Exterieure--DGIDIE). This organization, whose personnel were trained originally by German Democratic Republic (GDR--East German) and then by French advisers, possesses unlimited arrest and detention powers. To perform its duties, the DGID relies on a vast network of informers to ferret out dissenters, currency violators, and potential political opponents of the president. Over the years, the DGID has been accused of violating human rights, engaging in corrupt practices, and imprisoning foreign nationals accused of spying.

In February 1989, the French helped Madagascar establish an Antigang Brigade. This unit, which reports to the Ministry of Interior, is responsible for combatting hijackers, terrorists, and dangerous criminals. French security advisers provide training to the brigade.

TRAINING AND MORALE

Prior to independence, the French conducted all military training. In 1966 the Malagasy government, with French assistance, established the Military Academy (Académie Militaire) at Antsirabe. This school trains officers for the armed forces, the National Gendarmerie, and the Civil Service. In 1967 the first students enrolled in a three-year program that included courses in military and civic affairs. Students specialize in letters or sciences. A few foreign officers, usually from francophone African countries, also study at the Military Academy.

The May 1972 student strikes affected the Military Academy, which temporarily suspended examinations after students complained about the curriculum. Over the next several weeks, academy officials agreed to appoint a committee to review the possibility of modernizing course material, examinations, entry requirements, and general educational policies.

In addition to training officers at the Military Academy, the Malagasy government annually selects a small number of officer candidates to attend the French Military Academy at St. Cyr. Also, until military relations were severed in the mid-1970s, Malagasy and French units participated in joint annual exercises.

During the Cold War, hundreds, if not thousands, of FAP personnel received military training from several East European countries, including the former Soviet Union, the former GDR, Cuba, and the Korean Democratic Republic (North Korea). Beginning in the mid-1980s, France resumed training limited numbers of Malagasy military personnel. Additionally, the United States started an International Military Education and Training (IMET) program that sought to enhance the FAP's professional skills and reduce dependency on East European countries. By the early 1990s, the United States had expanded the IMET program to include management and technical training with emphasis on construction engineering skills and medical courses.

Historically, morale in the armed forces has been generally good, if for no other reason than the military provides job security in a country plagued by high unemployment. However, many côtiers who have been conscripted to serve in the ranks resent the lack of opportunity and the Merina domination of the officer corps. Also, with the decline of foreign military assistance since the end of the Cold War, poor morale has become a problem in many FAP units.

FOREIGN MILITARY ASSISTANCE

Since independence, the Malagasy armed forces have relied on numerous countries for military assistance. Historically, France has been the most powerful and most influential of Madagascar's military allies, despite the rift between the two countries in the 1970s.

Other nations that have provided military assistance to Madagascar include the former Soviet Union, North Korea, the former Federal Republic of Germany (West Germany), and the United States.

On June 27, 1960, the day after independence, Paris and Antananarivo signed an accord that empowered France to protect Madagascar and to establish military bases on the island. France also gained freedom of movement in Madagascar's airspace and coastal waters. A joint Franco-Malagasy defense command--which consisted of the island's president, the French ambassador, and the commander of France's Third Overseas Zone, the southwestern Indian Ocean--managed the security relationship between the two countries. France also agreed to transfer about 4,500 Malagasy personnel who had been serving in the French forces to Madagascar's newly established armed forces.

French officers and French-trained Merina officers dominated the Malagasy armed forces. Additionally, the presence of French officers in Madagascar helped to maintain professionalism and noninvolvement of the military in politics. President Tsiranana, with French support, tried to offset Merina domination in the officer corps by sending promising *côtier* military personnel to France for training and assigning them to important positions upon their return to Madagascar.

Apart from these activities, France also equipped the Malagasy armed forces. During the first five years of independence, France provided military aid worth approximately US$5 million annually, which included technical assistance, training, and nearly all the arms and equipment for the Malagasy armed forces. In addition, France maintained about 2,500 troops at Diego Suarez and Antsirabé; by 1972 this number had grown to approximately 4,000. A general with the title of senior commander of French Forces in the Southern Indian Ocean was in charge of these soldiers. His command also encompassed French forces on Reunion and Comoros. His forces included a marine parachute regiment, a Foreign Legion regiment, and several internal security units. French air units, based primarily at Ivato airfield, had helicopters and transport aircraft while naval units operated three destroyer-size vessels, a tanker, a logistical support ship, and escort vessels.

In the early 1970s, there was a radical change in FrancoMalagasy military relations. Ramanantsoa's government demanded the withdrawal of French military forces from Antananarivo, and announced that it would allow France to have access to the Diego Suarez naval base only on a renewable basis. By 1975 the French government, which opposed the tenuous nature of this proposed new relationship, had withdrawn all its military units from Madagascar.

Beginning in the mid-1980s, Franco-Malagasy relations improved. Between 1982 and 1988, for example, 783 Malagasy officers enrolled in a variety of military courses in France. In 1989 France financed the formation of the Antigang Brigade. On April 5, 1990, France announced that it had donated eight Auverland jeeps fitted with weapons, two ambulances, military engineering equipment, accessories for service vehicles, and 8,290 air force and navy uniforms. France also supplied the Malagasy gendarmes with equipment and a variety of other technical and material aid.

The political instability associated with the democratization movement again altered the nature of the Franco-Malagasy military relationship. On August 15, 1991, French president François Mitterrand ordered the withdrawal of French military advisers who were in charge of the personal security of Malagasy president Ratsiraka. This action occurred after the Presidential Guard opened fire and killed thirty-one demonstrators at a prodemocracy rally. Relations between the two countries improved after Zafy was elected president in early 1993, and French security technicians provided him with an independent communications system.

Former West Germany was another important source of military assistance in the immediate postindependence era. By 1964 Bonn had furnished approximately US$1.6 million of military assistance, including thirty jeeps and five coastal patrol boats. Additionally, fifty-five Malagasy naval personnel were studying at military schools in West Germany.

During the Ratsiraka era, the FAP gradually abandoned its almost total reliance on France for equipment and training, and looked to several communist nations for foreign military assistance. During the 1975-82 period, the FAP acquired artillery, small arms, and ammunition from North Korea and the People's Republic of China; two landing craft from North Korea; three Mi-8 helicopters, twelve MiG-21 jet fighter aircraft, and two An-26 transport aircraft from the former Soviet Union. North Korea also provided four MiG-17s on long-term loan, and about ninety military advisers who furnished crew and maintenance support for these aircraft. Approximately 130 Soviet technicians maintained the MiG-21s and the An-26s. FAP personnel received training from Cuban, Romanian, Soviet, and Chinese instructors. As Ratsiraka's radicalism waned, Madagascar distanced itself from these countries. The collapse of the Soviet Union signaled the end Madagascar's reliance on the communist world for military assistance.

Since 1960 the United States and Madagascar have maintained diplomatic relations. However, it was not until the mid-1980s that the two countries established a military relationship, largely because of Ratsiraka's radicalism and Madagascar's relations with the communist world. In fiscal year (FY--see Glossary) 1984, the United States initiated an IMET program to help the Malagasy to improve their defense establishment and military training capabilities. The following year, one Malagasy officer attended the Navy Staff College and another studied at the Army Command and Staff College; additionally, six midlevel officers enrolled in advanced engineering, infantry, field artillery, and communications courses. Also, in FY 1985, the United States approved a Military Assistance Program (MAP) for Madagascar, which included funds for medical supplies and Caterpillar earth-moving and road-building equipment. In July 1988, the United States provided US$1.2 million worth of military engineering equipment to Madagascar's Department of Military Engineering for National Development. Madagascar and the United States also cooperated on several military development projects such as construction of roads, schools, and health centers for the FAP. The FY 1989 MAP provided for maintenance support for the Malagasy Air Force's C-47 Dakota fleet. In the late 1980s, Washington earmarked US$200,000 for a civic-action project designed to build low-cost housing. In 1987 a "Seabee" battalion deployed to Manjakandriana to give a two-month training course to fifty-two men of the Third Regiment of the Malagasy Army's Development Force. By the early 1990s, the United States had confined its military aid objectives to developing Madagascar's military engineering capability, supporting the air force's transport aircraft, and providing managerial and technical training to the armed forces.

PENAL SYSTEM

The Malagasy Penal Code is based primarily on French penal codes and procedures and has been somewhat influenced by Malagasy customary law. The Malagasy Penal Code affords the accused most of the rights and protections granted under French and Western laws. The most severe punishments are death and forced labor for life.

Madagascar has three levels of courts. Lower courts are responsible for civil and criminal cases carrying limited fines and sentences. The Court of Appeals includes a criminal court for cases carrying sentences of five years or more. The Supreme Court functions as the highest court in the country. Also, there is a separate and autonomous Constitutional High Court that reviews laws, decrees, and ordinances and monitors elections and certifies their results. A military court has jurisdiction over all cases that involve national security.

Madagascar has a nationwide prison system. Each province has a central prison for inmates serving sentences of less than five years. At the seats of various courts, there also are at least twenty-five lesser prisons for individuals serving terms of less than two years and for prisoners awaiting trial. Courts at the local (subprefecture) level maintain jails for lesser offenders serving sentences of up to six months. Women normally serve long sentences in the Central Prison (Maison Centrale) in Antananarivo.

Conditions in Malagasy prisons are harsh. Cells built for one often house up to eight prisoners. Family members of prisoners need to augment the inadequate daily food rations. Prisoners without relatives often go for several days without food. Inmates also suffer from numerous medical problems that are not usually treated, including malnutrition, infections, malaria, and tuberculosis. Children normally live in prisons with

For additional analytical, business and investment opportunities information, please contact Global Investment & Business Center, USA at (202) 546-2103. Fax: (202) 546-3275. E-mail: rusric@erols.com

Foreign POlicy & International Relations

Close Franco-Malagasy ties formed the cornerstone of Madagascar's foreign policy in the early independence years, as witnessed by the signing of fourteen agreements and conventions with France. An Economic and Financial Cooperation Agreement signed in June 1960 specified and regulated Madagascar's status as a member of the Franc Zone. Other economic agreements ensured the sanctity of existing French economic interests and, therefore, continued strong levels of French influence over Madagascar's economy. The Malagasy role was largely limited to the impact of decision makers in the upper echelons of government and input at the grass-roots level by small-scale farmers producing for subsistence or export. Other sectors by and large remained the domain of French trading conglomerates, large-scale agriculturalists, or Chinese and Indian middlepersons.

In the realm of security, defense agreements underscored France's willingness to provide strategic protection for Madagascar. France was allowed access to military bases and installations in Madagascar. These included the natural harbor of Antsiranana at the northern end of the island and the Ivato airfield near Antananarivo. France also enjoyed complete freedom of movement in the island's airspaces and coastal waters. In return for these benefits, France provided military aid, technical assistance, and training for Malagasy security forces.

French influence was equally strong in the cultural realm. The country's intellectual elite was French-speaking, and many prominent Malagasy studied in French *lycées* and acquired degrees from French universities. Newspapers and periodicals published in French as well as Malagasy circulated in Antananarivo and other major cities. French was the language of instruction for higher education, and many teachers were French. At secondary and higher levels, the curriculum was modeled closely on that of France.

The strengthening of ties with France was complemented by a desire to enhance links with other Western countries, including Britain, Italy, Switzerland, the Federal Republic of Germany (West Germany), and most notably the United States. In October 1963, the Tsiranana regime consented to the construction of a National Aeronautics and Space Administration (NASA) satellite tracking station near the old airport outside the capital. In return, the United States initiated a modest foreign assistance program that guaranteed private investment in the island's economy and made available a number of fellowships to students from Madagascar. Madagascar also established diplomatic links with other newly emerging nations, particularly former French colonies in Africa, and strengthened relationships with Asian countries, most notably Japan, India, and Indonesia.

A significant shift occurred in Madagascar's foreign policy after the downfall of the Tsiranana regime in 1972. In a series of diplomatic moves that three years later were embraced by the Ratsiraka regime as the cornerstones of the Second Republic, the Ramanantsoa regime pronounced Madagascar's commitment to nonalignment, anti-imperialism, anticolonialism, and antiracism in international affairs. In the context of the privileged Franco-Malagasy relationship, these themes translated into harsh rhetoric concerning the necessity of revoking the "slavery agreements" of the Tsiranana regime, followed by the uncompensated nationalization of all French banks and insurance firms

For additional analytical, business and investment opportunities information,
please contact Global Investment & Business Center, USA
at (202) 546-2103. Fax: (202) 546-3275. E-mail: rusric@erols.com

in June 1975, contributing to the dramatic cooling of diplomatic relations. Moreover, in June 1976, the Ratsiraka regime laid claim to small, rocky, French-held islands around Madagascar, including the Glorieuses (claimed concurrently by Comoros), Juan de Nova, Europa, Bassas da India, and Tromelin (also claimed by Mauritius). Originally administered as part of French-ruled Madagascar, these possessions were split off just prior to independence in 1960 and include some minor military facilities.

Diplomatic links also soured with other Western powers, such as Britain, which closed its embassy in 1975. In the case of the United States, the immediate cause of strained ties was the Ratsiraka regime's decision to close the NASA tracking station. Another source of friction was the frequent verbal assaults by the Ratsiraka regime against the United States military presence at Diego Garcia Island. The Malagasy position was that, in accordance with a UN resolution passed in 1971, the Indian Ocean should be a demilitarized, nuclear-free zone of peace. Nonetheless, trade relations remained essentially unaffected, and diplomatic relations continued, albeit at the reduced level of chargés d'affaires.

The most dramatic development was the strengthening of ties with Eastern Europe and with other communist regimes. After establishing diplomatic links with the Soviet Union in October 1972--followed one month later by the establishment of ties with China and the Democratic People's Republic of Korea (North Korea)--ties were enhanced in the economic, cultural, and politico-military realms. Soviet development assistance was directed toward the fields of agriculture, medicine, science, and technology, and scholarships were provided to at least 2,000 Malagasy students to study in the Soviet Union. A new Malagasy- Soviet Intergovernmental Commission on Economic and Technical Cooperation and Trade facilitated these links. The Soviet Union was particularly interested in promoting security ties with the Ratsiraka regime. In addition to providing military advisers and technical advice, the former Soviet Union became the primary source of military equipment for the Malagasy Armed Forces, including providing access to MiG-21 Fishbed jet fighters, and aided in the construction of a series of sealane intercept stations along Madagascar's west coast astride the Mozambique Channel. These stations were eventually dismantled in 1983 after protests by the West.

Relationships with other communist countries developed in a variety of fields. Whereas Cuba provided technical assistance within the educational realm, China funded the construction of roads between Moramanga and Toamasina, and built a new sugar factory near Morondava. The Ratsiraka regime was especially impressed by North Korean leader Kim Il Sung and his ideology of national self-reliance known as *juche* (or *chuch'e*), hosting an international conference on this topic in Antananarivo in 1976. North Korean assistance was fairly extensive in the fields of agriculture and irrigation. The North Koreans were most noted, however, for their training of Ratsiraka's presidential security unit and the construction of a presidential bunker at Iavohola.

New directions in foreign policy were equally pronounced in Madagascar's relationships with other developing countries and its positions in a variety of international forums. In addition to breaking ties with Israel and South Africa, the Ramanantsoa/Ratsiraka regimes strengthened links with Libya, the Palestine Liberation Organization, and liberation movements in southern Africa and the Western Sahara. Madagascar also joined the Nonaligned Movement, became more active in the Organization of African

Unity (OAU), and took positions in the UN that favored the communist states, including abstaining on a resolution that denounced the Soviet Union's invasion of Afghanistan in 1979 and supporting Vietnam's invasion of Cambodia in 1978. In conjunction with his Cuban and Soviet allies, Ratsiraka even tried to broker an end to rising tensions between Marxist Ethiopia and Marxist Somalia just prior to the outbreak of the Ogaden War in 1977-78.

Despite some alarmist projections that the communist countries would replace the West and turn Madagascar into a Soviet satellite, the changes in Madagascar's foreign policies represented a short-term shift rather than a true break with the past. The Ratsiraka regime had gained little in the form of economic assistance from its friendly relations with the Soviet Union and other communist countries--aid from these sources constituted less than 1 percent of all bilateral assistance from 1977 to 1980--and was confronted with the harsh realities of economic decline. As a result, an increasingly pragmatic Ratsiraka sought to reaffirm and strengthen Madagascar's foreign policy relationships with the West. Indeed, relations with the West appeared to be on the upswing at the beginning of the 1980s, whereas those with the communist countries were more or less static--despite the similarity of views on a wide range of international issues routinely reaffirmed by the spokespersons of Madagascar and of communist countries. As was the case with other self-proclaimed Marxist regimes during the 1970s and the 1980s, Ratsiraka pursued politico-military links with the Soviet Union while seeking to maintain economic ties with the West.

Diplomatic overtures to France served as the logical starting point for achieving a balance in Madagascar's foreign policy relationships. As early as 1977, Ratsiraka provided assurances concerning compensation for French firms nationalized during the mid-1970s in order to foster greater official and private investment in Madagascar. France responded positively, as demonstrated by the tremendous increase in foreign assistance from US$38.4 million in 1979 to US$96.4 million in 1982. Indeed, as of the early 1980s, France remained Madagascar's most important foreign policy partner. It was the principal source of foreign assistance and the most valuable trading partner. The dispute over French control of neighboring islands, although unresolved, had little if any ill effect on Franco-Malagasy relations, mainly because the Ratsiraka regime no longer publicly pressed this issue in international forums. (The motion asking France to cede the islands had been adopted by the UN General Assembly by a ninety-seven to seven vote in 1979 with thirty-six abstentions.)

The diversification of ties, thereby avoiding dependence on any single power, served as another cornerstone of Madagascar's foreign policy initiatives during the 1980s. Relations were fully restored with Washington in November 1980 when United States Ambassador Fernando E. Rondon assumed his post for the first time since his predecessor had been recalled during the summer of 1975. Receiving the new envoy, Ratsiraka expressed the hope that "fruitful, loyal, and lasting cooperation" would develop between the two countries and that there would be "no further misunderstandings" as a result of differing opinions on international issues. Other major events included the reopening of the British embassy in 1979, Ratsiraka's visits with President Ronald Reagan in Washington in 1982 and 1983, the opening of a World Bank office in Antananarivo in 1983, and the strengthening of links with other industrialized countries, most notably Japan.

The levels of foreign assistance provided by the West demonstrate the success of Ratsiraka's diplomatic initiatives (see table 7, Appendix). Bilateral aid from the West constituted only US$36.3 million one year after Ratsiraka had taken power in 1975. Four years after the beginning of the foreign policy changes initiated by the Ramantsoa regime, this amount increased to US$168.1 million in 1982, to US$217.6 million in 1988, and to US$365.5 million in 1991. Similarly, multilateral assistance from Western financial institutions, such as the IMF and the European Common Market (European Union), increased from US$34.1 million in 1976 to US$80.6 million in 1982, to US$108.9 million in 1988, and to US$191.4 million in 1991.

Equally important, Ratsiraka's policies led to a diversification of Madagascar's sources of foreign assistance. Although France in 1991 still provided approximately 43 percent (US$157.0 million) of Madagascar's bilateral foreign assistance, in 1988 it had provided approximately 50 percent (US$108.5 million). The amount marked a significant decline from almost total dependence in 1970 when nearly 90 percent of all Western assistance was provided by France. Noteworthy, however, was France's provision of US$655.4 million of the total US$1,334.5 million multilateral aid that Madagascar received between 1985 and 1990. In addition, France gave Madagascar loan assistance for such projects as telecommunications, transportation, and banking, and canceled US$715 million in debts that the Madagascar government owed France. In 1993 Madagascar received about US$167 million in aid from France compared with about US$152 million in aid received from France in 1992. Whereas the United States provided US$71.0 million in multilateral aid in 1991, Japan and Germany extended US$56.8 million and US$30.3 million respectively.

United States direct development aid has become increasingly important for Madagascar and has risen from about US$10 million in 1990 to US$13.5 million in 1991 (US$28 million were authorized but could not be used because of strikes and the disrupted political and economic situation), US$40 million in 1992, and US$40.6 million in 1993. Of the 1993 total, US$20.4 million was earmarked for environmental protection and US$10 million for the private sector.

The growing partnership with the West was cemented by dramatic changes in the international system and in Madagascar's domestic political system. The fall of the Berlin Wall in 1989 signaled the beginning of a process eventually leading to the downfall of communist regimes and trading partners in Eastern Europe, the fragmentation of the Soviet Union, and the increasing international isolation of North Korea and Cuba as pariah regimes. Furthermore, this international trend facilitated the rise of popular pressures for a multiparty democracy in Madagascar, eventually leading to the downfall of Ratsiraka's Second Republic and its replacement in 1993 with a democratically inspired Third Republic under the leadership of Zafy.

The cornerstone of Madagascar's foreign policy in the post- Cold War era is the continued diversification of ties, with an emphasis on promoting economic exchanges. In addition to establishing formal diplomatic ties with the Republic of Korea (South Korea) in May 1993, negotiations were initiated to restore diplomatic links with Israel and South Africa. In each of these cases, diplomatic links are perceived as the precursor to lucrative trading agreements. For example, one month after establishing diplomatic ties with South Korea, Madagascar hosted a South Korean trade mission that included representatives of six major South Korean companies: Daewoo, Dong Yong Electronics, Hyundai, Kolon, Peace Industries, and Samsung. As underscored by Prime Minister Ravony, one of the most critical challenges facing Madagascar is the restructuring of its embassies and foreign policy to "objectives of economic redeployment" in the post-Cold War era. Of particular interest to Madagascar, in view of their proximity and commercial potential, are relations and trade with India, Mauritius, Australia, and South Africa.

The benefits associated with changes in the international environment have an impact on Madagascar's domestic political system.

Similar to other newly installed African democracies at the beginning of the 1990s, the Zafy regime confronts the challenge of consolidating still-fragile democratic practices and governing institutions in a significantly changed international environment. Although such potential benefits associated with the end of the Cold War as a renewed focus on economic as opposed to military investments have been heralded by Western observers, the leaders of African countries, including Madagascar, rightfully wonder if their countries will be further marginalized as former benefactors either turn inward or toward more lucrative economic markets in Asia and Latin America. Equally important, the Zafy regime faces balancing rising public demands to receive immediately the fruits of democratization with the harsh reality of the political constraints of a democratic system. Indeed, democratization has not proved to be a quick panacea to resolving such issues as the necessity of overhauling and privatizing largely inert and bloated state-operated economic enterprises, and has even led to the emergence of new problems, most notably federalist demands for greater regional autonomy. Nonetheless, Madagascar's political elite clearly seems committed to the continued reform and strengthening of multiparty democracy, as well as the expansion of the country's role as a leader in both regional and international forums.

FOREIGN TRADE

Madagascar historically has remained outside the mainstream of African affairs, although it is an active member of theOrganization of African Unity and the Non-Aligned Movement.In contrast to former President Ratsiraka's "all points" policystressing ties with socialist and radical regimes, includingNorth Korea, Cuba, Libya, and Iran, President Albert Zafy hasexpressed his desire for diplomatic relations with all countries.Early in his tenure, he established formal ties with South Korea and sent emissaries to Morocco. Active relationships have been maintained with Europe, especially France, Germany, and Switzerland, as well as with Russia, Japan, India, and China.

FOREIGN EXCHANGE

- Foreign currency may be imported into Madagascar without restriction (provided that a written declaration is made to customs).
- Local currency may not leave Madagascar with non-residents except FMG 25000.
- Exchange Control is administered by the External Finance Office of the General Directorate of the Treasury.
- The Floating System is in operation.

- Some approval authority for exchange control has been delegated to authorised intermediaries, and all exchange transactions relating to foreign countries must be effected through such intermediaries.
- No restrictions apply to the opening of credit or the means of financing imports; importers may use their own resources, borrow from the banking system, or avail themselves of external loans including suppliers' credits, to finance imports.

DOUBLE TARIFFS

Non-residents are quoted prices generally in French francs with an exchange rate that works out to an FMG figure about twice the price paid by residents. It may be worthwhile to note at this point that the average income of residents is $250 a year.

EXPORTS

(1992)--$328 million: vanilla, sugar, cloves,shrimp, chromite, graphite. Major export markets--France, U.S.,Germany, Japan, Singapore, Italy. Imports (1992)--$547 million:consumer goods, foodstuffs, crude oil, machinery and vehicles,iron and steel. Major suppliers--France, Iran, Japan, Germany, Saudi Arabia, Hong Kong..

IMPORTS

Labradorite is a type of feldspar displaying a unique labradoresence. The presence of feldspar lamellae gives rise to the Schiller effect, an iridescence due to light refraction.

Schiller is best developed in labradorites creating a lovely color play in shades of green, blue, gold and yellow. The color play is iridescent like the feathers of a peacock or the Northern Lights.

Each Labradorite item that we offer is unique in its coloration. In addition, they are hand carved, so the sizes listed are approximate. The quality of the carving and polish is especially fine.

These objects are all made from Petrified Wood found in Madagascar.

No, we haven't identified the kinds of trees these came from - scientists haven't even succeeded in doing that with all the existing trees in Madagascar!

These beautiful Star Rose Quartz spheres from Madagascar have naturally occurring 6 ray stars.

The stars are best seen in direct sunlight or through the use of a single ray of light.

The Ammonites from Madagascar are members of an extinct order of mollusks. These creatures died out about 65 million years ago.

They are related to the modern day squid, octopus and chambered nautilus.

For additional analytical, business and investment opportunities information, please contact Global Investment & Business Center, USA at (202) 546-2103. Fax: (202) 546-3275. E-mail: rusric@erols.com

The ammonites found in Madagascar are unique because of their well-defined chambers.

We also offer beautiful Madagascar Quartz Crystals. They are in matrix as shown, and are available in two different sizes.

WORLD BANK ROLE

There are 18 active International Development Association (IDA) projects in Madagascar and current commitments are US$629 million. About 33 percent of projects are in the social sectors, 18 percent in infrastructure, 8 percent in energy, 7 percent in agriculture sector, 7 percent in the private sector, 5 percent in environment, and 22 percent are multi-sector.

The International Finance Corporation (IFC) has committed $11.3 million to seven operations in Madagascar, and some new operations are under consideration. In the 1998-1999 financial year, IFC focused on projects in hotel and tourism, energy, agribusiness, telecommunications, air cargo transport, and export-oriented activities. IFC's advisory program is likely to focus on privatization in the telecommunications, tourism and banking sectors.

The Multilateral Investment Guarantee Agency (MIGA) has three guarantees in the tourism sector for a gross exposure of US$1.4 million. Once the project is constructed, the total amount of foreign direct investment facilitated is expected to reach US$117.6 million. It also has two active applications for Madagascar for a total investment potential of US$41 million in the oil and gas sector.

The World Bank Institute (WBI) organized two regional workshops in which a Malagasy delegation took part. The themes that were the most popular with the Malagasy were utility regulation and competition in telecom sector.

TRADE GENERAL

- Import licences are not required, except for a short list of goods which are subject to administrative control for security or health reasons.
- Before importing, importers are required to submit their "Fiche Statistique d'Importation" (Import Data File) with the proforma invoice to their bank. A copy must be submitted to the Ministry of Commerce.
- Madagascar is a contracting party of the Harmonised Commodity Description and Coding System.
- Customs duties and import taxes are assessed on an ad valorem basis; the basis for valuation is C.I.F..
- Samples having no commercial value are entered free of duty.
- Valuable samples may be admitted temporarily free under deposit or bond or bank guarantee.
- South African businessmen are encouraged to visit the island personally to re-initiate contact.
- According to the financial law of 1999, there are four types of duties

- - Import tax (TI): 0 - 25%
-
- - Custom fees (DD): 0 - 25%
- - Consumption tax (DA): 0 - 10%
- - Value Added Tax (VAT): 20%The government has eliminated most quantitative restrictions on imports.
- Director General of Customs - Tel: (0926120) 2222916, Fax: (09261 20) 2264680

DEVELOPMENT

Multilateral and bilateral donors, including the World Bank and the IMF, are active in Madagascar. Under Bank and IMF-sponsored economic reforms, stabilization has been satisfactory, and donor coordination is strong. The transport sector, education financing, rural development, locust control, and post-cyclone reconstruction projects are instances where there is multiple donor participation. Progress in structural reforms and debt relief during the year will be key to ensure that Madagascar can adopt a high growth path conducive to poverty reduction.

SELECTED OFFICIAL MATERIALS

PROGRAMME DE MISE EN ŒUVRE DE LA POLITIQUE GENERALE DE L'ETAT PRESENTE PAR MONSIEUR JACQUES SYLLA PREMIER MINISTRE CHEF DU GOUVERNEMENT

TABLE DES MATIERES

Monsieur le Président de l'Assemblée Nationale,
Mesdames et Messieurs les membres du Bureau Permanent l'Assemblée Nationale
Mesdames et Messieurs les Députés,

1 Introduction et Orientations Générales

1.1 Vision pour Madagascar

Les Malgaches ont du mal à se projeter dans l'avenir, ils n'ont aucun repère dans une société où aucun système de valeur n'est défini.
L'objectif premier du Gouvernement est d'éradiquer rapidement la pauvreté, selon la vision présentée comme suit:
Madagascar: nation riche, nation unitaire et indivisible dont la base est le Fihavanana,
Le "Fahamarinana" constitue le fondement d'un développement rapide et pérenne de notre pays,
Madagascar: une société de liberté et de tolérance dans la fierté et la confiance de son avenir,
Une démocratie malgache : participation de tous dans le choix des grandes décisions du pays, en alliant la "sagesse" et la "connaissance", en utilisant à bon escient et en enrichissant les plates-formes existantes d'écoute, d'échanges, de réflexions et de propositions (secteur privé, secteur public, société civile, élus...),
Une société prospère et moderne reposant sur une économie compétitive, dynamique et solide, tenant compte de l'évolution technologique et de la mondialisation,
Une société économiquement équitable, en transformant les 80% de notre population qui vivent en dessous du seuil de la pauvreté en une classe moyenne prospère et solide,
Madagascar : un véritable acteur reconnu et respecté sur l'échiquier international.

1.2 Un projet de société fondé sur la Justice et la liberté

Pour parvenir à la vision pour Madagascar citée ci-dessus, nous allons construire une société fondée sur la Justice et la Liberté.
Justice : c'est l'égalité de tous devant la loi, c'est faire en sorte qu'il n'y ait pas une catégorie de citoyens qui, pour des raisons d'ordre économique, financier, culturel et social, soit marginalisée.
C'est à l'Etat de veiller à la défense des droits de tous les citoyens et surtout des plus défavorisés ; de même il lui appartient de défendre la liberté de tout un chacun, de s'exprimer, d'entreprendre, de faire respecter les droits de l'homme les plus élémentaires.
L'Etat n'a pas à intervenir en principe dans des domaines qui relèveraient du secteur privé, mais sa présence est indispensable pour la sauvegarde de l'intérêt général et de la souveraineté nationale. C'est à l'Etat d'établir les règles du jeu en matière économique pour éviter de tomber dans les excès d'un libéralisme sauvage sans pour autant

entraver le libre fonctionnement du marché

La société malgache, en vue d'un développement durable, doit respecter l'Etat libéral et démocratique au service d'hommes et de femmes libres et responsables, aspirant légitimement à un mieux être, c'est à dire au bonheur.

1.3 Les grands axes du développement

Le Gouvernement a la ferme détermination, une volonté politique de fer, pour réussir le redressement d'une situation qui ne cesse inexorablement au fil des jours de se dégrader dans tous les domaines.

Le programme du Gouvernement s'inscrit dans le cadre d'un environnement susceptible de régénérer un nouvel élan de dynamisme de tous les acteurs socio-économiques et de tous les citoyens dans une société qui exclut toute forme de discrimination (ethnique, confessionnelle, raciale, etc...) et qui tend à réduire, autant que faire se peut, les inégalités sociales.

La politique de développement présentée ici met comme objectif la mise en œuvre rapide des mesures de développement pour insuffler un nouveau tonus au secteur privé et accroître la confiance des investisseurs.

1.3.1 Un préalable au développement

Pour la réussite de sa politique, les préalables sur lesquels le Gouvernement doit veiller est, le respect de la démocratie, la restauration de l'Etat de droit et la bonne gouvernance.

1.3.1.1 Respect de la démocratie

Dans ce cadre, deux facteurs seront considérés : le libre choix des gouvernants et la participation effective des citoyens aux affaires publiques,

1.3.1.2 Restauration de l'Etat de droit

Cela constitue la garantie pour tous les acteurs socio-économiques et tout individu dans leur entreprise pour le développement du pays.

Cet Etat de droit doit être vécu quotidiennement par les citoyens:

par le respect par les autorités des valeurs fondamentales prônées par la Constitution,

par l'appui que devra apporter l'Etat aux différentes organisations qui militent pour le respect des droits et pour la promotion de toute catégorie d'individus,

par la mise en place d'une Commission nationale des droits de l'Homme indépendante de l'administration tant dans sa composition que tous ses structures et son fonctionnement.

Cet Etat de droit doit se manifester par la dépolitisation de l'administration:

toute considération d'ordre politique doit être exclue de l'administration,

la gestion des carrières des fonctionnaires et les nominations aux différents postes techniques de responsabilité se feront principalement sur des critères de compétence et d'honnêteté,

les gouvernants comme les gouvernés seront égaux dans l'application de la loi.

Cet Etat de droit fonctionnera sous le contrôle d'une Justice indépendante prônée par la Constitution et garante principale de l'Etat de droit :

le système judiciaire doit être indépendant et efficace pour permettre d'assurer l'instauration d'un Etat de droit, la protection des droit de l'Homme et de la libre entreprise, puis l'administration de la Justice et l'administration pénitentiaire les décisions de la Justice devenues définitives seront appliquées sans discrimination

1.3.1.3 Bonne gouvernance

Indissociable de la démocratie, la bonne gouvernance constitue un gage de la réussite de toute action de redressement économique, voire du développement durable et soutenu ; elle est conditionnée par :
une éthique de gestion :
l'intérêt général ou l'intérêt public doit primer sur l'intérêt particulier,
le critère de gouvernant doit être basé sur des considérations de compétence et d'honnêteté
la primauté du droit par rapport à toute autre considération;
un respect de certaines règles de conduite en matière de gestion des affaires publiques dont notamment :
la transparence de la gestion,
l'imputabilité l'efficacité et l'obligation de résultats;
la mise en place d'un système de contrôle effectif et efficace éliminant toutes les formes d'impunité à quelque niveau que ce soit: les actes de corruption ou d'enrichissement illicite seront réprimés quel qu'en soit l'auteur. La lutte contre la corruption et les détournements des deniers publics sera intensifiée grâce notamment à :
la radiation pure et simple de la fonction publique et poursuite pénale à l'encontre des agents de l'Etat ou autorités commettant la corruption
la sanction pénale à l'encontre du corrupteur
la réglementation et le contrôle strict de la commission des marchés publics
le renforcement du contrôle d'exécution budgétaire
la simplification des procédures administratives
l'institution de programme d'éducation civique dès l'éducation de base
la mise en œuvre de la décentralisation effective : c'est un moyen d'ancrage et d'appropriation du développement par la population à la base;
la poursuite de la réforme de la Fonction publique,
l'existence d'un véritable programme de développement : concret, pragmatique et mesurable dans le temps, avec des priorités bien définies et échelonnées, ainsi qu'un dispositif de contrôle et de suivi de l'exécution.

1.3.1.4 Développement institutionnel

On assiste aujourd'hui à une prolifération de « projets de développement » financés par diverses institutions multilatérales ou bilatérales. Des axes de priorité ont été définis pour faciliter une coordination de ces projets qui, sur le terrain, se trouvent en concurrence au lieu de se compléter, pour un meilleur impact.
A cette fin, l'Etat malgache procédera à la décentralisation du financement des grands projets (infrastructures routières, services sociaux essentiels, etc.) qui va être transféré au niveau de chaque province. Le fonds alloué à ces projets va figurer ensuite dans le budget des Collectivités territoriales décentralisées pour réaliser les programmes définis comme prioritaires et pour permettre une meilleure coordination de ces projets.
A cet égard, le rôle de l'Etat se limite au suivi et évaluation des réalisations desdits

For additional analytical, business and investment opportunities information, please contact Global Investment & Business Center, USA at (202) 546-2103. Fax: (202) 546-3275. E-mail: rusric@erols.com

projets:
Chaque province, conformément à ces orientations, établira un Programme de Développement Provincial.
En fonction de ce Programme, chaque Commune mettra à la disposition du Fivondronana de son rattachement une monographie mettant en évidence un état des lieux, les potentiels de sa localité.
A partir des monographies de ses Communes, chaque Fivondronana formule son Programme de Développement
La Région aura la charge de coordonner les Programmes élaborés par les Fivondronana pour avoir une Politique de Développement Régional.
Par ailleurs, les autorités provinciales se chargeront de la coordination et de la gestion financière de cette politique.
Ce sera une approche à la fois institutionnelle au niveau de l'organisation de l'Etat et participative au niveau de la population

1.3.2 Les grands axes du programme de mise en œuvre de la politique generale de l'Etat

Le programme du Gouvernement est axé sur les principaux points suivants:
le développement des infrastructures,
la sécurité,
la politique sociale,
la préservation du droit de l'Homme,
la politique économique,
la politique étrangère.

(Note: Vous trouverez ce document téléchargeable en entier dans la partie "Téléchargements" du site)

For additional analytical, business and investment opportunities information,
please contact Global Investment & Business Center, USA
at (202) 546-2103. Fax: (202) 546-3275. E-mail: rusric@erols.com

DEMOCRACY & HUMAN RIGHTS

Madagascar is a multiparty democracy in which the President and a bicameral legislature shared power. The country's Constitution was amended in 1996 and 1998. These amendments significantly strengthened the executive, weakened the National Assembly, and gave the President the right to name one-third of the senators. Although 160 political parties were active throughout the country, the ruling President and his party dominated political life, as did former president Didier Ratsiraka and his AREMA party in the previous quarter century.

The new President, Marc Ravalomanana, relied on a coalition of political parties, Coalition of Marc Ravalomanana Supporters (KMMR), and his own organization Tiako-i-Madagsikara (TIM), "I love Madagascar" (which became a political party in July), to spearhead his challenge to former President Ratsiraka. Presidential elections were held in December 2001, and the results were disputed. Between January and June, both Ravalomanana in Antananarivo and Ratsiraka in the port city of Toamasina claimed to be the legitimate head of state. There was widespread, politically motivated conflict that led to approximately 100 deaths. In May Ravalomanana was declared President, and by June the Ravalomanana Government gained control of the country. The December 15 legislative elections, which international observers judged as generally free and fair, resulted in a substantial majority (124 of 156 deputies) for the TIM (102) and the pro-Ravalomanana National Alliance (22) in the new National Assembly. At year's end, four district elections were expected to be run again following the voiding of results by the High Constitutional Court. The judiciary was subject to executive influence and at times susceptible to corruption.

The Minister for Public Security (formerly a State Secretary at the Ministry of the Interior) headed the national police and was responsible for law and order in urban areas. The Gendarmerie Nationale, part of the Ministry of National Defense, insured security in all other areas of the island. Regular army units and reservists at times assumed law enforcement roles in matters that make large-scale logistical demands, such as cattle theft. Gendarmerie, regular army, and reservist units committed serious human rights abuses.

The country was very poor with a population of 16 million. Although the Government made the consolidation of a market-based economy a priority, the economy remained mixed. Agriculture was the largest sector of the economy, and shrimp and vanilla were the leading exports. More than 70 percent of the population fall below the Government's own poverty level of approximately 45 cents a day in income. In the first half of the year, trade declined by 50 percent and textile exports dropped 90 percent. Inflation was approximately 6 percent in 2001, peaked at a 60 percent annual rate during the political crisis, and fell to 12 percent by the end of the year.

The Government generally respected the human rights of its citizens; however, there were problems in some areas. Between January and June, the human rights situation worsened as both Ravalomanana and Ratsiraka fought for control of the Government, and both sides committed serious human rights abuses. After Ravalomanana achieved control of the country, the human rights situation improved; however, problems remained in some areas. Conflict between supporters of both sides was widespread and led to approximately 100 deaths. There were reports of brutality and abuse by security forces, particularly by armed irregulars (reservists) that the Government had recruited at the height of the conflict. Groups affiliated with both sides of the crisis abducted persons. Police or other security forces physically abused prisoners or detainees. Prison conditions were harsh and life threatening. In some prisons, women experienced physical abuse, including rape. The Government allowed the International Committee of the Red Cross (ICRC) to establish a permanent office in the country and to conduct inspections of detention facilities throughout the island. Arbitrary arrests and detentions of some supporters of the previous government occurred and some high-profile arrests were made months after the resolution of the political crisis. Suspects often were held for periods that exceeded the maximum sentence for the alleged offenses and lengthy pretrial detention remained a serious problem. Dina (local traditional) authorities imposed summary justice in rural areas where the Government's presence was weak. The Government limited freedom of speech and of the press. Journalists practiced self-censorship. The Government at times partially limited freedom of assembly. During the political crisis, both sides restricted freedom of movement. Women continued to face some societal discrimination. Child labor remained a problem. Workers' rights were limited in the export processing zones (EPZs). There were reports of trafficking in women and girls. Madagascar was invited by the Community of Democracies' (CD) Convening Group to attend the November 2002 second CD Ministerial Meeting in Seoul, Republic of Korea, as an observer.

RESPECT FOR HUMAN RIGHTS

SECTION 1 RESPECT FOR THE INTEGRITY OF THE PERSON, INCLUDING FREEDOM FROM:

A. ARBITRARY OR UNLAWFUL DEPRIVATION OF LIFE

During the political crisis of the first half of the year, supporters of both Ravalomanana and Ratsiraka committed an estimated 100 politically motivated killings. For example, on February 2, an armed group led by Lt. Col. Assolant Coutiti killed the Director of the BTM-BAO bank, who was a Ravalomanana supporter, in Nosy Be. Coutiti, the security coordinator for the Governor of Antsiranana Province, Jean Robert Gara, and Antsiranana Deputy Soaline were believed to have been responsible for numerous other politically motivated killings in Antsiranana Province. In September government authorities arrested Coutiti; his trial was pending at year's end.

On March 19, a group of 10 men who allegedly were members of the Gendarmerie associated with Ratsiraka killed the Regional Director of the Office of Copyrights, who was a well-known KMMR member in his home in Fianaranstoa Province. There was no investigation or action taken by year's end.

On April 9, security officers assigned to Prime Minister Jacques Sylla arrested Roland Ravalomasoa, a Ratsiraka supporter, in Antananarivo. He died the same day of injuries sustained during interrogations. There was no investigation or action taken by year's end.

During the year, security forces used lethal force to disperse demonstrations (see Section 2.b.).

On February 27, a number of Ravalomanana supporters attacked a group of Ratsiraka supporters outside the Palais de la Justice in Antananarivo. In the ensuing fight, one of the Ratsiraka supporters was killed. There was no investigation or action taken by year's end.

In April a Canadian missionary watching a demonstration in Fianarantsoa from his window was killed by gunfire. Circumstantial evidence suggested that pro-Ratsiraka militias targeted the man specifically. There reportedly was an investigation; however, there was no findings released by year's end.

After the crisis ended, there were no reports of unlawful killings; however, at least one prisoner detained on charges related to the political crisis died while in custody due to his poor health and the harsh prison conditions. The Government had not investigated or explained this incident by year's end (see Section 1.c.).

During the year, there were several high-profile killings of "Karana" (persons of Indo-Pakistani origin living in the country); however, these killings appeared to have criminal rather than political motives (see Section 5). In September the authorities arrested three individuals in connection with one of these killings; however, there was no further action taken by year's end.

B. DISAPPEARANCE

There were widespread, credible reports of abductions of persons for political reasons by groups affiliated with both sides during the political crisis; in some cases persons allegedly were tortured. These abductions generally were temporary in nature, the victims were released, and the perpetrators were identified. Supporters of the Ratsiraka government abducted numerous persons for political reasons, particularly in Antsiranana and Toamasina provinces, including several officials of the Church of Jesus Christ in Madagascar (FJKM), the Presbyterian Church of which President Ravalomanana is a Vice President and other known supporters of Ravalomanana (see Section 2.c.). Those abducted often were transferred to detention centers in other regions, sometimes using aircraft that belonged to a company owned by President Ratsiraka's son. Evidence provided by the nongovernmental organization (NGO) SOS to Victims of Illegality (SOSVND) indicated that the Pardes military camp in the middle of Antsiranana was the destination for the abductees.

On April 17, in the northern part of the island, Ratsiraka militias acting at the command of the local AREMA party Deputy Madame Soaline abducted an FJKM pastor named Ndriamisaina at his home. At the time of his arrest he was allegedly beaten with rifle butts. After spending 3 days in the Ambolimadinika military camp in the Sambava region of the country, he was transferred by aircraft to the Pardes detention camp in Antsiranana (see Section 2.c.).

In Fianarantsoa, Ravalomanana supporters abducted the state's prosecutor to the Court of Appeals after vandalizing his home and automobile. The Government made no effort to investigate or punish those responsible for the abductions of Ratsiraka supporters by year's end.

There were several kidnapings of members of the Karana community. Despite reports of ethnic friction between Karana and Malagasy citizens, these crimes were not considered to be ethnically motivated but to be caused, in part, by intra-Karana rivalry (see Section 1.a.). In September authorities arrested and charged 17 persons in connection with these crimes.

There were no arrests or other action taken in the following 2001 cases: The kidnaping of a girl in Antananarivo; the February kidnaping of a manager of a large automotive company in Antananarivo; and the August attempted kidnaping and killing of the victim in the Ivandry section of Antananarivo.

C. TORTURE AND OTHER CRUEL, INHUMAN, OR DEGRADING TREATMENT OR PUNISHMENT

The Constitution provides for the inviolability of the person; however, there were numerous, credible reports that both sides in the political crisis engaged in torture. The most common form of torture was the severe beating of detainees, usually with rifle butts. Prisoners also were burned with lighted cigarettes. The Ravalomanana Government used reservists who operated outside the normal armed forces chain of command and did not respect due process safeguards. Certain NGOs, such as the Association of Families of Persons Detained in the Context of the Political Crisis (OFPACPA), alleged that reservists engaged in numerous acts of violence, theft, and vandalism. For example, in June during their occupation of the city of Mahajanga on the country's west coast, pro-Ravalomanana reservists arrested Doctor Noel Randrianaivojaona, a prominent Ratsiraka supporter. He was publicly forced to walk on his knees over pavement for long distances. He then was incarcerated for several months before being tried on charges of "threatening the internal security of the state." He was acquitted in November.

In March in Diego Suarez, 16 resident members of KMMR were arbitrarily arrested, beaten, and tortured by pro-Ratsiraka militias and security forces. On April 20, pro-Ratsiraka forces arrested at least 10 persons and reportedly tortured some in Sambava. The detainees later were transferred to a military camp in the city of Antsiranama.

The political crisis exacerbated already harsh and life-threatening prison conditions. Prisoners' diets were considered inadequate, and families had to supplement daily rations. Prisoners without relatives went for days without food. Prison cells averaged less than one square yard of space per inmate. Adequate medical care also was a serious concern. These conditions caused a high incidence of malnutrition, malaria, tuberculosis, pneumonia, and a host of infections that resulted in an unknown number of deaths during the year. According to a Catholic Relief Services' (CRS) report, many prison health problems could be alleviated with adequate food. The Government maintained that harsh prison conditions reflected the country's low level of economic development, inadequate infrastructure, and a lack of resources. The Government was candid about the condition of prisons and generally open to requests for independent monitoring.

In the case of former Gendarmerie General Bory, the Ravalomanana Government temporarily denied family visitation and necessary medical care.

Prisoners can be used as forced labor, and there were reports that this occurred during the year. The Government was aware of the problem and said it would address it.

Pretrial detainees were not always kept separate from the general prison population. Women in prisons were abused, as were children who sometimes were confined with them. Women were not always held separately from men, and there were reports of rapes committed by other prisoners. Due to severe overcrowding, juveniles were not always held separately from the adult prison population. The 2002 CRS report indicated that prison facilities for minors adequately accommodated those detained.

In August Amnesty International (AI) visited the country for a "fact-finding and familiarization tour." AI attributed human rights abuses to both sides during and after the political crisis. AI alleged that in the post-political crisis environment in the country that nearly all of the proceedings for crimes stemming from the political crisis implicated officials or supporters of the former regime and that among those arrested and facing charges were persons arrested "arbitrarily, solely for having expressed, in a nonviolent manner, opinions critical of the current Government." Amnesty also spoke of quasi-systematic arrests of persons associated with the previous regime. Amnesty concluded the Ravalomanana Government record on human rights was deficient. Among AI's recommendations were that all crimes committed during the political crisis be impartially and independently investigated and that those who committed them brought to justice. There also were numerous recommendations touching on procedural issues such as the rights of the accused to be informed of the charges, to the assistance of counsel, and to the setting of reasonable bail. AI also called for reforms and upgrades of the penitentiary system.

Also in August, the Ravalomanana Government signed an agreement with the International Committee of the Red Cross (ICRC) that provided the ICRC with permanent offices and access to detention centers throughout the country. It also permitted the ICRC to interview detainees without a third party. The ICRC presented its findings directly to the Government. The ICRC representatives indicated that the Government was meeting its obligations under the agreement (see Section 4). In October the CRS presented to Justice Minister Alice Rajonah its Analysis of the Penitentiary System in Madagascar. CRS representatives noted that the Government expressed a desire to improve the conditions in its 97 prisons countrywide.

D. ARBITRARY ARREST, DETENTION, OR EXILE

The Constitution provides for due process for persons accused of crimes and prohibits arbitrary arrest and detention; however, the Government frequently ignored these provisions in practice. The law mandates that a criminal suspect must be charged or released within 48 hours of arrest. Ravalomanana government authorities admitted to detaining persons in connection with the political crisis for whatever length of time necessary for state prosecutors to develop a strong case. The Ravalomanana Government used reservists who operated outside the normal armed forces chain of command to make many of the arrests. These forces did not respect due process safeguards and were alleged by certain NGOs to have committed numerous abuses (see Section 1.c.).

Arrest warrants may be obtained but are not mandated strictly by law. Often a person was detained and jailed on no more than an accusation by another person. The law provides defendants in criminal cases the right to be informed of the charges against them and the right to a counsel when the charges formally are brought. The State provided counsel only in cases in which indigent defendants faced charges with sentences, if convicted, of greater than 5 years. Detainees, particularly those held in connection with the political crisis, were not always allowed family visitation or access to counsel (see Section 1.c.). A system of bail existed; however, in practice it was not extended to defendants accused of crimes related to the political crisis. Rather than grant bail, magistrates sometimes resorted to an instrument known as a retaining writ (mandat de depot) by which defendants were held in detention for the entire pretrial period or for periods longer than the maximum sentence on the charges faced.

Poor record keeping, lack of resources, and the difficulty of access to more remote parts of the island made it difficult to monitor pretrial detainees. According to CRS, 67 percent of the approximately 18,370 persons held in custody nationwide were in pretrial detention; however, only a small percentage of these were incarcerated on political crisis-related charges. Despite legal protections, investigative detentions often exceed 1 year. Many detainees spend a longer period in investigative detention than they would have spent incarcerated following a maximum sentence on the charges faced. An August amnesty declared by the Ravalomanana Government was a traditional, proforma gesture affecting 400 prisoners that did little to alleviate the problem of overcrowding and harsh conditions in prisons.

On June 24, pro-Ratsiraka militia in Antsiranana detained a group of 73 persons, many of highland origin, and chained them to the gate surrounding the governor's mansion apparently as a warning sign to approaching Ravalomanana forces that these hostages would be used as human shields in the event of an attack. No attack came, and the hostages were unshackled within a few hours, but some remained in detention until June 29.

The Ravalomanana Government used house arrest only in the case of former Prime Minister Tantely Andrianarivo. The former Prime Minister spent more than 5 months under house arrest and in October was relocated to Antanimora prison. He was charged with embezzling public funds, harboring known criminals, compromising national security, and abusing the public trust. The proceedings were mired in disputes over jurisdictional issues. The former Prime Minister's lawyers claimed that his appointment was never officially abrogated, and that he remained Prime Minister and must be tried in a special venue (la Haute Cour de Justice—-the High Court of Justice) reserved for ministers, rather than in the court of general jurisdiction. By year's end no trial date had been set.

The Government did not use forced exile.

E. DENIAL OF FAIR PUBLIC TRIAL

The Constitution provides for an autonomous judiciary; however, at all levels, the judiciary was susceptible to the influence of the executive and at times susceptible to corruption.

The judiciary had four levels. Courts of First Instance hear civil cases and criminal cases carrying limited fines and sentences. The Court of Appeals included a criminal court of first instance for more serious cases—-those carrying sentences greater than 5 years. The Supreme Court of Appeals heard cases on appeal from the Court of Appeals. The High Constitutional Court (HCC) reviewed the constitutionality of laws, decrees, and ordinances and certified election results. The judiciary also included specialized courts designed to handle specific matters such as cattle theft.

The judiciary was under the control of the Ministry of Justice and, as with many other branches of government, reports of corruption persisted. In its public statements, the Ravalomanana Government made the fight against corruption a top priority; however, there were no specific actions taken by year's end. The Constitution provides defendants with the right to a full defense at every stage of the proceedings, and trials were public. Defendants had a right to be present at their trial, to confront witnesses, and to present evidence. The law provides for a presumption of innocence; however, as CRS noted, "there was a large gap between the laws that served to protect the rights of the accused and the implementation of these laws in fact. The human rights of a person accused of a crime were often transgressed."

State prosecutors sought relatively lenient sentences for those convicted of crimes committed during the political crisis; however, some sentences provoked criticism from members of the public who were seeking greater retribution.

The Mayor of Toamasina, Roland Ratsiraka, nephew of former President Ratsiraka, was arrested on seven charges that included: inciting ethnic violence; violation of the Constitution by not accepting Ravalomanana as President of the Republic; firing of three municipal police officers; aiding and abetting militias; ordering the blockade of Toamasina Airport thereby preventing Prime Minister Sylla's visit; neglecting municipal finances; and absconding with $5 million (approximately 34 billion FMG). The local press widely criticized this action as arbitrary, particularly given Ratsiraka's known opposition to his uncle, his failure to sign the act of secession of Taomasina Province, and his advocacy during the political crisis of dismantling blockades erected throughout the country (see Section 2.d.). In Toamasina Province, his arrest provoked widespread anger, the circulation of petitions, and calls for a general strike. He was released 4 days after his arrest pending a hearing on the charges; however, there were no further developments by year's end.

The right of traditional village institutions to protect property and public order was codified in the Constitution as well as in earlier laws. Local traditional laws called Dina sometimes were used to resolve civil disputes between villages, and on occasion were used in urban areas. Because of the rise in crime, the uneven effectiveness of the judiciary, and the corruption of law enforcement, Dina jurisdiction sometimes was extended to criminal cases. Dina-based punishment could be severe and in the past had included death sentences; however, there were no reports of executions during the year. The less formal Dina process did not ensure internationally recognized standards of due process. Decisions based on Dina were not subject to codified safeguards for the accused; however, in some instances they could be challenged at the Appeals Court level. Cases also could be referred to the Office of the Mediator, which investigated and sought redress through formal judicial authorities.

Military courts were for the trial of military personnel only, were integrated into the civil judicial system, and differed only in the inclusion of military officers on jury panels. Defendants in military cases, as in civil cases, had access to an appeals process that reexamined points of law rather than questions of fact. A civilian magistrate, usually joined on the bench by a panel of military officers, presided over military trials.

The status of prisoners detained for their role in the political crisis was a major concern in the post-crisis period. The Ravalomanana Government pursued those associated with the former government and in particular those who were known to be behind the blockades placed on the roads linking the rest of the country with Antananarivo (see Section 2.d.). Those incarcerated, particularly those who served in the Gendarmerie or the Armed Forces at the time, continued to request, through their families, classification as political prisoners. Most were charged with treason; however, the detainees claimed they could not have committed treason because executive and governmental legitimacy were in question during the period, and they maintained their imprisonment was politically motivated. The NGO OFPACPA claimed the reprisals disproportionately targeted citizens of non-Merina ethnicity and thus added an ethnic factor to the political (see Section 5). Initially the Ravalomanana Government did not allow access either by counsel or by families to these prisoners; however, prisoners were allowed visitors and counsel by year's end.

F. ARBITRARY INTERFERENCE WITH PRIVACY, FAMILY, HOME, OR CORRESPONDENCE

The Constitution provides for the inviolability of the individual, his abode, and for the confidentiality of his correspondence; however, these provisions were not always respected. For example, on April 8, Ravalomanana supporters sympathizers looted and burned the homes of Jean Emile Tsaranazy and Gerard Andriamileravoson, respectively, Minister of the Ratsiraka Government and Director General (Chief of Staff) in the office of the Presidency

Militia members also arrested Dr. Roger Randriamihaja, another Ravalomanana supporter, as he emerged from the forest where he sought refuge after abandoning his home for fear of bands of pro-Ratsiraka militias. In these, as in approximately 50 similar cases catalogued by NGOs and foreign missionaries, forces on both sides disregarded constitutional provisions protecting the inviolability of the home and the person.

There were widespread reports that the Ravalomanana Government initiated a write-in informer system in Toamasina Province.

For additional analytical, business and investment opportunities information,
please contact Global Investment & Business Center, USA
at (202) 546-2103. Fax: (202) 546-3275. E-mail: rusric@erols.com

SECTION 2 RESPECT FOR CIVIL LIBERTIES, INCLUDING:

A. FREEDOM OF SPEECH AND PRESS

The Constitution provides for freedom of speech and of the press, however, both the Ratsiraka and Ravalomanana governments limited those rights. During the early stages of the political crisis, the Ratsiraka Government pressured private and state-owned media to curb or alter coverage of certain political developments. Journalists practiced self-censorship. At times the Government pressured the media to curb its coverage of certain events and topics, and there were reports that government personnel intimidated journalists.

There were four privately owned national daily newspapers and many other privately owned national and local news publications that published less frequently; however, in a country with a literacy rate of approximately 54 percent, the influence of print media was minimal.

After the post-crisis period, freedom of expression and critical political expression were permitted. In October the leadership of former president Ratsiraka's AREMA party took out a full-page advertisement in one of the country's main daily newspapers that was critical of President Ravalomanana's decision to dissolve the National Assembly. In August critical opinions of President Ravalomanana's decision to acquire an aircraft for presidential use was disseminated widely in the media, which prompted the Government to provide an official explanation on the decision through the Vice Prime Minister.

During the political crisis, there were widespread, credible reports of intimidation of journalists and employees of media outlets, especially by pro-Ratsiraka militias. For example, in May pro-Ratsiraka militia in Sambava arrested and transferred to the Pardes camp in Antsiranana, Tantelimalala Randriamanantsoa and Vola Julson Rafaralahy, both employees of a radio station called Tiako-I-Andapa (see Section 1.b.). According to SOSVN, each suffered physical abuse. They were charged with "broadcasting false news reports." After detaining the pair for 1 month, the Ratsiraka authorities dropped the charges.

The Government owned the only nationwide television and radio networks. There were more than 175 privately owned radio and television stations at the end of 2001; however, federal regulations restricted them from providing nationwide coverage.

In February the former Minister of Information cut off all transmissions from the state-owned Television Malagasy (TVM) and the state-owned national radio (RNM) after some of their commentators broadcast news of President Ravalomanana's first inauguration. The state-owned media stayed off the air for several weeks and then reopened. Some provincial affiliates preferred not to broadcast for fear of local reprisals.

During the crisis period, a number of private radio stations were ransacked, burned, or forced off the air. The Ravalomanana-owned Madagascar Broadcasting System (MBS) and its regional affiliates were the targets of attacks in Antsiranana Province and elsewhere. In Antananarivo fires set by a mob forced the pro-Ratsiraka Tsiokavo radio station off the air. It was not clear if the mob was composed of Ravalomanana supporters or Ratsiraka supporters.

The Government did not restrict academic freedom.

B. FREEDOM OF PEACEFUL ASSEMBLY AND ASSOCIATION

The Constitution provides for freedom of assembly; however, the Government at times limited the right in practice. The Government routinely issued permits for public meetings and demonstrations.

On January 25, a HCC decision calling for a second round of voting led Ravalomanana supporters to call a general strike. Beginning January 28, large crowds (up to several hundred thousand) of peaceful demonstrators gathered daily in Antananarivo for several months. The municipal government that was headed by Marc Ravalomanana permitted these demonstrations.

Despite being largely peaceful, some persons were killed when police used forces to disperse demonstrations. For example, on January 7, police in Antananarivo killed a young child with a tear gas canister they fired to disperse a peaceful pro-Ravalomanana demonstration.

In late February, President Ratsiraka declared a state of national emergency and martial law, which forbade most public gatherings and permitted government monitoring of suspicious individuals and groups; however, the monitoring was not effective in practice.

On March 15, 2 persons were killed and more than 40 injured when a group of Ravalomanana supporters, who accompanied Prime Minister-designate Jacques Sylla's attempt to take over the prime minister's offices in Antananarivo, clashed with elements of the military loyal to President Ratsiraka. There was no investigation or action taken by year's end.

The Constitution provides for the right of association and permits citizens to organize political parties and associations; however, the Constitution also explicitly forbids associations that "call into question the unity of the Nation, and those that advocate totalitarianism or ethnic, tribal, or religious segregation." There were 160 political parties throughout the island.

C. FREEDOM OF RELIGION

The Constitution provides for freedom of religion, and both Governments of the crisis period and the Ravalomanana Government generally respected this right in practice.

Religious groups must register and obtain authorization from the Ministry of Interior; however, there were no reports that any group was denied registration during the year.

President Ravalomanana is a Vice President of the FJKM. The church, along with its Catholic, Anglican, and Lutheran counterparts (collectively known as FFKM) actively

**For additional analytical, business and investment opportunities information,
please contact Global Investment & Business Center, USA
at (202) 546-2103. Fax: (202) 546-3275. E-mail: rusric@erols.com**

supported his candidacy for President and his policies during the political crisis. Members and facilities of the FJKM were frequent targets of pro-Ratsiraka forces (see Section 1.b.).

For a more detailed discussion see the 2002 International Religious Freedom Report.

D. FREEDOM OF MOVEMENT WITHIN THE COUNTRY, FOREIGN TRAVEL, EMIGRATION, AND REPATRIATION

The Constitution provides for these rights; however, during the political crisis both Governments restricted these rights. The fear of crime effectively restricted travel in some areas, especially at night.

During the period of political crisis, militias and provincial governors loyal to President Ratsiraka restricted freedom of movement. In response to rising insecurity during the political crisis, roadblocks were erected and curfews were imposed in the capital. In Antananarivo security forces and citizen supporters of Ravalomanana established nighttime roadblocks to control movement. Curfews and restrictions of movement tied to the state of martial law declared by Ratsiraka never were enforced.

In February student activists, militia, and security forces loyal to President Ratsiraka erected a barricade at Brickaville, a key junction leading to Toamasina, the country's principal port, and effectively blocked the flow of goods and people to and from Antananarivo until early August. Other national arteries similarly were blocked with varying degrees of success. There were reports of restrictions on the inter-provincial travel of vehicles and individuals from certain provinces and ethnic groups.

The country was a signatory to the 1951 U.N. Convention Relating to the Status of Refugees, although the Government has not signed the 1967 Protocol to the Convention. The law does not provide for the granting of asylum or refugee status; however, the Government cooperated closely with the U.N. High Commissioner for Refugees (UNHCR) in processing the small number of refugees or asylum seekers in the country. The issue of provision of first asylum never has arisen. There were no reports of the forced return of persons to a country where they fear persecution.

Section 3 Respect for Political Rights: The Right of Citizens to Change Their Government

The Constitution provides citizens the right to change their government peacefully; however, some degree of turmoil accompanied the three changes of government that occurred over the last 12 years.

The country nominally was a multiparty democracy in which power was divided between the executive, a bicameral assembly, an independent judiciary, and six autonomous provinces. Political and business leaders disproportionately influenced the administration of the country. Political parties coalesced around the single most powerful person, usually the President. "Pensee Unique," a national belief in which dissent was viewed as an attack on societal harmony, made a loyal opposition difficult in practice.

Representatives of the President's political party usually controlled the National Assembly; however, that was not the case from May to October, and on October 16, the President decided to dissolve the National Assembly. The December 15 legislative elections resulted in a substantial majority (124 of 156) deputies declared elected for the President's TIM party and the pro-Ravalomanana National Alliance. International observer teams from the European Union and La Francophonie found the election process to be transparent and the results credible, despite some organizational and local problems. Elections are scheduled to be held in early 2003 in the four districts in which the HCC voided the December 15 results.

The Constitution stipulates that in a presidential election only a candidate who carries more than 50 percent of the popular vote in the first round may be declared the winner. If no candidate receive a majority, a second round is held between the two leading vote gainers. The candidate receiving the majority of second round votes is declared the winner.

Presidential elections were held in December 2001 amid widespread allegations that voter list tampering prevented a significant number of eligible voters from exercising their right to vote. Prior to the elections former President Ratsiraka reorganized the HCC and packed it with known supporters in a bid to control the outcome of the election.

According to the unofficial tally of the Ministry of the Interior, President Ratsiraka received 40.69 percent of the vote, while his main challenger, Mayor of Antananarivo Marc Ravalomanana received 46.49 percent. Rather than await a second round, the Ravalomanana camp demanded a recount and, with the support of civil society groups, performed a recount the results of which gave Ravalomanana slightly more than the 50 percent required. Amid increasing tensions, particularly in the capital, the HCC made an official recount, and in January the HCC confirmed the unofficial first round results with very slight variation.

Alleging fraud, Ravalomanana immediately disavowed the HCC's official count and called for a general strike. During the following month, the situation deteriorated amid growing demonstrations in the capital and ineffective mediation efforts between the principals. On February 22, Ravalomanana declared himself President and appointed Jacques Sylla as his Prime Minister. Within a week, Sylla announced the composition of his cabinet. In response President Ratsiraka declared martial law in Antananarivo and appointed a military governor for the province. On March 4, the five governors of the country's other provinces announced that the national capital had been transferred to Toamasina. On March 14, the symbolic occupation of the Prime Minister's offices by Jacques Sylla led to an armed clash that left two dead and many injured. Later in March, pro-Ratsiraka forces began a systematic campaign targeting the infrastructure of Antananarivo by destroying a bridge at Fatihita. Roadblocks were erected along all the arteries supplying the city, severely reducing the flow of goods and persons both in and out of the capital with severe economic and serious humanitarian consequences for the entire country (see Section 2.d.).

On April 16, the Administrative Chamber of the Supreme Court declared the reorganized HCC was established illegally by President Ratsiraka and ordered its pre-November

2001 members reinstated. This reconstituted HCC was charged with review of the returns from the December 2001 elections.

On April 18, Ravalomanana and Ratsiraka met in Dakar, Senegal, under the auspices of the African Union (AU) and signed the first of two agreements (Dakar I) designed to end the deepening political crisis. The agreement reflected the Administrative Chamber's ruling and called for a recount of first-round ballots. It also outlined, in some detail, a framework to be implemented should, in that recount, neither of the two candidates received the required 50 percent of the popular vote. On April 29, 11 days after Dakar I was signed, the HCC announced the results of it recount, awarding Marc Ravalomanana 51.46 percent of ballots cast and declared him the first-round winner of the presidential election.

In response to that ruling, President Ratsiraka, with the support of five provincial governors, tightened the blockade of Antananarivo and increased attacks on the bridges leading to the capital and the nation's electrical infrastructure. On May 6, President Ravalomanana was sworn in a second time as President in Mahamasina Stadium in Antananarivo. In June the armed forces and the Gendarmerie Nationale pledged their support to the Ravalomanana Government. After a second, failed AU-brokered attempt to resolve the crisis (Dakar II), the Ravalomanana Government decided to use force to dismantle the blockades and seize control of the whole country. Within 2 weeks the major coastal cities of Tulear, Mahajanga, and Antsiranana were retaken with only token resistance from President Ratsiraka's forces. On July 8, government forces entered the Ratsiraka stronghold of Toamasina 1 day after President Ratsiraka left the country for France.

There were 11 women in the 150-member National Assembly dissolved in October and 9 women in the 90-member Senate at year's end. There were 8 women in the 160-member National Assembly elected in December.

GOVERNMENTAL ATTITUDE REGARDING INTERNATIONAL AND NONGOVERNMENTAL INVESTIGATION OF ALLEGED VIOLATIONS OF HUMAN RIGHTS

A number of local and international human rights groups, including SOSVN, OFPACPA, the ICRC, and CRS operated without government restrictions, and freely investigated, published, and otherwise disseminated their findings on human rights issues. These organizations reported that Ravalomanana government officials cooperated with their requests and were responsive to their views.

The Constitution requires the Government to create organizations that promote and protect human rights. The National Commission for Human Rights (CNDH) undertook public awareness campaigns and workshops with international NGOs that nevertheless were limited in their overall impact. The CNDH was apolitical and in practice generally remained separate from partisan politics. During the political crisis, the CNDH suspended its work in part because its meetings had become forums for political invective. The CNDH resumed work in the second half of the year and tentatively planned to publish its report in early 2003.

SECTION 5 DISCRIMINATION BASED ON RACE, SEX, DISABILITY, LANGUAGE, OR SOCIAL STATUS

The Constitution prohibits all forms of discrimination. No specific government institutions were designated to enforce these antidiscrimination provisions.

WOMEN

Domestic violence against women was not widespread. Police and legal authorities generally intervened when physical abuse was reported. The prohibition against rape was the only statute specifically to address violence against women. Spouses can be tried for nonrape abuses, generally under civil law. There were reports in media and public acknowledgements of a domestic violence problem, including reports of battered women. In December the Government launched the first national campaign highlighting domestic violence.

Prostitution is not a crime; however, related activities, such as pandering, are criminal. Incitement of minors to debauchery is a crime. The Ratsiraka Government acknowledged the existence of sexual tourism and undertook an awareness campaign; however, the political crisis and lack of resources precluded the Ravalomanana Government from addressing the problem.

Under the law, wives have an equal voice in selecting the location of the couple's residence, and they generally receive an equitable share of common property on divorce. Widows with children inherit half of joint marital property. A tradition known as "the customary third" occasionally was observed in some areas. Under this custom, the wife had the right only to one third of a couple's joint holdings; however, a widow received a government-provided pension, while a widower did not.

There was relatively little societal discrimination against women in urban areas, where many women owned or managed businesses and held management positions in state-owned companies. The latest information from the Ministry of Labor indicated that women owned 30 percent of formal sector companies and 53 percent of informal sector companies. A number of NGOs focused on the civic education of women and girls and publicized and explained their specific legal protections; however, due to cultural traditions, few women lodged official complaints or sought redress when their legal rights were compromised.

CHILDREN

The Ministry of Health, the Ministry of Education, and the Ministry for Population and the Condition of Women and Children were responsible for various aspects of child welfare. Lack of funds insured that public services in this area remained inadequate. Lack of funding also precluded the compilation of reliable statistics.

The Constitution provides for free public education for all citizen children and makes primary education compulsory for all. According to the Government's Interim Poverty

Reduction Strategy Paper (IPRSP) prepared in 2000, only 50 percent of primary school-age children were enrolled (see Section 6.d.).

There were no reports of societal patterns of child abuse. There were reports that in 2001 children charged with crimes were incarcerated with the general prison population (see Section 1.c.).

PERSONS WITH DISABILITIES

There was no official discrimination against persons with disabilities in employment, education, or in access to state services. The law broadly defines the rights of persons with disabilities. Handicap International Madagascar, an NGO advocate for persons with disabilities, led the fight for legislation mandating equal access for persons with disabilities and the establishment of the National Commission to Safeguard and Promote the Rights of Disabled Persons.

NATIONAL/RACIAL/ETHNIC MINORITIES

The Malagasy, of mixed Malay-Polynesian, African, and Arab descent, were divided into 18 tribes, a term without pejorative overtones in the country. The vast majority of Malagasy spoke a single Malagasy language, albeit with certain regional idiosyncrasies. None of the 18 tribes constituted a majority and there were large minorities of Indo-Pakistani and Chinese heritage.

A long history of military conquest and political dominance raised the status of highland ethnic groups of Asian origin, particularly the Merina, above that of coastal groups of African ancestry. The imbalance persisted to this day and fueled an undercurrent of tension between Malagasy of highland and coastal descents. Ethnicity, caste, and regional solidarity often were factors in hiring practices.

A significant Indo-Pakistani (Karana) community has been present for over a century. Traditionally engaged in commerce, the Karana numbered approximately 20,000 persons. Few of them held Malagasy citizenship, which was acquired through a native-born Malagasy mother. Indo-Pakistani merchants were mistrusted widely. During the political crisis, Karana businesses were vandalized on numerous occasions, and the authorities generally were slow to respond to these disturbances. In October President Ravalomanana met with Karana business leaders and expressed a willingness to look into citizenship issues raised by their community.

SECTION 6 WORKERS RIGHTS

A. THE RIGHT OF ASSOCIATION

The Constitution and the Labor Code provide workers in the public and private sectors with the legal right to establish and join labor unions of their choosing without prior authorization; however, essential service workers, including police and military personnel, may not form unions. Unions were required to register with the Government, and registration was granted routinely. Ministry of Labor statistics indicate that less than

5 percent of workers in export processing zone (EPZ) companies and less than 10 percent of all workers were unionized. There were a number of trade union federations, many of which were affiliated formally with political parties. During the political crisis, union participation was evident in numerous mass demonstrations throughout the country, particularly in those held in Antananarivo in support of President Ravalomanana.

The Labor Code prohibits discrimination by employers against labor organizers, union members, and unions. In the event of antiunion activity, unions or their members may file suit against the employer in civil court. Labor laws apply uniformly throughout the country; however, the Government's enforcement of labor laws and regulations was hampered by a lack of staff and financial resources.

In 2001 the International Labor Organization (ILO) noted a number of instances in which the Government failed to bring law and regulation into conformity with existing conventions or otherwise submit texts for ILO review, including those addressing forced labor, freedom of association, safeguarding of machinery, hygiene in commerce and offices, and weight limits. The political crisis prevented these issues being addressed during the year.

Unions may join international labor organizations and may form federations or confederations

B. THE RIGHT TO ORGANIZE AND BARGAIN COLLECTIVELY

The Constitution provides for the right of workers to bargain collectively. The Labor Code states that either management or labor may initiate collective bargaining. In practice the condition of the economy insured that collective bargaining agreements remained rare. Despite the existence of several public employees unions, few public employees were union members; however, during the year, public employees demonstrated a significant capacity to act in concert, particularly with respect to political matters.

The Constitution provides for the right to strike, within parameters fixed by law. This right extended to the EPZs, where several politically motivated strikes occurred during the year, even in the absence of organized unions. These strikes were primarily driven by political considerations; however, work-related issues emerged, such as demands for wage increases.

Workers in essential services have a recognized but restricted right to strike and exercised this right in the past. The Labor Code calls for workers to exhaust all options including conciliation, mediation, and arbitration before resorting to strikes. These provisions were not always observed. During the year, there was a short, nondisruptive strike over compensation by teachers grading middle school examinations. The strike ended with the examiners receiving a 50 percent--approximately $7 to $11 (50,000 to 79,000 FMG)--increase in the compensation they received to grade the exams.

There were reports that union members working in EPZs were mistreated and sometimes fired. Workers had recourse through the Ministry of Civil Service, Labor, and

Social Laws' Office of Work for dismissals and the Office of Social Protection for mistreatment. There were many EPZs that in practice were firms operating under special import and export rules. Such firms were required to follow all pertinent labor laws and regulations, including minimum wage laws; however, the Government allegedly did not enforce its labor laws adequately in the EPZs due to inadequate resources. The EPZs generally used worker representation councils whose members were elected by the employees but were not necessarily union representatives. These representatives frequently were perceived to be subject to pressure from management and to lack autonomy.

C. PROHIBITION OF FORCED OR BONDED LABOR

The Labor Code prohibits forced or bonded labor, including by children; however, at times the Government did not respect this prohibition. For example, in the past there were reports that prisoners were used in private industry or for domestic functions; however, there were no reports that officials of the Ravalomanana Government engaged in these practices.

Some press reports indicated workers at times were compelled under threat of loss of employment to work beyond the legal limits (see Section 6.e.).

D. STATUS OF CHILD LABOR PRACTICES AND MINIMUM AGE FOR EMPLOYMENT

The Labor Code defines a child as any person under the age of 18 years. The legal minimum age for employment was 15 years, and work by persons under the age of 18 statutorily was prohibited at sites where there was an apparent and imminent danger to health, safety, or morals. Individuals under 18 years of age also were forbidden from performing night work. The Government enforced child labor laws in the formal economic sector by means of inspectors from the Ministry of Civil Services. Enforcement in the much larger informal sector remained a serious problem. Child labor was a problem. Nearly 20 percent of urban children and 60 percent of rural children between the ages of 7 and 14 were employed. Children in rural areas generally dropped out of school to help on family farms and urban children often worked as domestic laborers and servants. In the agricultural sector, work for children on the family subsistence farm may begin at an even younger age. In cities many children worked in occupations such as transport of goods by rickshaw and petty trading. Effective implementation of the provisions of ILO Convention 182 on the worst forms of child labor was hampered by a lack of financial resources and the political crisis.

E. ACCEPTABLE CONDITIONS OF WORK

The Labor Code and its implementing legislation prescribe working conditions and wages, which were enforced by the Ministry of Civil Service, Labor, and Social Laws. The law makes separate provisions for agricultural and nonagricultural work.

The Government set the minimum wage at approximately $25 (180,000 FMG) per month for the nonagricultural private sector. The national minimum wage did not provide a decent standard of living for a worker and family, particularly in urban areas. Although most employees know what the legal minimum wages were, in practice those rates were not always paid. High unemployment and widespread poverty led workers to accept lower wages.

The standard workweek was 40 hours in nonagricultural and service industries and 42½ hours in the agricultural sector. Although labor legislation limits workers to 20 hours of overtime per week, employees often were required to stay on until production targets were met. In some cases, this overtime was unrecorded and unpaid.

The Labor Code sets rules and standards for workers safety and worksite conditions. Women and minors may not work in positions that might endanger their health, safety, or morals. Inspectors from the Ministry of Civil Service, Labor, and Social Laws monitored labor conditions; however, they usually were able to cover only the capital region effectively. In the past, the cost of protective clothing and other safety devices often led firms to forego their use. If violators do not remedy cited violations within the time allowed, they may be sanctioned legally or assessed administrative penalties. CNAPS, the country's equivalent of the Social Security Administration, published reports on workplace conditions, occupational health hazards, and workplace accident trends. Workers did not have an explicit right to leave a dangerous workplace without jeopardizing their employment. The Labor Code applies to all workers; however, foreign workers must have a valid visa to be protected.

F. TRAFFICKING IN PERSONS

The law prohibits trafficking in persons; however, in the past, there were reports of trafficking in women and girls for prostitution between Madagascar and the neighboring islands of Mauritius and Reunion. The number of persons involved was difficult to determine. There were no reports of arrests for trafficking. While the Government has expressed concern about trafficking, it lacked the resources to address it effectively.

STUDYING POLITICAL SYSTEM STHTOUGH THE CONSTITUTION

MADAGASCAR - CONSTITUTION

{ Adopted: 19 Aug 1992 / Status: 19 Aug 1992 }

Preamble

The sovereign Malagasy people, profoundly attached to their cultural and spiritual values, especially to the basis of national unity; affirming their belief in God the Creator; faithful to their international commitments; adopting the International Charter of Human Rights, the African Charter of Human Rights, the Convention on Children's Rights, and considering these to be an integral part of their law; convinced that the growth of their personality and identity is basic to their harmonious development, the essential conditions of which are recognized to be:
- respect for and protection of fundamental liberties, individual and collective;
- separation and balance of powers to be exercised through democratic procedures;
- openness in the conduct of public affairs as a guarantee of citizen participation in the exercise of power and efficient effective supervision;
- the establishment of a State in which the people and the public officials are subject to the same legal norms under the supervision of an independent judiciary;
- protection of national unity through the implementation of a policy of balanced development in all areas;
- dedication to peace and fraternity;
- struggle against injustice, inequality, and discrimination in all its forms; and
- the application of effective decentralization;
declares:

TITLE I GENERAL PRINCIPLES

Article 1 [People, State, Democracy]

(1) The Malagasy people shall constitute a Nation organized as a sovereign, secular State.

(2) This State shall be a Republic, unique and indivisible, and shall be named "Republic of Madagascar."

(3) Democracy shall be the basis of the Republic. Its sovereignty shall be exercised within the territorial limits recognized by international law.

Article 2 [Territorial Entities, Autonomie]

(1) The Republic of Madagascar shall be organized in decentralized territorial entities whose autonomy shall guaranteed by the Constitution.

(2) These territorial entities shall cooperate with the State developing the national community.

Article 3 [National Territory]
The national territory shall be inalienable.

Article 4 [Motto, Emblem, Anthem, Seals, Coat of Arms, Language]
(1) The Republic of Madagascar shall have for its Motto: *"Homeland - Revolution - Liberty"*.
(2) Its national emblem shall be a tri-colored flag, white, red, and green, consisting of three rectangular bands of equal dimensions. Starting on the edge closest to the flagpole, the first band shall be vertical and white; the other two shall be horizontal, the upper one red and the lower green.
(3) The national anthem shall be: *"Oh, Dear Homeland"*.
(4) The State Seals and Coat of Arms shall be defined by law.
(5) Malagasy shall be the national language.

Article 5 [Capital]
The Capital of the Republic shall be Antananarivo.

Article 6 [Sovereignty, Representation, Electoral Rights]
(1) Sovereignty shall belong to the people, who shall exercise it through their representatives elected by direct or indirect universal suffrage or through a referendum. No faction or individual may usurp the exercise of sovereignty.
(2) All citizens, of both sexes, who possess civil and political rights shall be electors under conditions determined by law.
(3) Electoral status may be removed only by judicial decision.

Article 7 [Rule of Law]
Law shall be the expression of popular will. The law shall be the same for all in protection, in obligation, or in punishment.

Article 8 [Citizen Equality, No Discrimination]
(1) Citizens shall be equal under the law, enjoying the same fundamental liberties protected by law.
(2) The State shall prohibit all discrimination based on sex, education, wealth, origin, race, religion, or opinion.

TITLE II LIBERTIES, RIGHTS, DUTIES

Section I Civil and Political Rights and Duties

Article 9 [Rule of Law]
The exercise and protection of individual rights and fundamental liberties shall be organized by law.

Article 10 [Expression, Association, Assembly, Move, Religion]
Freedom of opinion and expression, communication, press, association, assembly,

travel, conscience, and religion shall be guaranteed to all and may be limited only in respect of the rights and liberties of others and of the necessity to safeguard public order.

Article 11 [Information]
(1) Information in all forms shall be subject to no prior restraint.
(2) Conditions of freedom of information and its responsibility shall be determined by law and by codes of professional ethics.

Article 12 [Leave, Travel, Settle]
(1) Everyone shall have the right to leave the territory and to return under conditions established by law.
(2) Everyone shall have the right to travel and to settle freely within the territory of the Republic while respecting the rights of others and the limits of the law.

Article 13 [Liberty, Home, Communication, *Nulla Poena Sine Lege*, Legal Recourse, Counsel]
(1) Everyone shall be assured of protection of his person, his residence, and his correspondence.
(2) No search may take place except under law on the written order of the competent judicial authority, except in cases of *flagrante delicto*.
(3) No one may be prosecuted, arrested, or detained except in cases determined by law, according to the forms prescribed by law.
(4) No one may be punished except by virtue of a law promulgated and published prior to the commission of the act to be punished.
(5) No one may be punished twice for the same deed.
(6) The law shall assure everyone access to justice; lack of resources will not be no obstacle.
(7) The State shall guarantee full, inviolable rights of defense in all jurisdictions and all stages of procedure, including the preliminary investigation, Judicial police, and court.

Article 14 [Association, Political Parties]
(1) Citizens may organize freely without prior authorization in associations and political parties; however, associations or political parties which preach totalitarianism or segregation of an ethnic, tribal, or religious nature are forbidden.
(2) The law shall establish conditions for the creation and functioning of associations and political parties.

Article 15 [Eligibility, Electoral Rights]
Every citizen shall have the right to be a candidate in the elections provided for in this Constitution, without discrimination based on membership in a political party, under conditions established by law.

Article 16 [Duty to Respect the Laws]
Within the limits of the democratic liberties recognized by this Constitution, everyone shall have the duty to respect the Constitution, institutions, laws, and regulations of the Republic.

For additional analytical, business and investment opportunities information, please contact Global Investment & Business Center, USA at (202) 546-2103. Fax: (202) 546-3275. E-mail: rusric@erols.com

---

Section II Economic, Social and Cultural Rights and Duties

Article 17 [Personal Integrity, Dignity, Development]
The State shall organize the exercise of rights which guarantee to the individual personal integrity and dignity, and complete physical, intellectual, and moral development.

Article 18 [National Service]
National service shall be an honorable duty. It shall not affect employment or political rights.

Article 19 [Health, No Abortion]
The State shall recognize every individual's right protection of his health, starting from conception.

Article 20 [Family, Inheritance]
The family, the natural basis of society, shall be protected by the State. Everyone shall have the right to form a family and to bequeath personal goods through inheritance.

Article 21 [Protection of Family, Mother, Child]
The State shall protect the well-being of the family, the mother and child, by legislation and by appropriate social institutions.

Article 22 [Promotion of Development]
The State shall attempt, as its means permit, to assure the intellectual development of every individual, limited only by each person's ability.

Article 23 [Education, Training, Parents' Responsibility]
(1) Every child shall have the right to education and training, with the responsibility of the parents, and respecting their freedom of choice.
(2) Every adolecscent shall be entitled to professional training.

Article 24 [Public Education]
The State shall organize public education, free and accessible to all. Primary education shall be compulsory for all.

Article 25 [Private Education]
(1) The State shall recognize the right to private education and shall guarantee freedom of education subject to conditions of health, morality, and capacity established by the law.
(2) Private educational establishments shall have the benefit of the same fiscal regime, with conditions established by law.

Article 26 [Culture, Science]
(1) Everyone shall have the right to participate in the cultural life of the community, in scientific progress, and the resulting benefits.
(2) The State shall assure the promotion and protection of the natural cultural heritage, as well as artistic and literary production.

For additional analytical, business and investment opportunities information,
please contact Global Investment & Business Center, USA
at (202) 546-2103. Fax: (202) 546-3275. E-mail: rusric@erols.com

Article 27 [Work, Public Employment]
(1) Work and professional training shall be a right and a duty for every citizen.
(2) Access to public institutions shall be open to every citizen with no conditions other than those of ability and aptitude.

Article 28 [Workers' Equality]
No one may suffer injury in his employment because of sex, age, religion, opinion, origin, or political conviction.

Article 29 [Remuneration]
Every citizen shall have the right, based on the quality and product of his work, to fair remuneration to assure him and his family a living appropriate to human dignity.

Article 30 [Handicapped]
Through social agencies, the State shall attempt to provide for the needs of every citizen who, by reason of age or physical or mental handicap, is unable to work.

Article 31 [Union]
(1) The State shall recognize the right of every worker to defend his interests through union activity and especially freedom to form a union.
(2) However, membership in a union shall be voluntary.

Article 32 [Workers' Participation]
Every worker shall have the right to participate, through his representatives, in determining the rules and conditions of employment.

Article 33 [Strike]
The right to strike shall be recognized and exercised under conditions established by law.

Article 34 [Private Property]
The State shall guarantee the right to private property. No one can be deprived of property except for public use and with the condition of fair, prior compensation.

Article 35 [Minority Rights]
(1) The Fokonolona may take appropriate measures to prevent destruction of their environment, loss of their land, seizure of herds of cattle, or loss of their ceremonial heritage, unless these measures jeopardize the common interest or public order.
(2) The coverage and terms of these provisions shall be determined by law.

Article 36 [Taxation]
Every citizen's share in public expenditures must be progressive and calculated on his ability to pay.

Article 37 [Enterprise]
The State shall guarantee free enterprise within the limits of respect for the common good, public order, and the environment.

For additional analytical, business and investment opportunities information,
please contact Global Investment & Business Center, USA
at (202) 546-2103. Fax: (202) 546-3275. E-mail: rusric@erols.com

Article 38 [Capital, Investment]
The State shall guarantee the security of capital and investment.

Article 39 [Environment]
Everyone shall have the duty to respect the environment; the State shall assure its protection.

Article 40 [State Neutrality, Ombudsmen]
(1) The State shall guarantee the political neutrality of the administration, the Armed Forces, justice, the police, education, and training.
(2) The State shall be committed to instituting an independent agency responsible for the promotion and protection of human rights.

TITLE III STRUCTURE OF THE STATE

Article 41 [Powers]
The structure of the State shall include:
- the executive power, consisting of the President of the Republic and the Government;
- the legislative power, formed by the National Assembly and the Senate;
- the judicial power, exercised by the Administrative and Financial Constitutional Court, the Supreme Court, Courts of Appeal, Tribunals, and the High Court of Justice.

Article 42 [Remuneration]
The law shall determine the amount, the conditions, an the method of payment of the salaries to individuals elected to fulfill the duties or carry out the functions provided for in this Constitution.

Article 43 [No Corruption]
(1) No one called to carry out an office under this Constitution may accept presents or remuneration, except for his official salary, from any person or corporation domestic or foreign, under penalty of dismissal.
(2) The application of these provisions shall be determined by law.

TITLE IV EXECUTIVE

Section I President of the Republic

Article 44 [Presidential Office]
The President of the Republic shall be the Head of State. As "Ray aman-dreny" he shall assure respect for the Constitution. He is responsible for the regular functioning of public powers; he shall be responsible for national independence and territorial integrity and

shall assure protection of, and respect for, national sovereignty within national territory and abroad; he shall be the symbol of national unity.

Article 45 [Election, Term, Re-election]
The President of the Repllblic shall be elected by universal direct suffrage for a five-year term. He may be re-elected for one additional term.

Article 46 [Eligibility, Resignation, Candidacy]
(1) All candidates for the office of President of the Republic must possess all civil and political rights and must be at least 40 years old at the time the candidacy is declared.
(2) To become a candidate, the President then in office must resign one day before the beginning of the electoral campaign.
(3) Other conditions for candidacy shall he established by law.

Article 47 [Second Ballot]
(1) The election for President of the Republic shall take place, upon convocation of the Government, no less than thirty days and no more than sixty days before the expiration of the term of the President of the Republic then in office.
(2) The election shall be by a majority of the votes on the first ballot. If this is not obtained, the President of the Republic shall be elected on the second ballot by plurality of one of the two candidates having received the greatest number of votes on the first ballot.

Article 48 [Oath]
Before assuming office, the President of the Republic shall swear the following oath before the Nation and in the presence of the National Assembly, the Senate, and the Constitutional Court, specially convened:
"###"

Article 49 [Incompatibilities]
The office of President of the Republic shall be incompatible with any other elective public office, any other professional activity, and any activity within a political party or group of political parties.

Article 50 [Permanent Incapacity]
The permanent incapacity of the President of the Republic may be declared by the Constitutional Court following a resolution adopted by not less than two-thirds of the deputies in the National Assembly; for violation of the Constitution; and for any other cause duly stated and proved resulting in his permanent incapacity to exercise his duties.

Article 51 [Temporary Incapacity]
(1) The temporary incapacity of the President of the Republic may be declared by the Constitutional Court following a resolution adopted by at least a two-thirds majority of the deputies in the National Assembly.
(2) Removal of temporary incapacity shall be decided by the Constitutional Court. Temporary incapacity may not exceed a period of three months, after which permanent incapacity must be declared by the Constitutional Court.

Article 52 [Replacement]
(1) In case of vacancy, permanent incapacity or temporary incapacity, the duties of the President of the Republic shall be temporarily exercised by the President of the Senate.
(2) In case of vacancy or perrnanent incapacity, the election of the new President shall take place within the period provided for in Article 47.

Article 53 [Appointment of Prime Minister and Ministers]
(1) The President of the Republic shall appoint the Prime Minister under the conditions established in Article 90.
(2) Following the appointment of the Prime Minister, he shall appoint the other members of the Government, and may terminate their duties.

Article 54 [President and Government]
(1) The President shall preside over the Council of Ministers.
(2) He shall sign ordinances of the Council of Ministers in the cases and conditions provided for by this Constitution
(3) He shall sign the decrees debated in the Council of Ministers.

Article 55 [Head of Military]
(1) The President shall be the Supreme Head of the Armed Forces; he shall preside over the Superior Council of National Defense whose organization and duties shall be established by law. He shall declare defense policy in the Superior Council of National Defense, within general State policy.
(2) He shall decide upon the commitment of armed forces and resources in foreign interventions, after consulting the Superior Council of National Defense, the Council of Ministers, and the Parliament.
(3) He shall appoint military officials to represent the Malagasy State in international agencies.

Article 56 [Competences]
(1) The President of the Republic shall accredit and recall ambassadors and envoys extraordinary of the Republic of Madagascar to foreign States and international organizations.
(2) He shall receive credentials and requests for recall from States and international organizations recognized by the Republic of Madagascar.
(3) He shall negotiate and ratify treaties. He shall be informed of all negotiations leading to the conclusion of an international agreement which is not submitted for ratification.
(4) He shall make appointments through the Council of Ministers to high offices of the State; he may delegate this power to the Prime Minister.
(5) He may refer matters directly, if needed, to administrative agencies.
(6) He shall have the right of pardon.
(7) He shall confer the decorations of the Republic of Madagascar.

Article 57 [Promulgation of Laws, Request for Reconsideration]
(1) The President of the Republic shall promulgate laws within two weeks following transmittal to him of laws adopted by the National Assembly. This period may be reduced to five days in an emergency declared by the National Assembly.
(2) He may, before the expiration of this period, ask the National Assembly to reconsider

For additional analytical, business and investment opportunities information, please contact Global Investment & Business Center, USA at (202) 546-2103. Fax: (202) 546-3275. E-mail: rusric@erols.com

the law or certain articles of the law.

(3) In the absence of promulgation within the period provided, the President of the Senate may substitute for the President of the Republic.

Article 58 [Dissolution of Parliament]

The President of the Republic may dissolve the National Assembly at the request of the Council of Ministers under the terms of Article 95.

Article 59 [State of Emergency, Martial Law]

(1) The President of the Republic, meeting with the Council of Ministers, with the agreement of the Presidents of the National Assembly, the Senate, and the Constitutional Court, may proclaim a state of emergency or martial law for the defense of the Republic, for public order, or for State security, as circumstances require.

(2) The proclamation of a state of emergency shall confer special powers on the President of the Republic; their extent and duration shall be specified by law.

Article 60 [Countersignature]

Acts of the President of the Republic shall be countersigned by the Prime Minister and the Ministers responsible for executing them.

Section II Government

Article 61 [Tasks, Head of Government, Nomination]

(1) The Government shall consist of the Prime Minister and other Ministers.

(2) The Government shall determine and carry out State policy.

(3) The Government shall have at its disposal the administration and the armed force.

(4) The Government shall be responsible to the National Assembly under conditions provided for in Title V.

(5) The Prime Minister shall be the Head of the Government. He shall he appointed by the President of the Republic under conditions established by Article 90.

(6) Other members of the Government shall be appointed by the President of the Republic following nomination by the Prime Minister.

Article 62 [Ministerial Incompatibilities]

The duties of a member of the Government shall be incompatible with the exercise of any other elective public office, professional representation, public employment, or any other paid professional activity.

Article 63 [Prime Minister's Competences]

(1) The Prime Minister shall direct the activity of the Government and shall be responsible for coordinating the activities of the Ministries.

(2) He may initiate laws.

(3) He shall assure the execution of laws.

(4) He shall assure the execution of judicial decisions.

(5) He shall have at his disposal administrative agencies and shall assure the proper functioning of public services and the proper management of public finance.

(6) He shall assure puhlic security and maintain order, while respecting fundamental liberties and human rights: for this purpose, he shall have at his disposal all police,

For additional analytical, business and investment opportunities information, please contact Global Investment & Business Center, USA at (202) 546-2103. Fax: (202) 546-3275. E-mail: rusric@erols.com

security, and defense agencies.

(7) He shall preside over the Interministry Committee of Defense, which is responsible for establishing defense policy; he shall have at his disposal the Secretariat of defense. The organization and duties of these agencies shall be determined by law.

(8) He shall be the Head of the Administration; he shall appoint civil and military officials as well as other State officials.

(9) He shall preside over the Council of Government.

(10) He shall assure development

(11) He may delegate certain powers to Government members with the option to subdelegate.

Article 64 [Council of Government Competences]
In the Council of Government, the Prime Minister may:
- determine State policy and execute it;
- propose bills to be submitted to Parliament;
- exercise regulatory power;
- create plans for economic and social development as well as land development;
- negotiate and sign international agreements which are not submitted to ratification; and
- exercise other duties for which Government consultation is required under this Constitution and individual laws.

Article 65 [Countersignature]
Actions of the Prime Minister shall be countersigned, when approprite, by the Ministers responsible for executing them.

TITLE V LEGISLATURE

Section I National Assembly

Article 66 [Title, Election, Term]
(1) The members of the National Assembly shall have the title of Deputies of Madagascar.

(2) They shall be elected by direct universal suffrage for four-year terms.

Article 67 [Parliamentary Incompatibilities, No Directed Votes]
(1) The office of deputy shall be incompatible with the exercise of any other public employment, except education, and with any other elective public office.

(2) A deputy who is appointed member of the Government shall automatically resign the office of deputy.

(3) All directed votes shall be null and void.

Article 68 [Law on Election]
The law shall establish the number of members of the National Assembly, the distribution of seats throughout the national territory, as well as electoral districts and voting procedures. The law shall also establish conditions of eligibility, regulation of

ineligibility and dismissal, as well as conditions for the election of persons replacing deputies in case of vacancy, until the next Assembly election.

Article 69 [Indemnity, Immunity, Control]
(1) No deputy may be prosecuted, investigated, arrested, detained, or judged for opinions and votes cast by him in the exercise of his duties.
(2) For the duration of legislative sessions, no deputy may be prosecuted or arrested in a criminal or correctional matter, without the authorization of the bureau of the Assembly, except in case of *flagrante delicto*.
(3) Outside of legislative sessions, no deputy may be arrested without the authorization of the bureau of the Assembly, except in case of *flagrante delicto*, authorized prosecution, or final conviction.
(4) Anyone may bring to the attention of the National Assembly the acts or omissions of a deputy. The permanent bureau must furnish a prompt response.

Article 70 [President and Bureau of the Assembly]
The President of the National Assembly and members of the bureau shall he elected at the beginning of the first session for the duration of the legislature. However, they may be replaced when necessary by a vote of two-thirds of the deputies.

Article 71 [Sessions]
The National Assembly shall meet officially in two ordinary sessions per year. The length of each session may not be less than sixty days nor more than ninety days. The first session shall begin on the first Tuesday in May, and the second, devoted principally to the adoption of the budget, on the last Tuesday in September.

Article 72 [Extraordinary Sessions]
(1) The National Assembly shall meet in extraordinary session with an established agenda, upon the initiative of the President of the Republic and the order of the Council of Ministers, or called by the President of the Council of Ministers at the request of one-third of its members.
(2) The duration of the session may not exceed twelve days. However, closure may be declared as soon as the National Assembly has covered the agenda for which it has been convened.
Article 73 [Publicity]
(1) Sessions of the National Assembly shall be public. A record shall be kept and publicized under conditions provided for by law.
(2) The National Assembly may meet in closed session at the request of the Government or of one-fourth of its members.

Article 74 [First Session]
The new National Assembly shall meet officially in a special session on the second Tuesday following the proclamation of election results, to constitute its bureau and to choose the new Prime Minister. The session shall end after the installation or the naming of the new Prime Minister.

Article 75 [Procedural Rules]
The procedural rules of the National Assembly shall be established as general principles by law, and in specific terms by internal regulation.

Section II Senate

Article 76 [Title, Term]
Members of the Senate shall have the title of Senator of Madagascar. Their term of office shall be four years.

Article 77 [Election, Appointment, Nomination, Incompatibility]
(1) Two-thirds of the Senate shall consist of an equal number of members elected in each electoral district by elected representatives of the territorial entities, and one-third shall consist of members representing economic, social, cultural, and religious groups appointed by the President of the Republic upon nomination by legally constituted organizations and groups.
(2) The office of Senator shall be incompatible with that of deputy.

Article 78 [Re-election]
One-half of the Senate, in both categories, shall be eligible for re-election every two years. Its procedural rules, compensation, and means of designating its members shall be established by law.

Article 79 [Competences]
The Senate shall examine public and private bills; it must be consulted by the Government on economic, social, and territorial questions.

Article 80 [Sessions]
(1) The Senate shall meet during sessions of the National Assembly.
(2) It may also meet in special session at the request of the Government. In that case, its agenda shall be limited by the Government.
(3) When the National Assembly is not in session, the Senate may only discuss questions upon which the Government has consulted it, to the exclusion of legislative bills.

Article 81 [Applicable Provisions]
The provisions of Articles 68, 69, 70, 71, 73, and 75 shall be applicable to the Senate.

Section III Legislative Function, Relations With Government

Article 82 [Legislation]
(1) Laws shall be voted by Parliament under conditions established by this section. Parliament shall consist of the National Assembly and the Senate.
(2) In addition to matters referred to the Parliament by other articles of the Constitution:
I) The law shall establish rules concerning:
- civil rights and fundamental guarantees granted to individuals and groups for the exercise of rights and liberties;
- nationality and citizenship;

- obligations imposed by national defense upon citizens and their property;
- organization of the family, the State, and the status of persons, the regulation of marriage, inheritance and gifts, and the drafting and codification of customs regarding citizenship;
- the creation of new jurisdictions, the organization of administrative and financial agencies and the rules of procedure applicable to them, civil and commercial rules of procedure, the status of magistrates, and the guarantees of their independence;
- the determination of crimes and misdemeanors, as well as the applicable penalties, criminal procedure, and amnesty;
- judicial regulation of property and the conditions under which property may be subject to expropriation or requisition for public use or transfer of property to the State;
- the creation of categories of public establishments;
- election procedures in the territorial entities, the jurisdiction and resources of these entities, and their relation to the State;
- property transfers from the public sector to the private sector; and
- regulation of currency.

II) The law shall establish the fundamental principles of the following:
- the organization of national defense and the use of the Armed Forces or police forces by civil authorities, the status of the armed forces, and their neutrality;
- the status of civil servants and public agents;
- the status of teachers and researchers in higher education;
- the status of the national police;
- the status of correctional officers;
- the judicial regulation of civil and commercial obligations;
- the juridical framework of relations between employers and employees, trade union rights, and the right to strike;
- professional training;
- the organization of professions; and
- protection of the environment.

III) The law shall determine the basis, rate, and methods of collection for assessments of all types.

The budget shall establish the amount and nature of State resources and obligations for budgetary balance; this shall be discussed and voted upon under the conditions provided for in Article 88.

IV) The law shall determine the policies and goals of State action in economic, social and environmental areas.

V) War may only be declared by Parliament.

VI) A state of national emergency may be declared by the President of the Republic in accordance with Article 59; extension beyond two weeks may only be authorized by Parliament.

VII) The law shall establish limitations to individual and public liberties during emergencies.

VIII) Ratification or approval of alliances or commercial treaties, treaties or agreements regarding international organization which commit State finances, which deal with the status of persons, peace treaties, treaties which involve the ceding exchange or acquisition of territory must be authorized by law.

Prior to any ratification, treaties shall be submitted by the President of the Republic to the Constitutional Court. In case of non-conformity with the Constitution, ratification may take place only after Constitutional revision.

Article 83 [Regulations]

(1) Matters not within the jurisdiction of the law shall be regulatory matters. Regulations may be modified by decree with the consent of the Constitutional Court.

(2) Regulations which take effect after the adoption of this Constitution may be modified by decree only after the Constitutional Court declares that they are regulatory in nature by virtue of the preceding paragraph.

Article 84 [Initiative, Statement of Government, Acceptability]

(1) The power to introduce legislation shall be vested concurrently in the President of the Republic and the deputies.

(2) Government bills and amendments formulated by deputies shall be made known to the Government, which shall respond within a period of thirty days.

(3) At the expiration of this period, Parliament shall proceed to examine the bills or amendments for adoption.

(4) Bills or amendments shall not be acceptable if their adoption would entail reduction in public assets or the increasing of State debts except in regard to appropriation bills.

(5) In the course of the legislative procedure, if a bill or amendment does not appear to be a legal matter, the Government shall declare it unacceptable. In case of disagreement behveen the Government and the National Assembly or the Senate, the Constitutional Court, at the request of either assembly, shall rule within one week.

Article 85 [Priority of Governmental Bills]

The agenda of the assemblies shall give priority, in the order that the Government has established, to the discussion of bills and amendments presented by the Prime Minister.

Article 86 [Examination, Disagreement, Joint Commission]

(1) Each Government or private bill shall be examined first by the Assembly to which it has been presented and then shall be sent to the other Assembly.

(2) Discussion shall take place successively in each Assembly until a single text is adopted.

(3) When, following a disagreement between the two Assemblies, a Government or private bill has not been adopted after two readings in each Assembly, or if, after one reading by each of the Assemblies, the Government has declared an emergency, the Prime Minister has the option to create a joint commission responsible for creating a text on the provisions under discussion. The text prepared by the joint commission may be submitted by the Government for the approval of the two Assemblies. No amendment will be acceptable without the agreement of the Government.

(4) If the commission does not succeed in adopting a joint text, or if the text is not adopted under conditions provided for in the preceding article, the Government may ask the National Assembly for a final ruling.

Article 87 [Required Vote]

The Government, responsible under the conditions provided for in Article 91, may require that each of the Assemblies vote on all or part of the provisions under discussion:

- in extraordinary session, provided these texts have been presented within forty-eight hours of the opening of the session;
- in the last eight days of each of the ordinary sessions.

Article 88 [Appropriations Bill]

(1) Parliament shall examine the appropriations bill during its second ordinary session.

(2) Under the authority of the Prime Minister, as Head of the Government, the Minister responsible for the budget shall prepare the appropriations bill, which shall be enacted in the Council of Government. Parliament shall have a period of at least sixty days to examine it.

(3) The National Assembly shall have a period of thirty days from the presentation of the bill for the first reading. In the absence of a decision within this period, the bill shall be considered adopted and sent to the Senate.

(4) Under the same conditions, the Senate shall have a period of two weeks for the first reading and each Assembly shall have five days for each of the following readings.

(5) In the absence of a decision by an Assembly in a given period, the bill before it shall be considered adopted.

(6) If the Parliament has not adopted the appropriations bill before the end of the second session, the provisions of the bill may be put into effect by ordinance, including one or more of the amendments adopted by the two Assemblies.

(7) Any amendment to the appropriations bill which entails an increase in spending or a decrease in public resources must be accompanied by a bill to increase revenue or an equivalent savings.

(8) Conditions for the adoption of an appropriations bill shall be provided by law.

(9) If the appropriations bill for a fiscal year has not been presented in time to be promulgated before the beginning of that fiscal year, the Government shall ask Parliament for authorization to collect taxes and create credits by decree for services which have been voted.

Article 89 [Presidential Messages]

The President of the Republic shall communicate with the Parliament by messages which shall not give rise to debate.

Article 90 [Designation of Prime Minister, General Program]

(1) At the beginning of each legislature, or in case of resignation of the Government or vacancy in the office of Prime Minister for any other reason, the National Assembly, by a majority of its memhers, shall designate a Prime Minister from among its members or elsewhere within a period of seven days from the opening of the special session or from the date of the vacancy.

(2) Within two weeks of his election, the Prime Minister shall present his general program of action to the National Assembly.

(3) Election shall be by secret ballot by a majority of the members of the National Assembly. This vote is personal and shall not be delegated. The President shall appoint the Prime Minister elected by the National Assembly. If the appointment does not take place within ten days, the election by the National Assembly shall take effect immediately.

(4) In the event of rejection, the designated Prime Minister shall have a maximum of seven days to present a new program which shall be adopted under the preceding conditions.

(5) In the event of another rejection, or in case the National Assembly has not elected a Prime Minister for whatever reason within thirty days from the opening of the special session or the vacancy in the office of Prime Minister, the President of the Republic shall

appoint a new Prime Minister. In this case, no motion of censure may be voted upon before the presentation of the annual report provided for in Article 92.

Article 91 [General Program of Action, Vote of Confidence]
(1) The general program of action, once adopted, may not be reopened by the National Assembly.
(2) However, in the course of implementation, if the Government deems necessary fundamental modifications of the program, the Prime Minister shall submit these modifications to the National Assembly.
(3) After deliberation by the Government, the Prime Minister may commit his Government by requesting a vote of confidence.
(4) This vote shall not take place earlier than forty-eight hours after presentation of the question of confidence. If two-thirds of the members of the National Assembly so vote, the Government shall present its resignation to the President of the Republic.
(5) A new Prime Minister shall be chosen by the National Assembly to form a new Government under the conditions provided for in Article 90.

Article 92 [Annual Report of Government]
In the first ordinary session, the Government shall present to the National Assembly an annual report on the implementation of its program.

Article 93 [Interpellations]
(1) The National Assembly shall be informed of governmental action by means of oral questions, written questions, summonses, and commissions of inquiry.
(2) During ordinary sessions, one meeting a month shall be reserved for questions put to the Government by members of Parliament and for the Government's responses.

Article 94 [Motion of Censure]
(1) The National Assembly may raise the issue of Governmental responsibility by a Motion of Censure.
(2) Such a motion is only admissible if it is signed by at least one-fifth of the members of the National Assembly. A vote shall not take place earlier than forty-eight hours after presentation of the motion.
(3) The motion shall be adopted if it is voted by a majority of the memhers of the National Assembly.
(4) If the motion is adopted, the Government shall present its resignation to the President of the Republic. The President shall proceed with the selection of a new Prime Minister under conditions provided for in Article 90.

Article 95 [Ministerial Crises, Dissolution of Parliament]
(1) Within a period of eighteen months, if two ministerial crises occur following a vote of no confidence or censure, the Council of Ministers may rule on the dissolution of the National Assembly.
(2) Dissolution shall be pronounced, in accordance with this decision, by the President of the Republic.

Article 96 [Delegation of Powers to President, Enabling Law]
(1) Parliament, by majority vote in each Assembly, may delegate its legislative power to

For additional analytical, business and investment opportunities information,
please contact Global Investment & Business Center, USA
at (202) 546-2103. Fax: (202) 546-3275. E-mail: rusric@erols.com

the President of the Republic, acting in the Council of Ministers, for a limited period and for a specific purpose
(2) Delegation of power shall authorize the President of the Republic to take, by ordinance in the Council of Ministers, general measures of law. They shall take effect upon publication but shall elapse if a ratification bill is not presented to the National Assembly before the date set by the enabling law.

TITLE VI JUDICIARY

Section I General Provisions

Article 97 [Courts]
In the Republic of Madagascar, justice shall be rendered in conformity with the Constitution and the law in the name of the Malagasy people, by the Administrative and Financial Constitutional Court, the Supreme Court, Courts of Appeal, Tribunals, and the High Court of Justice.

Article 98 [Independence]
The judicial power shall be independent of the executive and legislative powers. The Administrative and Financial Constitutional Court and the Supreme Court shall assure this independence.

Article 99 [Personal Independence]
(1) Magistrates, judges, and assessors shall be independent in all their judicial activities and shall be answerable only to the Constitution and the law.
(2) To this end, with the exception of cases provided for by law and disciplinary power, they may not be hindered in any way in the exercise of their duties; they may not be called to account for decisions they render or in which they participate.

Article 100 [Protection of Magistrates]
Bench magistrates shall not be transferable; they shall occupy the post appropriate to their rank; they may not be reassigned, without their consent, except in case of necessity duly declared by the Superior Council of the Bench.

Article 101 [Public Prosecutor's Magistrates]
Magistrates in the Public Prosecutor's office shall be organized by rank; however, in their conclusions or indictments, they shall act according to their own convictions and in conformity with the law. They shall supervise the judicial police, which shall be at their disposal.

Article 102 [Magistratorial Incompatibilities]
The duties of magistrate shall be incompatible with any activity within a political party, public office, or any other remunerated professional activity.

Article 103 [General Inspection of Justice]
(1) The office of General Inspection of Justice, consisting of representatives from Parliament, the Government, and the magistrates, shall be responsible for supervising the regulation of magistrates, as well as the actions of judicial personnel.
(2) This office shall be connected to the Supreme Court.
(3) The President of the Republic, the Parliament, the Government, heads of court, legally constituted associations, and any individual may refer matters to the office of General Inspection of Justice.
(4) Rules regarding the organization, functions, and duties of the office of General Inspection of Justice shall be established.

Article 104 [National Council of Justice]
(1) The National Council of Justice, a consultative body consisting of the First President of the Supreme Court (as President), the General Prosecutor of the Supreme Court, the heads of the Courts of Appeal, representatives of the executive and legislative power, the Administrative and Financial Constitutional Court, the Superior Council of Magistrates, and auxiliaries, may make recommendations to improve the general functioning of justice. To this end, they may propose to the Government legislation or regulatory measures dealing with the organization and duties of judges, magistrates, and auxiliaries.
(2) Rules regarding the organization and duties of the National Council of Justice shall be established by law.

Section II Administrative and Financial Constitutional Court

Article 105 [Constitution]
(1) The Administrative and Financial Constitutional Court is a State institution consisting of:
- the Constitutional Court;
- the Council of State; and
- the Audit Office.
(2) The President of the Constitutional Court shall be the First President of the Administrative and Financial Constitutional Court.

Article 106 [Competences of the Constitutional Court]
(1) The Constitutional Court shall be responsible for ruling on the constitutionality of treaties, laws, ordinances, and regulations, as well as jurisdictional conflicts among two or more State institutions and between State institutions and the decentralized territorial entities.
(2) It shall decide contested elections.

Article 107 [Constitution of the Constitutional Court]
(1) The Constitutional Court shall consist of nine members with a single six-year term.
(2) Three of the members shall be appointed by the President of the Republic acting in the Couocil of Ministers, two by the National Assembly, one by the Senate, and three by the Superior Council of Magistrates.
(3) The President of the Constitutional Court shall be elected by its members. This election shall be announced by the President of the Republic.

Article 108 [Constitutional Court Incompatibilities]

The duties of a member of the Constitutional Court shall be incompatible with those of member of the Government, or Parliament, or any elective public office, or any remunerated professional activity, as well as party or union membership.

Article 109 [Competences of the Constitutional Court]

(1) The Constitutional Court shall supervise referenda and the elections of the President of the Republic, Deputies, and Senators.

(2) It shall announce the results of said referenda and elections.

Article 110 [Regular Ruling on Constitutionality of Laws]

(1) Before promulgation, laws shall be submitted by the President of the Republic to the Constitutional Court for a ruling on their constitutionality.

(2) A provision ruled unconstitutional by the Constitutional Court shall not be promulgated. In this case, the President of the Republic may decide to promulgate all other provisions of the law, to submit the entire law for reconsideration by Parliament, or not to promulgate the law.

Article 111 [Regular Ruling on Constitutionality of Ordinances and Internal Regulations]

Ordinances, before their promulgation, and internal regulations of each Assembly, before taking effect, shall be submitted to the Constitutional Court for a ruling on their constitutionality.

Article 112 [Advisory Opinion on the Constitutionality of Decrees]

The Constitutional Court may be consulted by public authorities for an advisory opinion on the constitutionality of any decree.

Article 113 [Ruling Pending Court Judgment]

In any jurisdiction, if one party raises an objection of unconstitutionality, that jurisdiction shall declare a delay of one month to refer the matter to the Constitutional Court, which must rule within one month.

Article 114 [Council of State]

(1) The Council of State may annul actions of the administrative authorities and may rule on various administrative decisions and on contested claims in fiscal matters. It shall be the Court of Appeal for judgments rendered by various administrative bodies and administrative jurisdictions at the first level of appeal. It shall also make final rulings on decisions rendered by the highest jurisdictions at the highest level of appeal.

(2) It may be consulted by public authorities for an opinion on:

- legislative or regulatory bills; and

- interpretation of legislation or regulatory provisions.

(3) When requested by public authorities, it may study bills and the organization and functioning of public services.

Article 115 [Audit Office]

(1) The Audit Office shall:

- examine the accounts of public accountants;

- supervise the implementation of appropriations laws and the budgets of entities and public bodies; and
- supervise the accounts and management of public enterprises.
(2) It shall rule on appeals of judgments rendered by administrative bodies.
(3) It shall assist the Parliament and the Government in supervising the implementation of appropriations laws.

Article 116 [Organizational Law]
Rules regarding the organization, functioning, and duties of the Administrative and Financial Constitutional Court shall be established by law.

Section III Supreme Court

Article 117 [Responsibilities]
The Supreme Court shall be the State institution responsible for:
- assuring the regular functioning of the judiciary;
- administering rules applicable to magistrates and to actions of judicial personnel; and
- ruling on judicial appeals.

Article 118 [Constitution]
(1) The First President and the General Prosecutor shall be the heads of the Supreme Court. The First President shall be elected by the Superior Council of Prosecutors and the General Assembly of the Supreme Court. This election shall be declared by the President of the Republic. His term shall be for three years and he may be re-elected once.
(2) The General Prosecutor of the Supreme Court shall be appointed by the President of the Republic acting in the Council of Ministers, from a list nominated by the Superior Council of Prosecutors. His term shall be for three years and he may be re-elected once.

Article 119 [Organizational Law]
Rules regarding the organization, functioning, and duties of the Supreme Court shall be established by law.

Article 120 [Annual Report]
The Supreme Court shall address an annual report of its activities to the President of the Republic, the Prime Minister, and the Presidents of the National Assembly, the Senate, and the Constitutional Court. This report shall be made public.

Section IV High Court of Justice

Article 121 [Responsibilities]
(1) The President of the Republic, the presidents of all the State institutions, members of the Government and of the Administrative and Financial Constitutional Court and Supreme Court shall be legally responsible for acts committed in the exercise of their duties which were crimes or misdemeanors at the time that they were committed.
(2) They may be judged by the High Court of Justice.
(3) They may be indicted by the National Assembly by secret ballot of the majority of its members.

Article 122 [Full Jurisdiction]
The High Court of Justice shall have full jurisdiction.

Article 123 [Constitution]
(1) The High Court of Justice shall consist of nine members, namely:
- the First President of the Supreme Court (as President);
- three Presidents of the Chambers of the Supreme Court;
- the First President of the Court of Appeals designated by the First President of the Supreme Court;
- two Deputies and two alternates elected by the National Assembly; and
- two Senators and two alternates elected by the Senate.
(2) Five alternate prosecutors shall be designated by the General Assembly of the Supreme Court or the First Presidents or President of Chambers of Courts of Appeal.
(3) The Public Prosecutor's Office shall be represented by General Prosecutors of the Supreme Court assisted by one or several other prosecutors.
(4) The Head Clerk of the Supreme Court shall be Clerk of the High Court; in case of disability of the Head Clerk, he shall be replaced by the most senior Chamber Clerk.

Article 124 [Organizational Law]
The organization and procedure of the High Court of Justice shall be established by law.

TITLE VII TERRITORIAL ENTITIES

Article 125 [Tasks]
The decentralized territorial entities, endowed with legal identity and financial autonomy, shall constitute the institutional framework for citizen participation in the management of public affairs and shall guarantee the expression of their diversity and individuality.

Article 126 [Creation]
(1) The creation of territorial entities must meet criteria of geographical, economic. social, and cultural homogeneity.
(2) The name, number, and limits of territorial entities shall be determined by law.

Article 127 [Assemblies]
Territorial entities shall be freely administered by Assemblies which shall deliberate on matters devolving to their jurisdiction by this Constitution and by law. These deliberations shall take effect upon publication. However, they may not conflict with constitutional, legislative, or regulatory provisions.

Article 128 [Local Elections]
(1) Members of the Assemhlies shall be elected by direct universal suffrage for a four-year term.
(2) These Assemblies shall include, in part, representatives of legally constituted economic, social, and cultural bodies within the jurisdiction of the territorial entity. These representatives shall also be elected by direct universal suffrage.

For additional analytical, business and investment opportunities information,
please contact Global Investment & Business Center, USA
at (202) 546-2103. Fax: (202) 546-3275. E-mail: rusric@erols.com

(3) The methods of election to the Assemblies of territorial entities shall be established by law.

Article 129 [Executive Bureau]
(1) The implementation of decisions made in the Assemblies shall be assured by an executive bureau directed by an official elected by direct universal suffrage for a four-year term; he may be re-elected once. The executive bureau shall consist of the leaders of the public services created and financed by the territorial entity or put at its disposal by the State. These members shall be appointed by the elected leader.
(2) The executive bureau shall be answerable to the elected Assembly.

Article 130 [High Official, Control, Public Order]
(1) The State shall be represented in the territorial entities by a high official whose appointment shall be established by law. The State representative shall be responsible for assuring adherence to legislative and regulatory provisions. He shall refer to the appropriate judicial authority any deliberations, actions, or agreements deemed illegal.
(2) The State representative shall be responsible for public order and administration under conditions established by law. He shall be the representative of all Ministries and shall supervise State services in the territorial entities.

Article 131 [Shared Competences]
The State shall be committed to the establishment of the following:
- distribution of jurisdictions between the territorial entities and the State;
- distribution of revenue between the territorial entities and the State; and
- distribution of public services between the territorial entities and the State.

Article 132 [Local Tasks]
(1) The territorial entities shall assure, with the cooperation of the State, public safety, the administration and management of territorial, economic, social, sanitary, cultural, and scientific development, as well as protection of the environment and improvement in the standard of living.
(2) The distribution of jurisdictions, considering national and local interests, shall be determined by law.

Article 133 [Local Finances]
(1) The distribution of resources, based on jurisdictions granted to the territorial entities, shall be determined by law.
(2) The territorial entities shall establish and manage the budget, its functioning, and its investment, in harmony with national planning.

Article 134 [Local Resources]
The resources of territorial entities shall consist of:
- the proceeds of taxes voted by the Assemblies of the territorial entities and levied for their budgets; the law shall establish the nature and maximum rate of these taxes, taking into account expenses assumed by the territorial entities and national expenses;
- their share in the proceeds of taxes levied for the State budget. This *pro rata* share shall be determined by law according to a percentage which takes into account the expenses assumed individually and collectively by the territorial entities and the level of

their own resources, in order to assure fair and equal treatment of the territorial entities and a balanced economic and social development among all territorial entities. The utilization of its share shall be freely determined by each territorial collectivity;
- the proceeds of endowments granted by the State to the territorial entities, as a whole or in part, to meet expenses resulting from the transfer of jurisdictions, or to compensate territorial entities for expenses resulting from particular programs or projects mandated by the State and implemented by the territorial entities;
- the proceeds of loans contracted by the territorial entities in the national or foreign market, with the agreement of national monetary authorities, with or without guaranty by the State;
- the proceeds of foreign aid obtained through the national monetary authorities and the ministerial department responsible for foreign relations;
- the proceeds of gifts; and
- revenue from territorial land.

Article 135 [Local Funds, Public Treasury]
Funds of territorial entities whose use falls within their jurisdiction shall be deposited in the public treasury under conditions provided for by law.

Article 136 [New Local Entities]
Regional and local administrative districts and structures may be created by decree in the Council of Ministers.

Article 137 [Organizational Laws]
Rules regarding the organization, functioning, and duties of territorial entities shall be established by law.

TITLE VIII AMENDING THE CONSTITUTION

Article 138 [Initiative]
The initiative to amend the Constitution shall be vested either with the President of the Republic acting in the Council of Ministers or with the National Assembly upon the proposal of one-third of its members.

Article 139 [Majority]
The bill or proposal for amendment shall be adopted only by a three-fourths majority of the members of the National Assembly and the Senate.

Article 140 [Facultative Referendum]
The President of the Republic acting in the Council of Ministers may submit the amendment to a referendum.

Article 141 [Obligatory Referendum]
The Preamble and Titles I, II, III, and VII may be amended only by means of referendum.

Article 142 [Republic]
The republican form of the State shall not be subject to amendment.

TITLE IX TEMPORARY AND MISCELLANEOUS PROVISIONS

Article 143 [1991 Constitution]
Until the institutions provided for in this Constitution are established, those provided for by the Convention of 31 Oct 1991 shall continue in effect, with the exception of the provisions which follow.

Article 144 [First Presidential Elections]
(1) Presidential elections must take place not later than sixty days from the date of the official proclamation by the High Court of Justice of the results of the national referendum adopting this Constitution.
(2) The elected President shall immediately exercise the duties devolving on the President of the Republic by the terms of the Convention of 31 Oct 1991 and those provided for in this Constitution. Before taking office, he shall swear the oath provided for in Article 48 before the nation and the transitional High Constitutional Court.

Article 145 [First Legislative Elections, Transitional Offices]
(1) Legislative elections must take place not later than two months after the proclamation of the results of the Presidential elections.
(2) The High Authority of the State and the Council on Economic Recovery shall terminate their duties upon the election of the bureau of the National Assembly.
(3) Upon the appointment of the new Prime Minister, the transitional Prime Minister shall present to the President of the Republic the resignation of the Government; this Government shall continue to be responsible for current business until the installation of the new Government.
(4) The National Assembly shall exercise full legislative power until the installation of the Senate.

Article 146 [Transitional Courts]
Until the institutions of the Third Republic are installed, the present High Constitutional Court and Supreme Court shall continue to exercise their duties in conformity with the legislation in effect.

Article 147 [Old Laws]
With the exception of future modifications, legislation in effect in the Republic shall remain applicable in all provisions which do not conflict with those of this Constitution.

Article 148 [Transition to Local Entities]
(1) Legislative provisions regarding territorial entities provided for in this Constitution must be implemented not later than eighteen months from the date of its promulgation. A commission will be created for this purpose.
(2) Until the installation of the territorial entities provided for in this Constitution, the

For additional analytical, business and investment opportunities information,
please contact Global Investment & Business Center, USA
at (202) 546-2103. Fax: (202) 546-3275. E-mail: rusric@erols.com

Special Delegations and Local Security Committees will continue to exercise their present duties.

Article 149 [Date of Effect]
This law will take effect upon promulgation by the transitional Prime Minister and will be published in the Official Journal of the Republic. It will be executed as the Constitution of the Republic of Madagascar.

For additional analytical, business and investment opportunities information, please contact Global Investment & Business Center, USA at (202) 546-2103. Fax: (202) 546-3275. E-mail: rusric@erols.com

INTERNATIONAL ASSITANCE

USAID ASSISTANCE TO MADAGASCAR

OBJECTIVES

The goal of the U.S. Agency for International Development's (USAID) FY 1998-2003 program in Madagascar is to help its people to break out of poverty to become one of Africa's emerging market economies. The USAID program helps establish a legal and policy environment that encourages private initiative and investment, fosters greater respect for human rights and the rule of law, and increases decentralized responsibility for decision making. It also helps the Malagasy people to manage effectively one of the earth's most unique sources of biodiversity. U.S. assistance is slowing the spread of the AIDS virus while helping Malagasy families to become smaller and healthier. Following the passage of 3 cyclones in early 2000, USAID is assisting the 300,000 victims to restore their livelihoods.

PROGRAM ACCOMPLISHMENTS

Improved Environment for Private Initiative: (FY 2002: $2,090,000) USAID's support helped our partners improve the legal, policy and financial conditions for trade and investment: Reform of key laws to facilitate business entry and exit, production of a CD-ROM on major laws and regulations, development of local civil society organizations fighting corruption and promoting greater public participation in economic and legal issues, accountability, and the rule of law. A Transparency International affiliate in Madagascar is now formally registered and the Malagasy Arbitration and Mediation Center, which offers alternative dispute resolution services in the commercial arena, has been created. USAID helps to expand the access of the poor to sustainable micro-finance via our partnership with the Caisse d'Epargne de Madagascar. We help to improve Madagascar's trade and investment regime to promote the country's effective integration into the global economy. We support strengthened civil society participation in policy debate and decisions as well as poverty analysis.

Smaller Healthier Families: (FY 2002: $16,197,953) The imbalance between Madagascar's high population growth (2.8%) and modest economic growth (2.9% per year, 1991 to 2001) contributes to the country's persistent poverty. USAID's programs engage communities, support local leadership, promote partnership and integrate related health, environment and food security activities. USAID addresses the health needs of the Malagasy family through high quality, accessible family planning and child survival services, prevention and mitigation of HIV/AIDS and STDs, and activities that enhance food security and disaster preparedness. At USAID program sites, DPT3 coverage rates reached 94% in 2001, exclusively breastfed infants increased to 83% in target groups. The contraceptive prevalence rate reached 12% in 2000. In a country where 49% of the under five children are malnourished, the Food Aid program reaches over 321,000 of these vulnerable citizens.

Biologically-Diverse Ecosystems Conserved in Priority Conservation Zones: (FY 2002: $10,539,121) Madagascar is a global biodiversity "hot spot" due to the high levels of species diversity and exceptional endemism that are coupled with high rates of destruction. The scale and intensity of deforestation, soil erosion and declines in soil productivity are enormous. USAID's support reinforces Madagascar's commitment to conserve its unique biological heritage by finding ways to balance the resource needs of an expanding population without compromising its unique biodiversity. USAID supports biodiversity conservation by shifting natural resource management responsibility to Malagasy institutions such as the National Park Service, expanding local community participation, and increasing ecotourism, while linking conservation to sustainable small farm agriculture and increased rural family income in ecologically significant landscapes. As a result of USAID support, environmental concerns are now incorporated into regional planning processes; local communities participate in decision-making for the management of natural resources; the National Parks System is better managed and expanded; and, the private sector is increasingly involved in sustainable natural resource use linking small farmers and producer organizations to agricultural export markets.

EU MADAGASCAR COOPERATION

GENERAL BACKGROUND

Madagascar is an Indian Ocean Island nation with a total area of 587,040-sq. km., somewhat bigger than France, and a population of some 16 million. Despite all its natural and physical potential, Madagascar is today, with a per capita GNP of US$ 300$ in 2002, one of the least developed countries of the world. It suffers from extremely high levels of poverty (61,1% of the population in 2001 and 73,2% expected for 2002), from chronic malnutrition and inadequate health and education facilities. It ranks 141st on the UNDP's Human Development Index.

Agriculture accounts for some 25% of GDP, employs more than 80% of Madagascar population and represents 20% of exports. However, the fluctuating nature of agricultural production, due to both to climatic conditions (cyclones) together with variations in commodity prices, including oil prices, is a major challenge to Madagascar's economic performance.

In spite of the dynamism (before the crisis) of the free-trade area and of some specific sectors (shrimps, textile, essential oils…), Madagascar's manufacturing sector (12% of GDP) is underdeveloped and suffers from a variety of inefficiencies that need to be addressed for the sector to play a greater role in the economy.
The services sector, approximately 63% of GDP, is dominated by transportation, construction and public works, telecommunications and tourism.

A large informal sector exists to the detriment of the formal sector.

Terms of trade have generally deteriorated since the prices of its own commodities (coffee, vanilla) have generally declined.

Despite constraints, and thanks to a first set of economic reforms, Madagascar's GDP growth increased markedly over the period 1995-2001, with an average annual growth rate from 1990 to 1999 of 3.2%, of 5% in 2000 and of 5,9% in 2001. However, due to the crisis, the growth rate has been negative (- 11,9%) in 2002. A negative growth is also expected for the years to come.

The urban population increased from 1.6 million (18%) in 1980 to 3.9 million (28%) in 1998 and to 4.8 million (30%) in 2001. An average of 1.4% of GDP was spent on health in the 1990s. HIV/AIDS is still relatively uncommon in Madagascar. Nonetheless, the cost of an effective prevention campaign and of treating those already infected is expected to impose great strain on the economy.

Madagascar is one of the most heavily indebted countries in the world. Total outstanding debt is about 3bn$, representing 140% of GDP in 1995 and debt servicing hovers around 40% of export revenues.

In December 2000 Madagascar was declared eligible for the Highly Indebted Poor Countries (HIPC) Initiative. Madagascar's inclusion in the HIPC programme was in part due to its continued progress in implementing the authorities' medium-term programme, and of stringent measures lay down by the World Bank and the IMF.
Due to the long crisis, although originally purely political, the economic situation has deteriorated rapidly: foreign investment completely cut off, paralysis of the industrial sector, fall of production, loss of 150.000 jobs (500.000 with families), loss of market, loss of confidence, financial problems.

In 2002 the secondary sector output has fallen by 13% since March and the tertiary sector by 11%. The inflation has been the order of 15,3%. Revenues represent only 50 of the budget amount. The poverty rate is expected to fall back to the 1997 rate of 73%.

In addition the Island is regularly affected from extensive damage and flooding caused by cyclones and heavy rains.

POLITICAL SITUATION

An independent Republic since 1960, Madagascar's current constitution adopted in 1992 and amended in March 1998, provides for a parliamentary form of government with a separation of legislative and executive powers. Parliament consists of two chambers: the National Assembly and the Senate. The constitution also provides for a degree of autonomy to the provinces (e.g. administration of municipalities and provincial police, and management of public utilities) however decentralisation has still to be implemented.

Madagascar's President is elected by direct, universal suffrage for a five-year term, which is renewable twice. The President is responsible for matters of national sovereignty such as foreign affairs and national defence. He also appoints a Prime Minister, who in turn appoints his cabinet of ministers with the approval of, and in consultation with, the President. The Prime Minister and his Cabinet constitute the Council of Government. The President, the Prime Minister and the Cabinet together constitute the executive branch. The constitutional framework provides for the possibility for the National Assembly, with the approval of the Senate, to impeach and remove the President. The President and the Council of Government can dissolve the National Assembly by decree. The National Assembly has 160 deputies, all elected to serve five-year terms. Following last parliamentary election of December 15, the President Party (TIM) and its allies won 131 over the 160 seats. The Malagasy Senate has 90 seats. The President of the Republic appoints 30 out of the 90 Senators by decree. 1.716 mayors and provincial advisers elect the other 60 through indirect suffrage.

As a consequence of last legislative elections results, Prime Minister Jacques Sylla was reappointed by President Ravalomanana and formed a new Government on 16 January 2003.

Madagascar's three-level judiciary is based on the French system. Appeal is from the Court of First Instance, through the Appeal Court, to the Supreme Court. Magistrates are appointed by the President (orders in the Council). Madagascar also has a Constitutional Court.

For administrative purposes, Madagascar is divided into six provinces: Antsiranana, Mahajanga, Toamasina, Antananarivo, Fianarantsoa, and Toliary.

Madagascar is emerging now from a period of political crisis that erupted after the contested presidential election of 16 December 2001, when the High Constitutional Court, considering that no candidate had won an absolute majority, called for a second round and the opposition candidate, Marc Ravalomanana, claiming victory declared himself President in February 2002, while incumbent President D. Ratsiraka moved a parallel government to the coast and blockaded the capital.

A solution was found when M. Ravolamana was declared the winner by the High Constitutional Court, assuming the Presidency on 6 May 2002, and the international community recognised him as President in July 2002, while D. Ratsiraka fled the country. M. Ravalomanana's popular backing was confirmed by the results of the 15 December 2002 legislative elections, with 131 of the 160 seats of the National Assembly won by his coalition candidates.

An EU Electoral Observation Mission, deployed in Madagascar from November 2002 to January 2003, issued declarations taking a generally favourable view of the legislative elections, despite some shortcomings and weaknesses in its preparation and occasional incidents of pressure and intimidation.

REGIONAL FRAMEWORK

In the south-west region of the Indian Ocean, comprising Comoros, Mauritius, Madagascar, Seychelles and France (Réunion and Mayotte), Madagascar alone represents 99% of the total land mass and approximately 90% of the population. Regional trade among the countries of the Indian Ocean Commission (IOC) represents only 3% of the total commercial flows of the various countries, with trade between Madagascar and Mauritius amounting to 90% of this figure.

Apart from membership of the IOC, Madagascar is also a member of COMESA (the Common Market for Eastern and Southern Africa) and of IOR-ARC (the Indian Ocean Rim Association for Regional Co-operation). It has also applied for membership of SADC (the Southern African Development Community).

Though considering itself non-African and a continent of its own, Madagascar has been in the past an important member of the OAU. As a consequence of the political crisis, the AU (African Union, former OUA) did not recognise Ravalomanana as President and decided that the seat of Madagascar should remain vacant. However, last February the Central Organ of the Mechanism for Conflict Prevention recommended to the AU Assembly to recognise him as the country's legitimate President and it is expected that Madagascar will soon reintegrate the AU.

RELATIONS WITH THE EU

The EU as a whole, and France in particular, is Madagascar's most significant trade partner. In 2001, 69% (607M€) of Malagasy exports went to the EU mainly fisheries products (prawns), garments, coffee, and vanilla, and 44% (431M€) of the country's imports came from the EU (mainly intermediate manufactures and capital goods).

In 1999, the EU became Madagascar's most important donor, followed by the World Bank. Virtually all of the instruments of EU-ACP co-operation have been employed in Madagascar.

- **EDF**:
  The main areas of concentration under the 6th (€ 125 m), 7th(€ 133.2 m) and 8th (€ 188.5 m) EDFs were transport infrastructure, support to social sectors (health, education), rural development. The 9th EDF Strategy Paper and Indicative Programme for Madagascar was signed on 19 July 2002. It involves a total amount of 327 M€ (allocation A: 267 M€ and allocation B: 60 M€). Main sectors of intervention are: Transport (135 M€); Rural Development and food security (60 M€); Macro-economic support (60 M€) and Good Governance (12 M€).

  - Madagascar also benefits from the **Regional Indicative Programme** for the Indian Ocean, which includes the regional EDF-funded PRIDE (Programme Régional Intégré de Développement des Echanges) project, an environmental programme and a programme for the University of the Indian Ocean.

  - A 70 M€ "Programme d'appui budgetaire d'urgence" was approved by the Commission in December 2002 in order contribute to the budget deficit and to support the recovery of the country. A first instalment of €35m has already been disbursed.

  - As a **Stabex** beneficiary, Madagascar was allocated some €48 under Lomé IV and IV bis for loss of export revenues, notably for coffee, vanilla and cloves. For the years 1997-98-99 a new Stabex commitment of € 19 m was granted.

  - A **Structural Adjustment Support Programme** of € 56.8 m (NIP funds € 20 m, Structural Adjustment Facility + ITF € 36.8 m) aiming at improving health and education services, was signed between Madagascar and the EC in October 1999. This programme was audited in June 2000 and has been disbursed. It included an instalment depending on the evolution of a series of indicators, mainly social ones, which was considered positive.

- The country is a member of the **Beef and Sugar Protocols** annexed to the ACP-EC Convention (but under Community embargo since 1997 for health reasons).

- **EIB**: Between 1979-1998 the Bank allocated some € 113.3 m in EIB risk capital, for the benefit of various sectors (aquaculture, small and medium-sized enterprises, etc). Food Security Programme: Since 1996, Madagascar has been one of the Community's "test" countries of the budget line for the implementation of its new food security policy. In this context, the country has benefited from a total amount of € 58.5 m of financing, including food aid.

- **ECHO**: Since 1994, Madagascar has received ECHO financial assistance 13 times. In 2000 the Commission approved a sum of € 1.5 m to help the country after the disaster due to cyclone Eline and the tropical hurricane Gloria (February and March 2000). A further € 0.9 m was later approved for work carried out through MSF-F, GAA and CARE-F. A sum of € 1-m is foreseen to address the consequences of the locust plaque.

- **Electoral observation and assistance**: An EU observation Mission was deployed from November 2002 to January 2003 to observe legislative elections held on December 15. An assistance programme to the electoral process was also provided.

- **Fisheries Agreement**: A Fisheries Agreement (in respect of tuna) was signed on in March 2001, covering the period 2001-2004. The Agreement allows 80 European boats to fish in Malagasy waters in return for financial compensation of € 2,475,000. In addition, amounts are made available for scientific programmes (€ 240,000); vessel monitoring (€ 801,000); study grants and training courses for sailors (€ 300,000) and assistance to traditional fishing (€ 210,000)

COUNTRY STRATEGY

The strategy of co-operation between the Republic of Madagascar and the European Commission for the next partnership takes account of all of the following considerations :

- it is founded on the objectives of co-operation of the union, notably the fight against poverty;
- it conforms to the political agenda of the Gouvernent, who have made the reduction of poverty their a principle objective ;
- it complements the strategies of other donors ;
- iit focuses on a small number of sectors chosen a) because of their impact on the reduction of poverty for the selected populations and b) from the 6 areas in which the European Commission has a comparative advantage

PRIORITIES FOR CO-OPERATION

Focal Areas

- Transport (50% of 'A' Envelope)
- Rural development and food security (22% of 'A' Envelope)
- Macro-economic support (22% of 'A' Enveloppe)

Non-focal Areas

- Governance (12% of 'A' Enveloppe)

FOCAL AREAS

A)Transport
The following objective will be pursued :

- To assure a high level of human and economic accessibility and to improve the performance of the roads sector. From the indicative programme around 135m has been reserved for this sector.The main activities foreseen are as follows:
    - Rehabilitation of sections of the RN6 (North) ;
    - Improved accessibility to two provinces in the South.

The principal measures, in terms of sectoral policy, taken by the Government as a contribution to the response strategy in this sector are:

- Pursuit and achievement of institutional reforms foreseen in the sectoral policy for transport;
- Stabilisation of other factors that influence the costs of transport (principally fuel);
- Consolidation of the Roads Fund.

B) Rural Development and Food Security
The objective is as follows:

- To improve, in a manner that is sustainable, the supply and demand of food and exported agricultural products, in particular in the provinces of Fianarantsoa and Tuléar. From the indicative envelope, around 60m will be reserved for this sector. The mainactivity foreseen is:
    - Support to the "Action Plan for Rural Development" (PADR) in the South.

- The principal measures, in terms of sectoral policy, taken by the Government as a contribution to the response strategy in this sector are:
    - Maintaining or improving the system of relative prices ;
    - Facilitating access to land for producers ;
    - Promoting ownership PADR process among a significant number of rural producers ;
    - Ensuring effective decentralisation and deconcentration of autonomous provinces(skills, human resources, finances);µ
    - establishing a national funds for repairing damage resulting from natural catastrophes

For additional analytical, business and investment opportunities information, please contact Global Investment & Business Center, USA at (202) 546-2103. Fax: (202) 546-3275. E-mail: rusric@erols.com

C) *Macroeconomic Support*

Macro-economic support will be provided in the framework set out by the PRSP and the PPTE initiative. Around 60m has been reserved for macro-economic support.

Non-focal sector of Co-operation

Good Governance

Consolidating the state of law and judicial reform are central to the poverty reduction strategy.

Around 12m has been reserved for this sector.

9th Financial Data

	Allocation	% of overall A allocation
A. Envelope		
Transport	186	44.5
Rural Development and food security	65.75	15.7
Macroeconomic support	145	34.6
Good governance	21.74	5.2
TOTAL	418.49	100
B. Envelope	10.1	
Total	428.59	

Previous EDF financial data

	6th EDF	7th EDF	8Th EDF
Allocation	125 M€	133.2 M€	185.5 M€
Focal sector	Transport, Health, Education, Rural development	Transport, Health, Education, Rural development	Transport, Health, Education, Rural development

The amounts shown above accounts solely for EDF (European Development Fund) allocations – programmable aid. Significant disbursements in non programmable assistance have been via mechanisms such as STABEX, EIB loans, structural adjustment, emergency aid and community budget lines.

MAJOR DEVELOPMENT PROJECTS

Examples projects co-funded by the EC

- Support programmes for macro-economic reforms
- Rehabilitation of the RN6
- Rural micro-finance projects
- Rural development programme (ACORDS : Appui aux Communes et Organisations Rurales du Sud)
- Food Security
- Support to PADR and to Rural Initiatives
- The Bemaraha Programme
- Good Governance and support to democracy

SUPPLEMENTS

GOVERNEMNT CONTACTS

PRESIDENCE

Adresse
Lapam-Panjakana Ambohitsorohitra
BP 955 - 101 ANTANANARIVO

TEL : (261 20) 22 273 38
FAX : (261 20) 22 670 33

PRIMATURE

Adresse
Lapan'ny Mahazoarivo

TEL : (261 20) 22 331 13 / 22 650 10

VICE-PRIMATURE CHARGÉ DES PROGRAMMES ECONOMIQUES, MINISTRE DES TRANSPORTS, DES TRAVAUX PUBLICS ET DE L'AMENAGEMENT DU TERRRITOIRE

Adresse
BP 3378 Anosy
101 ANTANANARIVO

TEL : (261 20) 22 356 12

JUSTICE

Adresse
Rue Joel Rakotomalala
Faravohitra - 101 ANTANANARIVO

TEL : (261 20) 22 376 84
FAX : (261 20) 22 644 58

INTERIEUR ET REFORME ADMINISTRATIVE

Adresse
BP 232 - 101 ANTANANARIVO

BP 833 - 101 ANTANANARIVO

TEL : (261 20) 22 230 84
FAX : (261 20) 22 277 77 (SG)
(261 20) 22 311 15 (DAF)

ENSEIGNEMENT SUPERIEUR ET RECHERCHE SCIENTIFIQUE

Adresse
BP 4163 Fiadanana
101 ANTANANARIVO

TEL : (261 20) 22 294 23
FAX : (261 20) 22 345 08

SECURITÉ PUBLIQUE

Adresse
BP 23 Bis - Anosy
101 ANTANANARIVO

TEL : (261 20) 22 210 29
(261 20) 22 376 14/18
FAX : (261 20) 22 318 61

AFFAIRES ETRANGERES

Adresse
BP 836 - Anosy
101 ANTANANARIVO

TEL : (261 20) 22 207 81
(261 20) 22 211 98
FAX : (261 20) 22 344 84

ENVIRONNEMENT, EAUX ET FORETS

Adresse
Rue Farafaty - Ampandrianomby

For additional analytical, business and investment opportunities information,
please contact Global Investment & Business Center, USA
at (202) 546-2103. Fax: (202) 546-3275. E-mail: rusric@erols.com

FAX : (261 20) 22 419 19

DEFENSE NATIONALE

Adresse
BP 8 - Ampahibe
101 ANTANANARIVO

TEL : (261 20) 22 273 95
(261 20) 22 222 11 **FAX :** (261
20) 22 354 20
(261 20) 22 604 73

FONCTION PUBLIQUE

Adresse
67 Ha 101 ANTANANARIVO

TEL : (261 20) 22 230 82
(261 20)22 230 47
FAX : (261 20) 22 338 56

SANTE

Adresse
BP 88- Ambohidahy
101 ANTANANARIVO

TEL : (261 20) 22 631 21
FAX : (261 20) 22 642 28

POPULATION

Adresse
BP 723 - Ambohijatovo
101 ANTANANARIVO

TEL : (261 20) 22 276 91
FAX : (261 20) 22 648 23

For additional analytical, business and investment opportunities information,
please contact Global Investment & Business Center, USA
at (202) 546-2103. Fax: (202) 546-3275. E-mail: rusric@erols.com

DECENTRALISATION, DEVELOPPEMENT DES PROVINCES AUTONOMES ET DES COMMUNES (AUPRÈS DE LA PRÉSIDENCE DE LA RÉPUBLIQUE CHARGÉ)

Adresse
BP 24 Bis
101 ANTANANARIVO

TEL : (261 20) 22 358 81
    (261 20) 22 375 16
FAX : (261 20) 22 375 16

CULTURE

Λ

Adresse
BP 305 - Antaninarenina
101 ANTANANARIVO

TEL : (261 20) 22 274 77
FAX : (261 20) 22 298 48

JEUNESSE, SPORTS ET LOISIRS

Adresse
Place Goulette - Ambohijatovo
BP 681 - 101 ANTANANARIVO

TEL : (261 20) 22 277 80
FAX : (261 20) 22 342 75

ENSEIGNEMENT SECONDAIRE ET EDUCATION DE BASE

Adresse
BP 267 - Anosy
101 ANTANANARIVO

TEL : (261 20) 22 629 11
    (261 20)22 213 02
FAX : (261 20) 22 247 65

TELECOMMUNICATION, POSTES ET COMMUNICATION

Adresse
Antaninarenina
101 ANTANANARIVO

101 ANTANANARIVO

TEL : (261 20) 22 232 67
FAX : (261 20) 22 358 94

ECONOMIE FINANCES ET BUDGET

Adresse
BP 674 - Anosy
101 ANTANANARIVO

TEL : (261 20) 22 665 24
FAX : (261 20) 22 285 08

AGRICULTURE, ELEVAGE ET PECHE

Adresse
BP 301 - Ampandrianomby
101 ANTANANARIVO

TEL : (261 20) 22 272 27
FAX : (261 20) 22 265 61

INDUSTRIALISATION, COMMERCE ET DEVELOPPEMENT DU SECTEUR PRIVE

Adresse
Immeuble ARO Ampefiloha
BP 527- 101 ANTANANARIVO

TEL : (261 20) 22 322 51
FAX : (261 20) 22 280 24

ENERGIE ET MINES

Adresse
Ampandrianomby
- 101- ANTANANARIVO

TEL : (261 20) 22 289 28
FAX : (261 20) 22 325 54

TOURISME

Adresse
BP 610 - Tsimbazaza
101 ANTANANARIVO

TEL : (261 20) 22 262 98
        (261 20)22 668 05
FAX : (261 20) 22 789 53

TRAVAIL ET LOIS SOCIALES

Adresse
Immeuble FOP - 67 Ha
101 ANTANANARIVO

TEL : (261 20) 22 338 59
        (261 20) 22 213 09 (S.P.)

IMPORTANT GOVERNMENT AND BUSINESS CONTACTS

COUNTRY GOVERNMENT AGENCIES

Ministère des Finances et de l'Economie
P.O. Box 61
Antananarivo - Madagascar
Tel: (261 20) 22 216 32
Fax: (261 20) 22 345 30

Ministère de la Décentralisation et du Budget
P.O. Box 61
Antananarivo - Madagascar
Tel: (261 20) 22 301 73
Fax: (261 20) 22 345 30

Ministère du Commerce et de la Consommation
P.O. BOX 245
Antananarivo 101 - Madagascar
Tel: (261 20) 22 272 92
Fax: (261 20) 22 312 80

Ministère de la Promotion de l'Industrie et de
l'Artisanat
P.O. BOX: 527
Antananarivo 101 - Madagascar
Tel: (261 20) 22 255 15
Fax: (261 20) 22 277 90

**For additional analytical, business and investment opportunities information,
please contact Global Investment & Business Center, USA
at (202) 546-2103. Fax: (202) 546-3275. E-mail: rusric@erols.com**

Ministère de l'Energie et des Mines
P.O. BOX 257
Antananarivo 101 - Madagascar
Tel: (261 20) 22 255 15
Fax: (261 20) 22 325 54

Ministère d'Etat à l'Agriculture et au Développement Rural
P.O. BOX 842
Antananarivo 101 - Madagascar
Tel: (261 20) 22 247 10
Fax: (261 20) 22 265 61

Ministère des Postes et Télécommunications
Antaninarenina
Antananarivo 101 - Madagascar
Tel: (261 20) 22 261 21
Fax: (261 20) 22 240 08

Ministère des Transports et de la Météorologie
Anosy
Antananarivo 101 - Madagascar
Tel: (261 20) 22 227 19
Fax: (261 20) 22 240 01

Banque Centrale de Madagascar
Antaninarenina
Antananarivo 101 - Madagascar
Tel: (261 20) 22 217 51
Fax: (261 20) 22 345 32

COUNTRY BUSINESS ASSOCIATIONS

Chambre de Commerce, d'Industrie et d'Agriculture d'Antananarivo
P.O. BOX 166
Antananarivo 101 - Madagascar
Tel: (261 20) 22 202 11
Fax: (261 20) 22 202 13

- FIVMPAMA (Association of Malagasy Businessmen)
12, rue Rainizanabololona - Antanimena
Antananarivo 101 - Madagascar
Tel: (261 20) 22 690 78
Fax: (261 20) 22 320 56

- GEM (Groupement des Entreprises de Madagascar)
P.O. Box 1695
Antananarivo 101 - Madagascar
Tel: (261 20) 22 238 41

Fax: (261 20) 22 219 65

- SIM (Syndicat des Industries de Madagascar)
c/o PAPMAD
P.O. Box 1756
Antananarivo - Madagascar
Tel: (261 20) 22 206 35
Fax: (261 20) 22 243 94

- GEFP (Groupement des Entreprises Franches et Partenaires)
Lot II B 1C
Amboditsiry – Andranobevava
Antananarivo 101 – Madagascar
Tel: (26120) 22 418 07
Fax: (26120) 22 403 73
E-Mail: gefpmg@dts.mg

COUNTRY MARKET RESEARCH FIRMS

Automated Data Analysis, Processing & Trading (ADAPT)
P.O. BOX 4212
Antananarivo 101 - Madagascar
Tel: (261 20) 22 291 92
Fax: (261 20) 22 291 92

Cabinet MICA
P.O. BOX 5258
Antananarivo 101 - Madagascar
Tel: (261 20) 22 243 62
Fax: (261 20) 22 259 31
E-Mail: narondro@dts.mg

Cabinet Fivoarana
P.O. BOX 3854 - Madagascar
Antananarivo 101
Tel: (261 20) 22 219 25
Fax: (261 20) 22 271 41

Cabinet d'Etudes, de Conseil et d'Assistance à la Réalisation
Lot IVD 17 Bis, Tsiazotafo
Antananarivo 101 - Madagascar
Tel: (261 20) 22 347 26
Fax: (261 20) 22 206 44

Cabinet Ravonison, Gast et Associés
Lot 1B 26-9, Rue de la Réunion
Isoraka
Antananarivo 101 - Madagascar
Tel: (261 20) 22 261 71
Fax: (261 20) 22 446 33

For additional analytical, business and investment opportunities information,
please contact Global Investment & Business Center, USA
at (202) 546-2103. Fax: (202) 546-3275. E-mail: rusric@erols.com

OSIRIS
P.O. BOX 3476
Antananarivo 101 - Madagascar
Tel: (261 20) 22 420 44
Fax: (261 20) 22 420 44

Ocean Consultants
P.O. Box 3528
Antananarivo 101 - Madagascar
Tel: (261 20) 22 428 06
Fax: (261 20) 22 271 26

USEFUL WEBSITES

Tourism: www.tourisme-madagascar.com
Intestment/Tourism: madagascar-guide.com
Industry: www.sinergic.mg/madagascar-industrie
General Information: www.embassy.org/madagascar
General/Economy: www.madagascar-contacts.com
National Assembly: www.an.online.mg
Economy: www.simicro.mg/sta
Malagasy Products: www.zoma.com
Privatization: www.madaprivat.org
Indian Ocean/Madagascar: www.lk-oi.com
Investment: www.bni.mg

EMBASSIS TO OTHER NATIONS

Embassy of Madagascar in Beijing, China - 3 Sanlitun Dong Jie, 100600 Tel: 6532-1353,6532-1643
Consulate of Madagascar in Hong Kong, Hong Kong - 14/F, East Ocean Centre, Penthhouse, 98 Granville Road, Tsim Sha Tsui East, Kowloon. Tel: 23160888
Embassy of Madagascar in Tokyo, Japan - 2-3-23, Moto-Azabu, Minato-ku. Post Code:106 Tel: 34467252/ 4 Fax: 34467078
Consulate General of Madagascar in Karachi, Pakistan - B-307,Block 6,Gulshan-e-Iqbal Karachi, Pakistan Tel: 467118, 464674

EMBASSIES OF OTHER NATIONS TO MADAGASCAR

Honorary Consulate of Belgium in Antananarivo, Madagascar - 19, Rue révérend Père Callet, Behoririka 101 Tananarive (Mailing : P.O. Box 3046, Antananarivo, Madagascar) Tel: 2220984 Fax: 2220368
Consulate of Canada in Antananarivo, Madagascar - c/o QIT-Madagascar Minerals Ltd.,Villa Paula Androhibe, Lot II-M62C, Villa 3H Ivandry, Antananarivo 101 (P. O. Box 4003, Antananarivo 101) Tel: 42559 Fax: 42506
Special Delegation of China in Antananarivo, Madagascar - Villa Bakoly VIII, Lot Pres VR 61 B Ambohidraserika, Ambohimiandra-Antananarivo, Madagascar (B.P. 3117, Antananarivo 101, Madagascar) Tel: 2234838 Fax: 2228971
Vice Consulate of Denmark in Toamasina, Madagascar - c/o La Ligne Scandinave, 2, Rue Lieutenant Berard, B.P. 18, Toamasina (Source from Udenrigsministeriet, check

following URL for update information) Tel: 53 32548 Fax: 53 339-37 E-mail: sealtmm@bow.dts.mg
French Embassy in Tanandava, Madagascar - 3 rue Jean-Jaur? - Ambatomena - BP 204 Tel: 22 398 98 Fax: 22 399 27
Embassy of Indonesia in Antananarivo, Madagascar - 26-28 Rue Patrice Lumumba, Tsaralalana, B.P. 3969/3242 Tel: (261-20) 222-4915, 222-4825 Fax: (261-20) 223-2857
British Embassy in Antananarivo, Madagascar - First Floor, Immeuble "Ny Havana" Cite de 67 Ha, BP 167, Antananarivo Tel: 22 27749, 22 27370, 22 33765 Fax: 22 26690 E-mail: ukembant@simicro.mg
British Consulate in Toamasina, Madagascar - SEAL TAMATAVE Tel: 53 32548/32569 Fax: 53 33937 E-mail: sealtmm@bow.dts.mg

FOREIGN ORGANIZATIONS IN MADAGASCAR

Organization Name	Phone	FAX	Address (all in Antananarivo)
American Lutheran Mission	22-331-74 22-292-86	22-330-81	9 Rue de Belgique, Isoraka
Care International	22-320-75 22-332-65	22-349-11	11 Rue Radama 1er, Tsaralanana
Catholic Relief Services	22-265-34 22-206-66	22-316-96	II W 27 D, Ankorahotra
Conservation International	22-352-89	22-204-22	II L 1 A, Ankadivato
Rotary Club	22-414-65		Rue VVS, Andrainarivo
UNESCO	22-217-61		11 Rue Naka Rabemanantsoa, Behoririka
UNICEF	22-280-83 22-303-51	22-304-01	Rue Robert Ducrocq, Behoririka
UNPD	22-219-07 22-234-90 22-241-15	22-347-96	22 Rue Rainitovo, Antsahavola
USAID - US Agency for International Development	22-254-89	22-348-83	Immeuble Vonisoa, Ambohijanahary-Andrefana
US Cultural Center	22-202-38 22-202-39	22-213-97	4 Rue Razafindratandra, Ambohidahy
US Embassy	22-200-89 22-212-57	22-345-39	14 Rue Rainitovo, Antsahavola
US Peace Corps	22-313-30 22-313-54		II Y 14 bis, Ambaranjana
WWF - World	22-346-38 22-348-85	22-348-88	II M 85 ter.

Wildlife Fund			Antsakarivo

BANKS IN MADAGASCAR

- Standard Bank of South Africa holds a minority shareholding in the Union Commercial Bank SA, Madagascar.

Tel.: 092612022 27262

Fax.: 092612022 28740

- **Bankin'Ny Tantsaha Mpamokatra (BTM)**
  (Banque Nationale pour le Développement Rural)
  Place de l'Indépendance
  BP 183
  Antananarivo
  tel: 20251
  fax: 29408

- **Bank Pan Oceanic (BPO)**
  BP 21 bis
  Antananarivo 101

- **Banky Fampandrosoana Ny Varotra (BFV)**
  (Banque Nationale pour le Commerce)
  14 Lalana Jeneraly Rabehevitra
  BP 196
  Antananarivo
  tel: 20691
  fax: 34554

- **Banque Malgache de l'Océan Indien (BMOI)**
  BP 25 bis
  Antananarivo 101
  fax: 34610

- **BNI - Crédit Lyonnais Madagascar**
  74 Rue du 26 Juin 1960
  BP 174
  Antananarivo 101
  tel: 22800
  fax: 33749

Union Commercial Bank SA
77 rue Solombavambahoaka Frantsay
BP 197
Antananarivo

For additional analytical, business and investment opportunities information,
please contact Global Investment & Business Center, USA
at (202) 546-2103. Fax: (202) 546-3275. E-mail: rusric@erols.com

tel: 27262
fax: 28740

- **Chamber of Commerce, Industry and Agriculture of Antananarivo**
  Antananarivo 101
  tel: 20211
  fax: 20213

- **Fédération des Chambres de Commerce, d'Industrie et d'Agriculture**
  20, Rue Paul-Dussac
  Antananarivo

Central Bank of Madagascar
Avenue de la Révolution Socialiste
BP 550
Antananarivo 101
tel: 21751
fax: 34532

Principal Commercial Centres

- Antananarivo is the commercial and financial centre and also a major industrial centre.
- Toamasina is the country's major port and an important industrial centre.
- Other centres include Tulear, Antsiranana, Fianarantsoa, Antsirabe and Mahajanga.

SENATE MEMBERS

ANTANANARIVO

1 - ANDRIMIARISATRANA Noël Christian

2 - ANDRIANIRINA Lucien

3 - RABE François

4 - RABETSAROANA Sylvain Willy

5 - RAJEMISON RAKOTOMAHARO Guy

6 - RAHARIMINA Olga Emilienne

7 - RAKIVOLAHARIVONY Jeanine Hortense

8 - RAKOTOAMBOA Louis

9 - RAKOTOARIVENTINY Charlie

10 - RAKOTOMANANA Honoré

11 - RAKOTOZANANAY Augustin

12 - RAMAMONJISOA Benjamin

13 - RAMANANAKASINA Maurice

14 - RAMILISON Max Marie

15 - RANDRIAMIANDRISOA Philippe

16 - RANIRIHARINOSY Daniel

17 - RANOHISOA Seth.

18 - RASAMOELY Frederic

ANTSIRANANA

1 - ADINANY Jery

2 - BADADY Roland

3 - BENJAMIN Clovis

4 - BETIANA Bruno

5 - FAGNANO Andriana

6 - JAOTOMBO Ferdinand

7 - JOSEPH Yoland

8 - RAKOTO Julien

9 - RAKOTOMAMONJY Jean Max

10 - RAZANAMAHOLY Robia

11 - TOTOBESOLA Jean Pierre

12 - VAOVAO Benjamin

FIANARANTSOA

1 - ANDRIAMORA Paul Bernard

2 - JOSEPH Sylvain

3 - MAC TONG KI Jean Yves

4 - MANANJARA

5 - NDONGO Gabriel

6 - RAFAMANTANANTSOA Faniry

7 - RAKOTOMIHANTAHARIZAKA R.S Organès

8 - RAKOTOZANDRINDRAINY Raphaël

9 - RANDIMBISOA Jean Chrysostome

10 - RANDIMBISON André dit Jehovah

11 - RANDRIANANDRASANA Jean Louis

12 - RAVELOARISOA Olga

13 - RAZAFIMILY Constance

14 - VELONAODY Fabien

MAHAJANGA

1 - BEFENO

2 - HASSANY Bin Mohamady

3 - HOUSSAIN

4 - JAFASY Bruno

5 - JEAN Clément

6 - LININA Zoé

7 - MARINASY

8 - MOHAMED Abdou

9 - RALAIJAONA Alfred

10 - RAMBOASOLO Lucien

11 - RATIANARIVO Jeanson

12 - SAJY Pierre

13 - SOUDJAY Bachir Adehame

For additional analytical, business and investment opportunities information, please contact Global Investment & Business Center, USA at (202) 546-2103. Fax: (202) 546-3275. E-mail: rusric@erols.com

14 - SYRITIS Alexandre

TOAMASINA

1 - ANDRIAMASY née RAKOTOARIVO Marie Suzette

2 - BEKY née RAZAFITSALOVA Monique

3 - BOTOROA Romule

4 - JEAN Félicien

5 - KOTO Dauphin

6 - MORA Richard

7 - PAUL Samuel

8 - RAKOTOMANANA Henri

9 - RAKOTOSIHANAKA Andriamiandra

10 - RAMASY Adolphe

11 - RANDRIANARIMANANA Jérôme

12 - RAOELINA Médard

13 - RATOVOSON Seth Arsène

14 - VELO Arsène

15 - RANDRIAMARO Arme

TOLIARA

1 - ARMAND Jean

2 - BOTOTSAKO Augustin

3 - DIMBY Marie Naphtaline

4 - KOLO Roland Eugène Christophe

5 - MARA David

6 - MOSA David

7 - NAIKA Eliane veuve Abdoulanziz

8 - NANG-TCHEE Jean de Dieu

9 - RABERSON Emilien Jeannot

10 - RAHERIVELO Tantely Guinéus

11 - RAJAOFERA Charlesv

12 - RASANDRATRINIAVO Hozllaz

13 - RAZAFITOMBO née Alibena Elisa

14 - REBOZA Mahaforona Cyrille

15 - ROBERT Razaka

16 - SOJA Jean André

GLOSSARY -- MADAGASCAR (INDIAN OCEAN)

CFA
Communauté Financière d'Afrique (African Financial Community). The CFA covers those African countries whose currencies are linked with the French Franc at a fixed rate of exchange.

Comoran franc (CF)
One Comoran franc = 100 centimes; in June 1995 US$1.00 = CF363.98.

crown colony
A colony of the British Commonwealth over which the crown maintains some control, as through appointment of the governor.

European Community (EC)
See European Union.

European Currency Unit (ECU)
Standard currency unit of the European Union; in April 1995 ECU1 = US$0.75.

European Union (EU)
Formerly the European Community, it was established by the Maastricht Treaty of December 1991 to expand European cooperation from economic and commercial into monetary, security and judicial matters. It officially came into being at the end of 1993.

exclusive economic zone (EEZ)
A wide belt of sea and seabed adjacent to the national boundaries where the state claims preferential fishing rights and control over the exploitation of mineral and other natural resources. Madagascar claims a 150-nautical-mile exclusive economic zone. Mauritius, Comoros, Seychelles, and Maldives all claim 200 nautical miles. Boundary situations with neighboring states sometimes prevent the extension of the exclusive economic zones to the full limits claimed.

fiscal year (FY)
Same as the calendar year for all except Mauritius, in which it runs from July 1 to June 30.

Franc Zone
A monetary union among countries whose currencies are linked to the French franc. Members are France and its overseas appendages and fourteen African countries, including Comoros.

gross domestic product (GDP)

> A value measure of the flow of domestic goods and services produced by an economy over a period of time, such as a year. Only output values of goods for final consumption and intermediate production are assumed to be included in the final prices. GDP is sometimes aggregated and shown at market prices, meaning that indirect taxes and subsidies have been eliminated, the result is GDP at factor cost. The word "gross" indicates that deductions for depreciation of physical assets have not been made. See also gross national product.

gross national product (GNP)

> Gross domestic product (q.v.) plus the net income or loss stemming from transactions with foreign countries. GNP is the broadest measurement of the output of goods and services by an economy. It can be calculated at market prices, which include indirect taxes and subsidies. Because indirect taxes and subsidies are only transfer payments, GNP is often calculated at factor cost, removing indirect taxes and subsidies.

import substitution

> The replacement of imports by domestically produced goods, often supported by tariffs or import quotas, and motivated by foreign exchange considerations.

International Development Association (IDA)

> See World Bank.

International Finance Corporation (IFC)

> See World Bank.

International Monetary Fund (IMF)

> Established along with the World Bank (q.v.) in 1945, the IMF is a specialized agency affiliated with the United Nations and is responsible for stabilizing international exchange rates and payments. The main business of the IMF is the provision of loans to its members (including industrialized and developing countries) when they experience balance of payments difficulties. These loans frequently carry conditions that require substantial internal economic adjustments by the recipients, most of which are developing countries.

Lomé Convention

> The first Lomé Convention (Lomé I) came into force in 1976, Lomé II came into effect in 1981, and Lomé III came into force in 1985; Lomé IV came into effect in 1990. The convention covers economic relations between the members of the European Economic Community (EEC) and their former colonies in Africa, the Caribbean, and the Pacific (ACP). The convention allows most ACP exports to enter the EEC duty-free or at special rates and, among other things, provides funds through the Stabex system (q.v.) to offset adverse fluctuations in the prices of ACP exports.

London Club

> An informal group of commercial banks that come together to negotiate a debt rescheduling agreement with a country. The group has two committees, an economics committee that develops economic data projections and a negotiating committee. Committee members usually come from the five principal banks that hold the largest amounts of a country's debt.

Malagasy franc (FMG)

> 1 Malagasy franc (franc malgache-FMG) = 100 centimes; in May 1995 US$1.00 = FMG4,236.9.

Mauritian rupee (MauR)

1 Mauritian rupee = 100 cents; in August 1995 US$1.00 = MauR14.43.

parastatal

A semi-autonomous, quasi-qovernmental, state-owned enterprise.

Paris Club

The informal name for a consortium of Western creditor countries (Belgium, Britain, Canada, France, Germany, Italy, Japan, the Netherlands, Sweden, Switzerland, and the United States) that have made loans or guaranteed export credits to developing nations and that meet in Paris to discuss borrowers' ability to repay debts. Paris Club deliberations often result in the tendering of emergency loans to countries in economic difficulty or in the rescheduling of debts. Formed in October 1962, the organization has no formal or institutional existence. Its secretariat is run by the French treasury. It has a close relationship with the International Monetary Fund (q.v.), to which all of its members except Switzerland belong, as well as with the World Bank (q.v.) and the United Nations Conference on Trade and Development (UNCTAD). The Paris Club is also known as the Group of Ten (G-10).

rufiyaa (Rf)

Maldives currency; 1 rufiyaa = 100 laari; in June 1995 US$1.00 = Rf11.77.

Seychelles rupee (SRe)

1 Seychelles rupee = 100 cents; in August 1995 US$1.00 = SRe4.25.

Shia (from Shiat Ali, the Party or Ali)

A member of the smaller of the two great divisions of Islam. The Shia supported the claims of Ali and his line to presumptive right to the caliphate and leadership of the Muslim community, and on this issue they divided from the Sunni (q.v.) in the major schism within Islam. Later schisms have produced further divisions among the Shia over the identity and number of imams. Most Shia revere Twelve Imams, the last of whom is believed to be hidden from view.

South Asia Association for Regional Cooperation (SAARC)

Comprises the seven nations of South Asia: Bangladesh, Bhutan, India, Maldives, Nepal, Pakistan, and Sri Lanka; founded as South Asia Regional Cooperation (SARC) organization at a meeting of foreign ministers in New Delhi on August 1-2, 1983; a second organizational meeting of foreign ministers was held in Thimphu in May 1985; inaugural meeting of heads of state and government in Dhaka on December 7-8, 1985. The goal is to effect economic, technical, and cultural cooperation and to provide a forum for discussions of South Asia political problems.

special drawing rights (SDRs)

Monetary units of the International Monetary Fund (q.v.) based on a basket of international currencies including the United States dollar, the German deutsche mark, the Japanese yen, the British pound sterling, and the French franc.

Stabex system

A system of export earnings stabilization set up by the European Community (EC) in accordance with the African, Caribbean, and Pacific (ACP) states. Under the system, the EC helps developing countries withstand fluctuations in the price of their agricultural products by paying compensation for lost export earnings.

Sunni

The larger of the two great divisions of Islam. The Sunni, who rejected the claims of Ali's line, believe that they are the true followers of the sunna, the guide to proper behavior set forth by Muhammad's personal deeds and utterances. *See also* Shia.

World Bank

Informal name used to designate a group of four affiliated international institutions: the International Bank for Reconstruction and Development (IBRD), the International Development Association (IDA), the International Finance Corporation (IFC), and the Multilateral Investment Guarantee Agency (MIGA). The IBRD, established in 1945, has the primary purpose of providing loans to developing countries for productive projects. The IDA, a legally separate loan fund but administered by the staff of the IBRD, was set up in 1960 to furnish credits to the poorest developing countries on much easier terms than those of conventional IBRD loans. The IFC, founded in 1956, supplements the activities of the IBRD through loans and assistance specifically designed to encourage the growth of productive private enterprises in the less developed countries. The MIGA, founded in 1988, insures private foreign investment in developing countries against various noncommercial risks. The president and certain senior officers of the IBRD hold the same positions in the IFC. The four institutions are owned by the governments of the countries that subscribe their capital. To participate in the World Bank group, member states must first belong to the International Monetary Fund (IMF-- *q.v.*).

GLOBAL BUSINESS, RESEARCH AND POLITICAL LIBRARIES

RUSSIA
BUSINESS LAW HANDBOOK

SOUTH AFRICA
INVESTMENT
&
BUSINESS
GUIDE

JAPAN
BUSINESS
&
INVESTMENT
OPPORTUNITIES
YEARBOOK

BAHAMAS
OFFSHORE
INVESTMENT
&
BUSINESS
GUIDE

LIBYA
A "SPY" GUIDE"

CHINA
FOREIGN POLICY
GOVERNMENT
GUIDE

RUSSIA
A COUNTRY
STUDY

INDIA
BUSINESS
INTELLIGENCE
REPORT

US-ISRAEL
POLITICAL
&
ECONOMIC
COOPERATION
HANDBOOK

ARMENIA
EXPORT-IMPORT
&
BUSINESS
DIRECTORY

Guides, reports and handbooks are available for the following countries:

Albania	Central African	Gabon	Lebanon	Niger	Solomon
Algeria	Republic	Gambia	Lesotho	Nigeria	Islands
Andorra	Chad	Georgia	Liberia	Norway	Somalia
Angola	Chile	Germany	Libya	Oman	South Africa
Antigua and	China	Ghana	Liechtenstein	Pakistan	Spain
Barbuda	Colombia	Greece	Lithuania	Palau	Sri Lanka
Argentina	Comoros	Grenada	Luxembourg	Panama	Sudan
Armenia	Congo,	Guatemala	Macedonia	Papua New	Suriname
Australia	Democratic	Guinea	Madagascar	Guinea	Swaziland
Austria	Republic	Guinea-Bissau	Malawi	Paraguay	Sweden
Azerbaijan	Costa Rica	Guyana	Malaysia	Peru	Switzerland
Bahamas	Côte d'Ivoire	Haiti	Maldives	Philippines	Syria
Bahrain	Croatia	Honduras	Mali	Poland	Taiwan
Bangladesh	Cuba	Hungary	Malta	Portugal	Tajikistan
Barbados	Cyprus	Iceland	Marshall	Qatar	Tanzania
Belarus	Czech Republic	India	Islands	Romania	Thailand
Belgium	Denmark	Indonesia	Mauritania	Russia	Togo
Belize	Djibouti	Iran	Mauritius	Rwanda	Tonga
Benin	Dominica	Ireland	Mexico	Saint Kitts &	Trinidad &
Bhutan	Dominican	Israel	Micronesia	Nevis	Tobago
Bolivia	Republic	Italy	Moldova	Saint Lucia	Tunisia
Bosnia &	Ecuador	Jamaica	Monaco	Saint Vincent	Turkey
Herzegovina	Egypt	Japan	Mongolia	& Grenadines	Turkmenistan
Botswana	El Salvador	Jordan	Morocco	San Marino	Tuvalu
Brazil	Equatorial	Kazakhstan	Mozambique	San Tome	Uganda
Brunei	Guinea	Kenya	Myanmar	and Principe	Ukraine
Bulgaria	Eritrea	Kiribati	(Burma)	Saudi Arabia	United Arab
Burkina Faso	Estonia	Korea, North	Namibia	Senegal	Emirates
Burundi	Ethiopia	Korea, South	Nauru	Seychelles	United
Cambodia	Faroe Islands	Kuwait	Nepal	Sierra Leone	Kingdom
Cameroon	Fiji	Kyrgyzstan	Netherlands	Singapore	United States
Canada	Finland	Laos	New Zealand	Slovakia	Uruguay
Cape Verde	France	Latvia	Nicaragua	Slovenia	Uzbekistan

Madagascar

FY 2006 Assistance by Sector

Global Health
$10,015
49%

Democracy, Conflict and Humanitarian Assistance
$514
3%

Economic Growth, Agriculture and Trade
$9,865
48%

FY 2006 Assistance by Account

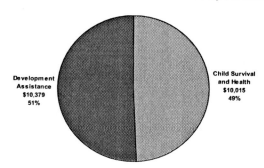

Development Assistance
$10,379
51%

Child Survival and Health
$10,015
49%

Objectives and Budget

Objective	SO Number	FY 2004	FY 2005	FY 2006
Governance in Targeted Areas Improved	687-004	1,647	1,500	514
Selected Health Services and Products	687-005	10,365	11,315	10,015
Biologically Diverse Forest Ecosystems	687-006	8,233	6,847	8,725
Critical Private Markets Expanded	687-007	498	677	1,140
Total (in thousands of dollars)		20,743	20,339	20,394

Excludes P.L. 480. See Program Annex.

Administrative Expenses and Workforce

Administrative Expenses	FY 2004	FY 2005	FY 2006
Mission Allocation	2,816	2,264	2,302
USDH Salaries & Benefits	542	555	567
Program Funds	1,946	1,981	1,992
Total (in thousands of dollars)	5,304	4,800	4,861

FY 2006 Workforce

Program Funded, 43, 45%

USDH, 5, 5%

Other US, 1, 1%

FSN, 47, 49%

Mission Director: Stephen Haykin

For more information, please visit our Website, www.usaid.gov

Madagascar

The Development Challenge: The Government of Madagascar (GOM), led by President Marc Ravalomanana, is engaged in an ambitious effort to address the country's immense development challenges. Stricken with widespread poverty and endemic corruption, Madagascar has an average per capita income of only $255; 70% of its population lives below the poverty line; 49% of children under five years of age are malnourished; rates of child mortality of 84 per 1,000 live births and maternal mortality of 488 per 100,000 live births are unacceptably high; life expectancy is only 55 years; HIV prevalence is 1.1%; the annual population growth rate is high at 2.8%; and, 46% of the population is illiterate. The projected 2004 real gross domestic product (GDP) growth rate of 5.3% is considerably less than the 9.6% growth rate achieved last year. Overall macroeconomic management has been sound, but the economy was buffeted by a rapid depreciation of the currency in early 2004 and rising world prices for rice and petroleum products, resulting in a projected inflation rate of 27%. In mid-2004, Madagascar reached the Completion Point under the Highly Indebted Poor Countries Initiative (HIPC), resulting in extensive cancellation of sovereign debt ($1.9 billion U.S. dollars). Based on sound economic, governance, and social investment indicators, Madagascar was selected as one of the first 16 countries worldwide eligible to receive Millennium Challenge Corporation (MCC) funding.

Under the country's Poverty Reduction Strategic Plan (PRSP), GOM development priorities emphasize good governance, economic growth, and social welfare. To promote good governance, the GOM has established an Anti-Corruption Commission in the Presidency as well as an independent, anti-corruption agency, both of which are supported by USAID's Anti-Corruption Initiative. The GOM requires public disclosure of assets by state officials and is introducing public finance and customs sector reforms. The government is working to reduce the illicit trade of precious and semi-precious gemstones. The GOM has canceled illegal forestry permits and has banned the export of endangered species. To stimulate economic growth, the GOM has strengthened partnerships with the private sector and, with donor support, will have invested over $1 billion in roads and other transportation infrastructure by 2006. The GOM also declared a two-year tax holiday on investment and limited consumer imports, and has opened the sale of land to foreign investors. Recognizing the importance of its unique environment to the long-term health of the Malagasy economy and the welfare of its people, and building upon support from USAID and other donors, the GOM has dramatically increased planned protected areas from 1.7 million to 6 million hectares. In the social sector, the GOM is committed to preventing the spread of HIV/AIDS; fighting malaria; strengthening health care at the community level; and increasing access to and the quality of primary education through its "Education for All" program.

Installed in 2002, the Ravalomanana government maintains considerable public support for its ambitious programs. However, it faces a number of risks: that a weak and poorly equipped bureaucracy will be unable to accomplish many of the planned reforms and results; that ambitious social programs will outstrip government revenues; that the public will grow impatient with the pace of reform under the weight of grinding poverty and rising food prices; that vested interests will retard the reform agenda; that foreign investment will fail to materialize at the rate necessary to meet economic growth objectives; and, that natural disasters -- the country is vulnerable to cyclones -- will undermine GOM progress. U.S. Government (USG) development assistance mitigates these risks.

U.S. national interests in Madagascar include the preservation of the country's unique biodiversity; its growing importance as a bilateral commercial partner under the African Growth and Opportunity Act (AGOA); and alleviation of its deep poverty, which is exacerbated by natural disasters, food insecurity and weak social services. The United States and Madagascar enjoy close relations, and Madagascar is an ally in the global fight against terrorism. The top three U.S. foreign policy objectives in Madagascar are promotion of democracy; broad-based economic development (including health); and environmental protection. Complementary interests include containing the nascent HIV/AIDS epidemic, supporting the country's democratic transition, and combating Trafficking in Persons. Madagascar is one of the three highest biodiversity conservation priority countries in the world.

The USAID Program: The overall goal of the USAID program in Madagascar is sustainable and inclusive economic development. Madagascar's acute poverty and legacy of corruption continue to pose formidable challenges to government and donor community efforts to transform the country. Human and financial resources and the institutional capacity to implement programs, especially in the public and nongovernmental organization (NGO) sectors, remain weak, undermining the overall ability of the Malagasy Government to deliver results. The USAID program directly addresses these problems by strengthening local NGOs and selected government institutions; promoting public-private dialogue; supporting the implementation of a national anti-corruption agenda; increasing access to quality health services and products; improving natural resource management; promoting private investment; and increasing rural incomes.

Other Program Elements: USAID's centrally funded education activities, and support received from the Leland Initiative, provide increased Internet access in Madagascar. A three-year program under the Women's Legal Rights Initiative began early 2004. Central population funds contribute to joint environment-health programs. Funds from centrally managed USAID health programs will support community-based health and family planning activities. USAID central funds enable the conservation of a national park in west Madagascar. Funds provided by USAID's centrally managed disaster assistance program assists populations affected by drought in the south of the country. Finally, the P.L. 480 food assistance program will continue to support child survival and nutrition, education, and rural development.

Other Donors: USAID places strong emphasis on donor coordination and enjoys productive collaboration with all major donors. The World Bank, the United Nations and the European Union are Madagascar's largest multilateral donors, followed by France, the United States and Japan at the bilateral level. Donor coverage and priorities by sector are as follows: World Bank (governance, institutional development, public finance, judicial reform, gemstone trade, maternal/child health, HIV/AIDS, environment, education, privatization, agriculture, food security, rural development, micro-credit); European Union (public finance, judicial reform, environment, agriculture, rural development, food security, transportation infrastructure); United Nations (governance, maternal/child health, family planning, environment, rural development, food security, disaster mitigation); France (judicial reform, public finance, maternal/child health, family planning, environment, rural development, food security, micro-credit, agriculture, urban development); and Japan (collaborates with USAID in health and behavioral change activities). Governance and institutional development are the central themes of World Bank and International Monetary Fund support. The World Bank is the lead HIV/AIDS and education sector donor in Madagascar. Madagascar also receives funding from the Global Fund for AIDS, Tuberculosis and Malaria (GFATM), the Global Alliance for Vaccinations and Immunizations (GAVI), and the MacArthur Foundation.

Madagascar
PROGRAM SUMMARY

(in thousands of dollars)

Accounts	FY 2003 Actual	FY 2004 Actual	FY 2005 Current	FY 2006 Request
Child Survival and Health Programs Fund	9,293	10,365	11,315	10,015
Development Assistance	10,504	10,378	9,024	10,379
Economic Support Fund	1,000	0	0	0
PL 480 Title II	10,381	12,477	11,607	15,719
Total Program Funds	**31,178**	**33,220**	**31,946**	**36,113**

STRATEGIC OBJECTIVE SUMMARY				
687-003 Biodiversity Conservation and Sustainable Dev't				
DA	1,819	0	0	0
687-004 Governance in Targeted Areas Improved				
DA	1,685	1,647	1,500	514
ESF	250	0	0	0
687-005 Selected Health Services and Products				
CSH	9,293	10,365	11,315	10,015
687-006 Biologically Diverse Forest Ecosystems				
DA	6,000	8,233	6,847	8,725
ESF	250	0	0	0
687-007 Critical Private Markets Expanded				
DA	1,000	498	677	1,140
ESF	500	0	0	0

Mission Director,
Stephen Haykin

Data Sheet

USAID Mission:	Madagascar
Program Title:	Governance in Targeted Areas Improved
Pillar:	Democracy, Conflict and Humanitarian Assistance
Strategic Objective:	687-004
Status:	Continuing
Planned FY 2005 Obligation:	$1,500,000 DA
Prior Year Unobligated:	$0
Proposed FY 2006 Obligation:	$514,000 DA
Year of Initial Obligation:	2003
Estimated Year of Final Obligation:	2007

Summary: USAID's current democracy and governance program is the foundation for its portfolio in Madagascar (environment, health, and economic growth). Finances and governance-related results are shared across strategic objectives. The program is working across sectors to deepen and strengthen civil society, increase the flow of information to citizens and local leaders, and strengthen the government's ability to respond to citizens' demands. In addition, USAID is implementing initiatives in the areas of anti-corruption, women's legal rights, education, and information and communications technologies development in Madagascar. Through support from the Africa Education Initiative, USAID is improving the quality of and access to basic education by supporting in-service teacher training and provision of scholarships to disadvantaged girls.

Inputs, Outputs, Activities:
FY 2005 Program: Promote and Support Anti-Corruption Reforms ($500,000 DA). Under the Africa Bureau Anti-Corruption Initiative, USAID is strengthening Madagascar's two new government anti-corruption agencies, lending support to a targeted 32 local anti-corruption civil society organizations, and increasing citizen knowledge about corruption. FY 2005 efforts will prioritize support to regional Government of Madagascar (GOM) anti-corruption offices in USAID's three target intervention zones. USAID is also providing funds and technical assistance to lead development of a national anti-corruption baseline survey to be implemented February - April 2005. Principal grantees: Pact and Catholic Relief Services (CRS).

Improve the Quality of Basic Education ($1,000,000 DA). SO4 is currently developing a three-year education program that will be launched in 2005. This program will build off the successes of its civic education program which introduced the concepts of advocacy and a participative teaching method into the classroom. The new program will improve the quality of classroom teaching instruction at the primary and lower secondary levels through the combined use of face-to-face training and radio-based distance learning. Principal grantees: to be determined.

FY 2006 Program: Strengthen Civil Society ($114,000 DA). USAID will continue to build the advocacy capacity of selected 25 CSOs by improving their ability to analyze, articulate, and present their issues. USAID will work with selected national associations to build their organizational capacity, and strengthen their ability to network with civil society and other actors. Training and mentoring will be provided in organizational development to create more sustainable CSOs. Principal grantees: Pact and Catholic Relief Services (CRS) for all components.

Promote and Support Anti-Corruption Reforms ($400,000 DA). USAID is strengthening government capacity to fight corruption. This includes providing technical assistance to national-level agencies as well as three of the government's six regional anti-corruption bureaus. Same implementers as above.

Performance and Results: Excellent results have been achieved in the program's first year of implementation. USAID provided valuable assistance to Madagascar's new National Anti-Corruption Council to develop and launch a national work plan. USAID interventions have also helped strengthen civil society, most notably through its support to FAMAK, a recently established anti-corruption coalition, and in the establishment of the CSO National Platform, a federation of 300 independent civil society advocacy organizations. USAID support in FY 2004 for the Information, Communications and Technologies (ICT) sector was pivotal in development of the national ICT legal and regulatory framework which is the basis of a telecommunications policy in Madagascar. Through the Education for Development and Democracy Initiative, youth have become better educated in civic and advocacy issues; media and civil society have increased their involvement in civic education; and the Ministry of Education has increased its skill in providing civic education in lower-secondary schools. To date, approximately 30,000 students from 170 lower-secondary schools have been reached by the civic education program, and 60 CSOs and journalist associations have been trained on civic education messages. In the focus region of Fianarantsoa, civic education radio messages have been broadcasted to over one million youth. Madagascar's first-ever survey on women's rights, which also included the rarely discussed issue of violence, is helping to increase knowledge about the constraints women face in Malagasy society. By the end of the program in 2008, civil society will be able to play a more effective role as an advocate for citizens' demands and act as a more effective government watchdog. Government anti-corruption agencies will be more capable of fighting corruption. Regional level anti-corruption mechanisms will be established and accessible to ordinary citizens in our targeted regions.

US Financing in Thousands of Dollars

687-004 Governance in Targeted Areas Improved	DA	ESF
Through September 30, 2003		
Obligations	1,685	250
Expenditures	0	0
Unliquidated	1,685	250
Fiscal Year 2004		
Obligations	1,647	0
Expenditures	820	0
Through September 30, 2004		
Obligations	3,332	250
Expenditures	820	0
Unliquidated	2,512	250
Prior Year Unobligated Funds		
Obligations	0	0
Planned Fiscal Year 2005 NOA		
Obligations	1,500	0
Total Planned Fiscal Year 2005		
Obligations	1,500	0
Proposed Fiscal Year 2006 NOA		
Obligations	514	0
Future Obligations	2,189	0
Est. Total Cost	7,535	250

Data Sheet

USAID Mission:	Madagascar
Program Title:	Selected Health Services and Products
Pillar:	Global Health
Strategic Objective:	687-005
Status:	Continuing
Planned FY 2005 Obligation:	$11,315,000 CSH
Prior Year Unobligated:	$0
Proposed FY 2006 Obligation:	$10,015,000 CSH
Year of Initial Obligation:	2003
Estimated Year of Final Obligation:	2007

Summary: The Health, Population and Nutrition (HPN) Program will increase the use of selected health services and products while improving health knowledge and practices. The program strengthens institutional capacities to develop, implement, and evaluate priority health programs, including Sexually Transmitted Infection (STI) and Human Immune Virus/Acquired Immune Deficiency Syndrome (HIV/AIDS) prevention and management at the national and community levels.

Inputs, Outputs, Activities:

FY 2005 Program: Reduce Transmission and Impact of HIV/AIDS ($2,000,000 CSH). Increasing mobility and the high rates of partner change threaten to accelerate the spread of HIV/AIDS. USAID is strengthening the organizational and strategic planning capacity of AIDS committees at the national (1) and local level (30). Assistance to AIDS committees will enable them to implement effective behavior change communication activities and track the epidemic with HIV surveillance data. USAID will maintain its innovative social marketing program to increase access to quality STI and HIV testing and counseling services through over 100 private sector clinics and strengthening public sector commodity logistics management. Public sector competency-based training and private physician training improve the quality of health services. Principal contractors and grantees: Chemonics, JHPIEGO (an affiliate of Johns Hopkins), Helen Keller International, Medical Care Development International (MCDI), Georgetown University, Population Services International (PSI), HIV/AIDS Alliance, Family Health International (FHI) and the Centers for Disease Control and Prevention (all prime), Training Resource Group Inc. (subs).

Prevent and Control Infectious Diseases of Major Importance ($2,300,000 CSH). USAID is providing quality technical assistance to the Ministry of Health and Family Planning (MOHP) to develop national policies and guidelines. Continued support of social marketing operations is expanding mass media and rural outreach education, reinforcing home-based care of uncomplicated malaria, and improving access to effective malaria treatment and insecticide-treated bed nets for children and pregnant women. Competency-based training in medical and nursing schools will improve the quality of health services, and technical assistance to Madagascar's drug agency will advance drug quality assurance. Innovative interventions are improving health and hygiene, linking potable water, health, nutrition and food security, and watershed management. USAID is also expanding access to potable water with simple, affordable treatment solutions, increasing access to clean water, promoting hygiene and sanitation, and improving local water management capacity. Principal contractors and grantees: Chemonics, PSI, Malaria Action Coalition, CARE, and Adventist Development and Relief Agency (ADRA).

Improve Child Survival, Health and Nutrition ($3,475,000 CSH). To reduce the child mortality rate, USAID is expanding vaccination coverage and Essential Nutrition Actions (ENA), and scaling up prevention, early detection and treatment of childhood diseases under the Integrated Management of Childhood Illnesses (IMCI) approach. USAID is continuing competency-based training in medical and nursing schools for IMCI and ENA and supporting the development of national child health and nutrition policies; improving cold chain and commodity management; supporting mobile health clinics for remote populations; supporting improved use of data for decision making; and continuing to improve the national polio surveillance system. At the community level, USAID efforts engage leaders, link communities with health care providers, mobilize communities to action, and expand outreach and education through innovative approaches. Principal contractors and grantees: Chemonics (prime), PSI, Linkages, ADRA, MCDI, CARE, CRS, and others to be identified (subs).

Reduce Unintended Pregnancy and Improve Healthy Reproductive Behavior ($3,540,000 CSH). USAID is increasing availability of and access to family planning services and products through social marketing and community-based distribution and education; strengthening the public sector commodity management and distribution system and the technical and management capacity of selected family planning health organizations, expanding integrated health, population, and environment interventions in remote biodiverse areas; and improving quality of services, focusing on competency-based approaches in pre-service health professional training institutions and revising public health norms, standards and guidelines. USAID-provided technical assistance to the MOHP is strengthening its capacity to develop, implement and evaluate programs. Principal contractors and grantees: Chemonics (prime), PSI, CARE, CRS, ADRA, Voahary Salama (a consortium of local NGOs) (subs), and others to be identified.

Enhance Food Security of Vulnerable Populations. P.L. 480 Title II food aid program is helping food insecure families maintain nutrition levels. Monetization proceeds from the authorized sale of U.S.-supplied food aid in country are used to help families increase food production and income, and improve maternal and child health. Using community-based field agents and food-for-work activities, the Title II program is increasing the availability of and access to locally produced food by increasing incomes of targeted families and are improving health through nutrition education.

FY 2006 Program: Reduce Transmission and Impact of HIV/AIDS ($2,000,000 CSH). USAID will continue support for innovative behavior change interventions, maintain access to socially marketed products and services and continue to provide leadership in developing data for decision making. Implementers will remain the same as above.

Prevent and Control Infectious Diseases of Major Importance ($1,000,000 CSH). Additional infectious disease resources will allow USAID to continue community mobilization and education activities, including assuring access for pregnant women and children to effective malaria prevention and treatment. Implementers will remain the same as above.

Improve Child Survival, Health and Nutrition ($3,475,000 CSH). USAID will continue to support IMCI immunization, and promotion of ENA and Vitamin A distribution, as well as improvements in the delivery of quality health services. Implementers will remain the same as above.

Reduce Unintended Pregnancy and Improve Healthy Reproductive Behavior ($3,540,000 CSH). USAID will continue activities to strengthen commodity distribution systems and community-based distribution, and will maintain community outreach and social marketing activities. Implementers the same as above.

Enhance Food Security of Vulnerable Populations. P.L. 480 Title II-funded activities to improve maternal and child health, nutrition and food security will continue at planned levels. All family planning assistance agreements are incorporating clauses that implement the President's directive restoring the Mexico City Policy.

Performance and Results: The previous strategic objective (SO), which ended in FY 2004, met its targets: contraceptive prevalence increased from 10% in 1997 to 18% in 2003; the Diphtheria, Pertussis and Tetanus immunization rate for children under one year of age improved from 48% in 1997 to 61% in 2003; exclusive breastfeeding rates increased from 22% in 1997 to 67% in 2003. The current SO is on track - national distribution of health products exceeded targets: 529,009 bottles of the safe water solution, SurEau, were sold, above the 518,040 target; 11,357,045 condoms were sold exceeding the target of 11,000,000; and 344,019 insecticide-treated bed nets were sold, surpassing the target of 333,201. Vitamin A distribution of 88% surpassed the 85% target. By the end of the program in 2008, child and maternal health will have been improved in targeted regions, public and private sector capacity to deliver high quality health services will be strengthened at both national and local levels, communities will be mobilized to promote their own health, and essential drugs and medical supplies will be more consistently available in targeted areas.

US Financing in Thousands of Dollars

Madagascar

687-005 Selected Health Services and Products	CSH	ESF
Through September 30, 2003		
Obligations	8,293	400
Expenditures	505	90
Unliquidated	7,788	310
Fiscal Year 2004		
Obligations	9,357	0
Expenditures	4,921	162
Through September 30, 2004		
Obligations	17,650	400
Expenditures	5,426	252
Unliquidated	12,224	148
Prior Year Unobligated Funds		
Obligations	0	0
Planned Fiscal Year 2005 NOA		
Obligations	11,315	0
Total Planned Fiscal Year 2005		
Obligations	11,315	0
Proposed Fiscal Year 2006 NOA		
Obligations	10,015	0
Future Obligations	19,183	0
Est. Total Cost	58,163	400

Data Sheet

USAID Mission:	Madagascar
Program Title:	Biologically Diverse Forest Ecosystems
Pillar:	Economic Growth, Agriculture and Trade
Strategic Objective:	687-006
Status:	Continuing
Planned FY 2005 Obligation:	$6,847,000 DA
Prior Year Unobligated:	$0
Proposed FY 2006 Obligation:	$8,725,000 DA
Year of Initial Obligation:	2003
Estimated Year of Final Obligation:	2007

Summary: Madagascar has consistently been identified by the international community as one of the highest biodiversity conservation priorities in the world. USAID's program to conserve biologically diverse forest ecosystems includes training, technical assistance, and grants to local organizations. It is concentrated at the national level and in three priority eco-regions around the country. Core activities are designed to improve forest and "protected area" management systems; maintain the biological integrity of critical biodiversity habitats; promote alternatives to the practice of slash-and-burn agriculture; support development of eco-enterprises; and improve environmental governance.

Inputs, Outputs, Activities:

FY 2005 Program: Improve Sustainable Management of Natural Resources and Biodiversity Conservation ($5,700,000 DA). USAID is working toward improved protected area management by continuing to fund activities to implement President Ravalomanana's pledge to triple the country's protected area network. This includes the creation of new conservation sites and developing new management systems. USAID is providing training to promote collaboration between managers of protected areas and private ecotourism operators. It is working with the Government of Madagascar (GOM) to build on efforts to strengthen potential income sources for habitat conservation by developing the management capacity of Malagasy environmental trust funds/foundations, finalizing creation of a specific biodiversity trust fund, and identifying new funding sources.

USAID is improving forest management systems by finalizing a regional handbook covering the zoning process that will serve as the basis for the zoning of conservation and production forests. USAID is working to establish a sustainable strategy to control forest exploitation. This includes the implementation of a new transparent forest-permitting system--one that encompasses a formal bidding system and is appropriate to the Malagasy context. USAID is also funding work on landscape restoration to reconnect degraded forest corridors in priority areas.

Outside of the main protected areas, USAID is promoting alternatives to slash-and-burn agriculture by training farmer-to-farmer extension agents in natural resource management and agricultural development, with an emphasis on the adoption of small-scale, integrated farming systems. It is also continuing to reinforce the pioneering "Green Commune" approach (criteria for certification as a green commune include a record of "zero fires," combined with communal reforestation efforts). Principal contractors and grantees: Conservation International, International Resources Group, Development Alternatives Inc. (prime), World Wide Fund for Nature, Wildlife Conservation Society, GOM/ANGAP (sub),

Increase Private Sector Growth ($600,000 DA). USAID is increasing private sector investment in natural resource management by supporting ecologically and economically sustainable forest and natural product enterprises. It is providing technical or financial assistance to 20 eco-enterprises and small businesses; assisting in the implementation of an ecotourism strategy at the eco-regional level; and supporting the National Office of the Environment to ensure the integration of environmental considerations, including training on the effective use of environmental impact assessments into economic investment decisions. Principal contractors and grantees: Chemonics, International Resources Group, Wildlife Conservation Society (prime).

Support Democratic Local Government and Decentralization ($547,000 DA). USAID's joint environmental and governance activities help selected government units to increase access to information about natural resource management. USAID is working to ensure that rural radio networks in the new eco-regional zones are independent and sustainable. USAID is establishing a Multi-Sector Information Service to link information sources to generate crosscutting data for advocacy and decision making among governmental partners and environmental civil society organizations (CSOs). USAID is also continuing to help key environmental CSOs advocate effectively. Thirty environmental groups are being selected in FY 2005 for grants and training in advocacy, gender, and organizational strengthening. Principal contractors and grantees: Pact (prime), Catholic Relief Service (prime), local civil society organizations (subs), International Resources Group (prime), National Office of the Environment (sub).

FY 2006 Program: Improve Sustainable Management of Natural Resources and Biodiversity Conservation ($6,725,000 DA). Efforts will be pursued to triple protected areas with the formal establishment of an additional one million hectares. New models for protecting critical biodiversity outside of the national park system and that involve local communities and private sector operators will be put into place, and additional funding mechanisms will be explored for protected area management. Support will be reinforced for a revitalized forest authority and management systems. USAID will continue to support communities that reduce destructive farming methods, and will increase the number of communities assisted. Same implementers as above.

Increase Private Sector Growth ($1,200,000 DA). To better conserve biodiversity, USAID will further expand the promotion of business relations between producer associations and eco-enterprises to access domestic and international markets for agricultural/natural products. The partnership agreement between managers of protected areas and private sector operators will be expanded to enhance ecotourism products and services. Forest industry activities will also be increased to promote reforestation and ecological restoration zones. Same implementers as above.

Support Democratic Local Government and Decentralization ($800,000 DA). USAID plans to continue its crosscutting environmental governance program. USAID plans to keep helping the government, CSOs, and the private sector gain access to information to promote better environmental decision making, and bring communication access to towns bordering the country's remaining primary forest. USAID also plans to continue providing assistance to CSOs to improve their ability to serve as environmental advocates. Same implementers as above.

Performance and Results: USAID's environmental activities contributed to a number of important results in FY 2004: 1) The program's focus on integrating multiple land use into conservation planning contributed to the decrease in forest loss in two priority forest corridors. 2) Significant progress was made in fulfilling President Ravalomanana's commitment to triple the protected area network - 6 million hectares were identified and prioritized as critical biodiversity habitats for new conservation sites. 3) With the support of the U.S. Forest Service, a strategic forest zoning framework was developed that delineates conservation and production zones. 4) 68% of targeted farmers (approximately 20,000 farmers) were using at least two of the elements of an integrated "farming systems" approach, with an average increase in income of 31%, to help provide alternatives to slash-and-burn agricultural practices. 5) To promote investment in natural resource management, USAID supported linkages between 20 eco-enterprises and producer associations to improve market access for natural products. 6) The National Office of the Environment, with USAID assistance and advice, reviewed 30 environmental impact assessments submitted by investors from different sectors, including agriculture, mining, and roads.

By the end of the program in 2008, slash and burn agriculture in targeted areas will be reduced, total forest area under conservation in Madagascar will have been increased, and national forest management practices and environmental governance will be improved.

US Financing in Thousands of Dollars

Madagascar

687-006 Biologically Diverse Forest Ecosystems	DA	ESF
Through September 30, 2003		
Obligations	5,996	250
Expenditures	0	0
Unliquidated	5,996	250
Fiscal Year 2004		
Obligations	8,233	0
Expenditures	3,299	9
Through September 30, 2004		
Obligations	14,229	250
Expenditures	3,299	9
Unliquidated	10,930	241
Prior Year Unobligated Funds		
Obligations	0	0
Planned Fiscal Year 2005 NOA		
Obligations	6,847	0
Total Planned Fiscal Year 2005		
Obligations	6,847	0
Proposed Fiscal Year 2006 NOA		
Obligations	8,725	0
Future Obligations	24,867	0
Est. Total Cost	54,668	250

Data Sheet

USAID Mission:	Madagascar
Program Title:	Critical Private Markets Expanded
Pillar:	Economic Growth, Agriculture and Trade
Strategic Objective:	687-007
Status:	Continuing
Planned FY 2005 Obligation:	$677,000 DA
Prior Year Unobligated:	$0
Proposed FY 2006 Obligation:	$1,140,000 DA
Year of Initial Obligation:	2003
Estimated Year of Final Obligation:	2007

Summary: USAID seeks to accelerate economic growth through business and market development. The Economic Growth program emphasizes export market development and is complementary to the USAID Environment and Rural Development Program, which increases the output of environmentally sustainable agricultural and natural resource-based products. The program is building Madagascar's promising product chains and trade capacity, and encouraging investment through strengthening linkages between producers, enterprises, and external markets; increasing access to finance and more productive technology; improving the enabling environment for trade and investment; and promoting public-private partnerships.

Inputs, Outputs, Activities:
FY 2005 Program: Improve Private Sector Growth ($577,000 DA). USAID is promoting the introduction of more productive technology to build the capacity of producers, processors and enterprises to produce and trade value-added agricultural and non-agricultural products. The program is promoting linkages between cooperatives and enterprises to increase their ability to meet market quality and quantity demands. USAID is also providing technical assistance and training to businesses and rural cooperatives to expand the use of best business practices and to reduce production costs. Principal contractors and grantees: Chemonics (prime), International Business Initiatives (sub).

Enhance the Financial Sector's Contribution to Economic Growth ($100,000 DA). USAID is supporting the Malagasy Government's efforts to expand financial services. USAID uses microfinance activities to enhance economic opportunities in targeted sectors, working with credit institutions that offer sustainable access to credit. USAID is reducing obstacles to financing faced by small and medium enterprises, and is working with business associations to increase the number and quality of services they offer to their clients. By expanding their businesses, these entrepreneurs not only increase their productivity, sales, and income, but also build and contribute to Madagascar's growing economy. Same implementers as above.

FY 2006 Program: Improve Private Sector Growth ($700,000 DA). USAID will expand the program to include new products in response to market needs. Training and technical assistance will continue to support private sector expansion, increase its access to improved inputs and new technologies, and build the regional competitiveness of Malagasy products. Same implementers as above.

Enhance the Financial Sector's Contribution to Economic Growth ($200,000 DA). USAID will increase funding access and technical assistance to Malagasy entrepreneurs to increase their ability to buy raw materials, upgrade equipment, invest, formalize, and expand commercial activities. USAID will also promote the issuance and trading of different forms of bonds by increasing the secondary trading of treasury bills. Same implementers as above.

Increase Participation in Global Trade and Investment ($240,000 DA). USAID will continue to address the policy and informational constraints to the expansion of Madagascar's private sector. Targeted interventions will emphasize the sustainable expansion of trade in Madagascar's strategic forest and mineral products. Specific intervention areas include the reduction of legal barriers to the export of key products and services such as spices, "sustainable forest" products, ecotourism, and the establishment of a bio-safety regime. Same implementers as above.

Performance and Results: The Economic Growth Program builds on the success of USAID's biodiversity conservation and private initiative programs.   Program successes in FY 2004 include strengthened linkages between natural products enterprises and rural cooperatives. For example, USAID facilitated the signature of a $40,000 production contract between a farmers' cooperative and the private enterprise Biosave for the sale of ginger. Progress was made in increasing private enterprise efficiency, particularly in the areas of business practices and financial services. Twenty-four enterprises that are involved or are planning to get involved in business activities in various areas such as essential oils, agricultural inputs, rice, horticulture and ecotourism were assisted during FY 2004, exceeding USAID's target of "17 eco-enterprises and businesses to receive technical, financial assistance and/or advice." USAID support for the Eco-enterprise Investment Fund and the Agricultural Commercial Fund resulted in a 29% and 5% expansion of each fund's capital over FY 2003 levels ($31,700 and $35,300 respectively). Each fund provides much-needed access to credit for small and medium enterprises. This program will support businesses and farmer groups and make Madagascar a more competitive environment for trade in agricultural and natural resource-based products. It will increase value-added processing and expand exports, and reinforce efforts to conserve Madagascar's unique biodiversity and to benefit rural areas. Completed training of two senior officials of the Ministry of Energy and Mines with the Gemological Institute of America contributes to improved governance and professionalism in the mining sector.

By the end of the program in 2008, economic growth in targeted areas will have been accelerated through sustainable business and market development, private sector revenues for selected products will have been increased through increased access to local, regional and international markets, and the enabling environment for trade and investment in Madagascar will have been improved.

US Financing in Thousands of Dollars

Madagascar

687-007 Critical Private Markets Expanded	DA	ESF
Through September 30, 2003		
Obligations	1,000	500
Expenditures	0	0
Unliquidated	1,000	500
Fiscal Year 2004		
Obligations	499	0
Expenditures	145	9
Through September 30, 2004		
Obligations	1,499	500
Expenditures	145	9
Unliquidated	1,354	491
Prior Year Unobligated Funds		
Obligations	0	0
Planned Fiscal Year 2005 NOA		
Obligations	677	0
Total Planned Fiscal Year 2005		
Obligations	677	0
Proposed Fiscal Year 2006 NOA		
Obligations	1,140	0
Future Obligations	9,913	0
Est. Total Cost	13,229	500

USAID/Madagascar

Annual Report

FY 2004

June 14, 2004

Please Note:

The attached RESULTS INFORMATION is from the FY 2004 Annual Report and was assembled and analyzed by the country or USAID operating unit identified on the cover page.

The Annual Report is a "pre-decisional" USAID document and does not reflect results stemming from formal USAID review(s) of this document.

Related document information can be obtained from:
USAID Development Experience Clearinghouse
8403 Colesville Road, Suite 210
Silver Spring, MD 20910
Telephone: (301) 562-0641
Fax: (301) 588-7787
Email: docorder@dec.cdie.org
Internet: http://www.dec.org

Portions released on or after July 1, 2004

Madagascar

Performance:

Background: Madagascar's new government, led by President Marc Ravalomanana, is demonstrating the will and commitment to tackle the country's immense development challenges, notably widespread poverty and corruption. Madagascar has an average per capita income of only $260; 70% of its population lives below the poverty line; 48% of children under five years of age malnourished; infant, child and maternal mortality rates are unacceptably high and life expectancy is only 58 years; HIV prevalence is 1.1%; the annual population growth rate is high at 2.8%; and, 46% of the population illiterate. Moreover, the country is emerging from a deep political crisis in 2002, which resulted in a 12% decline in GDP and increased poverty. The country is now stable and economic recovery is underway, with GDP growth in 2003 estimated by the GOM and the World Bank at in excess of 9%. Madagascar is expected to reach the Completion Point under the Highly Indebted Poor Countries Initiative in mid 2004, resulting in extensive cancellation of sovereign debt.

GOM priorities, as articulated in the country's Poverty Reduction Strategy Paper, and demonstrated through recent actions are: 1) good governance; 2) economic growth; 3) social welfare.

- To promote good governance: the GOM has established an Anti-Corruption Commission in the Presidency, which USAID is supporting through the Anti-Corruption Initiative; requires public disclosure of assets by public officials; is introducing reforms in public financial management, including customs procedures; is instituting a program to reduce corruption in the trade of precious and semi-precious stones, with support from the World Bank and the USG; and, has canceled illegal forestry permits and banned exports of endangered species.

- To stimulate economic growth, the GOM: has strengthened its partnership with the private sector; with donor support is investing over $1 billion in transportation infrastructure, especially roads, between 2002 and 2005; has declared a two-year tax holiday on imports of investment and some consumer goods; and is opening up land sales to foreign investors. Recognizing the importance of its unique environment to the long-term health of the Malagasy economy and the welfare of its people, and building upon support of USAID and other donors, the GOM plans to increase land in environmentally important protected areas, from 1.7 million to 6 million hectares over the next five years.

- In the social sectors, the GOM is committed to: preventing the spread of HIV/AIDS; fighting malaria; strengthening health care at the community level using models developed through past USAID programs; and increasing access to and quality of education through its "Education for All" program.

While the new government has considerable public support and momentum for its ambitious programs, it faces a number of risks: that a weak and poorly equipped bureaucracy will be unable to realize many of the planned reforms and results; that the public will grow impatient with the new government under the weigh of grinding poverty; that vested interests will retard the reform agenda; that foreign investment will fail to materialize at the rate necessary to met economic growth objectives; or, that natural disasters -- the country is vulnerable to cyclones -- will undermine the pace of progress. U.S. assistance contributes to mitigating these risks.

U.S. Interests and Goals: The United States and Madagascar enjoy close relations, and Madagascar is an ally in the global fight against terrorism. The top three U.S. foreign policy objectives with respect to Madagascar, as articulated in the Mission Performance Plan are: promotion of democracy; broad-based economic development, including health; and environmental protection. U.S. development assistance is motivated by Madagascar's unique biodiversity, its growing importance as a commercial partner, and its deep poverty, which is exacerbated by natural disasters, food insecurity and weak social services. Complementary interests include the nascent HIV/AIDS epidemic and the country's democratic transition. USAID works closely with the Department of State in Madagascar across all programs. The U.S. Peace Corps (health and environment/rural development), U.S. Geological Survey (environment, rural development), U.S. Forest Service (environment and rural development), U.S. Department of Defense (HIV/AIDS) U.S. Army Corps of Engineers (bridge rehabilitation), and Center for Disease Control (polio, HIV/AIDS, cholera and diarrheal diseases), are all working with USAID in the achievement of U.S. development objectives.

Challenges: Madagascar's acute poverty and endemic corruption pose formidable challenges to the efforts of the new government and donors to transform the county. Human and financial resources, and the institutional capacity to implement programs, especially in the public and NGO sectors, are weak. This constrains the leadership's ability to translate plans into action. Manifestations of this problem include the limited capacity of the majority of the population to influence the decisions that affect them, limited access to and quality of social services, and the poor governance of natural resources. These challenges are compounded in the aftermath of the 2002 political crisis by uncertainty over the likely impacts of policy and leadership changes. Uncertainty and persistent administrative barriers are among the principle factors holding back new private sector investment. USAID's new programs will help to strengthen NGOs and selected government institutions, promote public-private dialogue, support efforts to combat corruption, strengthen access to and quality of health services and products, improve management of natural resources, promote private investment, and help increase rural incomes.

Key Achievements: USAID's long-term investments in Madagascar continued to bear fruit, even as Mission programs entered a transition phase from one strategic plan cycle to another. Overall, USAID Madagascar's Democracy and Growth Special Objective, and its Environment and Health Strategic Objectives demonstrated considerable achievement in FY 2003, generally meeting or exceeding expectations.

1.   Democracy and Economic Growth: The Democracy and Economic Growth SO largely met its targets this year, despite challenging circumstances. Although the economic and political crisis ended in June 2002, its effects were felt well into the fiscal year 2003 reporting period. Ministry reshuffles, changing regulations, jailed political prisoners, and December 2002 legislative elections all contributed to creating an aura of uncertainty and flux around the new government as it moved to consolidate its position. This uncertainty continues to affect development programs, government initiatives, and the business investment climate. Despite this, significant results were achieved. Under the "Madagascar Media and Message" civic education activity, more than 12,000 students, 130 teachers, and 20 trainers from 50 junior high schools benefited from a pilot project. The pilot project used interactive and student-centered teaching to address key public issues at the communal level. It culminated in the organization of three mass civic events focusing on student presentations to key regional government officials on such issues as election fraud, potable water, and sanitation. Through USAID programs to stimulate public participation in government decision-making, issues concerning the management of a lake and inter-communal forest governance were addressed through public dialogue in the province of Fianarantsoa, and a public land use issue was discussed in a public forum in the province of Mahajunga. Coalitions were built to observe municipal and legislative elections, and voter education was reinforced. Civil society organizations and government officials have since established permanent associations in these areas to continue with the information sharing and public dialogue platforms. Five new "Networking Academies" were established as part of continuing Internet-related development in Madagascar that is largely attributable to financial and technical support from the USAID's Leland Initiative through a partnership with Cisco Systems. Madagascar's rank and score on Transparency International's "Corruption Perception Index" improved. Nevertheless, a concerted effort will be required on the part of the GOM to achieve prompt and tangible results under its anti-corruption campaign.

Three significant laws to improve the business environment that were drafted with USAID support were passed by the Parliament in December 2003; they are the Companies, Bankruptcy, and Secured Transactions laws. USAID's trade capacity building activities have increased public and private sector understanding of the World Trade Organization agreements and the African Growth and Opportunities Act, helped to develop GOM negotiating capacity, provided direct assistance to over 40 firms on exporting to the U.S., and provided the catalyst for trade missions to and from the U.S. USAID trade capacity building support is coordinated with that of the World Bank, UNDP and other donors in the context of the Integrated Framework for Trade, under which Madagascar is a pilot country. Many investors remain uncertain about the business climate, however, and further efforts will be needed to reduce administrative barriers in order to promote private sector activity.

2.   Health, Population and Nutrition: A major achievement in FY 2003 was the adoption by the GOM and World Bank of USAID's community-based health service approach for nationwide use in their own programs. Progress on reinstating health cost recovery measures was less satisfactory. Although the GOM instituted a new cost-recovery system following the suspension of the old system in response to the economic hardships caused by the 2002 political crisis, the new system is limited in scope, and constitutes a weak link in efforts to strengthen the health system in Madagascar. USAID will continue to advocate for full implementation and reinforcement of the cost recovery system for basic health services and contraceptives.

Overall, USAID health, population and nutrition programs performed well. Evidence suggests that most targets, under the previous strategic objective "Smaller, Healthier Families, 687-002," were achieved in FY 2003, though national level data are incomplete. The polio campaign saw complete national coverage of children under 5 years; the percentage of children completely immunized rose from 19% in 1999 to 73.7% in 2003; 110,680 Insecticide-Treated Bed Nets were sold; sales of contraceptives rose 15% (oral) and 11% (injectables); and condom sales rose 54% to 10,699,191. Under PL 480, Title II: the Contraceptive Prevalence Rate (CPR) at one site was 24.37%, exceeding the target of 20%; and rice production in another site rose from 1.16 tons/hectare in 2000 to 1.55 tons/hectare. National data for two key program indicators, CPR and immunization rates will not be available until completion of Madagascar's third Demographic and Health Survey in FY 2004. USAID continues to support disaster prevention and mitigation activities in three disaster-prone regions. Title II emergency relief rations were provided to 55,000 beneficiaries, while food from Title II Operational Reserves was provided to an additional 33,000 people.

3.   Environment: The Strategic Objective, "Biologically-Diverse Ecosystems Conserved in Priority Conservation Zones," led to the development of tools and approaches for sustainable management of the environment. A national park system -- which represents 83% of recognized critical habitat types, compared to USAID's target of 100% -- now protects 1,774,575 hectares of natural habitats. This will be increased to 6,000,000 hectares over the next five years. Twenty-nine thousand hectares of natural forest were transferred to 25 community management associations in 2003, and there is an overwhelming demand for more transfer contracts. USAID helped establish farmer associations in 882 villages where about 23,000 farmers have agreed to stop destructive slash and burn farming around critical biodiversity habitats. Tany Meva, a Malagasy environmental foundation established with USAID support, provided $162,000 in small grants to 310 local groups for environmental activities. Biodiversity interventions attracted more than $1.25 million in private investments by environmentally friendly enterprises involved in ecotourism and agro-processing. Finally, 14 projects benefited from formal Environmental Impact Assessments, indicating increased public sector capacity to review proposals and greater private sector commitment to the environment.

Deforestation rates in USAID intervention zones (0.33% and 1.12%) are currently about a third of what they are outside these zones (3.18%). Deforestation rates over the last two years in one USAID intervention zone decreased by 22% while rates in the nearby non-USAID control area increased by 35%. Yet, overall, the rates of forest loss are significantly higher than expected. In addition, although there has been significant progress in promoting collaboration between the mining and forest sectors to allow for a more transparent allocation of forestry and mining permits in environmentally sensitive forest zones, mining exploration inside these forests continues. These are important and immediate challenges for USAID that will be addressed through future activities.

Donor Relations: The new government's commitment, and the trust that it has engendered, is leading the World Bank, European Union (EU), and African Development Bank to experiment with budget support for sector programs. There is also a trend towards more active government participation in donor coordination and information exchange. Madagascar's major donors are the World Bank, EU, United Nations System, France, the United States and Japan. The World Bank has identified governance and institutional development as its central theme. The World Bank, International Monetary Fund, and EU provide budget support linked to improved public financial transparency and accountability. The World Bank, EU and France support reform and strengthening of the judicial system. The World Bank also leads efforts to clean up trade in gems. The United Nations Development Program (UNDP), EU, Japan, Germany, and Switzerland collaborate in electoral observation and support. The World Bank, United Nations specialized agencies, and France are active partners in the health sector, particularly in maternal and child health. The World Bank is becoming the lead donor in fighting HIV/AIDS, while UNFPA is a major partner in family planning, and Japan collaborates with USAID in certain areas, including behavioral change activities. Madagascar receives funding from the Global Fund for AIDS, Tuberculosis and Malaria, and the Global Alliance for Vaccinations and Immunizations. The World Bank, EU, UNDP, France, Germany and Switzerland are, with the United States, active members of a multi-donor group on environment, rural development and food security. The World Bank leads in the education sector. The World Bank and EU lead in transportation infrastructure development, and the World Bank aids privatization efforts. The World Bank and France support the financial system, especially mutual credit institutions. Agricultural development is a priority of the World Bank, EU, France, and International Fund for Agricultural Development. France is an active supporter of urban development projects. Finally, UNDP is a major partner in disaster preparedness, and the World Food Program is the major partner in promoting food security.

Gender: Gender considerations are fully integrated into the new country strategy, and explicit weight is being given to gender considerations in the development of new contracts and awards. Women accounted for 40% of the 1,173 direct beneficiaries of 25 training and related programs under the Democracy and Economic Growth program. More than 6,000 female, junior high school students (50% of participants) benefited from the civic education pilot program in the province of Fianarantsoa. Poverty research continued to provide gender-disaggregated data for use in national program planning. Madagascar has also been selected as a pilot country for USAID's Women's Legal Rights Initiative.

Country Close and Graduation:

NA

Results Framework

687-001   Improved environment for private initiative
   SO Level Indicator(s):
   Issues addressed through an open, informed and participatory process
   Number of clients of Savings Bank of Madagascar
   Number of new firms created each year
   1.1 Improved legal, policy, and financial conditions for trade and investment
   1.2 More informed public participation in economic and legal issues

687-002   Smaller, healthier families
   SO Level Indicator(s):
   Condom sales through social marketing
   Percentage of children 12-23 months receiving three DPT doses before 1 year of age
   Percentage of women age 15-49 currently using modern methods
   2.1 Family level: Increased use of services and healthy behaviors
   2.2 Community level: Increased community participation leading to improved health and food security
   2.3 Health center level: Increased access to quality health services
   2.4 Institutional level: Increased capacity to plan and manage programs
   2.5 Policy level: Improved Policies, Program Advocacy, and Decision-Making

687-003   Biologically diverse ecosystems conserved in priority conservation zones
   SO Level Indicator(s):
   Number of investment projects passed through environmental review
   Number of villages in priority zones participating in community-based conservation
   Percent of natural ecosystems represented in National Park system
   3.1 Improved Management of Critical Biodiversity Habitats
   3.2 Sustainable use of natural resources in broader landscapes
   3.3 Sustainable financing mechanisms mobilized
   3.4 Development and application of environmental policies, legislation and procedures
   3.5 Productive Infrastructure and Systems Rehabilitated

687-004   Governance in Targeted Areas Improved
   SO Level Indicator(s):
   Number of partnerships created between government and civil society
   Percentage of citizens showing confidence in their government
   Transparency International Corruption Perceptions Index
   4.1 Deeper and Stronger Civil Society
   4.2 Information Flow Increased
   4.3 Government Responsiveness Increased

687-005   Use of Selected Health Services and Products Increased and Practices Improved
   SO Level Indicator(s):
   Condom use
   Contraceptive prevalence rates
   Percentage of children 12 - 23 months receiving three DPT doses before 1 year of age
   5.1 Demand for Selected Health Services and Products Increased
   5.2 Availability of Selected Health Services and Products Increased
   5.3 Quality of Selected Health Services Improved
   5.4 Institutional Capacity to Implement and Evaluate Health Programs Improved

687-006   Biologically Diverse Forest Ecosystems Conserved
   SO Level Indicator(s):
   Change in natural forest cover

6.1 Forest Management System Improved
6.2 Biological Integrity of Critical Biodiversity Habitats Maintained
6.3 Alternatives Adopted to Reduce Slash and Burn Agriculture
6.4 Investment Initiatives and Partnerships in Natural Resource Management Increased
6.5 Environmental Governance Improved

687-007   Critical Private Markets Expanded and Strengthened
SO Level Indicator(s):
    Gross domestic product from selected products
    Value of selected goods and services exports
7.1 Agricultural Production and Practices Improved
7.2 Value-added through Agribusiness Increased
7.3 Trade Flows in Selected Commodities Increased
7.4 Selected Policies, Regulations, and Procedures Changed

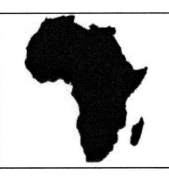

U.S. Agency for International Development
Bureau for Africa

MADAGASCAR

INTEGRATED

STRATEGIC PLAN

FY 2003-2008

November 2002 (Revised)

USAID/Madagascar
Antananarivo, Madagascar

Table of Contents

USAID MADAGASCAR
INTEGRATED STRATEGIC PLAN FY 2003 – 2008
November 2002

PART I   EXECUTIVE SUMMARY

U.S. development assistance to Madagascar supports the policy goals of promoting good governance and market-driven growth as mechanisms that will lead to better management of Madagascar's unique natural resources, an overall reduction in poverty, and a qualitative improvement in the health of the population. A successful program will have numerous ancillary benefits, such as reducing vulnerability to HIV/AIDS, improving the country's ability to manage natural disasters, and enhancing its attractiveness as a commercial partner for the U.S.

Madagascar is one of the world's top three "biodiversity hotspots." Poverty, unproductive agriculture, and weak governance continue to threaten the country's natural resource base and its unique biodiversity. The vast majority of Madagascar's fast-growing population depends on low-productivity, extensive agriculture for its livelihood. Yet this is the main and most severe source of environmental degradation. Deforestation, bush fires, and extensive cropping of marginal lands result in destruction of the ground cover necessary to prevent soil erosion, which in turn contributes to watershed instability, more topsoil loss, and smaller forests.

Madagascar's economy has considerable untapped potential. For example, AGOA-induced investments in Madagascar increased exports to the U.S. by 96.6% in 2000 and 72.3% in 2001. This activity also created over 60,000 jobs—making Madagascar one of the most successful beneficiaries of AGOA. Textiles and clothing accounted for the majority of this export growth.

Almost 70% of Madagascar's people lived in poverty in 2001, making it one of the poorest countries in the world. Poverty is most widespread in rural areas: 75% of the rural population live below the poverty line, compared to 50% in urban areas. Forty-six percent of adults are illiterate. Infant, child, and maternal mortality rates remain very high; life expectancy at birth is only 58 years (see Annex 6). This dire social situation springs mainly from the combination of low economic growth—itself in large part a result of the country's 20 years of failed socialist policy—and an average annual population growth of 2.8%.

Conflict over the disputed December 2001 presidential election, though largely resolved, has had dramatic impacts on Madagascar's economy and on its poor. The economy contracted by an estimated 12% in 2002, and over 100,000 people lost employment in the formal sector. Agricultural production and rural incomes were adversely affected, and health and nutritional status—already low—has deteriorated. The distress of the Malagasy population, combined with a legacy of corruption, presents challenges for the new administration in its efforts to establish good governance and restore economic growth.

Against this backdrop of social change and poverty, USAID/Madagascar sees hope, and sets its plans for the future. There is new opportunity in the political transition, and new prospects for growth and sustainable development. The Mission is nearing the end of its Country Strategic Plan FY 1998 – 2003. Over the course of the last two years much thought and planning has gone into preparing the Mission's new Integrated Strategic Plan for fiscal years 2003 – 2008. The ISP process, which was interrupted by the eight months of instability that flowed from the election crisis, has resulted in a new Mission Goal: "Sustainable and Inclusive Economic Development."

This new goal complements and builds upon the Mission's current goal of reducing poverty, and aligns well with host country priorities, U.S. foreign policy, and USAID Agency goals. This statement underscores the importance of economic and democratic transformation that involves and benefits all segments of society and is sustainable, both environmentally and in its respect for the aspirations of the Malagasy people.

The new ISP proposes the following four strategic objectives (SOs):

- SO 4: "Governance in Targeted Areas Improved"
  (Democracy and Governance, or DG);

- SO 5: "Use of Selected Health Services and Products Increased, and Practices Improved"
  (Health, Population and Nutrition, or HPN);

- SO 6: "Biologically Diverse Forest Ecosystems Conserved"
  (Environment and Rural Development, or Env/RD); and

- SO 7: "Critical Private Markets Expanded"
  (Madagascar Agriculture and Trade, or MAT).

The gist of the **Democracy and Governance** SO is that the weakness of the country's democratic institutions, compounded by a lack of good governance, hampers economic development and reduces any program's chances for success. The DG SO will pursue its goal of improved governance through intermediate results aimed at building a deeper and stronger civil society, increasing information flow, and increasing government responsiveness.

The **Health, Population and Nutrition** SO will emphasize STI/HIV/AIDS prevention and management, public health systems strengthening, and expansion of private sector health services to continue to improve child, maternal, and reproductive health and nutrition. It will do this through the following intermediate results: Demand for Selected Health Services and Products Increased; Availability of Selected Health Services and Products Increased; Quality of Selected Health Services Improved; and Institutional Capacity to Implement and Evaluate Health Programs Improved.

The focus of the **Environment and Rural Development** SO will be on conserving Madagascar's biologically diverse forest ecosystems. According to lessons learned, the most efficient and effective way to do this is through an ecoregional conservation and development approach (see Annex 8). This approach conserves critical biodiversity habitats by linking sustainable management of natural resources with environmentally sensitive development, thus improving people's livelihoods. Five intermediate results are planned: Improve Forest Management System; Maintain Biological Integrity of Critical Biodiversity Habitats; Alternatives Adopted to Reduce Slash and Burn Farming; Increase Investment Initiatives and Partnerships in Natural Resource Management; and Improve Environmental Governance.

The Mission's new program in **Agriculture and Trade** will concentrate on accelerating economic growth through market development and trade. Its intermediate results are: Improved Agricultural Production Practices; Increased Agribusiness Efficiency; Increased Trade Flows in Selected Commodities; and Selected Policy, Regulatory, and Procedural Changes. This SO grows out of and will complement activities to protect critical biodiversity.

In addition, USAID's last 10 years in Madagascar have demonstrated that there are strong cause and effect linkages within and between these strategic objective sectors and a number of vital cross-cutting areas. Under the ISP the Mission intends to continue its innovative cross-sectoral efforts in the areas of food security, HIV/AIDS prevention, good governance, Information and Communications Technology, disaster and conflict vulnerability, gender equity, and public-private alliances. Each Strategic Objective will also incorporate a "crisis modifier," which will facilitate the reorientation of program resources to crisis response in the event of conflict or natural disaster.

Finally, the Mission presents its proposed ISP as a sustainable development, scenario-based strategy. As prescribed in the Parameters Guidance (see Annex 3), the proposed strategy sets forth a range of three different funding and staffing levels, and includes a management structure for each of the three scenarios.

PART II   ASSISTANCE ENVIRONMENT AND RATIONALE FOR STRATEGIC CHOICES

A. Assistance Environment

1. Political Trends

Madagascar is emerging from an eight-month period of political instability. The crisis began following the disputed presidential election in December 2001. It escalated from massive public demonstrations calling for greater transparency in the vote count, to general strikes, economic blockades, and ultimately intimidation and some violence; a breakdown of governmental authority followed. Mediation attempts by the Organization of African Unity and others failed, and the situation became increasingly tense. Roads, ports, and airports were blocked, disrupting transportation and the flow of fuel and basic commodities from the coast to the high plateau. Following the June 2002 recognition of Marc Ravalomanana over Didier Ratsiraka as president, more than 400 people were arrested. Many of these arrests appear arbitrary.

The government of President Ravalomanana is now firmly in control. It enjoys broad support among the Malagasy people, and normal relations with most Western countries. It has stated its commitment to restoring economic growth, improving social services, eradicating corruption, and adopting transparent government systems. As an example: in September 2002 the Council of Ministers adopted a decree requiring high public officials to document their financial status.

To consolidate these democratic gains, the new government must be able to produce results—to demonstrate that "business has changed." Many of the new leaders, however, are inexperienced in national politics. They have inherited a country in severe economic and social crisis, and a government not fully supported by other African states. In addition, many of the democratic weaknesses inherent in the old system of government persist, and contribute to Madagascar's vulnerability to internal conflict (see Annex 10/Post-Crisis Political Issues):

- Rule of Law: The Constitution calls for judicial independence. In reality, judges are subordinated to an administrative hierarchy dominated by the Executive Branch.

- Decentralization: The Constitution calls for autonomous provinces within a unitary state. The old regime attempted to "deconcentrate" power, placing party members in key local positions. It remains unclear how successfully the future decentralization process will devolve decision-making and finances to local authorities.

- Civil Society: While the role of civil society has been increasing during the past decade, it remains mostly limited to urban centers. Its ability to act as an effective advocate or counterweight to governmental power is still weak. Independent sources of information also remain limited outside of Antananarivo.

President Ravalomanana has called for National Assembly elections in mid-December 2002. This will be the first major test of his government's commitment to democracy. In the aftermath of the last presidential election, expectations are high to see a free, fair, and representative legislature seated. It is widely expected that these elections will consolidate President Ravalomanana's popular mandate through 2006.

2. Economic Environment

Madagascar, a low-income country with a GDP per capita of $260, has over the past three decades, seen a decline in real per capita income of almost 50%. According to the National Institute for Statistics (INSTAT), 69.6% of the population lived below the poverty line in 2001 (defined here as consumption of a minimum daily requirement of 2,100 calories)—and this was before the recent months of political turmoil slowed the economy even more. Education and health indicators, including literacy rates and life expectancy, are at or below averages for Sub-Saharan Africa, and access to basic public services is scarce. This is especially true in rural areas, where 85% of Madagascar's poor live.

On the positive side, Madagascar undertook significant reforms to liberalize its economy during the 1990's. As a result, GDP growth between 1996 and 2001 averaged 4.7%. This represented—in light of 2.8% annual population growth—an increase in GDP per capita. Average inflation during the same period was in single-digits at 7.8%. The GOM also made progress in fiscal management (a deficit of nearly 3% in 2001 compared to 5% in 1996). These accomplishments, though, have not yet had a major impact on overall poverty. Recent findings show that while macroeconomic policies have had some effect in reducing urban poverty, they have had little impact in rural areas; economic growth has also benefited richer households more than poorer ones.

- **Agriculture** plays a central role in Madagascar's economy. From 1996-2001, agriculture's share of total output (30% in 2000) declined slightly, but it remains the mainstay of the economy: Agriculture contributes more than 60% of the country's export earnings (see Annex 9).

- **The industrial sector**, accounting for 13% of output in 2000, grew by 7.6% in 2001. This was mostly due to the strong performance of the food, tobacco, and beverage industries and the growth of the free trade zone; the textile industry in the latter was a major source of new employment, growing by 40% in 2001.

- **The service sector**, accounting for 57% of output, increased steadily—4.6% growth in 1997; 6.1% in 2001—and was the economy's major source of growth (service sector expansion was led by the tourism industry, transport services, telecommunications, and construction).

- **The African Growth and Opportunity Act (AGOA)** fueled economic growth in Madagascar and provides real opportunities for further expansion. The degree to which this dynamic will continue depends largely on how competitively the country bounces back from the 2002 crisis, and how successful it is in attracting new (and retaining current) foreign investment.

Estimates for 2002 indicate a contraction of Madagascar's GDP by 11.9%, mostly in the industrial and service sectors. The industrial sector was virtually paralyzed and has declined by nearly 25%, while the service sector contracted by 12.5% (tourism, transport, and construction operated at around 20% of capacity during the crisis). Free trade zone (primarily textile) production also dropped dramatically: an estimated 80% of the 100,000 workers in this sector are out of work or are working reduced hours. The GOM estimates that it will take up to a year to restore export orders and attract new investment in a sector that was, until recently, thriving.

Despite this picture, there is a sense in Madagascar that the country is now more surely placed to pursue a course of equitable growth. In September 2002 the GOM renewed its commitment to poverty reduction under the Highly Indebted Poor Countries (HIPC) Initiative, and plans to finalize its Poverty Reduction Strategy Paper (PRSP) in December 2002. And in November 2002 the GOM/World Bank program was restructured to promote economic recovery, improve social services, and reduce poverty.

3. Environment

The island of Madagascar (about twice the size of Arizona) has been cited as the highest biodiversity priority in Africa—and among the top five globally—by international conservation organizations. Its owes this status to its unique combination of high diversity, endemism, and degree of threat. More than 80% of Madagascar's flora and fauna are found nowhere else in the world. Some taxonomic groups, including reptiles and amphibians, are over 95% endemic. The country's original flora and fauna evolved largely in isolation for 160 million years, proliferating into a wide array of unusual and often unique organisms. All of this combines to make Madagascar especially important to the United States:

- the island is one of the top locations on the planet for adding to the world's knowledge of evolution; and
- it provides a storehouse of plants and animals not yet known to science that could lead to cures for major diseases.

Madagascar's forests are also extremely important to the island itself. They are complex biological systems that provide society with a wide range of essential products (including timber, fuel, food, medicine, and raw materials). Forests provide critical ecological services to the island, such as soil formation and nutrient cycling, pest and pathogen control, pollination, climate regulation, and maintenance and control of water flow and quality.

Unfortunately, Madagascar is also noted for its high degree of environmental degradation (see Annex 8). The area covered with primary natural forest has declined from about 25% in 1950 to less than 15% today. Forest destruction is eliminating viable habitat critical to innumerable plants and animals. Poverty, unproductive agriculture, high population growth, inappropriate national policies, and weak governance also threaten Madagascar's natural resource base in a number of ways. These include encouraging slash and burn agriculture, deforestation, unsustainable forest management, and habitat loss. This, in turn, leads to plant and animal extinction, watershed degradation, erosion, soil fertility loss, vulnerability to conflict and disaster, and a further increase in poverty.

Madagascar is suffering from a severe agrarian crisis as well as an environmental crisis, and the two are inextricably linked. The vast majority (70%) of Madagascar's fast-growing population depends on traditional agriculture for its livelihood—and traditional agriculture is the main and most severe source of environmental degradation. Deforestation, bush fires, and extensive cropping of marginal lands are removing the ground cover that protects the most highly erodible soils. Degradation threatens not only biological diversity and soils but also watershed stability vital to the agrarian economy. In rural Madagascar, poverty continues to threaten the sustainability of the natural resource base. Community members need more options to utilize available natural resources in a sustainable manner. Given the widespread food insecurity at the household level, forest removal is seen as a means of survival. This is particularly true as agricultural productivity stagnates and other natural resources are depleted without long-term attention to their potential economic value as a sustainable resource. As stated in a Malagasy proverb: "Without the forest, there will be no more water; without water, there will be no more rice."

4. Health Sector

Despite improvements in a number of health indices in recent years, Madagascar continues to face serious health sector problems. Taken together, these problems have substantial implications for the country's economic and environmental well being and social stability. The statistics tell a chilling story:

- Infant mortality has improved slightly, but is still at 88/1,000;

- Child mortality remains among the highest in Sub-Saharan Africa (only 44% of children are fully vaccinated);

- Due to a combination of poor feeding practices and repeated episodes of diarrheal disease, respiratory infections, malaria, and other illnesses, the majority of children under five—and 50% of all children—suffer from chronic malnutrition;

- Maternal mortality is still high, with a rate of 4.88/1,000. The contraceptive prevalence rate for women in union is just over 12% nationally;

- Access to potable water has increased since 1993, but 80% of the population still has no such access; and

- While the HIV/AIDS epidemic in Madagascar is in its early stages (estimated HIV prevalence is about 1%), Madagascar has one of the highest rates of classic sexually transmitted infections (STIs) in the world. Of prostitutes in three study sites, 82% had at least one STI; in another study, 21% of pregnant women had active syphilis (see Annex 6).

The public sector and NGOs provide services at approximately 2,800 health facilities nationwide. Quality of services is often below standard, however, and basic medicines and supplies are frequently in poor supply. Approximately 65% of the population are estimated to live within a five-kilometer radius (within a one-hour walking distance) of an MOH facility. Although the number of sites providing family planning services has multiplied several times over since 1992, access to reproductive health services remains unacceptably low. Both public and local NGO capacity to plan and manage effective programs remains weak, particularly with regard to financial and administrative management and use of data for planning. Madagascar has a limited but emergent private health sector; most of these providers are located in urban and peri-urban centers. The nationwide health infrastructure, information and logistics systems, and pre-service training programs are extremely weak.

Public sector spending on the health sector has incrementally increased as a share of GOM expenditures, from 5% in 1988 to 8% in 1994 to 10% in 2000. Now, however, in the aftermath of the recent political crisis, the new GOM faces even more serious challenges to its health sector programs. The health care finance and cost recovery system needs to be reconstructed. The overall logistics system needs to be strengthened. Salama, the central drug procurement agency, needs millions of dollars in recapitalization. The GOM has acknowledged these needs, and has stated that one of its key priorities is sustainability of the public health system. It has, for example, committed HIPC savings to the procurement of essential drugs.

5. Natural Disasters

Madagascar is vulnerable to recurring drought, cyclones, flooding, and plagues of locusts (see Annex 10 and Addendum: Mapping Disaster Vulnerability, Figure 1). For a large percentage of Madagascar's people, the damage caused by these disasters is an ever-present aspect of life; such calamities continuously undermine the nation's capacity to improve the well being of its citizens. To make matters worse, the severity of natural disaster impact and levels of human vulnerability have increased in recent decades. This is mostly due to the continuing environmental degradation of the island: deforestation, eroded soils, and contaminated surface water are among the most pressing problems. The country's physical infrastructure is dilapidated, and rapid population growth exacerbates the impact of each natural disaster that comes along. Chronic poverty and food insecurity, inadequate social services, and the physical isolation of many rural communities increase vulnerability. The severity of logistical and administrative constraints increases short- and long-term impacts and escalates the cost of disaster response: The total cost of reconstruction following a series of particularly devastating cyclones during the year 2000 was estimated at over $128 million.

The National Strategy for Disaster and Risk Management stresses the critical link between emergency and development programs. Together, these help to reduce community and household vulnerability and facilitate post-disaster recovery. The strategy emphasizes prevention, preparedness, and mitigation. Its intent is to reduce the human, economic, and environmental impacts of natural disasters by building on—and strengthening—community coping systems.

B. Strategic Planning Process and Decisions

1. Description of the Strategic Planning Process

USAID/Madagascar started its broad process of consultative planning and analysis before the end of FY2000. Many of the studies and analyses that would eventually feed into the ISP were set into motion then, and a number of brainstorming sessions were held. This led to a Mission-wide Strategic Planning retreat in March 2001. Discussions continued all the while with

Malagasy partners, U.S. Mission Agencies, Washington staff, local cooperating partners, and private sector and international donors.

The Mission used a variety of methods to listen to and engage interested parties during the design of the ISP. These included:

- surveys to decide which development problems should be addressed (ranging from nationwide in scope to a survey of Mission FSN staff);
- committees to help shepherd the planning process (such as the in-house group tasked to ensure that the ISP dealt comprehensively with gender issues);
- workshops to elicit feedback from stakeholders (including several aimed specifically at our local PVO/NGO partners); and
- meetings with key partners (all relevant GOM ministries have been consulted).

Much of the effort expended during this process was aimed at developing linkages that would serve to multiply the effects of the various proposed programs. The next step was submission of the Concept Paper, which was reviewed in Washington in November 2001. Parameters Guidance was received in January 2002 (Annex 3).

The process slowed during the recently ended eight-month political crisis. The U.S. Mission's Ordered Departure in April 2002 depleted the number of USAID/Madagascar staff in-country, and slowed or stopped the operations of many of our local partners. Consultations with USAID/W continued nonetheless and, because of the presence in Washington of a number of Mission staff, even increased. Finally, in September and October 2002, planning parameters were revalidated, and the last of the analyses and assessments were completed. These remaining pieces of the puzzle served to augment the collaborative consulting process, and allowed the Mission to finalize the ISP for November 2002 submission.

2. Priorities of Host Country and Other Donors

Madagascar's new government presented a recovery plan to the international community in July 2002 based on a goal of "rapid and sustainable economic growth." Emergency measures were adopted to: a) support the most vulnerable in society; b) assist private sector firms in restarting production and creating employment; and c) ensure adequate public services. Good governance is at the foundation of new GOM reconstruction and development initiatives. The Government also places heavy emphasis on the improvement of transportation infrastructure as a means to achieving emergency and longer-term objectives.

The new Administration is committed to completing the preparation of a full Poverty Reduction Strategy Paper (PRSP). An Interim PRSP was completed, and Madagascar reached the Highly Indebted Poor Countries Initiative Decision Point in December 2000. The objectives of the PRSP are to accelerate economic growth for the benefit of the poor, and to improve the quality of life. This is to be achieved through three axes:

- Economic opportunity. Improving economic performance with participation of the poor (including an emphasis on rural development and the environment);

- Investing in people. Developing essential public services (including education, health, and potable water); and

- Good Governance. Putting in place an institutional framework favorable to economic growth and poverty reduction, and strengthening capacity for improved governance and relations between the government and the governed.

The United States is among Madagascar's top five donors, together with the World Bank, the European Union, France, and Japan. Donor coordination in Madagascar is highly effective. The World Bank is the largest donor by far, with a pipeline and estimated new resources of $800 million.

Key priorities among other donors:

- **Governance**: The World Bank has identified governance as the central theme of its lending. The World Bank, IMF and the EU are the primary providers of budgetary support, and link this assistance to efforts to improve public financial transparency and accountability. The EU will support also judicial reform, and the World Bank will play a key role in efforts to clean up trade in precious and semi-precious stones. UNDP, EU, Japan, Germany, and Switzerland are partners in electoral support. Switzerland also provides assistance to NGOs.

- **Health, Population and Nutrition**: The World Bank, UN specialized agencies, and France are active partners in the health sector, in such areas as maternal and child health. The World Bank is becoming the lead donor in HIV/AIDS prevention. UNFPA is a major partner in family planning. USAID also collaborates with Japan, especially on behavioral change activities.

- **Environment**: The World Bank, the EU, UNDP, France, Germany, and Switzerland are, with the U.S., active members of the Multi-Donor Group on Environment, Rural Development and Food Security. Each of these entities actively supports the implementation of the GOM's National Environmental Action Plan as a sector program.

- **Economic Growth**: The World Bank is the most active donor in supporting emergency economic recovery efforts. The World Bank and EU are leaders in support for infrastructure, especially roads. The World Bank also supports privatization efforts. The World Bank and France provide support to the financial system, especially in the development of mutual credit institutions. Agricultural development focused on the poor is a priority of the World Bank, as well as the EU, France, and the International Fund for Agricultural Development. The World Bank is also the lead donor in the education sector.

- **Disaster Preparedness and Mitigation**: UNDP is a major partner in disaster preparedness and risk reduction. The EU has led the development of an early warning system for the drought-prone South, and, with the African Development Bank, supports ongoing efforts to contain locust outbreaks and mitigate their impacts. The World Food Program is the major partner in improving food security for vulnerable populations. UNICEF is the key multilateral agency in water and sanitation programs.

3. Relation of Strategy to U.S. Foreign Policy

The proposed program is predicated upon U. S. foreign policy concerns in relation to Madagascar. United States development assistance to Madagascar is motivated by three primary interests: (1) Madagascar's rich natural resources—notably its unique biodiversity, which is of immeasurable global importance; 2) the country's growing importance as a commercial partner, as demonstrated by its exceptional response to the African Growth and Opportunity Act; and 3) the deep poverty of its people, exacerbated by their vulnerability to recurrent natural disasters, continued food insecurity, and lacunae in government management of social sector priorities. Madagascar is also a good partner in the global war on terrorism. Complementary interests include the nascent HIV/AIDS epidemic, which further threatens improved economic well-being, and the evolution of the country's transition to democracy.

The Mission's Integrated Strategic Plan is directly linked to broader U.S. foreign policy objectives. For example, in September 2002, the White House released *The National Security Strategy*; it states that "[u]ltimately the path of political and economic freedom presents the surest route to progress in sub-Saharan Africa . . . ." The strategy discusses the need to strengthen democracy worldwide, and in Africa, along with a U.S. desire to "ignite . . . global economic growth through free markets and free trade." These goals are in complete accord with the Mission's new strategic objectives in democracy and governance and economic growth. Moreover, the State Department's Bureau of African Affairs recently released its *2004 Strategic Plan*. Four of that document's five "overarching goals" dovetail with USAID/Madagascar's four strategic objectives (the fifth Africa Bureau goal deals with terrorism).

U.S. foreign policy with respect to Madagascar is synthesized in the U.S. Mission's FY2004 *Mission Performance Plan*. Broad-based economic development is its top priority. The MPP sees market-oriented economic growth as the best way to reduce poverty and spur investment, and links it to health issues and bio-diversity conservation. This is closely followed by the U.S. Mission's number two priority: promotion of democracy. These synergies with the ISP reflect the close collaboration and planning among agencies at Post.

4. Options Considered and Choices Made

The Mission considered retaining its FY 1998 – 2003 Goal of "Reducing Poverty." While fully consistent with poverty reduction, the new goal ("Sustainable and Inclusive Economic Development") was chosen instead to emphasize the important role that economic growth and development plays in improving the well being of the poor. This choice also responds to the post crisis need to reestablish economic growth.

Madagascar also has a compelling need for increased investment in education (in access to education, and in quality of education) at all levels. However, the Mission has not proposed to mount a major initiative in this sector because: a) the Mission determined that USAID does not have a comparative advantage in this sector, in part due to the language and pedagogical barrier posed by French language instruction; b) other donors, notably the World Bank, are active in this area; and c) program, Operating Expense and staff resources are constrained.

Other configurations of the Madagascar portfolio were presented in the Mission's November 2001 Concept Paper:

- The Mission considered implementing democracy and governance activities as a special objective or integrating them into other strategic objectives. However, according to the Parameters Guidance: "The importance of maintaining a presence in democracy and governance was underscored . . . . It was agreed that Democracy and Governance should be a separate Strategic Objective . . . ."

- Limiting the program to two strategic objectives—in the environmental sector, and in Health/Population/Nutrition—was considered. The Mission felt, however, that this would severely constrain its capacity to effectively address critical governance and economic growth issues. In addition to the foregoing reasons for a DG SO, USAID is unique among donors in Madagascar in its market-oriented vision. Without an Agriculture/Trade SO, the Mission would be much less effective in its efforts to leverage private sector and other donors' resources to help lift the rural economy out of poverty.

- The Mission considered eliminating HPN interventions in favor of a greater emphasis on economic growth. However, health concerns are critical to sustainable economic growth: improved health and nutrition are necessary for productivity increases, and failure to arrest the HIV/AIDS epidemic would have devastating economic impacts. USAID has a comparative advantage in supporting STI/HIV/AIDS prevention, social marketing, drug and contraceptive logistics, child, maternal, and reproductive health, and public-private sector partnerships.

- A combined Health, Population, and Environment SO drawing on the Mission's rich cross-sectoral experience was also considered. However, it was decided that health should not be subordinated to the biodiversity conservation objective.

Based on a thorough discussion of these options, the January 2002 Parameters Guidance (2002 STATE 02926; see Annex 3) gave the Mission the go-ahead to elaborate four strategic objectives: in Democracy/Governance, Health/Population/Nutrition, Environment/Rural Development, and Agriculture/Trade.

PART III   INTRODUCTION TO PROPOSED STRATEGIC PROGRAM

Under its proposed Integrated Strategic Plan, USAID/Madagascar will maintain and sharpen its focus on democracy-building, on improving health services, on conserving biologically diverse ecosystems, and on reducing poverty through economic growth. The Mission believes that its new program best responds to the immense development challenges that Madagascar will face in the coming years.

The ISP is the result of an extensive and integrated collaborative process. It is a program that springs from USG priorities and Agency goals. It builds on lessons learned. And its four sectoral programs are mutually reinforcing, with cross-cutting links connecting each of the strategic objectives and many of the Intermediate and Sub-Intermediate Results.

A. Linkages to Agency Goals and Objectives

USAID/Madagascar's new Goal is "Sustainable and Inclusive Economic Development." This directly supports the achievement of the Agency strategic goal of "[b]road-based economic growth and agricultural development encouraged." Through the individual SOs, the Mission Goal also supports several other specific Agency goals:

- Democracy and Governance. The new DG SO's emphasis on improved governance directly supports the Agency goal: "Democracy and good governance strengthened." Much of this SO's governance work will be in environmentally sensitive areas, which supports the Agency goal of protecting the world's environment for long-term sustainability. The DG SO also has a sub-IR aimed at helping to create a deeper and stronger civil society. This supports the Agency cross-cutting theme of "Civil Society Development."

- Health. The Mission will focus on improving the use of selected health services and increasing the use of selected health-related products, which directly supports the Agency goal of "[w]orld population stabilized and human health protected." Similar to the cross-cutting work planned by the DG SO, many of the health interventions will be in priority conservation areas (thus supporting the Agency's environmental goal).

- Environment. The Environment/Rural Development SO will center its activities around conserving biologically diverse forest ecosystems. This supports the Agency goal of protecting the world's environment. With its sub-IR aimed at improving environmental governance, the Env/RD SO also supports the Agency "good governance" goal. In addition, much of the work being planned by the environment SO is directly tied to protecting human health (as seen by the number of cross-cutting links between this program and the Mission's health activities).

- Agriculture and Trade. The new Agriculture and Trade SO will work to expand critical private markets. This is in direct correlation with the Agency objective of encouraging broad-based economic growth and agricultural development (a relationship further shown by two of this SO's sub-Intermediate Results: "Increased Agribusiness Efficiency" and "Improved Agricultural Production Practices").

B. USAID Past Accomplishments and Relationship to Proposed Program

Limited U.S. foreign assistance to Madagascar predates the establishment of USAID. USAID maintained an office in Antananarivo in the 1960s and early 1970s. After a 12-year absence, presence was reestablished in 1984. At that time, the program focused on food aid and local financing of several small interventions in agriculture. In 1985, the Madagascar Agriculture Rehabilitation Support Program began. This was followed in 1988 by the Madagascar Agricultural Export Liberalization Program.

The Mission Goal of the USAID FY 1993 – 1998 Country Program Strategic Plan was: "Broad-Based, Market-Led, Sustainable Economic Growth." It was comprised of four integrated strategic objectives: 1) Establish Competitive, Pro-Business Climate; 2) High Potential Zone Growth Multiplies National Market Activity; 3) Reduce Natural Resource Depletion in Targeted Areas; and 4) Reduce Total Fertility. It was supplemented with a "Target of Opportunity:" Support Transition to Democracy.

The Mission Goal of the FY 1998 – 2003 Country Strategic Plan is Reduced Poverty. It operates through a Special Objective: Improved Environment for Private Initiative, and two Strategic Objectives: Smaller, Healthier Families; and Biologically Diverse Ecosystems Conserved in Priority Conservation Zones.

Poverty and Economic Growth. USAID has addressed poverty through its environment and rural development activities, its health and family planning initiatives, its P.L. 480, Title II, Food Security interventions, and selected poverty research projects. The environment program addresses poverty through its "landscape approach," which integrates rural development, rural income generation, and protection of critical biodiversity habitats. Work with the National Savings Bank (CEM) has stimulated increased access to savings for families of modest means: 48 percent of the CEM's clients are women. Poverty will continue to be addressed through all SOs in the new ISP.

USAID programs have contributed substantially to the underpinnings of economic growth in Madagascar. In 1996-1997, for example, USAID assistance to the Central Bank was instrumental in putting the country's World Bank and IMF programs back on track. USAID has helped the GOM recognize the legal and administrative constraints to trade and investment, and assisted with the promulgation of more progressive business laws. Mission support for business development services spurred a $13 million Swiss/Malagasy investment in organic fruit, vegetable, and oleoresin manufacturing for export to European markets. USAID pioneered "Ecologic Investment Zones," encouraging tourist investments near major parks and stimulating natural product exporter association development. USAID programs also contributed to the remarkable pre-crisis success of the AGOA initiative in Madagascar. The new Agriculture and Trade SO will continue this work, while concentrating on addressing production and marketing constraints along the entire commodity chains.

Environment. USAID's leadership in the environment sector in Madagascar over the past ten years has concentrated on support of the GOM's 15-year National Environmental Action Plan

(NEAP). The Mission's support to the first and second phases of NEAP focused on developing environmental tools and approaches, including environmentally friendly technologies for rural production and hillside and watershed stabilization. An internationally respected national park system now protects 8% of Madagascar territory (up from 4.7% in 1992), including 15 of 16 critical biodiversity habitats. Economic growth associated with the system—primarily in the areas of ecotourism and natural products—directly benefits the rural poor. The size of the "protected area network" has increased, too: from 1.1 million to 1.7 million hectares since 1991. With USAID support, management of eight classified forests was transferred to local communities. Local communities now manage forest resources in nine classified forests overall (200,000 hectares). Over 16,000 farmers have formed nearly 600 producer organizations committed to abandonment of destructive land use practices in biodiversity-rich unprotected forests. USAID activities are helping to slow the rate of forest loss. The cumulative rate of forest loss in two USAID intervention zones over seven years (from 1993-2000) was 2.2% and 3.8%, respectively; this compares to a 6.7% cumulative loss over the same period in non-intervention zones.

The Mission is currently finishing implementation of its FY 1998 – 2003 Strategic Objective, *Biologically Diverse Ecosystems Conserved in Priority Zones*. This cutting edge, multi-faceted program stresses an ecoregional approach to conserving and managing Madagascar's unique biodiversity while promoting environmentally sensitive economic growth. It is an excellent lead-in to the Mission's proposed new program, which will concentrate on conserving biologically diverse forest ecosystems while working with people closest to the natural resource base.

Democracy. Despite limited funding, the Mission has made meaningful contributions in the democratic arena during the past decade. For example, the Center for Arbitration and Mediation of Madagascar (CAMM), the country's first alternative dispute resolution center, has been established. The capacity of Madagascar's Chamber of Accounts and Inspector General to audit the use of USG grant funds was strengthened. The Mission financed the compilation and codification of eight commercial codes that were distributed to the nation's courts, and to other public and private organizations. These codification efforts led to the production of a full text, word-searchable CD-ROM containing 300 Malagasy legal texts; 1000 copies of this USAID-funded CD-ROM have been distributed throughout the country.

In addition, dialogue between civil society and government has been strengthened. Debate over the issue of corruption has been raised to the national level. USAID assistance has also strengthened national capacity to conduct election monitoring and civic education. Work with the media has led to increased access to information through more and varied reporting on social, economic, and political issues. Through the Education and Democracy for Development and Leland Initiatives, the Internet market is competitive and growing, strengthening information links within the country and between it and the rest of the world. USAID health and environment programs have worked with the DG team, and directly with community, district, and provincial authorities, in support of decentralization and increased advocacy around key social sector issues. Governance and decentralization issues are directly addressed by the proposed new Democracy and Governance SO, and will strongly affect selection of specific strategies and activities across all proposed SOs.

Health. USAID investments in health in Madagascar over the past 10 years have demonstrated impressive gains in child and maternal health. Health interventions emphasized health worker training, community mobilization and health education, and expansion of quality child, maternal, and reproductive health care delivery in the public and private sectors. The program also focused on the areas of food security and disaster mitigation and response.

USAID-funded activities were pivotal, for example, in the successful development of a pioneer program in the Integrated Management of Childhood Illnesses. Contributions to the National Immunization Program resulted in increased vaccination coverage. USAID family planning and STI/HIV/AIDS prevention efforts increased contraceptive prevalence rates and condom sales. Household food security nutrition interventions resulted in increased rice production and increased exclusive breast feeding of infants. These positive results are due to the effectiveness of the Mission's community mobilization approach, its social marketing efforts, and its success in harmonizing health approaches with the Ministries of Health, Interior and Administrative Reform, Primary and Secondary Education, and Population. Investments in primary schools are also paying off, through the child-to-child approach, through adolescent reproductive health, through expansion of health information through mass media, and through increased involvement with the private sector.

Many of the current activities will continue under the ISP's new streamlined health sector program, and, as outlined in Part V, the Mission will seek to take past successes to scale from the commune to the national level. It has become apparent, however, that systemic problems related to health systems management is one of the issues most hampering improved quality of care. The new program will concentrate on this by working to expand private/public sector alliances and strengthening procurement and logistic systems.

HIV/AIDS. USAID has historically been the main donor in Madagascar supporting the fight against HIV/AIDS and STIs. Recently, USAID leadership led to government recognition of the potential seriousness of HIV/AIDS in Madagascar, despite a still-low rate of infection. Ongoing prevention and management activities include social marketing of condoms, targeted behavior change interventions, support for research to improve data for decision-making, high-level advocacy to raise political awareness of STI/HIV/AIDS, and widespread Behavior Change Communication and adolescent reproductive health programs. The Mission has been successful in integrating STI/HIV/AIDS prevention and management across all its SOs.

As elaborated in Annex 6, the national response to HIV/AIDS changed significantly in late 2000 when the GOM evidenced a new commitment by including STI/HIV/AIDS prevention components in its Poverty Reduction Strategy. The GOM also allocated savings realized under the HIPC Debt Initiative to prevention activities, and created a multi-sectoral HIV prevention committee at the Prime Ministerial level. In September 2002, President Ravalomanana elevated national HIV/AIDS coordination to the Chief Executive's Office. The World Bank is initiating a $20 - 30 million HIV/AIDS project, and the National Strategic Plan for HIV/AIDS Prevention is being finalized. The Mission's new ISP builds on its current program, and takes advantage of the increase in GOM momentum by stepping up its public sector activities. At the same time, the ISP reflects the Health SO's greater role in leveraging support for programs sponsored by a range of donors.

Disaster Response. USAID has been one of the leaders, along with the UNDP and PVOs such as CARE, in the development of disaster response capacity in Madagascar. The Mission coordinates with these and other organizations to help the GOM implement its National Strategy for Disaster Risk Management. For example, a well-organized Mission Disaster Management Team is in place to work with government structures and the donor community in the event of a natural disaster. After the year 2000 cyclones, the Mission obtained more than $20 million in International Disaster Assistance funds: $3 million was used immediately for emergency relief and $17 million (from the Southern African Flood Supplemental Appropriation) was integrated into the environment and health portfolios. These supplemental funds were used in the rehabilitation of irrigation, road, rail, port, and agricultural infrastructure. This work was accompanied by the formation of community associations to help ensure the maintenance and sustainability of these investments, which link 100,000 rural families to key markets and help to stem further environmental and watershed damage. Community health facilities were reinforced, and capacity for production and distribution of safe water products was increased. Health education campaigns were conducted, accompanied by research into accelerating the adoption of practices, at the household level, to reduce the risk of diarrheal disease. Interventions were also coordinated with local governments to help develop community disaster preparedness plans.

The Mission has also recently become more involved in prevention and mitigation activities. It is integrating these activities into the ISP by including disaster management components into the community-level planning and governance work to be carried out under each SO.

C. Goal Statement

USAID/Madagascar's proposed new goal of "Sustainable and Inclusive Economic Development" is the result of a long and participatory process (see Part II.B.1). The Mission feels strongly that the end result of that process sums up well what it hopes to accomplish over the next five years: building on the current goal of "Reduced Poverty" by bringing together three descriptive and inter-related themes:

- Sustainability. The concept of sustainability reaches across-the-board to each of the proposed SOs; in its absence, USAID/Madagascar's work will fall short of its goals. The term itself is directly linked to the Mission's flagship environmental program: according to the Agency's own definition, one of the four key principles underlying "sustainable development" is responsible stewardship of the natural resource base. (See Glossary of ADS Terms.) That same definition also speaks to the relationships between sustainable development, good governance, and "improved quality of life"; the latter concept is inherent in every intervention being proposed by the Mission's health SO.

- Inclusion. Inclusiveness implies the active participation of all groups and members of society in the political process; it is not only a vital component of any democratic system but also of the Mission's newly focused democracy and governance program. The importance of inclusivity in the proposed program is reflected by sub-results under all of the DG IRs; two examples are: "Increased Advocacy Capacity of CSOs" (working to bring more informed and representative voices to the governance table), and "Increased Capacity of Independent Media Outlets" (bringing more information to more people).

- Economic Development. Helping Madagascar's economy to grow and develop is key to USAID assistance to the country. It is a USAID overall goal, it is the top priority of the U.S. Mission to Madagascar (as set out in the FY 2004 MPP) and of the GOM, and it remains the most direct way to fight poverty. Helping more Malagasy people increase their incomes, their chances of finding a job, and their agricultural output—while conserving the country's natural resources and increasing participation in the governance process—will result in a better life for all.

D. Cross-Cutting Themes

The Parameters Guidance for preparation of this Integrated Strategic Plan (see Annex 3) "complimented the Mission on the multi-sector and integrated nature of the program and agreed with the Mission that it should continue this approach . . . in order to maximize sustainable development results." The Mission agrees with that guidance, having long felt that Madagascar's developmental needs—and the work USAID is doing to address those needs— lends itself to a strategy with multiple cross-sector linkages.

Madagascar is one of the poorest countries in the world. It problems are interwoven: Poverty encourages production practices that threaten Madagascar's resource base and biodiversity. It perpetuates population pressures and health practices that contribute to ill health, draining family resources and reducing productivity. It encourages political and social behaviors—including gender disparities—that undermine economic development and good governance. Similarly, lack of transparency, responsiveness, and inclusiveness in governance inhibits economic growth and accelerates environmental degradation, as do cyclical natural disasters. Food insecurity is both a cause and a consequence of destruction of the environment, poor health, weak governance, and poverty. The threat of rapid escalation of HIV/AIDS, too, poses a real risk to continued development. And gender inequity directly and indirectly constrains family, community, and national economic growth and well being.

To address these concerns, the Mission held a number of "cross-cutting" meetings early in its ISP process. These meetings were initially designed to allow the various SO teams to familiarize themselves with the earliest drafts of each other's strategic frameworks. Then, as the individual strategies evolved, the teams met to identify potential cross-cutting areas and agree on the meaning of common terms. Finally, the SO teams worked with each other, and with USAID/W, to identify specific cross-cutting linkages and how best to implement them. The latter, in most cases, turned out to be "shared resources supporting shared results."

The primary cross-cutting issues that will be integrated throughout the Mission portfolio are: good governance, Information and Communication Technologies (ICT), food security, HIV/AIDS prevention and management, disaster and conflict vulnerability, gender equity, and public-private alliances.

The Mission sees **good governance** as one of its strongest cross-cutting issues. Its role has come up again and again in discussions with groups in all sectors of Malagasy society and the development community: it is a necessary base to development in Madagascar. The new Democracy and Governance SO has been put together just for this reason. It will provide integral support to the other SO teams in such areas as strengthening sector-specific civil society organizations, increasing the flow of sector-specific information, and increasing government responsiveness across-the-board.

A basic premise of democracy (and good governance) is that citizens have access to diverse and independent information sources. There is, however, a huge lack of information of all kinds in Madagascar, especially at the provincial and most rural levels. The Mission has successfully begun addressing this need by implementing a limited number of **Information and Communication Technology (ICT)** activities under its current strategy. It proposes to expand these activities beyond the urban centers, e.g., by supporting increased access to and use of ICTs. Among other things, this will allow the other SO teams to spread their programmatic messages further and more effectively.

USAID has addressed **food insecurity** through its maternal, child, and reproductive health programs, through strengthening farmer access to local markets, through community participation in both the management of and economic benefits from the natural environment surrounding their communities, and through disaster mitigation activities. P.L. 480, Title II programs include direct food aid distribution and monetization. Title II resources contribute to child survival, family planning, agriculture, and disaster preparedness activities.

USAID will guide its future Title II Food Aid to activities that contribute to the reduction of food insecurity. Title II will continue to support all SOs and to strengthen cross-sectoral linkages. Pre-positioning strategies will be considered in remote regions and those vulnerable to disasters. Crop diversification and agricultural intensification will be encouraged in communities with good market access. Title II Development Activity Proposals (DAPs) for programs beginning in FY 2004 will concentrate efforts toward poor population sub-groups considered most vulnerable for food insecurity: children under age 2, women, communities vulnerable to disasters, and communities close to fragile ecosystems (see Annex 7).

The Mission proposes to include Food for Work and direct food aid distributions in the new Title II programs, oriented toward support to maternal and child health and nutrition, HIV/AIDS, and agriculture activities. The Mission will consider very cautiously the use of monetization to finance the next round of programs, and will discourage proposals that request 100 percent monetization. Priority areas for monetization activities will be disaster preparedness, agricultural production (linked with the environment and agriculture/trade SOs), and activities in support of the health SO, especially in STI/HIV/AIDS and child survival.

HIV/AIDS prevention and management will be directly addressed in the health SO. Examples of HIV/AIDS linkages with other SOs:

Democracy and Governance
- Collaboration in mobilizing civil society to create open discussion of HIV/AIDS issues

(for example, in DG's project to mobilize municipalities);

- Collaboration in NGO capacity-building by working with DG's existing partners such as the Malagasy Council of NGO's for Development and the Environment (COMODE);
- Building political commitment in the GOM for HIV/AIDS prevention; and
- Working with the Federation of Women in Business and other leading women's associations to address gender issues in STI/HIV/AIDS.

<u>Environment/Rural Development and Agriculture/Trade</u>
- Expanding HIV prevention and treatment programs to all partners in the Health, Population and Environment initiative known as Voahary Salama;
- Maximizing HIV/AIDS education through farmer-to-farmer associations and environmental groups; and
- Including HIV/AIDS questions in baseline studies or environmental impact assessments.

To better ensure the sustainability of its development investments, and to mitigate the potential impact of natural disasters on economic growth and the fight against poverty, the Mission proposes to integrate **disaster and conflict vulnerability** into the community-level planning and governance work to be carried out under each SO. Title II resources will augment this cross-cutting approach by continuing to support the natural disaster-related activities of U.S. PVOs, which in turn support local NGOs, businesses, and communities.

In addition, a recently conducted internal Mission analysis identified five sources of instability as most likely to cause conflict and crisis in the country over the coming years: natural resource degradation, HIV/AIDS, land tenure issues, post-crisis political issues, and corruption. (See Annex 10.) The analysis concluded that the most obvious root cause of these conflict-related disasters is bad governance. Its recommendations to address these problems are being incorporated into each SO's individual strategy.

Given that crises due to natural disaster or, less probably, conflict are likely to occur during the life of this strategy, each SO has an associated "crisis modifier." With the concurrence of the Africa Bureau and Government of Madagascar, and subject to account and earmark restrictions, program resources may be reoriented to respond to crises. However, funds will be used for development assistance programs and not for Disaster Assistance. Based on past experience, such as cyclone response in 2000 and the political crisis in 2002, interventions will be fully integrated into on-going programs. This will maintain continuity in program management and obviates the need for presenting crisis-based scenarios in the ISP.

USAID/Madagascar has paid special attention to **gender equity** concerns in its new strategy, and has worked to apply gender analysis to all sectors and all illustrative activities. As part of this analysis, the Mission has attempted to ascertain how gender relations will affect the achievement of sustainable results under the ISP. In turn, it has looked at how those results might affect the relative status of women. To help do this, gender-disaggregated indicators will be used whenever possible.

The Mission actively participates in the UN-supported Gender Thematic Working Group, and the Malagasy Gender Network. The Mission's approach to gender integration is also informed by the *Beijing Declaration and Platform for Action*, by the Agency *Gender Plan of Action*, and by a WIDTECH - Women in Development strategy outline for mainstreaming gender that was prepared for the Mission in March 2001. The Mission also intends to incorporate the Ministry of Population, Women's and Children's Affairs' evolving national and regional action plans into activity planning.

Public-private alliances will continue to be an important modality for implementing the Mission's strategic objectives. Recent experiences with Phelps-Dodge and QMM-Qit Fer (Rio Tinto Mining) demonstrate that private sector entities have a clear interest in partnerships with USAID to help address those environmental and rural development challenges that accompany their private investments. The partnership between a USAID grantee and local industry for the production of a safe water product may spawn similar initiatives (for instance, the local production of pesticide-treated bed nets). Private foundations and institutions such as universities, zoos, and museums are likely partners for future alliances, especially in the environmental and health sectors. USAID/Madagascar already has successful partnerships with, for example: the Packard Foundation in support of integrated health, population, and environment activities; CISCO Systems for computer systems training; and the Global Alliance for Vaccines and Immunization.

PART IV STRATEGIC OBJECTIVE #4 – GOVERNANCE IN TARGETED AREAS IMPROVED

A. Problem Identification and Past Achievements

While Madagascar has many of the trappings of a modern democracy, its institutions are weak and continue to derive their authority from a dominant central government. Under the regime of Didier Ratsiraka, decisions were made by an elite group at the highest political levels, judicial systems were best avoided by all but the rich, and a lack of accountability and sanctions resulted in a culture of corruption. Civil society remains weak and unorganized, unable to act as an effective counterweight to government excesses. As a result, the notion of "government for the people" has little resonance in this country. According to USAID's Democracy and Governance Assessment, which was conducted in August 2001:

> *The team's overriding conclusion is that the disconnect between the ruling elite and the masses is so great, government corruption is so pervasive, and USAID resources are so limited, that in order to protect its investment in technical sectors (HPN, EG, AGR, ENV, Title II, disaster), as part of development of the new Integrated Strategic Plan, the Mission should carefully consider an increase in its focus on democracy and good governance in order that its results in <u>all sectors</u> are sustained over time.*

The weakness of the country's democratic institutions, compounded by a lack of good governance, is having a direct impact on USAID's ability to effectively implement its programs. This lack of good governance is at the root of poverty and conflict vulnerability in Madagascar.

Efforts to address these ills within the FY 1998 – 2003 Democracy and Economic Growth Special Program Objective (SPO) have focused on improving the environment for private investment. This approach—with the ultimate goal of reducing poverty—worked in two ways. First, SPO worked closely with the GOM to improve the legal, financial, and policy framework for trade and investment.

The other half of the program concentrated on strengthening civil society to ensure that dialogue between citizens and government was increased, leading to greater public participation in the decision-making process. From national elections to the country's Poverty Reduction Strategic Plan, Malagasy were mobilized to give greater voice to their concerns and demands. The Mission has also been a strong supporter of the Leland Initiative, helping to expand the use of the Internet within Madagascar from zero Internet accounts in 1994 to approximately 12,000 Internet accounts (each account has multiple users) by 2002.

While much work has already been done in the areas of civil society and access to information, work on good governance has been more limited within SPO. With a few exceptions—such as the USAID-funded local chapter of Transparency International—civil society's ability to demand transparency and accountability from decision-makers remains very limited. This lack of expertise, coupled with the former government's near dictatorial hold on power for so many years, has, in the past, made for slow progress in the area of good governance.

With the recent installation of a new government, however, there are new opportunities for USAID to work with an administration that has publicly committed itself to instilling better governance. In agreement with the recommendations of the Democracy and Governance Strategic Assessment, USAID has determined that targeted investments over the next five years should lend integral support to the Mission's other SOs in the key areas of civil society strengthening, dissemination of information, and working with local government in priority zones.

B. Strategic Objective and Intermediate Results

"Governance in Targeted Areas Improved" (targeted areas due to limited funding) is the new democracy and governance strategic objective for FY 2003 – 2008.

A strong democracy requires open and accessible flows of information, citizen participation in the policymaking process, and a government that acts in an accountable and transparent manner. These attributes of democracy together can help ensure that government policy reflects the will of the people. This in turn contributes to fairer uses of public resources—for example, improved health care, greater education opportunities, access to land, and more effective management of natural resources—to better meet the needs and concerns of local communities. Limited funding for this SO requires that its interventions be targeted.

While this SO will promote good governance explicitly and directly, activities undertaken in the environment, agriculture/trade, and health sectors will serve also as effective vehicles for advancing good governance. Benefits produced by these SOs provide compelling reasons for individuals and groups to come together, discuss roles and responsibilities, and advocate for progressive change. For example, forming democratically run producer associations that allow small-holders to benefit from trade and forest management provides a foundation upon which to promote and improve governance practices. Health groups that move beyond health issues to influence other areas of economic and social life are also powerful vehicles for change, and can foster democratic values and good governance principles at the grassroots.

To integrate and target these activities, common democracy results indicators have been incorporated across all SOs, and priority zones for implementation have been identified (see Annex 11). A portion of funding from each strategic objective will be channeled toward good governance activities, and results achieved under this SO will be shared across the Mission portfolio. Further, while a number of elements under this SO will focus at the national level, field-based work with local CSOs, government, and information systems will be concentrated in the Mission's priority provinces of Fianarantsoa and Tamatave, as well as the Fort Dauphin / Anosy region. Where appropriate and complementary, SO activities may be implemented in geographical areas where the Mission's Title II program is working.

Illustrative Indicators for SO 4:
- Increase in percentage of citizens showing confidence in their government;

- Increase in number of partnerships created between government and civil society; and
- Progress in corruption as shown by Transparency International's Corruption Perception Index (proxy measure).

IR 1: Deeper and Stronger Civil Society

In Madagascar, although civil society remains weak and dominated by the urban elite, progress has been made in fostering a more vibrant sector during the last decade. At the local level, the growth of microfinance institutions, farmer associations, environmental coalitions, and other issue-based groups are encouraging signs for the future. In step with recommendations from the Conflict Prevention and Vulnerability Assessment, USAID will continue to deepen and strengthen the level of civil society in the country, especially in regard to its ability to act as an effective advocate for good governance, including increased public sector transparency and accountability.

Deepening civil society means moving beyond the capital-based clients to the provincial, regional, and rural levels. Current estimates place 60% to 70% of all NGOs in the provincial capital of Antananarivo. This IR will work to move beyond this single set of actors and increase rural-urban, inter-provincial, and sectoral networking. For example, deforestation is not simply the work of one national "environmental" CSO. An effective advocacy effort should include vertical and horizontal linkages among agricultural associations (due to deforestation's negative effects on farmland productivity and watersheds), health groups (as the health of the community is so directly linked to the land's productivity), information centers (as they can provide the data and information needed to change public and government opinion), and democracy groups (to ensure people know their rights and can take legal action if needed). At the same time, the new Democracy and Governance SO will foster the inclusion of youth, women, and the disenfranchised in all its activities.

In addition, this IR will strengthen civil society capacity. This will include fostering organizations that are democratically managed, are able to transparently handle outside funding from donors or private groups, and are working toward greater sustainability.

Civil society strengthening also entails increasing its role as a watchdog and advocate for good governance. While civil society has expanded during the past 10 years, its ability to advocate remains at a rudimentary level: when compared to other African countries, most civil society groups in Madagascar are "behind the curve" in this area. They are unfamiliar with the concept of advocacy, and lack the tools and training to undertake a cohesive effort. (Some of civil society's major accomplishments, such as input into the PRSP process and drafting of an NGO law, have not been followed up by the kinds of advocacy efforts needed to finish the job. For example, the NGO law, while drafted, has never been enacted into law.)

Links to other SOs: This SO will strengthen advocacy skills among NGO partners in the sectors of environment, health, and agriculture/trade. The goal of this strengthening will be to give NGOs a better understanding of advocacy, the training needed to coalesce around a chosen issue, and moving that issue forward.

Illustrative Activities for IR 1:

- Provide training and support to strengthen the capacity of CSOs to advocate effectively at the national and local levels. National level activities will target organizations advocating for a variety of reforms, including increased public sector transparency and anti-corruption. Local level activities will focus on building skills among CSOs that advocate for issues using a community mobilization approach to improving healthcare and sustainably managing natural resources in Fianarantsoa and Tamatave provinces, and the region of Fort Dauphin / Anosy;
- Work with national federations and associations to increase the capacity of their provincial-based, rural partners; and
- Provide training and mentoring on financial, management, and organizational reforms necessary to create more representative, participatory, and financially sustainable civil society organizations.

Illustrative Indicators for IR 1:

- Increase in number of times CSO coalitions appeal to the Government of Madagascar; and
- Increase in number of targeted organizations showing improvement on an NGO index scale (which would measure factors affecting capacity-building and sustainability of NGOs).

IR 2: Information Flow Increased

Since the end of press censorship in 1990, Madagascar has seen a continual decline in the state's monopoly over radio and television. During the last decade the country's independent media has become one of the major institutions promoting democratic development and good governance practices. More than 100 small, private radio stations have sprung up almost overnight in the provinces. Although most of them are subsidized by local patrons, they are offering an alternative to the state-dominated coverage. There have also been efforts to organize and professionalize journalists, although most of the training has been limited to Antananarivo.

Despite these efforts there remains a gaping lack of information at the provincial and rural levels. Only state television and radio have "national coverage" (which the Ministry of Communication admits covers but two-thirds of the country). And those programs that are broadcast, at the Ministry's own admission, often have little relevance to the daily lives of rural farmers. A more liberal communications bill, first drafted in 2000, remains to be passed into law.

In order to formulate interests and participate in policy debates, the Mission will work through this SO to help ensure citizen access to diverse and independent information sources. These include the electronic and print media, newsletters or bulletins published by civil society organizations, and a multi-sector information service center. Access to other independent instruments, such as the Internet and e-mail, will also be a catalyst for further information sharing and consensus building.

The DG SO will also work to help information find its way to local leaders. Elected mayors, isolated from information sources and by geography, often do not know their roles and responsibilities, or what the most recent laws are, or even what neighboring communes are doing. Communication links—whether with civil society or other government entities—stop short of their door.

Links to other SOs: This IR will continue to build on work undertaken through Leland Initiative and the Education for Democracy and Development Initiative (EDDI) to increase information flow by establishing a more open framework and increasing the capacity of independent media. This includes not only expanding the Internet, but also moving information, communication, and technology methods out beyond the capital to selected provinces. This improved infrastructure will allow the other SOs to increase the use of ICTs, spread their messages more efficiently, and reach deeper into rural areas at lower cost.

Illustrative Activities for IR 2:
* Provide technical assistance to the government to improve its regulatory framework for ICTs (see Annex 2);
* Increase the reach of ICTs into rural areas for citizens, civil society, and government; and
* Provide financial, organizational, management, and journalism training to increase the sustainability of independent print and broadcast media outlets in targeted areas.

Illustrative Indicators for IR 2:
* Increase in percentage of population using internet; and
* Increase in percentage of country covered by independent media sources.

IR 3: Government Responsiveness to Citizens' Demands Increased

Transparency and accountability have been lacking in the GOM. Normal checks and balances seen in other countries are, for the most part, nonexistent. The historically strong role of the state, plus the executive branch's domination of government, has created a near monopoly on power that threatens economic growth and social stability (see Annex 10). Laws tend to be enforced selectively: sometimes as a result of lack of institutional capacity, sometimes by design. Low levels of transparency and responsiveness contribute to the discretionary power of public officials, and to a lack of accountability. Basic information is often unavailable to citizens, further impeding their ability to check abuses of power.

The new government offers an opportunity for change. President Ravalomanana has identified good governance as one of his new "pillars," and has taken steps to address corruption. Work through this IR will seize opportunities that now exist to work directly with selected government units on governance reforms, including improved environmental governance and stakeholder dialogue.

Links to other SOs: USAID/Madagascar as a whole will work to support champions of good governance. Building the capacity of reformist mayors and councils in USAID's "priority areas" will be undertaken in conjunction with other SOs, and will include facilitating dialogue to ensure that community priorities for key forest ecosystems, health services, and trade and agriculture reforms are heard, understood, and integrated into local, regional, and national-level planning and decision making. Within the DG arena, providing innovative, information-based systems that improve government services is one specific area that will be addressed. The rising field of electronic-government (e-government)—which results in a more transparent and accountable way of doing business—will also be linked to other SO issues and could be supported in pilot areas.

Illustrative Activities for IR 3:
- Support pilot e-government programs that increase transparency and accountability of local government;
- Increase local government partners' access to information; and
- Support mechanisms (town hall meetings, public hearings, etc.) that increase communication linkages between civil society and government "reformers."

Illustrative Indicators for IR 3:
- Increase in number of government units that solicit citizen input; and
- Increase in number of CSO issues responded to by the government.

C. Critical Assumptions

- *A stable government will remain in place during the next six years.*
- *The GOM will continue to demonstrate greater commitment to democratic principles.*
- *Sustainable economic recovery will continue during the next six years.*
- *Funding will not drop below the low-level funding scenario (see sub-section F. below).*
- *The DG SO will be supported with cross-sectoral funding.*
- *Other donors will continue to support their current DG- and education- focused activities.*

D. Integration and Cross-cutting Issues

Crisis Modifier: Resources under this SO may be redirected to reconciliation or to organizational strengthening and advocacy in the event of a political or natural disaster. Where appropriate, the DG SO could also use Economic Support Funds, Conflict funds, or International Development Assistance.

Other SO Teams: Success in the other core areas of USAID's development agenda (agriculture and trade, population, health and nutrition, the environment, disaster prevention) is inextricably linked to democratization and good governance. As outlined in sub-section B. above, this SO has been formulated to lend support to the Mission's other SOs in the key areas of civil society strengthening, dissemination of information, and working with local leaders in priority zones. This ongoing endeavor to ensure better governance is really the basis on which the other SO activities are being built. As noted in the individual SO frameworks, the SOs will be sharing common IRs, as well as resources, to avoid "stove-piping" and to ensure greater collaboration.

Gender: During the development of the ISP, the DG team first engaged in a general discussion of gender, followed by several exercises to help reinforce the definition of gender. Once there was understanding and agreement on the term, the implications of a "gender approach" were discussed for each IR and possible set of activities. Special importance was paid to the growing "digital divide" in Madagascar, as well as to the lack of local women leaders. Future activities will strengthen women-oriented rural groups and civil society organizations at the national level;

will work with and train women local leaders; and will help ensure that more women benefit from ICT (e.g., that more women are trained in new technologies).

Other U.S. Agencies: The second performance goal of the Embassy's FY 2004 MPP is: "The development of democratically accountable government institutions in Madagascar that follow the rule of law." This SO, through its work on good governance, will directly support this. Close collaboration will continue with the Embassy's Political and Public Affairs sections. Personnel from the Office of Democracy and Governance, the Office of Sustainable Development (AFR/SD), and the Leland Program will be utilized for technical field support throughout the life of this program.

E. Local Partners

Government: Past programs in SPO have seen coordination between a number of different ministries, including Justice, Communications, Industry, and Commerce. As the trade and economic growth activities evolve into a new SO, more effort will shift to the ministries responsible for the communication and decentralization sectors. Exploratory meetings have been held with all relevant ministries to discuss the new DG strategy, and government officials have expressed a readiness to collaborate.

Other Donors: Meetings have also been held with other bilateral and multilateral donors working in the DG sector to ensure coordination, and the Mission has encouraged the establishment of a DG working group. As major providers of budgetary support, the World Bank and EU are engaged in programs to improve accountability and transparency in public finance. The Ravalomanana government is in the process of consolidating its mandate, with legislative elections scheduled for December 2002. A number of other processes are still to take place, including new provincial gubernatorial elections, decentralization, and the resumption and finalization of the Poverty Reduction Strategic Plan. Donors are moving forward cautiously in this still-changing environment, and USAID personnel will continue to coordinate as the programs of its donor partners are finalized.

Local Organizations: The new DG SO will continue to support local organizations working towards good governance, including the local chapter of Transparency International, and expand efforts to identify new partners, both within the DG arena and other sectors. As detailed above, the move to strengthen advocacy efforts in local NGOs is in its infancy. The Mission will be looking to expand its base of collaboration, both at the national level and in targeted priority areas.

F. Alternative Approaches

This SO was developed after lengthy consultations with donor, government, and local partners. The cornerstone of the research used was the DG assessment conducted in July 2001. While the political situation has changed since the assessment was completed, many of the underlying truths for the country—a weak legal system, weak ICT sector, high levels of corruption—still remain despite the change in leadership.

This SO will continue to build on work accomplished to date through, e.g., civil society, the Leland Initiative, and EDDI. Responding to the DG assessment's recommendations, a more explicit emphasis, however, will be placed on promoting good governance. Work in the area of legal reform was not considered because of the limited budget available to this SO, and due to work already planned by the EU in this arena.

The mid-level funding scenario is needed to implement the DG activities as outlined above at the national and local levels. At this funding level, additional resources will be forthcoming also from other SO teams to address such cross-cutting issues as strengthening the ICT, civil society development, and the incorporation of grassroots environmental, health, and economic growth concerns into regional development and governance agendas. These funds are crucial for the full implementation of the DG program.

Under the high-level scenario, greater results would be achieved. First, the DG SO would expand the number of issue-areas pursued by civil society, and increase the number of targeted government units receiving information and technical assistance. These programmatic changes would be determined in consultation with the other SO teams. Second, this level of funding would allow the DG SO to pursue anti-corruption efforts more aggressively. Third, the high-level scenario would allow USAID to play a role in Madagascar's decentralization effort. Within the time frame of this strategy, it is certain that the decentralization process will take place. Because the Mission's environment, health, and agriculture programs work at the most basic rural level, it is crucial that the current "deconcentration" efforts be turned into true decentralization. The outcome of this process will have a profound impact on the Mission's portfolio. The DG SO should be in a position to commit resources and technical assistance to help ensure a positive outcome for all programs.

Under the low-level scenario, activities would be severely constrained. This would be due not only to the drop in funds directly available to the SO, but also (because the new DG program has been designed with close linkages to the other Mission SOs) to the decreased share of funding that the other SOs would be able to contribute to DG activities. Low levels of funding would result in fewer CSO and government partners, would hamper the Mission's ability to support meaningful change in the ICT sector, and would substantially curtail DG activities in the Fort Dauphin / Anosy region.

G. Measuring Results

In light of the intertwined nature of the new ISP, monitoring and measurement of common IRs and pooled resources are being refined among the different teams. Also—as in the past—the DG SO will continue to work with its implementing partners to design a usable and affordable system of monitoring results. Efforts will also be made to include Madagascar on the Afrobarometer survey in the future (the Afrobarometer is an international collaborative enterprise of the Institute for Democracy in South Africa, the Center for Democracy and Development-Ghana, and Michigan State University).

USAID/Madagascar Democracy and Governance (DG) Results Framework

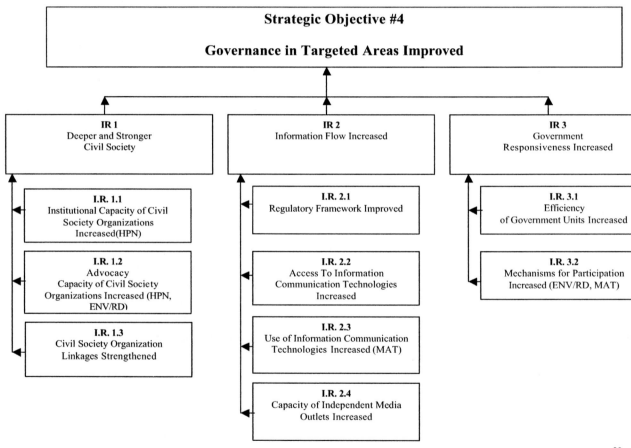

Strategic Objective #4

Governance in Targeted Areas Improved

IR 1
Deeper and Stronger
Civil Society

IR 2
Information Flow Increased

IR 3
Government
Responsiveness Increased

I.R. 1.1
Institutional Capacity of Civil
Society Organizations
Increased(HPN)

I.R. 1.2
Advocacy
Capacity of Civil Society
Organizations Increased (HPN,
ENV/RD)

I.R. 1.3
Civil Society Organization
Linkages Strengthened

I.R. 2.1
Regulatory Framework Improved

I.R. 2.2
Access To Information
Communication Technologies
Increased

I.R. 2.3
Use of Information Communication
Technologies Increased (MAT)

I.R. 2.4
Capacity of Independent Media
Outlets Increased

I.R. 3.1
Efficiency
of Government Units Increased

I.R. 3.2
Mechanisms for Participation
Increased (ENV/RD, MAT)

30

PART V   STRATEGIC OBJECTIVE #5 –
USE OF SELECTED HEALTH SERVICES AND PRODUCTS INCREASED AND PRACTICES IMPROVED

A. Problem Identification and Past Achievements

As described more fully in Part II.A., and despite some real advances in health sector indicators, the Madagascar health care system remains one of the weakest in the world – in a recent WHO report, it ranked 159th out of 191 countries.

USAID leadership in child, maternal, and reproductive health has been key to strengthening Madagascar's capacity to address priority health issues. USAID has contributed to a major turnaround in the National Immunization Program: the percentage of children receiving Diptheria, Pertussis and Tetanus (DPT3) immunizations increased from 48% in 1997 to 55% in 2000 (in USAID focus areas, 2001 data show DPT3 rates at 94%). Overall, 87% of infants are completely vaccinated in USAID sites, compared to 44% nationwide. Exclusive breast- feeding of infants increased from 46% to 83% in target groups. And in USAID target areas, 76% of children 12-23 months of age received Vitamin A supplements, compared to 50% nationally.

USAID family planning services and HIV/AIDS prevention efforts have continued to meet performance targets as well. Condom sales through social marketing increased from 1.1 million in 1996 to over 6 million in 2001. The contraceptive prevalence rate (CPR) increased from 5% in 1992 to 12% in 2000. In USAID focus areas, 2001 data show a range of CPR from 15-23%. And the number of sites where couples have access to reproductive health and family planning services grew nationally from approximately 150 in 1992 to 1,145 in 2000.

With funding from the Southern Africa Flood Supplemental Appropriation, the production capacity and sale of a new safe water product increased to 250,000 bottles per month in 13,600 retail outlets, providing clean water for approximately 2,550,000 people every month. USAID support in developing a health information system and for various studies and surveys, including the national Demographic and Health Survey, has also greatly increased availability of reliable data for decision-making.

B. Strategic Objective and Intermediate Results

"Use of Selected Health Services and Products Increased and Practices Improved" is the new health sector strategic objective for FY 2003 - 2008.

The next five years: The Mission proposes a streamlined HPN program; key program areas are:

- increasing the demand for and quality of selected child, maternal, and reproductive health services and products;
- improving availability of priority products and services through expanding private/public sector alliances and strengthening procurement and logistics systems;
- STI/HIV/AIDS and malaria prevention and management; and
- improving nutrition practices and household food security.

The new program reflects an expansion of private sector participation and social marketing, greater emphasis on participant training and U.S./Malagasy partnerships, and greater collaboration with civil society organizations. It will also reinforce the Mission's environmental objective of protecting biologically diverse ecosystems, as well as support the GOM as it prepares for and attempts to mitigate natural disasters.

The new program reflects current needs in the health sector in Madagascar. It considers USAID's comparative advantage and budget levels and, based on 10 years of experience, proposes logical next steps. The focus is on people-level impact in terms of "use of services" and "behavior change" at two levels. At the national level, the program will reach the entire Malagasy population through policy dialogue, institutional capacity development, social marketing, and media activities. At the commune level, intensive and fully integrated SO activities will improve the supply of and demand for quality health services and products among approximately 8 million people (half of Madagascar's total population). The program will identify successful interventions at the commune level and institutionalize them at the national level, including the "champion community" approach, child-to-child program, and behavior change activities designed to empower women and families as pro-active stakeholders and managers of their own healthcare needs.

Support is still needed to strengthen the public sector health system, particularly logistics management of essential drugs, contraceptives, and the vaccine cold chain. The program will contribute to improving key indicators such as immunization rates, contraceptive use, exclusive breastfeeding, bed net use, condom use, treatment of STIs, and use of selected services. The Intermediate Results should lead to improvements in health status and decreases in fertility.

Illustrative Indicators for SO 5:
- Increase in Contraceptive Prevalence Rates;
- Increase in DPT3 coverage;
- Increase in exclusive breastfeeding;
- Increase in Vitamin A supplementation in women and children;
- Increase in condom use;
- Improvement in appropriate STI treatment; and
- Increase in use of treated mosquito bednets.

IR 1: Demand for Selected Health Services and Products Increased

An increase in demand for health services and products requires knowledge of healthy behaviors, positive attitudes toward modern health care, and a desire to seek and use health services and products. Based on recent community work in the area of behavior change communication in Madagascar, it is clear that knowledge of healthy behaviors alone is not enough to create demand. Communities that have motivated change in personal and community norms and attitudes have been the most successful in improving key health indicators. Community leaders who also work closely with the public health system have challenged the system to improve services. Private social marketing programs and NGOs reinforce messages, motivation, and access to health services and products. The health sector needs to work more with such "non-traditional" health groups to expand knowledge and promote positive attitude for change.

Illustrative Activities for IR 1:

- Mobilize communities through the "champion community" approach to supporting selected health services, products, and environmental initiatives;
- Child-to-child school health education programs;
- Social marketing of services and products;
- Behavior change and communication campaigns using mass media, cinemobile, and other channels for targeted messages; and
- Health education in agricultural and environmental organizations.

Illustrative Indicators for IR 1:

- Increase in percentage of target population that know about the transmission, prevention, and treatment of malaria, STIs, HIV/AIDS, vaccine preventable diseases, and diarrhea; and
- Increase in percentage of communities meeting "champion" criteria for health and environment.

IR 2: Availability of Selected Health Services and Products Increased

As demand is increased, services and products (such as contraceptives, condoms, vaccines, essential drugs, bednets, safe water, and nutrient dense foods) must be made more available. It is frequently systemic problems related to health systems management, rather than health worker or client knowledge, which hamper improved quality of care. One of the principal systemic constraints is the inability to make available timely and adequate stocks of essential drugs and other commodities at the health services delivery level.

Illustrative Activities for IR 2:

- Develop logistics management tools for procurement and management of health products;
- Strengthen institutional capacity to plan for and manage health commodity needs, including the formulation of a national plan for contraceptive security (see Annex 2);
- Promote local production of health products;
- Support a national social marketing program; and
- Pre-position essential commodities in cyclone vulnerable areas.

Illustrative Indicators for IR 2:

- Decrease in percentage of service delivery sites that report a stock out of selected products during the previous 12 months; and
- Increase in numbers of modern contraceptives and condoms sold.

IR 3: Quality of Selected Health Services Improved

Use of health services is highly dependent upon the quality of care provided. Quality is generally measured against accepted protocols or standards. While continuing education for health professionals exists, there is a need to systematically strengthen their pre-service training in technical areas that are quickly changing. Examples include: STI case management, nutrition, Integrated Management of Childhood Illnesses, infectious disease control, and family planning.

Illustrative Activities for IR 3:

- Technical support for pre-service training to medical, public health, and nursing schools to incorporate the latest standards and guidelines in selected technical areas;
- Promote the Essential Nutrition Action package as a national standard;
- Expand the implementation of guidelines for STI case management for high risk women; and
- Conduct operations research on malaria and STI/HIV/AIDS program issues.

Illustrative Indicators for IR 3:
- Increase in number of medical, public health, and nursing schools that have incorporated state-of-the-art technical updates in their curriculum;
- Increase in number of STI cases treated according to national guidelines; and
- Cold chain fully functional in 112 health districts.

IR 4: Institutional Capacity to Implement and Evaluate Health Programs Improved

The strength of health delivery systems depends on the institutional capacity of public, non-governmental, and private sector organizations to use trained personnel to provide appropriate services. The Mission proposes to expand public health training through U.S. - Malagasy university partnerships. Because 80% of health services are most needed in rural areas, the Mission will continue to support private organizations and NGOs that provide rural health services, particularly in regions containing critical biodiversity habitats. Experience here has shown that—in addition to health organizations—environmental, agricultural, and a range of women's and community groups are also able to promote health messages and provide referrals to the nearest health centers. Expanding access to health information through the media and organizational networks multiplies the impact of the formal health sector. Madagascar also has a wealth of national survey data, but disease surveillance systems are weak (particularly HIV, STI, and malaria). The Mission plans to support technical assistance to strengthen these systems.

Illustrative Activities for IR 4:
- Develop partnerships between Madagascar's medical, public health, and nursing schools and U.S. schools of public health and nursing;
- Develop partnerships with the National Medical Association and private practitioners;
- Strengthen disease surveillance systems and the Demographic and Health Survey; and
- Support NGO organizational and technical capacity to provide key maternal and child services.

Illustrative Indicators for IR 4:
- Increase in number of formal agreements between U.S. and Malagasy-based health organizations;
- Increase in quality health data available for GOM and civil society organizations; and
- Increase in percentage of NGOs supported that demonstrate increased technical and program management skills.

C. Critical Assumptions

- *The GOM maintains a strong commitment to and continues to view health of the Malagasy population as key to economic development.*

- *Economic growth supports greater private sector expansion and individual ability to pay for health services and products.*

D. Integration and Cross-cutting Issues

Crisis Modifier: Program resources under this SO may be redirected in response to a crisis resulting from natural disaster or conflict. For instance, ongoing programs may be reoriented to affected populations, or assistance may be provided to overcome logistical constraints induced by a crisis. Where appropriate, the HPN SO could also be funded with IDA resources.

Health, Population and Environment: During the current strategy period, integrated program activities have been supported in regions important to the preservation of biologically diverse ecosystems. "Integrated" means that various sector-specific activities—in health, family planning, environment, and agricultural development—are better coordinated between and within the organizations working on them. The underlying hypothesis has been that integration focused on the interaction between such sector specific activities—in communities and in the organizations providing technical and financial support to them—will yield better results than separate sector-specific efforts.

To date, these efforts have been supported under the Mission's objectives in environment and in health, in partnership with the USAID Bureau for Global Health's Population-Environment Program and Environment Health Project. USAID was also instrumental in leveraging $2 million over four years from the Packard Foundation to further Health/Population/Environment efforts. Technical support for integration has been provided to a wider array of implementing partners through the newly established Voahary Salama ("health along with all that is natural") consortium, which is now recognized by the GOM as an official non-governmental organization.

Through Voahary Salama, USAID provides: (1) direct financial support to NGOs for program integration in the Moramanga and Fianarantsoa regions (see Annex 11); (2) technical support through training and materials to a broader array of partners; (3) support for monitoring and evaluation to test and document the effectiveness of integrated approaches; and (4) support for a secretariat to coordinate timely and effective communication among all Voahary Salama partners.

Gender: The new HPN program considers women's participation throughout: in health activities, in access to information, in participation in decision-making, in access to resources for investments in family health, and in opportunities for training and leadership in the public health field. In addition, men's roles in family health are included, such as fathers' participation in monitoring child growth and nutritional status, men's condom use, men's role in contraception, and men's roles in promoting community health. Actively engaging men and women on family and community health issues will lead to more sustainable maternal, child, and reproductive health results. Global evidence demonstrates that improvement in these areas has a positive impact on women's productivity and quality of life.

HIV/AIDS programs will include activities to strengthen safer-sex negotiation skills and other activities aimed at helping women take greater control in sexual decision-making. Public health survey data will be disaggregated by sex to determine differences in use of health care, vaccine coverage, nutritional status, attitudes toward condom use, etc. Professional training opportunities developed in the new strategy will emphasize female participation on an equal basis with males. Leadership training for women will also be emphasized.

Food Security: USAID's efforts to improve the food security of Madagascar's most vulnerable populations, and respond to potential disasters, have been a focus for the HPN SO over the past five years. HPN has spearheaded efforts to address food insecurity through its nutrition, maternal, child, and reproductive health programs (see Annex 7). Increases in agriculture productivity through Title II programs contribute powerfully to food security by augmenting the quantity of food available and improving food access. Food security issues dovetail with HPN's efforts in disaster preparation and mitigation. HPN and Title II partners work in the most cyclone-vulnerable areas, at the community level, to train leaders in cyclone preparation and response and to pre-position food, pure water product, and health supplies; and at the national level, to help the National Disaster Management Council build a sustainable disaster early warning system and improve national response to cyclones. During and following a natural disaster, HPN has taken the lead in working with the Office of Foreign Disaster Assistance to manage the USG response, and with Title II partners, Food For Peace, and the World Food Program in delivering food aid to affected populations.

E. Local Partners

Government: HPN works closely with the GOM Ministries of Health, Interior and Administrative Reform, Primary and Secondary Education, and Economy, Finance and Budget (including the National Statistics Institute, or "INSTAT"). The schools of medicine, public health, and nursing are also key institutions for developing U.S. - Malagasy partnerships. Interventions such as the national immunization program, HIV prevention, social marketing, and selected others will involve the government and elected officials at the central, regional, district, and community levels.

Local Non-governmental Partners: Local non-governmental partners include international and local NGO/PVOs, the network of faith-based NGOs, a range of community groups involved in the promotion of health, agriculture, environment, and education initiatives, private physicians, media associations, and private and public schools. Private organizations, companies, and factories that provide health services will also be considered.

Other USG Agencies: The Peace Corps and USAID collaborated closely over the past eight years in child and maternal health and in HIV prevention, and these efforts will continue. USAID and CDC have combined forces in the areas of polio surveillance, assessment of the HIV surveillance system, and in cholera and diarrhea diseases and development of the clean water product Sur' Eau; this relationship is expected to deepen. In the area of HIV prevention, USAID has worked closely with the Department of Defense and the Embassy's Public Affairs Section. USAID also serves on the Embassy's interagency HIV/AIDS prevention committee.

Other Donors: USAID will continue to work closely with other donors to coordinate human and financial resources to support health initiatives in Madagascar. The key international health donors are UNICEF, the UNFPA, the World Bank, the European Union, the Japanese Embassy, GTZ, the World Health Organization, and the French Cooperation.

F. Alternative Approaches

This SO is based on in-depth analysis and assessment of the status and trends in nutrition, maternal, child, reproductive health, food security, and disaster preparedness. The Mission studied the elements contributing to sustainable health programs, the socio-economic and political context of health systems, and identified realistic outcomes. Lessons learned during the past 10 years of USAID work in Madagascar informed the new direction and approach.

Initially the Mission considered placing the SO at the highest impact level to measure changes in fertility and child mortality rates. However, in spite of much progress, change in health indicators and the nutritional status of women and children continues to come slowly. The Mission recognizes that the country's level of economic development and the availability of resources to support the health system is limited. These factors, together with USAID's manageable interest, led the Mission to conclude that the program is not ready to graduate to the next level, i.e., that the Strategic Objective should rest at the outcome, or behavior change, level.

The Mission also considered how best to focus resources for maximum impact. Alternative scenarios for supporting the public and the private sectors were analyzed. Given past experience working with the Ministry of Health, the current political context, and the need in the private and NGO sector for capacity development, the SO is designed to provide optimum flexibility and will balance support among the public, private, and NGO sectors. During the past five years the Mission placed substantial program resources at the District and community levels. In the development of this SO, resources will continue to be focused at the community level. To broaden impact, however, a greater focus will be at the national level to strengthen systems and pre-service training. The strategy also allows for future expansion of the private sector components of the program such as increasing work with NGOs, private companies, the media, and social marketing of selected health products.

Over the past decade, the Mission has demonstrated remarkable results in Contraceptive Prevalence Rates, immunization, and breast-feeding in targeted areas. HPN has forged strong partnerships with the GOM, local NGOs, and donors, and mobilized communities have led a groundswell for improved health services and products. At the mid-level funding scenario, the Mission could maintain these results and expand to additional geographic areas and populations, supporting both the public and private sectors. At the high-level, the program could broaden its reach even further, and deepen activities aimed at building greater systemic change and sustainability. In particular, it could provide significantly more support to greater numbers of NGOs, broaden the access to and use of health information services and technology, and appreciably strengthen national management of drug, vaccine, and contraceptive logistics systems. The low level is less than HPN received, on average, during the past five-year strategy. Consequently, the expected results will be severely constrained; the program will be tightly focused geographically, and the reach of activities limited.

G. Measuring Results

The baseline for measuring program impact will be the 2003 national Demographic and Health Survey (a follow-up survey is scheduled for 2008). USAID is coordinating this survey with INSTAT), the GOM, and other donors. All key indicators for program baseline information will be included in the 2003 survey. In addition, a national household survey funded by the World Bank will be completed in 2004 and a UNICEF Multiple Indicator Survey in 2005. Periodic program surveys, social marketing sales data, and the GOM health information system will also be used to monitor program indicators.

USAID/Madagascar Health, Population and Nutrition (HPN) Results Framework

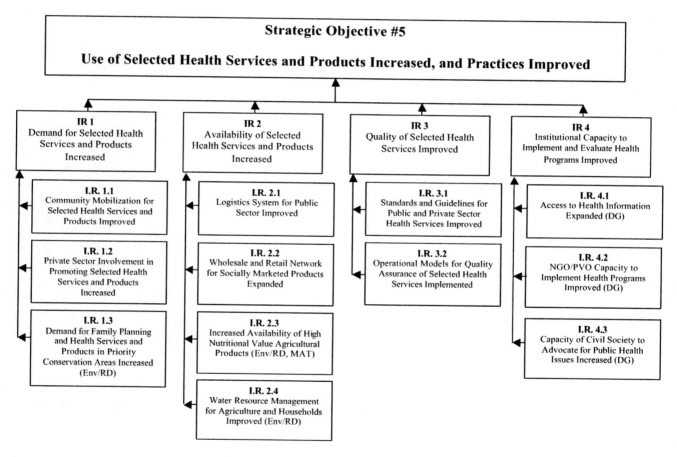

Strategic Objective #5

Use of Selected Health Services and Products Increased, and Practices Improved

IR 1
Demand for Selected Health Services and Products Increased

IR 2
Availability of Selected Health Services and Products Increased

IR 3
Quality of Selected Health Services Improved

IR 4
Institutional Capacity to Implement and Evaluate Health Programs Improved

I.R. 1.1
Community Mobilization for Selected Health Services and Products Improved

I.R. 1.2
Private Sector Involvement in Promoting Selected Health Services and Products Increased

I.R. 1.3
Demand for Family Planning and Health Services and Products in Priority Conservation Areas Increased (Env/RD)

I.R. 2.1
Logistics System for Public Sector Improved

I.R. 2.2
Wholesale and Retail Network for Socially Marketed Products Expanded

I.R. 2.3
Increased Availability of High Nutritional Value Agricultural Products (Env/RD, MAT)

I.R. 2.4
Water Resource Management for Agriculture and Households Improved (Env/RD)

I.R. 3.1
Standards and Guidelines for Public and Private Sector Health Services Improved

I.R. 3.2
Operational Models for Quality Assurance of Selected Health Services Implemented

I.R. 4.1
Access to Health Information Expanded (DG)

I.R. 4.2
NGO/PVO Capacity to Implement Health Programs Improved (DG)

I.R. 4.3
Capacity of Civil Society to Advocate for Public Health Issues Increased (DG)

PART VI   STRATEGIC OBJECTIVE #6 –
BIOLOGICALLY DIVERSE FOREST ECOSYSTEMS CONSERVED

A. Problem Identification and Past Achievements

Madagascar has been identified consistently by the international community as one of the highest biodiversity conservation priority countries in the world. Some experts believe that the country harbors more genetic information per unit area than anywhere else in the world. A hectare of forest lost in Madagascar has a greater negative impact on global biodiversity than a hectare of forest lost virtually anywhere else on earth. Poverty, unproductive agriculture, high population growth, and weak natural resources governance threaten Madagascar's natural resource base by encouraging slash and burn agriculture, deforestation, unsustainable forest management, and habitat loss. This leads to plant and animal extinction, watershed degradation, erosion, soil fertility loss, conflict and disaster vulnerability, and more poverty (see Annexes 8 & 10).

USAID has provided extensive leadership in the environment sector in Madagascar over the past ten years, primarily through support to the fifteen year (1991- 2006) National Environmental Action Plan (NEAP). The USAID/Madagascar environment program has been one of the Agency's flagship environmental programs. To help conserve Madagascar's heritage, USAID has implemented a cutting edge approach that has consistently linked a healthy environment to improved well being of the Malagasy people. It has done this through approaches that address biodiversity conservation while contributing to the country's socio-economic development. Another critical component has been the inclusion of rural communities in the management and sustainable use of their natural resource base.

USAID's support to the first and second phases of NEAP has focused on developing environmental institutions, tools, and approaches. For example, the Mission has helped develop a more efficient National Park Service, which in turn increased the total area of critical habitats being effectively managed and protected. USAID support has helped transfer management of forest areas to local communities. And it has been instrumental in the establishment of ecotourism investment zones, promotion of environmentally friendly farmer groups, and development of more financially sustainable environment institutions.

B. Strategic Objective and Intermediate Results

"Biologically Diverse Forest Ecosystems Conserved" is the new environment and rural development strategic objective for FY 2003 - 2008.

As demonstrated over the last ten years, there are inextricable links between natural resources, economic growth, agricultural productivity, water quality and availability, poverty, health, and governance. It is clear that forest ecosystems are essential to the long-term economic, social, and environmental well being of local populations in Madagascar, the national economy, and the earth's biosphere as a whole. Therefore it is critical, in addressing the problems of Malagasy people, to focus more holistically on forest ecosystem management over the next five years. This will deepen the Mission's efforts in the environment domain while increasing the emphasis on conservation and sustainable use of forest and natural resources to empower, enrich, and elevate people out of poverty. **Working with people closest to the natural resource base will be the nexus of the new Environment/Rural Development (Env/RD) SO.**

A multifaceted program will be pursued to achieve the new SO—one which continues the current successful ecoregional (i.e., biogeographical areas which represent distinct assemblages of natural communities and share a majority of species and ecological processes) approach. The strategy's intent is to "conserve biologically diverse forest ecosystems" by improving sustainable natural resource management and environmentally sensitive development. The SO's five components are based on accepted approaches to ecoregional conservation and development.

Illustrative Indicator for SO 6:
• Percent change in forest cover.

IR 1: Forest Management System Improved

Ecological services provided by forest ecosystems are extremely valuable benefits. These services include maintaining and controlling water flow and quality, soil formation and nutrient cycling, pest and pathogen control, pollination, and climate regulation. Ignoring or undervaluing these can increase pressure for land conversion—a result based on the mistaken perception that agriculture or other land use practices would be a more valuable land use. A strategic vision for the preservation of forest ecosystems must be integrated into the decision-making process of all stakeholders, and must be implemented at the field level.

Satisfying the broad range of human and ecological demands requires new approaches to the stewardship of Madagascar's forests. Forest management will be based on two key premises:

• forests must be managed to fulfill a range of environmental, social, economic, and cultural functions, rather than serving sole interests such as logging or conservation; and

• forest products outside of primary forest exploitation must be made more profitable, which will tend to reduce the pressure for primary forest timber products.

To help facilitate the development of a forest management vision, a number of activities will take place under the new ISP. USAID will assist in establishing an effective system and structure responsible for forest management. Support will be provided to ensure that the forest service is able to transfer its vision to the field through national, regional, and communal forest zoning plans. Along with establishing an effective institution, USAID will help implement a system to provide adequate resource information on which to base decision-making: Skills and infrastructure will be developed to ensure that information is gathered, analyzed, and provided in a way to allow use by decision-makers at all levels. Finally, the flow of information and dialogue with partners will be facilitated to ensure that the priorities for key forest ecosystems are heard, understood, and integrated into local, regional, and national-level planning.

Illustrative Indicator for IR 1:
• 20-year management vision defined and implemented through national and regional zoning plans.

IR 2: Biological Integrity of Critical Biodiversity Habitats Maintained

Ensuring that core biodiversity areas are protected is critical to conserving forest ecosystems. The program will strive to reach the internationally accepted measure for how much of a country's critical habitats should be protected, which is that an adequate percentage (usually 10%) of habitats are under conservation status. To achieve this, USAID will provide support to implement the strategic management plan for the protected areas network developed with past USAID support.

One aspect of protecting critical habitats is to maintain the ecological processes within and between habitats. A total of 90% of the country's biodiversity lies within forest areas, of which less than 8% is represented in the protected area network. Moreover, many of Madagascar's highest priority biodiversity areas fall outside the network. The program will use new and innovative mechanisms, such as conservation contracts and regional protected areas, to help ensure that these high priority areas are maintained.

Ecological restoration and reforestation will be used to re-establish connectivity between habitats where ecological processes have been destroyed. Another aspect of conserving critical habitats is to ensure that biodiversity habitat management plans are integrated into landscape planning. When local, regional, and national level development plans are established, the needs for protecting these critical habitats will be integrated to ensure that conservation goals and development activities are complementary.

Within the protected area network, program activities will promote continued institutional development, while also focusing on developing the capacity to implement field-level management activities. These activities will include park outreach and education, monitoring and research, infrastructure development and maintenance, habitat maintenance, and integrating protected-area management activities and local and regional development.

Continued support in the area of "sustainable financing" is also critical; public resources are insufficient. A multi-pronged approach will be pursued here: (i) restructuring of the environmental institutions to enable them to be more financially and institutionally secure; (ii) exploring new avenues for securing increased and sustainable revenue generation for the environment, which might include carbon sequestration, private sector resources, green taxes, etc.; and (iii) pursuing the establishment of a biodiversity/protected areas trust fund.

Illustrative Indicator for IR 2:
- Area of selected habitats under conservation management.

IR 3: Alternatives Adopted to Reduce Slash and Burn Agriculture

The largest threat to the remaining natural forests of Madagascar is slash and burn agriculture (*tavy*). *Tavy* is the result of a number of social, cultural, economic, and biological factors. Local communities and forest dwellers are working to reclaim their rights to use and manage the forestlands. These critical landscapes include biodiversity-rich forest ecosystems, water catchment areas, land use systems where agriculture has high potential for sustainable growth, marginal lands with valuable non-agricultural resources that are under threat of degradation, and lands that can support economic diversification.

USAID's efforts to reduce slash and burn farming will continue to be based on reinforcing synergies between natural resources management, agricultural productivity, food and financial security, economic growth and poverty alleviation, health, and natural resource sustainability. The approach will address socio-economic factors that increase human pressure on highly valuable forest corridors in two USAID priority ecoregions. It will help to alleviate poverty while improving food security in both regions. USAID will build on foundations established by the current ecoregional conservation program, which has demonstrated that slash and burn can be halted, and expansion of lands encroaching on priority ecosystems limited, through agricultural intensification and income-generating activities based on sustainable use of natural resources.

Farmers and their communities are the common element in these desired conditions, so USAID will focus on community-level "farming systems" interventions. This will increase farmer incomes and create strong economic, ecological, social, and geographical linkages between rural development and reduction of pressures on forest corridors. The approach will focus on inter-related interventions based on sustainable land use planning and management.

The first of these interventions is community-based forest management. Contracts will continue to be established with local communities to transfer management of designated forests with well-defined resource management plans, access, and use. Alternative energy sources and technologies, such as community woodlots, will be explored to reduce dependence on harvesting fuel-wood from primary forests. Second, agricultural productivity will be increased by encouraging farmers to adopt approaches that are more sustainable and profitable than the slash and burn system. Emphasis will be placed on empowering farmers to be self sufficient. This will be done through a "farmer-to-farmer" approach using ecologically friendly techniques and by fostering market linkages between producer groups and agribusinesses (in collaboration with the Mission's Agriculture and Trade SO). Third, community land use management plans will build-in the protection of micro-level water catchments, thereby improving water quantity and quality. Finally, linkages will be established with the Mission's health sector SO to address a number of community health concerns, as well as the over-arching need to address population growth around forest areas. This will be achieved by increasing the demand and availability of family planning and health services, products, and practices.

Illustrative Indicator for IR 3:
• Decrease in area and incidents of new slash and burn agriculture sites in priority areas.

IR 4: Investment Initiatives and Partnerships in Natural Resource Management Increased

In order to protect Madagascar's unique biodiversity, it is necessary to facilitate the involvement of the private sector: under this IR, economic benefits will be emphasized and investments in natural resource management encouraged. Forest lands and other natural resources will be identified with a view toward capitalizing on their potential for production of goods, maintenance of environmental services, generation of jobs and public sector revenues, contributions to exports, and associated multiplier effects.

Forest-based industries such as plantations will be supported as a way of enhancing sustainable use of forest assets and reducing pressures on the natural forests. Assistance will be focused on improving methods of management, harvesting, extraction, utilization, recovery of wastes, and value-added processing of forest products. There will be an emphasis on training field-level forest workers in more efficient forest production and processing methods, and exploring use of wood residues to create biomass energy for value-added processing of forest products.

USAID also plans to support businesses in the natural products sector, through production of quality natural products for domestic and international markets. This will consist of promoting the environmentally sensitive collection, production, and processing of indigenous and introduced natural products such as essential oils and spices (as well as such crafts as raffia woven products). Continued support will be provided to the ecotourism sector, too, as a way to actively engage the private sector in the conservation agenda. Other areas of collaboration to be pursued will include emerging carbon sequestration/carbon credit trading options, eco-certification of forest products, biotechnology, and bio-prospecting. USAID will also play a pro-active role in identifying ways to engage other institutions, including zoos, museums, and universities, to invest in Madagascar's biodiversity.

Illustrative Indicator for IR 4:
- Increase in number of investments contributing to natural resource management.

IR 5: Environmental Governance Improved

Forests are amazingly busy places. Carbon sequestration, aesthetic and religious values, agents of soil and water protection, biodiversity in all its aspects: these are things not transacted in markets. Even though they carry no market price as such, these forest "values" are essential to Malagasy society. Thus, government must intervene to establish rules of the game and incentives that encourage sustainable natural resources management.

Activities within this IR will promote the involvement of all interest groups to improve environmental governance and stewardship. Public institutions must demonstrate that they can manage natural resources and revenues transparently, particularly forest and mining resources (e.g., gemstones). Law enforcement must be improved. The government must demonstrate that public forests can be managed for national benefit, rather than for private gain. Incentives and disincentives must be put into place. Communities must perceive that the government is making decisions that favor their interests rather than the influential segments of society. Finally, natural resource observatories, local monitoring measures, and independent "watchdogs" measures must be promoted. In so doing, this IR will respond to a source of tension between farmers and state agents, and contribute to the Mission's efforts to help prevent conflict stemming from natural resource degradation (see Annex 10).

Checks and balances will be enhanced by: (i) facilitating *participation* in environment management through greater information flow and communication with communities about their role as environmental watchdogs; (ii) educating the public about its role as an *advocate* for better environmental management; and (iii) educating development actors about the benefits that arise from an effective *partnership* with environmental institutions through use of environmental impact assessments and information for decision-making.

Illustrative Indicator for IR 5:
- Decrease in illegal exploitation of natural resources.

C. Critical Assumptions

- *Large scale natural forest exploitation in Madagascar is not sustainable.* Due to the relative lack of large forest blocks and the complex and poorly understood forest dynamics, the application of worldwide research and experience demonstrates that large scale natural/primary forest exploitation is not sustainable in Madagascar. Any natural forest exploitation should be small scale and limited to the community level.
- *Positive economic growth in the broader landscape will complement the activities located near the forest corridor.*
- *The GOM will maintain its commitment to sustainable management of Madagascar's natural resources; the donor community will continue to view biodiversity support as necessary for the "international public good."*

D. Integration and Cross-cutting Issues

Links to other USAID/Madagascar Strategic Objectives: Given the importance of natural resources to the socio-economic fabric of Malagasy society, linkages between the Env/RD SO and economic growth, agriculture, health, food security, and governance activities are critical. Joint implementation of complimentary activities in priority watersheds will be promoted with linkages to transport infrastructures and domestic and international markets. The program's focus on water quality and availability has a direct link to health programs related to infectious diseases and child survival. The SO also responds to the need to curb corruption through its governance-related activities.

Other U.S. Agencies: With its increased emphasis on combating corruption through improved governance, USAID will work closely with the Embassy's Public Affairs Section to implement a strategic, media-targeted approach to help increase transparent communication in the sector. USAID and the Peace Corps have collaborated over the last eight years, primarily through the Malagasy Park Service to improve park management. This collaboration will continue. The U.S. Forest Service will provide technical support to the Malagasy Forest Service and to USAID implementing partners to improve strategic planning and sustainable forest management. The U.S. Geological Service will provide information management and remote sensing support.

Conflict Prevention and Disaster Vulnerability: Good management of forest ecosystems and watersheds directly contributes to disaster prevention and mitigation. Stabilization of hillsides is also critical: it decreases erosion, siltation of agricultural lands, and cyclone-caused landslides. Crisis Modifier: The Env/RD SO could be adjusted in response to crises to assist in restoring the livelihoods of affected populations, and to mitigate damage to the environment.

Gender: Integrating gender concerns to development investments will be systematically addressed through organized groups such as rural associations, producer organizations, women-owned businesses, and community-based natural resource groups. The organization of formal groups will be developed to ensure participation of women. Provision of on-site income generation opportunities will promote participation of women in socio-economic activities.

E. Local Partners

The National Environment Action Plan provides a 15-year strategic framework. Malagasy partners include the Ministry of Environment, Ministry of Water and Forests, Ministry of Agriculture, National Office of the Environment, National Association for the Management of Protected Areas (ANGAP), National Association of Environmental Actions (ANAE), and Support Services for Environmental Actions (SAGE). Another key partner is Madagascar's first private national environmental organization, Tany Meva (Beautiful Country), which was established with USAID funding and which began grant making in 1997.

Bilateral and multilateral donor support of NEAP's first phase (EP1) totaled $150 million; another $120 million has been provided for EP2. The World Bank has provided technical assistance to key environmental institutions and funding for projects to address the problems of soil and water conservation. The Global Environmental Facility (GEF) is supporting the management of critical biodiversity habitats within and outside the protected area network. Bilateral donors have been primarily involved in the forestry sector. Germany has been instrumental in the development and implementation of a new forestry policy. France is helping to improve forestry sector fiscal policies and promoting community-based NRM.
The three principal international conservation organizations active in Madagascar are WWF, Conservation International, and the Wildlife Conservation Society. They are primarily involved in improved management of biodiversity habitats, community-based forest management, sustainable financing options, and environmental education. U.S. PVO development partners include PACT, CARE, ADRA, and CRS, and a host of national NGOs.

F. Alternative Approaches

The development process for this SO was based heavily on lessons learned during the past 10 years of USAID support to the NEAP. The cornerstone of the process was a stocktaking exercise undertaken during 2000. Early on, the Mission held discussions on whether the program should change focus from biodiversity conservation to sustainable natural resource management. However, discussions with partners in Madagascar and Washington recommended that, given the high biodiversity priority of Madagascar worldwide, the focus of the program should remain biodiversity. An array of possible strategic objectives for biodiversity conservation was considered and rejected, including the pursuit of agricultural and trade development under this SO. However, conserving forest ecosystems was selected as the focal point due to the importance of forests in terms of biodiversity, USAID's relative comparative advantage *vis a vis* other donors' activity areas, and the crucial role forests play in providing critical ecological services.

The Mission also considered ways in which the program could be best focused to help ensure maximum impact. In light of budgetary concerns, and given past USAID support, a geographical focus on vital forest corridors was selected for field-level activities. At a national level, strategic support will be provided for forest and protected area management.

To build on and expand its activities in two eco-regions in the provinces of Fianarantsoa (see Annex 11) and Tamatave, and in the southern Madagascar eco-region of Anosy, the Env/RD SO will need to operate at the mid-level funding scenario. Under the high-level scenario, a further expansion of activities could occur north of Tamatave, into the largest remaining forest blocks in the country. The Mission was actively involved in this area in the early 1990s. Under the low-level scenario, USAID would have to substantially curtail support to the Anosy eco-region (where USAID has been instrumental in incorporating environmental concerns into regional development, in part through its implementation of a public-private alliance with a mining company). The Anosy investments would be compromised if the Mission is unable to continue its support to this region. In addition, under the low-level scenario, support to improve forest industry efficiency would have to be limited to pilot activities only.

G. Measuring Results

Achievement of results under the Env/RD SO will be addressed by integrating implementation activities and monitoring of key indicators at the SO level, IR level (see relevant IR sections), and sub-IR level. The results of these efforts will be used to ensure that the program is on track, and, if it is not, to decide what changes should be made or problems addressed to ensure future targets are met.

At the SO level, forest cover monitoring has already established a solid baseline from which to base future comparisons. At the IR and sub-IR level, each procurement mechanism will be required to establish a baseline for each IR they are involved with. Reasonable but ambitious targets will be established based on analysis of baseline data and discussions with partners. Targets and indicators will be evaluated on a yearly basis, and any necessary adjustments or changes will be considered.

PART VII   STRATEGIC OBJECTIVE #7 -
CRITICAL PRIVATE MARKETS EXPANDED

A. Problem Identification and Past Achievements

According to the U.S. Embassy's Mission Performance Plan for FY 2004:

> *Within this [MPP] framework, economic development,*
> *generated by market-oriented, private sector-led economic*
> *growth is our top priority. Adoption and implementation of*
> *such an approach will allow Madagascar to reduce poverty*
> *and spur investment by enhancing the ability of the private*
> *sector to thrive. This priority encompasses activities across*
> *a variety of sectors, including health and the environment.*

Madagascar has substantial economic growth potential, yet it remains poor. Economic growth is essential to empowering and improving the living conditions of the poor, and reducing the country's dependence on external assistance. Properly managed, economic growth can also contribute to stewardship of the environment. Madagascar experienced accelerating growth between 1996 and 2001, but the political crisis of 2002 resulted in an estimated contraction in GDP of nearly 12%.

Textiles led much of the economy's growth in recent years, with the trade advantages afforded by AGOA playing a significant role. Madagascar has also become one of the world's major suppliers of rubies, sapphires, emeralds, and other precious and semi-precious stones, though the bulk of this trade remains outside of formal channels. There are opportunities for growth in artisanal products. It is agriculturally based products, however, that offer the greatest potential for growth to reach the majority of Madagascar's population in the medium-term. Agriculture accounts for 30% of GDP. Eighty-five percent of Madagascar's poor live in rural areas, and 77% of the rural population is poor. Madagascar is already a world leader in vanilla, clove, and litchi markets. Its diverse climatic conditions host a wide array of attractive commodities, including: fresh fruits and vegetables; robusta and arabica coffees; tea; cereals (rice, maize, wheat); tubers (cassava, yams, potatoes); dried beans; oilseeds (soybean, sunflower, peanuts); essential oils (aloe, ylang ylang, ravinala); spices (pepper, ginger, cinnamon); fibers (cotton, silk); tree crops (cashews, cocoa, coconut, palm oil); dairy products; livestock; and poultry. Madagascar also supplies seafood and forest products to the world economy, though these sectors need to be better managed to remain sustainable. Linkages exist with regional and international markets (and U.S. markets under AGOA), but these need to be strengthened. More efficient domestic commodity distribution channels need to be established.

Agricultural productivity is low. Farmers rely on traditional farming practices, often including slash and burn, and adoption of new technologies is low. Landholdings are small, and, increasingly, soils are being depleted. Input and output markets are weak, in part because of poor transportation infrastructure, small marketable surpluses and long distances between rural families and urban markets. Weak organization of producers and traders constrains efforts to surmount these problems (see Annex 9).

Madagascar's entrepreneurs tend to lack the information and experience necessary to compete successfully in international markets. Increased knowledge of market requirements such as standards and packaging specifications, and of the benefits of international agreements, is essential. Limited access to investment credit and to trade financing instruments, such as letters of credit, also hinders expansion of international trade.

Despite steady improvement in the policy environment for private enterprise and international trade over the past decade, and the commitment of the new government, much more needs to be done to improve policies and their implementation. The World Bank - UN "Integrated Framework" study identifies a number of policy constraints: poor customs administration, high import taxes, weaknesses in the rule of law, inability to enforce contracts and secure loans, disadvantageous labor policies and practices, and restrictive access to land.

Precious and semi-precious stones offer an opportunity for rapid growth in incomes, and government revenues. The vast majority of exports of precious and semi-precious stones is clandestine. Neither the small-scale miners nor the state coffers realize sufficient benefits. Establishment of transparent mechanisms for the grading and sales of these stones, with the private sector playing a substantial role in management, would bring sales revenues into the formal sector. Moreover, GOM efforts to reform this sector would be a bellwether of its commitment to good governance.

USAID has promoted agribusiness and economic growth in the past. For example, the Commercial Agricultural Promotion (CAP) Project was a six-year $24 million project designed to increase production of agricultural products in targeted high potential zones. It provided technical assistance to agribusiness and producer groups and rehabilitated roads and rail lines. Also, between 1994 and 2001, USAID invested in the development of improved crop varieties through a grant to the International Rice Research Institute. However, lack of funding has slowed the dissemination of improved varieties. Environment and PL 480, Title II partners are working with farming communities to improve agricultural practices and mitigate pressures on the environment. In order to scale up support for agricultural production, more attention is needed to improve markets for inputs and agricultural products.

USAID programs are currently working with business associations in national products (spices and essential oils) and eco-tourism to expand trade. The Global Technology Network facilitates access to American technology. USAID has also provided technical assistance for the formation of a Madagascar - U.S. Business Council, and for workshops and information dissemination on World Trade Organization and regional trade agreements.

B. Strategic Objective and Intermediate Results

"Critical Private Markets Expanded" is the new agriculture and trade strategic objective for FY 2003 - 2008.

Market-led development will increase family incomes and improve food security. Over the life of this SO, selected interventions will be undertaken along selected commodity chains:

production, market organization, competitiveness, international trade performance, and national policy. Choice of interventions will be based on three priority considerations: a) potential for a significant contribution to economic growth; b) contribution to improving the lives of poor populations, with reference to gender equity and food security; and c) complementarity with environment/rural development activities.

This SO will support improved marketing and trade of selected agricultural and non-agricultural goods and services. It will be mutually reinforcing with the Env/RD SO. It will assist in job creation and help identify new livelihood opportunities (which will, in turn, draw growing populations away from threatened forests). It will have a strong private-sector orientation and will be a vehicle for developing public-private partnerships. Through its emphasis on markets, it is expected to reinforce and leverage World Bank, European Union, and GOM (HIPC) investments in agricultural production and transportation infrastructure.

Illustrative Indicators for SO 7:
- Increase in Gross Domestic Product from selected products; and
- Increased value of selected goods and services exports.

IR 1: Agricultural Production and Practices Improved

In coordination with the Env/RD SO and in support of a key recommendation of the Mission's agribusiness and food security assessments (see Annexes 7 & 9), this IR will increase agricultural production through the introduction of new technologies and best practices. It will help to address constraints affecting agricultural productivity, including limited access to agricultural inputs, and limited use of productivity-enhancing technologies. It may promote farm productivity through: 1) agro-ecological approaches using traditional or improved methods of inter-cropping, fallow, rotations, agro-forestry, crop-livestock integration, green manure, cover crops, integrated pest management, and water management; and 2) genetically engineered cultivars that resist pests and drought and produce higher yields. Technology choice will, among other considerations, reflect domestic and international consumer preferences, small farmer capacities, agribusiness competitiveness, and Malagasy policy (including biosafety regimes that regulate genetically modified organism research and use).

The introduction of productivity-enhancing agricultural technologies is important to increase rural incomes and decrease food insecurity – both key contributors to Madagascar's vulnerability to conflict and disaster. Increased access to environmentally appropriate technologies will allow rural families in environmentally fragile areas to improve output and increase household incomes. Agricultural diversification and off-season cropping will help to reduce the use of slash and burn practices and stabilize hillsides, thereby mitigating pressures on the forests.

Market-responsive technology dissemination will take place through agribusinesses, NGOs, or state institutions. Based on experience gained under the FY 1998 - 2003 Country Strategic Plan, this IR will work primarily through farmers' associations, in collaboration with local authorities and NGOs.

Illustrative Activities for IR 1:

- Increase farmers' access to existing and new technologies;
- Promote off-season crops and crop diversification;
- Identify new products for small farmers to produce and market;
- Increase farmers' participation in producers' organizations;
- Increase small farmers' access to market information; and
- Help local organizations facilitate collective action and complement public services.

Illustrative Indicator for IR 1:
- Increased production of selected agricultural commodities in priority areas.

IR 2: Value-Added through Agribusiness Increased

This IR will promote increases in the value of selected commodities for the domestic and export markets. This intervention is intended to increase net returns to suppliers at each level, e.g., producers, handlers, processors, and exporters. With regard to export, intervention is intended to increase the share of the value chain for exportable products that remains in Madagascar. Agribusiness development will help to diversify and upgrade Madagascar's domestic as well as exportable supply of agriculture-based products, measured in terms of varieties, length of season, market window, presentations, forms, packaging, container type, and transport mode.

Madagascar's poor road and communication networks, small marketable surpluses, long distances between rural families and urban markets, weak rural institutions, and rugged terrain increase agricultural extension, rural finance, and marketing risks and costs. To reduce costs and encourage mutually beneficial agribusiness-small farmer linkages, this SO will support farmer-initiated, democratically managed, financially viable, rural group businesses (e.g., cooperatives). Group businesses will reduce technology and information dissemination costs through farmer-to-farmer extension. They will rely on group liability for and management of rural finance (micro-finance, out-grower schemes, forward contracts, etc.) to reduce financial intermediation risks and costs, and group input and output marketing to reduce marketing costs. This SO support will network rural group businesses into regional and national farmer federations or unions. USAID has developed experience in working with village farmer groups, road user associations, and water user associations and forging national linkages.

Illustrative Activities for IR 2:
- Increase business skills of rural, non-farm enterprises, e.g., planning, management, storage, processing, packaging, and marketing;
- Increase use of formal and informal business contracts;
- Support the establishment of private and non-governmental business service providers;
- Increase access to and use of market information, including the use of information technologies;
- Help non-farm enterprises identify and gain access to credit; and
- Promote and tailor technology to local conditions.

Illustrative Indicators for IR 2:
- Number of agribusinesses showing improvement on a Best Business Practices Index (TBD); and

- Number of group businesses assisted (cumulative).

IR 3: Trade Flows in Selected Commodities Increased

The volume of trade, both domestically and into the international market, is hampered by a number of factors. These include lack of access to finance, poor quality standards, and lack of adequate infrastructure. Private sector knowledge of and adaptation to international norms, e.g., certification, custom procedures, and sanitary and phyto-sanitary standards, is also needed. Under this IR, USAID/Madagascar's objective is first to identify trade constraints and bottlenecks, and then to promote solutions that will result in an increase in the flow of trade of selected agricultural and non-agricultural commodities. Opportunities will be identified that will result in more efficient flow of goods and services within the country and internationally. Where feasible, intervention by USAID/Madagascar will seek to differentiate Malagasy products in target markets, and will work to increase the leverage of Malagasy suppliers in target markets by enhancing competitive advantage. If these interventions are effective, there will be measurable increase in domestic and international trade.

Illustrative activities for IR 3:
- Assist development of business associations;
- Support development of trade facilitation services;
- Promote investment;
- Stimulate consumers' preferences for Madagascar's exports;
- Support access of Malagasy businesses to U.S. markets; and
- Facilitate market access by reducing transaction costs.

Illustrative Indicator for IR 3:
- Increased trade volumes of selected goods and services.

IR 4: Selected Policies, Regulations, and Procedures Changed

Inappropriate national and local policies, regulations, and procedures (e.g., macro-economic, trade, agricultural, nutritional, environmental, or gender-biased) contribute to limiting trade opportunities, food insecurity, poverty, and environmental degradation. Under this IR, USAID/Madagascar's objective is to help public, private, and non-governmental organizations identify and analyze the policy and regulatory issues that need change. This will, in turn, create additional forums for dialogue among stakeholders. It will provide more and varied tools for advocacy so that policy-makers have the right information on which to act. And it will help to open up the international market.

Illustrative activities for IR 4:
- Support business association participation in informed decision-making;
- Support policy analysis;
- Support improvements in policies and practices, e.g., customs, taxation, telecommunications, finance, and land-use (see Annex 2);
- Support market access, input provision, and crop diversification interventions; and

- Promote an improved land tenure system that provides better incentives for farmer investments in land use conservation practices, tree plantations, and perennial crops.

Illustrative Indicators for IR 4:
- Index of Policy Changes (TBD); and
- Index of Economic Freedom (Heritage Foundation).

C. Critical Assumptions

- *Land tenure policies and practices will not pose a binding constraint to economic growth.* A viable land tenure system is important to secure property rights, so that rural households and agribusiness firms are more likely to benefit from their investments. Without such a system, any investor's access to land is problematic and time-consuming. Generally, foreigners cannot own land in Madagascar, though they are permitted to obtain long-term leases. The majority of rural holdings are small: over 80% of rural households have access to less than 2 hectares (4.94 acres) of land. Yet, there has been progress (since 1998) in establishing industrial and eco-tourism zones for long-term investment, and in privatizing state-owned plantations and industrial concessions. Improving access to land will be addressed over time under IR4.

- *Weak financial markets will not pose a binding constraint to market development.* Although commercial banks have ample money to lend, Malagasy businesses have difficulty in meeting loan criteria and rely on auto financing. This is exacerbated by weak laws governing security of assets. Donor-supported micro-finance schemes do not yet satisfy demand, and there is a "missing middle"—credit is less available to small and medium enterprises. USAID will help to expand access to credit by assisting in investment project preparation and promoting innovative financing schemes, such as inventory credit. Meanwhile, it is expected that credit pressures will ease over the life of the strategy as other donors' lending for micro, small and medium enterprises expands.

- *The GOM will support prudent macro policies,* including exchange rate, fiscal, and monetary restraint in order to maintain stable aggregate price and employment patterns, allowing market-based macroeconomic and sectoral reforms to provide the overall structure of market and price incentives.

- *World Bank, EU, and GOM investments in road, rail, and port infrastructure will lower marketing costs and increase participation in the market by remote, rural populations.* Telecommunications are adequate in major cities, but costly. With privatization and increased competition, telecommunications are likely to improve and become less expensive. Electricity and water supplies are generally adequate for industrial uses.

D. Integration and Cross-cutting Issues

Crisis Modifier: In the event of a crisis due to **conflict** or **natural disaster**, interventions may be adjusted to help restore productive capacity and market access for affected populations.

The process of selecting interventions to develop markets will be done in collaboration with the Env/RD SO. These two SOs will also share activities under agricultural productivity IRs. Policy change and association development activities will be coordinated with the DG SO. Development of agricultural production and agribusiness will contribute to **food security**, and complement health and nutrition activities under the HPN SO. SO 7 will contribute to the Mission's Health, Population and Environment Initiative. **Gender** considerations will be integrated into commodity choice, and into agricultural production, association, and business development activities, on the ground.

SO 7 will also collaborate with central and regional USAID projects. For example, the SO will work with AFR/SD's Tree Crops Initiative to increase small farmer production and agribusiness export of coffee, cocoa, and cashew products. In several of Madagascar's biodiversity-rich conservation areas, cashew and coffee production is closely linked to improved forest management. The SO will also work with AFR/SD's Agribusiness in Support of Natural African Products (ASNAPP) project to increase production and export of Madagascar's potentially vast array of natural products, providing rural families with income opportunities beyond slash and burn and charcoal and firewood production. To promote trade and investment, including participation in regional trading arrangements, the Mission will collaborate with REDSO/E's COMESA and RCSA's SADC development activities, as well as with the Political and Economic section of the U.S. Embassy.

E. Local Partners

SO 7 is directly supportive of Madagascar's Poverty Reduction Strategy Paper (PRSP) and the National Recovery Plan (July 2002). One of the major axes of the PRSP is to improve economic performance by increasing participation of the poor. Its rural development objectives include: a) ensuring food security; b) contributing to economic growth; c) reducing poverty and improving rural living conditions; d) promoting sustainable natural resource management; and e) promoting training and information to improve rural production. The National Recovery Plan emphasizes "rapid and sustainable development," including "restarting agriculture." Agriculture production and marketing interventions are further supportive of Madagascar's Rural Development Action Plan (PADR).

USAID and the U.S. Embassy work in close collaboration with the GOM, business associations, and other donors through the recently created *Comité d'Appui et de Pilotage pour la relance des Entreprises* (CAPE). In particular, business facilitation services will be coordinated with CAPE. Principal counterparts in the Government are the Ministries of Agriculture and Livestock, Industry and Private Sector, and Commerce and Trade. USAID will also collaborate with the Ministry of Economy, Finance and Budget, and provincial and local authorities.

SO 7 will directly complement the European Union's $100 million, the World Bank's $89 million, and the International Fund for Agricultural Development's $11 million investments in rural development—all of which place an emphasis on increasing agricultural production among poor, rural households. USAID's critical contribution will be to leverage these investments by emphasizing market development. The World Bank and the EU are also investing in road and rail transport infrastructure. The World Bank is making additional investments in community development and economic recovery.

Malagasy NGOs will be important partners in the implementation of SO 7. The Mission already has established partnerships with organizations such as the national congress of farmers' associations, and PRONABIO/SYPIEM, the association of natural products producers.

F. Alternative Approaches

Early in the development of the ISP, the Mission considered pursuing agriculture and trade development as part of the Environment/Rural Development Strategic Objective. This approach was rejected because: a) the economic growth orientation of this SO, while it contributes to biodiversity conservation, represents a separate objective; b) results of economic growth (especially agriculture, and trade and investment) funding will be more directly observable; and c) the skills required to manage this SO differ from those of the Environment/Rural Development Strategic Objective.

The Mission also considered a tighter focus of this SO, either on a geographic basis or on agriculture. While it is expected that agricultural production activities will tend to coincide geographically with the Env/RD SO's eco-regions, the market-based orientation of this SO argues for not being overly restrictive. Similarly, best practice suggests that it is not desirable to pre-select the commodity or product lines for intervention at the strategic planning stage. This is better done in consultation with implementing partners and taking into account market conditions at the implementation stage. This ISP sets out broad criteria for identification of "critical markets," for further refinement during implementation. Indeed, some flexibility is required to respond to the short-term economic recovery emphasis of the GOM and the Mission Performance Plan, and to adapt to changing conditions over the life of the strategy.

The Mission also considered including a credit component, e.g., microcredit. Given the additional management implications and the efforts—albeit imperfect—of other donors, USAID-financed lending operations are not proposed at this time.

At the mid-level funding scenario, the Mission will pursue selected interventions along several high priority commodity chains. At the high-level scenario, the Mission would be better placed to reinforce the private-sector orientation of the GOM, engage more aggressively in policy dialogue, and provide more active support for Madagascar's participation in regional and global trade initiatives. In addition, the range of commodities and the numbers of beneficiaries would be increased, and USAID's contribution to economic growth would be more substantial. Under the low-level scenario, agricultural production interventions (IR 1) will be fully dependent on the Env/RD SO, PL-480, Title II agriculture activities, and GOM and other donors' investments. This would still enable USAID to concentrate on its comparative advantage on market development issues, but it would constrain efforts to link farmers groups with buyers. The choice of commodity chains would be limited as well in the first two years of implementation, with a likely focus on only three or four commodity groups.

G. Measuring Results

This SO requires measurement of agricultural output, commodity sales, and exports, as well as monitoring of policy changes. The primary responsibility for performance measurement will be placed on the lead implementing partner, under the supervision of the SO Team. It is expected that data collected will be closely integrated with the efforts of the GOM (notably INSTAT), the World Bank, and producers' and business associations.

PART VIII   RESOURCE REQUIREMENTS AND PROGRAM MANAGEMENT

A. Funding Scenarios

Madagascar's importance as a biodiversity hotspot, its economic potential, its extreme poverty, its need for assistance in recovery from the recent political crisis, the development foundations set before the crisis, and the promise of the new government—particularly its commitment to good governance—provide sound reasons for sustaining and increasing U.S. foreign assistance. Program funding scenarios are derived from the January 2002 Parameters Guidance for Madagascar 01 STATE 02926 (See Annex 3).

Development Assistance/Child Survival and Health: The Parameters Guidance identified three funding scenarios. Under the low-level scenario, DA and CSH resources total $16.25 million. The mid- and high-level scenarios are for $23 million and $30 million, respectively. The funding would be distributed as follows:

FY 2003 – 2007 Annual Funding (DA/CSH, $U.S. millions) and Staffing

Scenario	Low	Mid	High
Total Funding (DA/CSH), o/w	**$16.25**	**$23.0**	**$30.0**
Democracy & Governance	$0.75	$1.0	$2.0
Health, Population, Nutrition	$6.5	$9.0	$11.0
Environment/Rural Development	$7.5	$10	$12
Agriculture/Trade	$1.5	$3.0	$5.0
P.L. 480- Title II	**$6.5**	**$8.5**	**$9.0**
USDH Staff	*3*	*5*	*8*

Source: Parameters Guidance, 01 STATE 02926

The mid-level scenario of $23 million per year ($115 million over five years) corresponds most closely to the Mission's initial estimate of requirements to fund the proposed program, as presented in the November 2001 Concept Paper. This level begins to send a signal that the USG values the commitment that the GOM is making to good governance, economic growth, HIV prevention, and investing in the health and well being of its people. At this level, economies of scale would be realized in reaching households and communities through core implementation mechanisms. The Mission would be assured of resources necessary to support policy dialogue and change.

The high-level scenario of $30 million per year ($150 million over five years) would capitalize on Mission expertise and the integrated nature of USAID/Madagascar's portfolio, and increase overall program impacts. The Health, Population and Nutrition SO could provide significantly more support to greater numbers of NGOs, broaden the access to and use of health information services and technology, and appreciably strengthen national management of drug, vaccine, and contraceptive logistics systems. The Environment and Rural Development SO could expand activities to the north of Tamatave, into the largest remaining forest block in the country—an area in which the Mission was actively involved in the early 1990s. The Agriculture and Trade

SO would be better placed to address specific bottlenecks in agricultural production, reach significant numbers of farmers' groups, broaden the range of commodities assisted, reinforce the private-sector orientation of the GOM, engage more aggressively in policy dialogue, and provide more active support for Madagascar's participation in regional and global trade initiatives. The Democracy and Governance SO would be in a better position to provide targeted support to decentralization efforts, expand the number of issue-areas pursued by civil society, and increase the number of targeted government units receiving information and technical assistance.

The low-level scenario of $16.25 million per year ($81.25 million over five years) would enable the Mission to make substantial contributions in the environment and health sectors, and targeted, yet influential interventions to support good governance and economic growth. Even at these funding amounts, the Mission would be in a position to leverage private resources and influence the course of GOM and other donor investments in Madagascar. Maintenance of this minimum level of funding is important to the mutually reinforcing nature of the four SOs. Given the low level of funding for the DG SO in this scenario, and its planned contributions to other SOs, some DG activities would likely be funded by more than one SO. It would be limited in its capacity to support anti-corruption efforts. Similarly, the MAT SO would be dependent on other interventions (Env/RD and P.L. 480, Title II) for agricultural production and farmer association activities. Under the low scenario, the HPN SO would be constrained in the number of communities and target groups it could reach. This in turn would have a negative effect on key health indicators such as vaccination rates, quality of STI services, and improvements in nutritional status. And the Env/RD SO would be constrained in its capacity to provide further assistance to its public-private alliance in the southern Madagascar Anosy eco-region.

The DG SO could be financed using Democracy and Governance funding and, for some activities, either Conflict or Education funding. The HPN SO could be financed through DA or CSH funds, including Child Survival, HIV/AIDS, Infectious Disease and Micro-nutrient funds. The Env/RD SO could be financed through Environment (including Biodiversity), Agriculture, and Other Economic Growth Funds. The Agriculture and Trade SO could be financed using Agriculture, Trade, or Other Economic Growth Funds. The majority of Mission activities will be implemented through bilateral instruments, except that approximately one-third (to one-half) of the HPN activities will be implemented through Global Field Support mechanisms.

PL-480, Title II Assistance: The Parameters Guidance provides for between $6.5 million and $9 million in PL-480, Title II resources. In July 2002, USAID/Madagascar issued guidelines to potential Cooperating Sponsors based on the Parameters Guidance and indicating avenues for Title II programs to reinforce the ISP. Title II Development Assistance Program Proposals for FY 2004 – 2008 were submitted to the Mission in November 2002. Direct feeding and Food-for-Work programs may support STI/HIV/AIDS prevention, maternal and child health and nutrition, and agricultural development. Monetization proceeds may be directed to health, environment, agriculture and rural development, and disaster preparedness activities. Before proceeding with monetization under a new ISP, the Mission will commission independent analyses of the market impacts of monetization. Currently, Title II imports are managed through a consortium of Cooperating Sponsors.

B. Staffing and OE

Staffing: The low-level scenario would require USAID/Madagascar to reduce USDH staffing from six positions at the end of FY 2002 to three, whereas the high scenario would restore staffing to the FY 01 level of eight. It is the Mission's assessment that a reduction in USDH positions to as few as three would increase Mission vulnerabilities and is not advisable. Higher USDH staff levels also increase Mission capacity to engage in policy dialogue with senior Government officials, and to better coordinate with other donors. The Mission recommends that, under the low- and mid-level funding scenarios, USDH staffing be maintained at no less than five positions, and that the full complement of eight positions be considered in the context of the mid- and high-level funding scenarios.

If reduced to five under the mid-level scenario, USDH positions would be allocated for a Mission Director, Supervisory Project Development Officer (S/PDO), Supervisory General Development Officer (S/GDO), Controller, and Executive Officer (EXO). Four internationally recruited Personal Service Contractors (PSC) SO Team Leaders and the PSC Food For Peace Officer would each report to either the S/PDO or S/GDO. A resident-hire USPSC would serve as Deputy Team Leader in the Env/RD office. Note: The Mission proposes that the GDO (Democracy and Governance Officer) return to post after Home Leave and serve until July 2005, at which point the DG Team would be shifted to USPSC leadership. The current Third Country National PSC Food for Peace Officer would be retained until the end of his contract in FY 2004.

Under the high-level scenario, eight USDH positions would be allocated: Mission Director, S/PDO, Controller, Health Officer, Environment Officer, Private Enterprise Officer, GDO (Democracy and Governance), and EXO. Three US and TCN PSCs will provide additional technical leadership.

Under the low-level scenario, three USDH positions would be retained: Mission Director, S/PDO, and Controller. This scenario would require an OE-Funded USPSC Executive Officer. After a period of transition, each of four strategic objective teams would be headed by internationally recruited, program-funded PSCs, reporting to the Mission Director or S/PDO. Locally recruited PSC's would serve as Deputy Team leaders for the health and environment SOs.

A qualified staff of Foreign Service Nationals makes each of these scenarios viable. At the end of FY 2002, the Mission had 63 FSN positions (37 OE-funded, of which two were vacant but deemed essential, and 26 Program-funded). There is only limited scope for reducing these numbers, as FSN staffing requirements are not highly sensitive to changes in program funding or USDH staffing levels. Under the low-level scenario, FSN staffing would be reduced to 57 (30 OE/27 Program), while under the high-level scenario it would reduce to 60 (35 OE/25 Program). A net reduction in OE-funded FSN positions can be realized if up to two financial analyst and two procurement specialist positions are shifted to Program Funding, and, with fewer USDH, up to three secretarial positions are shifted from OE to Program.

Illustrative Workforce by Scenario, FY 2004 – 2008

Low-level Scenario Estimate	GDO	D&G	Health	Env.	Agric. Trade.	Total SO/SPO	Org. Mgmt.	Fin. Mgmt	Admin. Mgmt	Contract	Total Mgmt.	Total Staff
OE Funded: 1/												
U.S. Direct Hire	1					1	1	1			2	3
Other U.S. Citizens						0			1		1	1
FSN/TCN Direct Hire						0					0	0
Other FSN/TCN	1					1	5	10	12	2	29	30
Subtotal	2	0	0	0	0	2	6	11	13 *	2	32	34
Program Funded 1/												
U.S. Citizens		1	2	2	1	6					0	6
FSNs/TCNs		4	10	5	4	23		2		2	4	27
Subtotal	0	5	12	7	5	29	0	2	0	2	4	33
Total Direct Workforce	2	5	12	7	5	31	6	13	13 *	4	36	67
TAACS/Fellows						0					0	0
Subtotal	0	0	0	0	0	0	0	0	0	0	0	0
TOTAL WORKFORCE	0	5	12	7	5	29	8	13	13 *	4	38	67

* Excludes 31 Manpower Contract personnel
Not shown: The USDH GDO (DG Officer) position would also be retained until July 2005; the DG Team secretary would not shift to program funding until FY 05.

Mid-level Scenario Estimate	GDO	D&G	Health	Env.	Agric. Trade	Total SO/SPO	Org. Mgmt.	Fin. Mgmt	Admin. Mgmt	Contract	Total Mgmt.	Total Staff
OE Funded: 1/												
U.S. Direct Hire	1					1	2	1	1		4	5
Other U.S. Citizens						0					0	0
FSN/TCN Direct Hire						0					0	0
Other FSN/TCN	1					1	6	10	12	2	30	31
Subtotal	2	0	0	0	0	2	8	11	13 *	2	34	36
Program Funded 1/												
U.S. Citizens		1	1	2	1	5					0	5
FSNs/TCNs		5	10	6	4	25		2		2	4	29
Subtotal	0	6	11	8	5	30	0	2	0	2	4	34
Total Direct Workforce	2	6	11	8	5	32	8	13	13 *	4	38	70
TAACS/Fellows						0					0	0
Subtotal	0	0	0	0	0	0	0	0	0	0	0	0
TOTAL WORKFORCE	2	6	11	8	5	32	8	13	13 *	4	38	70

* Excludes 31 Manpower Contract personnel
Not shown: The USDH GDO (DG Officer) position would also be retained until July 2005; the DG Team secretary would not shift to program funding until FY 05.

High-level Scenario Estimate	GDO	D&G	Health	Env.	Agric. Trade	Total SO/SPO	Org. Mgmt.	Fin. Mgmt	Admin. Mgmt	Contract	Total Mgmt.	Total Staff
OE Funded: 1/												
U.S. Direct Hire		1	1	1	1	4	2	1	1		4	8
Other U.S. Citizens						0					0	0
FSN/TCN Direct Hire						0					0	0
Other FSN/TCN		1	1	1	1	4	6	11	12	2	31	35
Subtotal	0	2	2	2	2	8	8	12	13	2	35	43
Program Funded 1/												
U.S. Citizens			1	2	0	3					0	3
FSNs/TCNs		4	9	5	3	21		2		2	4	25
Subtotal	0	4	10	7	3	24	0	2	0	2	4	28
Total Direct Workforce	0	6	12	9	5	32	8	14	13	4	39	71
TAACS/Fellows						0					0	0
Subtotal	0	0	0	0	0	0	0	0	0	0	0	0
TOTAL WORKFORCE	0	6	12	9	5	32	8	14	13	4	39	71

* Excludes 36 Manpower Contract personnel

Mission Motorpool and Shipping and Property Management Services are provided under two local contracts, which provide employment for an additional 38 persons (31 OE/7 Program). Under the low- and mid-level scenarios, only limited reductions in staffing under these contracts are deemed feasible.

Operating Expenses: The Parameters Guidance instructs the Mission to straight-line the FY 2001 OE Budget, i.e., $2,570,000 for the high-level scenario, and indicate how lower OE levels could be accommodated under the low- and mid-level scenarios. The chart below indicates the distribution of FY 2001 OE according to major expenditure groupings. The two largest cost elements are local Personnel (Foreign Service National salaries and benefits, and Motorpool and Shipping and Property Management Contracts, 28%), and US Direct Hire support costs (22%).

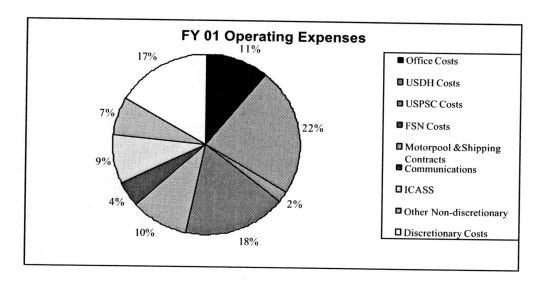

Actual OE requirements for FY 2003 and beyond will be determined by a number of factors, including: size and complexity of the assistance program; numbers of OE-funded US PSCs (e.g., EXO); timing of USDH transfers; FSN and service contract cost increases; staff training; relocation of USAID offices; and, in the event of Mission restructuring, FSN termination costs and changes in ICASS costs.

The table below presents OE requirements under the high-level scenario based on conservative projections of personnel, facilities and administrative costs, inflation, and exchange rate changes. Under this scenario, OE requirements exceed the FY 2001 straight-lined level, beginning in FY 2004. In FY 2008, projected requirements exceed the baseline by $876,000, or 34.1%. During the life of the ISP, the cuts in personnel, support contracts, and discretionary costs necessary to conform to the Parameters Guidance would become so severe as to be unsustainable.

Illustrative Operating Expense Budget Projections, by Scenario FY 2003 – 2008

	FY 2001 Actuals	FY 2003 Budget	FY 2004 Budget	FY 2005 Budget	FY 2006 Budget	FY 2007 Budget	FY 2008 Budget
Low-level Scenario							
Office Rent – maint. – util.	273,832	271,862	281,499	281,699	291,710	294,310	295,710
USDHs	591,383	422,639	392,872	335,716	387,674	367,974	383,174
USPSCs	47,338	152,653	175,925	169,900	167,885	170,423	209,525
FSNs Salary & Benefits	459,768	578,506	609,325	668,712	722,544	779,687	841,488
Motorpool & Shipping/ Property Mgmt. contracts	254,439	280,520	294,699	309,434	324,905	341,151	358,208
Communication & Courier	114,486	124,100	124,100	124,100	124,100	124,100	124,100
ICASS	231,871	210,990	147,333	154,667	162,400	170,520	179,046
Other Non-discretionary	168,467	175,880	159,945	157,428	157,088	174,408	174,338
Discretionary Costs	428,417	287,806	224,146	239,984	268,705	244,024	205,692
Total	2,570,000	2,504,956	2,409,844	2,441,639	2,607,011	2,666,597	2,771,281
FY 01 level		2,570,000	2,570,000	2,570,000	2,570,000	2,570,000	2,570,000
Variance		(65,044)	(160,156)	(128,361)	37,011	96,597	201,281
Mid-level Scenario							
Office Rent – maint. – util.	273,832	271,862	281,499	281,699	291,710	294,310	295,710
USDHs	591,383	628,888	576,116	526,516	528,511	617,811	540,011
USPSCs	47,338	-	18,946	33,500	-	-	35,000
FSNs Salary & Benefits	459,768	578,506	619,379	679,975	734,725	792,861	855,736
Motorpool & Shipping/ Property Mgmt. contracts	254,439	280,520	294,699	309,434	324,905	341,151	358,208
Communication & Courier	114,486	124,100	124,100	124,100	124,100	124,100	124,100
ICASS	231,871	210,990	184,167	193,333	203,000	213,150	223,808
Other Non-discretionary	168,467	175,880	159,945	157,428	157,088	174,408	174,338
Discretionary Costs	428,417	290,566	234,906	239,984	272,105	247,424	209,092
Total	2,570,000	2,561,313	2,493,756	2,545,969	2,636,144	2,805,214	2,816,002
FY 01 level		2,570,000	2,570,000	2,570,000	2,570,000	2,570,000	2,570,000
Variance		(8,687)	(76,244)	(24,031)	66,144	235,214	246,002
High-level Scenario							
Office Rent – maint. – util.	273,832	271,862	281,499	281,699	291,710	294,310	295,710
USDHs	591,383	544,638	853,096	799,746	851,992	870,792	962,492
USPSCs	47,338	-	18,946	33,500	-	-	35,000
FSNs Salary & Benefits	459,768	578,506	652,994	726,683	785,239	847,493	914,820
Motorpool & Shipping/ Property Mgmt. contracts	254,439	280,520	306,588	321,918	338,014	354,915	372,660
Communication & Courier	114,486	124,100	124,100	124,100	124,100	124,100	124,100
ICASS	231,871	210,990	184,167	309,333	324,800	341,040	358,092
Other Non-discretionary	168,467	175,880	159,945	157,428	157,088	174,408	174,338
Discretionary Costs	428,417	290,566	385,984	239,984	272,105	247,424	209,092
Total	2,570,000	2,477,063	2,966,741	2,994,391	3,145,048	3,254,481	3,446,304
FY 01 level		2,570,000	2,570,000	2,570,000	2,570,000	2,570,000	2,570,000
Variance		(92,937)	396,741	424,391	575,048	684,481	876,304
Exchange rate		6,350	6,450	6,550	6,550	6,550	6,550

Projected mid-level scenario requirements begin to exceed the FY 2001 straight-line by FY 2006. In FY 2008, projected requirements exceed the straight-line by $246,000, or 9.6%. By limiting FSN salary increases at Post, containing ICASS costs, and reducing non-expendable property, training and related travel costs, the Mission could likely operate within the FY 2001 baseline budget level under the mid-level scenario. Scope for further budget reductions under this scenario are limited.

The projected OE requirements of the low-level program funding and staffing scenario also begin to exceed the FY 2001 OE funding level in FY 2006. By FY 2008, OE levels would be 7.1% higher than in FY 2001. As with the mid-level scenario, it is likely that the adjustments necessary to straight-line the FY 2001 OE level would be feasible.

Cost considerations with respect to the major expenditure groupings are explored below:

- Office rent, maintenance and facilities: The foregoing OE estimates are based on the assumption that USAID remains at its current location. For security reasons, however, the Mission is actively seeking to relocate. Negotiations over one site broke down in late 2001. One contributing factor was the Mission's inability to commit to what would have been increased recurrent costs at the new location. The Mission will seek to reduce office facilities costs in selecting new office space. However, renovating and relocating would entail additional, one-time costs that are not included in the Mission's OE budget scenarios.

- USDH and USPSC Staffing: Budget projections are sensitive to assumptions on USDH and USPSC staffing. Reducing USDH staff from eight to five yields estimated savings ranging from $273,000 in FY 2005 to $422,000 in FY 2008. However, USDH reductions from five to three would be fully offset by the costs in the Mission's budget of a USPSC Executive Officer.

- FSN salaries and benefits and manpower contracts (for motorpool, and shipping and property management services): FSN and manpower budget requirements are relatively insensitive to changes in the number of USDH—whether under the high- or low-level USDH and program funding scenarios. There is little scope for reducing the numbers of OE-funded support staff since essential program, controller, contracting, information system, and executive office functions would need to be performed under each of the scenarios.

- Communications: The Mission is implementing measures to contain communications costs, including installation of Voice over Internet Protocol telephony, switching to a lower-cost cellular telephone company, and using scanning and e-mailing in place of telefaxing to send important documents.

- ICASS: ICASS costs are sensitive to assumptions about USDH and USPSC staffing. USAID will continue to seek ways to contain costs through ICASS. However, it is unlikely that significant savings would occur by sourcing additional resources from

ICASS. USAID will also explore the cost implications of competitively outsourcing services now provided in-house or under ICASS.

- Discretionary Costs: Discretionary costs include non-expendable property, training and conferences, and related travel costs. Estimated budget requirements range between $200,000 and $300,000 per year. Only limited cuts could be sustained.

Conclusions:

- The eight USDH scenario is not viable without at least a 4.3% annual growth in OE (FY 2001 - 2008). However, program activities corresponding to the high-level scenario ($30 million/year) could be sustained with the substitution of USPSCs (or PASAs or TAACS Advisors). This would involve trading off OE savings versus vulnerabilities, knowledge of USAID priorities and procedures, and influence in dealing with host country counterparts.

- The five USDH scenario is viable within a range of up to 10 percent above the FY 2001 straight-lined OE levels.

- The three USDH scenario is viable at or slightly below the FY 2001 straight-lined level, but it implies increased vulnerabilities and reduced effectiveness compared to the five USDH scenario.

- Requirements for USDH staff are not directly tied to program funding levels. USPSCs (and potentially PASA or TAACS employees), as well as professional FSN staff can, to some extent, offset reductions in USDH. However, a minimum of five USDH is recommended to limit vulnerabilities and maximize program effectiveness under the low- and mid-level scenarios. Eight USDH positions should be considered in the context of the mid- and high-level program funding scenarios.

C. Management Considerations

Implementation plans for the ISP will be developed at the onset to limit the number of management units. Proliferation of management units has been an outcome of the Mission's successful competition for additional resources under special initiatives and emergency response programs over the life the current strategy. New instruments will be designed with flexibility to adjust to changing circumstances, whether special initiatives or crisis response. Participant training will usually be integrated into these instruments, rather than being administered directly by the Mission.

The Mission expects to implement the DG SO through one to two primary contract or grant instruments, with buy-in from the HPN and Environment/Rural Development SOs likely. The HPN SO will rely on one major Mission-based contract and a limited number of field support instruments. The Env/RD SO requires a wide range of organizational competencies and will be best managed through four to five primary instruments: contracts, grants, and interagency agreements. The Agriculture/Trade SO will likely be implemented through one primary contract, with buy-in from the Env/RD SO under consideration. It is expected that three PL-480

Title II Cooperating Sponsors will be selected on the basis of the Development Assistance Proposals submitted for FY 2004 - 2008 programs. Provision will be made for contractors and grantees to enter into public-private alliances using program resources, with USAID concurrence. Resources permitting, the Mission expects to identify additional public-private alliance opportunities over the life of the strategy, which may result in an increase in the number of management units.

D. Field Support Requirements

USAID/Madagascar will continue to require Regional Contracting Officer and Legal Advisor support. Currently, the Mission is receiving excellent service from RCSA/Gaborone. The Mission will continue to rely on REDSO/Nairobi and RCSA/Gaborone for technical backstopping for disaster response, Food for Peace, and other programmatic areas. The Mission also plans to increase interaction with Regional Hubs on such issues as trade, anti-corruption, and HIV/AIDS to augment Mission-sponsored training and information exchange.

USAID/Washington technical support will also be needed. For instance, the Mission has enjoyed solid technical backstopping in the health, democracy, environment and economic growth sectors. This will continue to be important, as the health portfolio may become increasingly dependent on centrally funded projects. Bureau for Democracy, Conflict and Humanitarian Assistance support for P.L. 480, and disaster preparedness and mitigation will continue to be important.

INTERNATIONAL MONETARY FUND

REPUBLIC OF MADAGASCAR

Ex Post Assessment of Longer-Term Program Engagement

Prepared by a Staff Team from African, Fiscal Affairs, Monetary and Financial Systems, and
Policy Development and Review Departments[1]

Authorized for circulation by Thomas Krueger and Mark Plant

May 12, 2005

Contents   Page

---

[1] The team comprised M. Quintyn (Head, MFD), L. Allain, K. Nassar, and A. Jayaratnam (all AFR),
A. Hajdenberg (FAD), J. Mbabazi-Moyo (MFD), and P. Kongsamut (PDR).

GLOSSARY

BFV	National Bank of Commerce
BTM	Bank for Rural Development
CBI	Cross-border initiative
COMESA	Common Market for Eastern and Southern Africa
EPZ	Export processing zones
GDP	Gross Domestic Product
HIPC	Heavily Indebted Poor Countries
IFI	International financial institutions
IMF	International Monetary Fund
I-PRSP	Interim Poverty Reduction Strategy Paper
IT	Information technology
JSA	Joint Staff Assessment
MDG	Millennium Development Goals
PC	Performance criterion
PEM	Public expenditure management
PSRP	Poverty Reduction Strategy Paper
REER	Real Effective Exchange Rate
SADC	Southern African Development Community
SB	Structural benchmark
VAT	Value-added tax

- 4 -

I. INTRODUCTION

1.   **During the 1970s, Madagascar followed an inward-looking development strategy, which resulted in declining growth, as well as large economic and financial imbalances.** Real GDP grew at an average annual rate of less than 2 percent and real per capita GDP declined steadily. Administrative controls multiplied in the economy and several sectors were nationalized. Since the early 1980s, several adjustment programs, supported by Fund arrangements and World Bank resources, succeeded in reducing the economic and financial imbalances, including through extensive debt relief, but not in remedying the structural rigidities.

2.   **In 1988, the authorities adopted an ambitious strategy to move toward an open and market-oriented economy.** A 10-month stand-by arrangement with the Fund served as the bridge between the first annual arrangement under a SAF, and arrangements under a new ESAF, starting in 1989.

3.   **This report presents an ex post assessment of Madagascar's long-term program engagement with the Fund.** Given the important shift in the economic course in 1988–89, those years are taken as the starting point. The report focuses on performance during the programs supported by the 1989 and 1996 ESAFs, and the 2001 PRGF. Under the 1989 ESAF, only the amounts under the first and second annual arrangements were fully disbursed (Table 1). Under the 1996 ESAF, two disbursements were made under the first annual arrangement. No understanding could be reached on a second arrangement. The program was extended by one year. It eventually expired in November 2000, with the completion of just two of the three envisaged annual arrangements. The 2001 PRGF was the only program in the period under review, under which all disbursements were made. Meanwhile, Madagascar reached the HIPC decision point in December 2000 and the completion point in October 2004. Fund and Bank endorsed the full PRSP in 2003.

Table 1. Madagascar: History of IMF Lending Arrangements
Since 1987
(In thousands of SDRs)

Facility	Date of Arrangement	Date of Expiration or Cancellation	Amount Agreed	Amount Drawn	Percent Drawn
PRGF	3/1/01	3/1/05	91,650	91,650	100.0
ESAF	11/27/96	11/30/00	81,360	78,860	96.9
ESAF	5/15/89	5/14/92	76,900	51,267	66.7
SBA	9/2/88	5/15/89	13,300	2,800	21.1
SAF	8/31/87	5/14/89	46,480	13,280	28.6

Source: IMF, FIN Department.

4.   **Despite nearly continuous involvement by the IMF, other international financial institutions (IFI), and bilateral donors, economic progress has been slow**. Only the most recent years have witnessed inroads into poverty reduction of some significance (Appendix I). External shocks and political crises frequently interrupted stabilization and growth efforts, and stalled reforms. Structural reform has accelerated with the onset of the PRSP process around 2000. The country's growth base remains narrow, and its institutional framework and governance weak. Madagascar remains one of the poorest countries in the world (Table 2), and today's real GDP per capita still stands 50 percent below its 1960 level.[2]

5.   **Poverty remains prevalent in Madagascar and poverty reduction has been slow**. Poverty has dramatically increased since the 1960s and, in particular, during the period of inward-looking policy actions in the 1980s. Structural reforms since the mid-1990s are having a beneficial, though still limited, impact on poverty levels (Table 3 and Appendix I). In 2004, an estimated 75 percent of the population still lived in poverty. This percentage is markedly lower for the urban population, which has benefited more from economic growth (approximately 40 percent). The levels of most social indicators and of access to basic utilities remain low. Net primary school enrollment has increased from 48 percent to 70 percent since the mid-1990s. The percentage of electricity and water connections has doubled in the same period, but remains low (respectively, 19 percent and 27 percent). On the other hand, the infant mortality has hardly come down and remains at 86 deaths per 1,000 births, and immunization rates are only at 36 percent of children. About 80 percent of the rural population still has no reliable transport services, and of these, one-third has no road access at all.

---

[2] Per capita GDP was US$430 in 1960, compared to US$220 in 2003. Since 1975, annual population growth has averaged 2.8 percent, compared with an average annual GDP growth of 1.2 percent.

Table 2. Madagascar: Growth Comparison (1983–2004)

	Burkina Faxo	Cameroon	Ethiopia	Kenya	Uganda	Tanzania	Rwanda	Zambia	Mozambique	Madagascar	Sub-Saharan Africa
1983–92											
Average real GDP growth (in percent)	4.7	0.4	0.8	3.6	3.0	3.5	2.6	0.8	0.4	1.2	2.1
Standard deviation of real GDP growth	5.1	6.2	8.3	2.5	3.9	2.8	5.6	3.5	8.9	2.9	1.9
Average GDP per capita growth (in percent)	2.2	-2.4	-1.7	0.2	0.9	0.4	-0.6	-2.2	-1.0	-1.3	-1.2
Per capita GDP in 1992 (in 1990 U.S. dollars)	367	850	147	346	412	183	348	459	173	242	409
1993–2004											
Average real GDP growth (in percent)	5.7	3.5	5.2	1.9	6.7	4.5	4.1	1.2	8.0	2.6	3.6
Standard deviation of real GDP growth	2.4	3.1	5.0	1.4	2.2	2.0	19.8	5.4	3.2	5.4	1.8
Average GDP per capita growth (in percent)	3.2	0.6	2.2	-0.3	3.1	1.8	-0.1	-1.4	5.8	-0.5	0.6
Per capita GDP in 2001 (in 1990 U.S. dollars)	487	855	188	336	556	197	323	364	291	244	425
1983–2004											
Average real GDP growth (in percent)	5.3	2.1	3.2	2.7	5.0	4.0	3.4	1.0	4.5	2.0	2.9
Standard deviation of real GDP growth	3.8	4.9	6.9	2.1	3.5	2.4	14.8	4.5	7.4	4.4	1.9
Average GDP per capita growth (in percent)	2.7	-0.8	0.5	-0.1	2.1	1.1	-0.4	-1.7	2.7	-0.9	-0.3

Source: World Economic Outlook, IMF.

II. ECONOMIC AND POLITICAL DEVELOPMENTS

6.   **Economic growth picked up quickly in the wake of the implementation of market-oriented reforms in 1988–90 (Figure 1)**. For the first time in almost a decade, real per capita GDP growth was positive (Figure 2). However, the episode was short-lived. A combination of policy slippages and adverse weather conditions dampened growth already in 1990, and the political crisis of mid-1991 paralyzed economic and social life entirely.

7.   **Political and social instability kept the country in its grip until roughly 1996–97.** The political turmoil found its origin in a growing popular resentment at the government's liberal measures—including price and trade liberalization, privatization, civil service reform, and tax and customs reform—combined with a gathering desire for political change. It resulted in massive general strikes and social unrest. Most economic reforms, started during 1988–90, were either suspended or reversed.[3] Real GDP growth stalled, inflation soared, internal and external balances widened, and payments arrears accumulated. Real per capita GDP declined by almost 9 percent in 1991, and close to 4 percent in 1992. Work started on a new constitution in 1992, and a new president took office in 1993.

8.   **The political situation remained unstable and structural reform lost momentum**. The rift between the new president, who was elected on a platform of populist measures, and the government, which intended to pursue a drastic reform agenda, continued to dominate political and economic life.

9.   **In mid-1994, the government prepared a new medium-term policy statement, with support from the IMF and World Bank**. This statement provided a framework for economic liberalization and structural reforms in several key areas. However, the political climate did not yet prove right for implementation. The impeachment of the president by parliament in 1997 brought an end to this long period of political instability and opened the way for reform.

10.   **Since 1997, the record in terms of economic stabilization and growth has been more positive than before, even though this period has not been without crises either**. Between 1997 and 2001, economic growth averaged 4½ percent, inflation remained subdued, exports doubled, and international reserves rose sharply, even in the face of adverse exogenous shocks (three cyclones hit Madagascar in early 2000). Structural reform started to take root, laying the foundations for a period of accelerated growth.

---

[3] These include certain tax measures and the open general license system for imports.

Table 3. Madagascar: Social Indicators—Comparison with Averages for Sub-Saharan Africa Countries

	1990		1995		2001		2002	
	MDG	SSA	MDG	SSA	MDG	SSA	MDG	SSA
Population below $1 a day (%)	...	44.6	...	45.3	49.1	46.5	...	...
Adult literacy rate (% of people ages 15 and over)	...	...	...	...	...	64.1	...	64.9
Youth literacy rate (% ages 15-24)	72.2	...	76.3	...	80.8	76.9	...	80.2
Ratio of girls to boys in primary and secondary education	98.9	79.1	99.2	...	...	...	...	...
Under 5 mortality rate (per, 1,000)	168.0	187.1	156.0	184.9	136.0	175.4	...	173.9
Prevalence of HIV, female (% ages 15-24)	...	...	...	...	0.2	9.4	...	...
Access to an improved water source (% of population)	44.0	53.2	...	...	47.0	58.2	...	...
Fixed line and mobile telephones (per 1,000 people)	2.8	10.0	3.0	11.2	13.3	23.8	14	30.9
Life expectancy at birth (years)	52.8	50.0	53.3	49.2	54.7	46.5	55.5	45.8

Source: http://devdata.worldbank.org/

Figure 1. Madagascar: Real GDP Growth and Major Events, 1988–2004
(In percent)

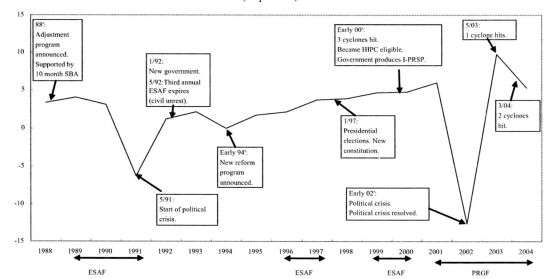

11.   **These positive developments were abruptly interrupted by the 2002 political crisis**. Despite strong suspicion of vote-rigging, official results denied victory to the opposition candidate (Mr. Ravalomanana) in the 2001 presidential elections, forcing him into a second round. When he proclaimed himself president in February 2002 after the second round, the country had effectively two administrations because the incumbent (Mr. Ratsiraka) refused to accept defeat. His supporters organized a blockade of Antananarivo, and economic life in the capital city stalled nearly completely. The rest of the country was also affected, but less severely.

12.   **The crisis was short-lived,[4] but its economic and social consequences were devastating, underscoring the persistent fragility of Madagascar's economy**. Real GDP contracted by 13 percent in 2002 and inflation soared to double-digit levels. Per capita real GDP dropped by 15 percent—washing away the gains made in the previous five years—and income poverty increased by as much as 6 percent, affecting 75 percent of the population at the end of 2002. Recovery from this political crisis was quick and economic growth resumed its earlier trend in 2003. However, recovering the losses registered in income poverty and other social indicators is much slower.

---

[4] In May, the new president was sworn in, and by July he was internationally recognized.

Figure 2. Madagascar: Real GDP Per Capita Growth, 1980-2004
(In percent)

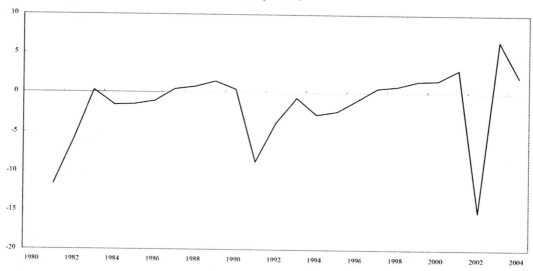

III. ASSESSMENT OF FUND INVOLVEMENT

A. Objectives of the Programs

13.   **Given Madagascar's low level of economic development, Fund involvement sought to achieve and maintain an environment of macroeconomic stability and external viability, conducive to sustained growth.** The three programs also supported the government's structural reform agenda aimed at reducing poverty. To achieve these objectives, the first program focused specifically on domestic and external liberalization. The second program aimed more at a structural transformation of the economy in order to create conditions for sustained economic growth and the reduction of poverty by rebuilding a capable public administration, and addressing corruption and weak governance. The third program supported the government's objectives—in line with the goals set out in the I-PRSP and, later on, in the PRSP—of strengthening economic growth while improving the distribution of its benefits in order to secure a permanent reduction in poverty.

14.   **The results of the Fund's involvement in achieving these objectives have been uneven.**[5] Fund involvement has contributed to macroeconomic stabilization, strengthening

---

[5] For illustrative purposes, Appendix II compares Madagascar with two other Sub-Saharan countries that went through an economic regime change roughly around the same time as Madagascar, and which also benefited from extensive Fund assistance.

the resilience of the economy and external viability. It has also been fairly successful in bringing about some structural reforms (external sector liberalization, financial sector reform, and exchange rate regime), while in others, notably, tax policy, tax and customs administration, public expenditure management, privatization, and civil service, progress has been limited. This section analyzes progress in meeting the respective program objectives.

B. Areas of Strong Progress

Macroeconomic stabilization

15.   **Inflation has been brought down, but remains volatile and above the objectives**. Inflation was brought down from 23 percent in 1987 to 11 percent in 1990 (Figure 3).[6] However, it veered out of control during the subsequent political crisis. Since 1996–97, inflation has, on average, been below 10 percent. The surge during the 2002 political crisis was controlled rapidly. Despite these achievements, inflation remains volatile and above the objectives (to some extent, due to exogenous factors, such as the rise in agricultural and oil prices in 2004).

16.   **Economic growth has picked up since the late 1990s, but this positive track record is still short**. Since 1997—with the exception of 2002—growth has been in the 5 percent to 6 percent range, close to program targets (Figure 4), but still below the rates targeted in the PRSP to achieve significant poverty reduction.[7] It seems, however, that a basis for sustainable growth has been laid. Recovery from recent shocks (natural shocks in 2000, 2001, and 2004, and the political crisis of 2002) has been faster than before.

17.   **Significant progress has been made in achieving the external sector objectives, which focused on improving external viability**. In the early 1990s, international reserves were drawn down, bottoming out at SDR 42.7 million by the end of 1994—just over one month of imports (Figure 5). In recent years, they have been buffeted by the weather, commodity price, and political shocks in 1998, 2002, and 2004. At end 2004, Madagascar's gross reserves position had reached a historically high level of over SDR 300 million. However, this level is still below the set objective, and, given Madagascar's sensitivity to shocks, it still provides only a limited cushion of around three months of imports.

---

[6] The projections in the figures are those prepared by the staff at the beginning of the program for the length of the program, as well as at the beginning of a new annual arrangement for the next year.

[7] The PRSP's goal is to reduce the level of poverty by half in 10 years (i.e., by 2013). To achieve that goal, an average annual GDP growth of 9.3 percent is needed. The Millennium Development Goals (MDG) are somewhat less ambitious. They call for a halving of poverty by 2015, which corresponds with an average annual growth rate of 8 percent.

Figure 3. Madagascar: Inflation, 1988–2004
(Annual average, in percent)

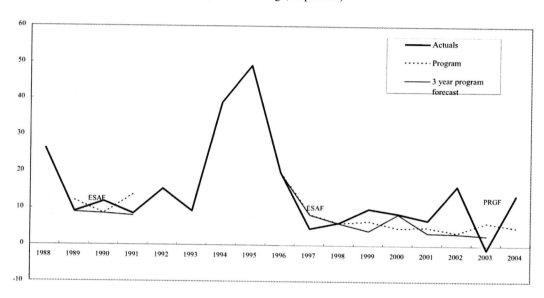

18.   **Madagascar's external debt situation has improved significantly**. Its position could remain sustainable, provided sound macroeconomic policies are maintained and structural reforms continued, according to the HIPC completion point debt sustainability analysis. Since 1981, the country rescheduled its debt to the Paris Club creditors 11 times. With the latest round of debt relief, the NPV of debt to exports was expected to be reduced to a little over 150 percent in 2004 (IMF Country Report No. 04/406, December 1, 2004). Debt service to exports will be below 5 percent and debt service to revenue about 10 percent. Sensitivity analysis indicates that a sustainable debt position depends critically on achieving sustained GDP growth rates of at least 6 percent.

Figure 4. Madagascar: Real GDP Growth, 1988–2004
(In percent)

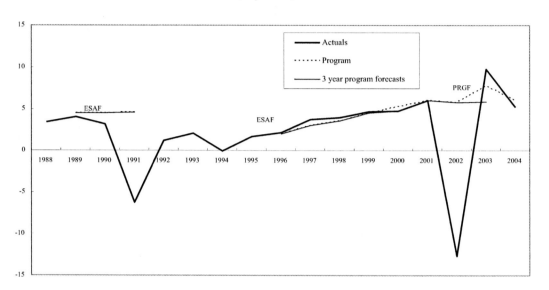

Figure 5. Madagascar: Gross International Reserves, 1988–2004

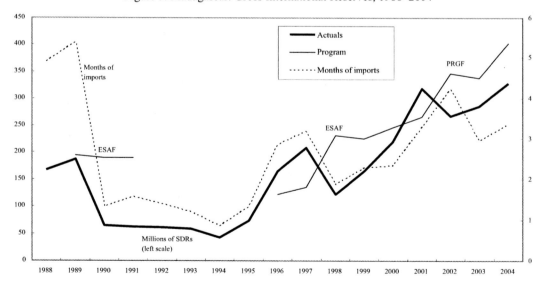

19.   **The external current account deficit remains wide and its size continues to fluctuate**. Since 1996, current account deficits (excluding grants)—have been between 6 percent and 8½ percent of GDP—in all but one year (2001) (Figure 6). These deficits have been largely financed by aid inflows (mainly grants). The trade structure has changed tremendously during this period, with traditional exports fading in relative importance as the exports from the export processing zones (EPZ) and other exports have grown.

Figure 6. Madagascar: Current Account Deficit, 1988–2004
(In percent of GDP)

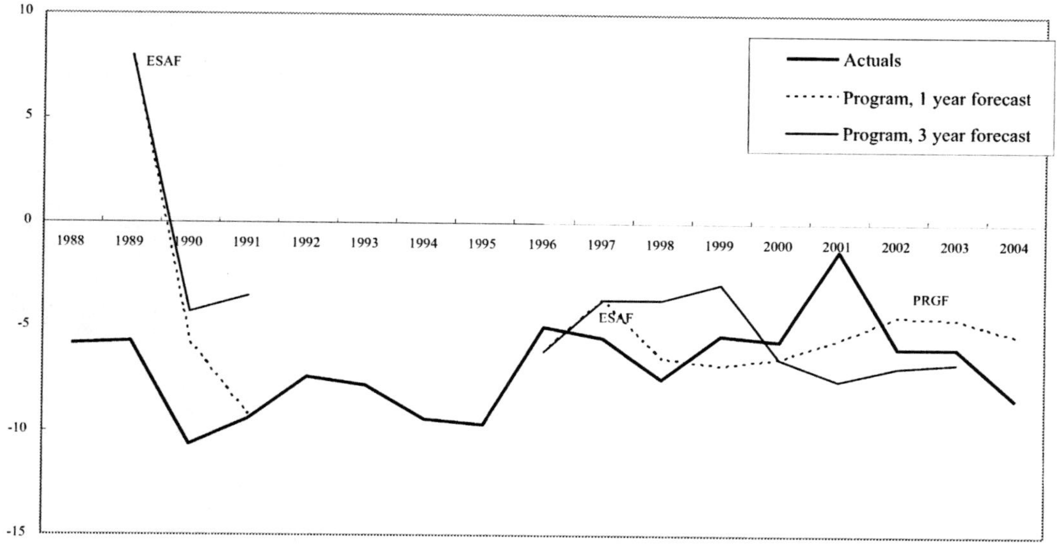

20.   **The Malagasy franc has remained broadly competitive, as measured by the REER** (Figures 7 and 8). Following a period of loss in competitiveness under a pegged exchange rate, with a widening gap between official and parallel exchange rates, widening external imbalances and trade restrictions driving trade increasingly into informal channels, the authorities decided to adopt a floating exchange rate regime in 1994. This regime has helped in maintaining the currency's competitiveness.

- 15 -

Figure 7. Madagascar: Nominal and Real Effective Exchange Rate, 1988M1–2004M8
(Index, 1990=100)

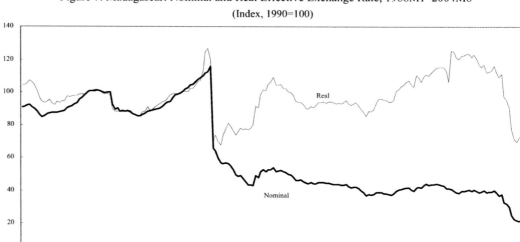

Figure 8: Madagascar: Real Effective Exchange Rates for Selected Countries (Sep 2002–Feb 2005)
(Index, Sept 2002 =100)

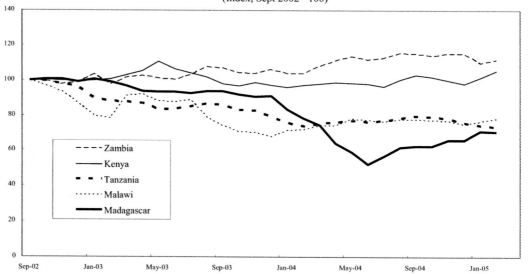

Structural reform

External sector liberalization

21.   **Initially, external trade liberalization was slow, with some reversals.** In the early reform years, trade liberalization was considered essential to integrate Madagascar into the global economy. However, the strides taken were limited. Import tariffs were lowered from 80 percent to the 50–60 percent range. Some export taxes were abolished while others, such as on vanilla, remained in existence. The political and economic crisis of 1991 was marked by an intensification of restrictions on current account transactions.

22.   **Since 1996, trade liberalization was conducted in the context of the Cross-Border Initiative (CBI) and COMESA, and has made major strides.** Import duty rates have been lowered, in line with the CBI guidelines. The weighted average rate is currently estimated at 18 percent (Country Report No. 04/403, 12/10/04). Export taxes and the export surrender requirement were fully eliminated in 1997. Since 2004, the country only has four tariff bands, and the two import taxes have been merged. Madagascar accepted the obligations of Article VIII in 1996.

Exchange rate regime and markets

23.   **The exchange rate mechanism, established in 1994, has operated satisfactorily, despite occasional problems at the level of the market infrastructure.** Initially, the operation of the floating rate regime was undermined by the sluggishness of the unified interbank foreign exchange market. One large, state-owned bank, BTM (Bank for Rural Development) dominated the market, but was not very active given its distressed state. Only after BTM's restructuring in 1996 did the market start to operate more smoothly. The system was also hampered by the fact that residents could transfer foreign exchange deposits among each other, thereby significantly reducing the volumes that went through the market. The introduction of the continuous quotation interbank market in 2004 seems to have improved the efficiency of the system.

Price liberalization

24.   **Price liberalization started in 1989 and is now almost complete.** Many price controls were abolished between 1989 and 1995, and by now, most prices are market-determined. A significant achievement was the liberalization of domestic oil prices in 2004.

Financial sector reform

25.   **Following an unconvincing start in the early 1990s, financial sector reform gathered speed in the late 1990s.** The privatization of two ailing state banks, BTM and BFV (National Bank of Commerce), had been part of the conditionality under Fund-supported programs since the late 1980s. However, outright privatization proved politically difficult and technically complex. Under the 1996 ESAF, intermediate steps, intended to first clean up

these banks, were taken. Privatization finally took place between 1996 and 1999. The authorities have also permitted private domestic and foreign banks to operate in the country.

26. **The supervisory framework for banking has been improving since the mid-1990s.** The establishment of the independent Banking and Financial Supervision Commission in 1996 laid the basis for a modern supervisory framework. The alignment of the prudential supervisory framework with the Basel Core Principles in recent years has contributed to the soundness of the banking system (Table 4). While the banking system is sound, intermediation remains low, mainly because of other impediments to financial services (Table 5).

Legal reform

27. **The 1996 ESAF had a substantive legal reform component.** The most critical achievement was the introduction of legal instruments for long-term land lease by foreigners, as well as procedures to effect a lease within 60 days. This, and other improvements to the legal framework and the work conditions and professional capacity of magistrates have improved the business climate and the rule of law in Madagascar.

C. Areas of Weak Progress

Macroeconomic stabilization

28. **Little progress has been made in strengthening public finances.** While the authorities in general managed to keep the fiscal deficits close to the program targets, the way they achieved them was often not consistent with the programs (Figure 9). The disappointing tax revenue record (see below) forced the authorities constantly to compress expenditures (and to borrow more from the banking system than programmed), in order to hit the deficit objective. This poor-quality fiscal adjustment constrained the provision of basic public services and economic development in general.

Structural reform

Tax policy and administration

29. **The absence of any significant improvement in tax collection is one of the greatest failures during the period under review.** Despite the fact that achieving an increase in domestic revenue mobilization has been recognized as a key objective in each program, the outturn for 2004, a tax-to-GDP ratio of 11 percent, is equal to the level attained in 1989 (Figure 10). Madagascar remains among the countries with the lowest tax revenue/GDP ratio (Figure 11).

30. **The authorities have been unable to mobilize domestic revenue in a magnitude consistent with the expenditure needs of the country.** Since 1996, Fund-supported programs have sought to address deficiencies in tax policies, the tax base, and tax and customs administration, but achievements to date are minimal. On the upside, the

introduction of VAT ensured that the drop in trade taxes, as a result of external liberalization was, to some extent, offset. On the downside, however, tax policy has been plagued by the complexity of the tax code, frequent resort to ad hoc (tax and customs) exemptions, and policy reversals. The tax base remains narrow and tax revenue does not benefit from the high growth areas of the Malagasy economy (EPZs and mining sector, for instance, are subject to very low tax rates). These problems are compounded by the fact that—despite some achievements—tax and customs administration remains weak and plagued by corruption.[8]

Table 4. Madagascar: Financial Soundness Indicators, 1998–2004
(In percent, unless otherwise indicated)

	1998	1999	2000	2001	2002	2003	2004 Jun.	2004 Sept. Est.
Capital adequacy								
Regulatory capital to risk-weighted assets								
Lowest Ratio	8.6	9.7	10.1	12.0	11.4	10.7	9.4	8.4
Highest Ratio	30.5	28.7	32.2	34.1	38.7	38.5	49.1	38.7
Asset quality								
Nonperforming loans to total gross loans	21.1	8.4	8.4	10.3	19.5	16.7	14.2	12.9
Earnings and profitability								
Return on assets	3.2	4.3	4.0	2.8	1.1	3.2	4.3	4.4
Return on equity	91.0	53.0	47.0	39.0	16.0	45.7	33.4	..
Noninterest expenses to gross income	46.5	42.9	45.4	48.9	52.2	46.9	42.4	42.9
Personal expenses to noninterest expenses	44.6	36.7	38.4	35.3	38.3	38.9	36.1	35.6
Liquidity								
Liquid assets to total assets	35.9	37.0	36.9	44.2	52.1	50.5	49.4	48.7
Liquid assets to short-term liabilities	61.9	61.2	62.2	70.0	77.8	74.5	71.8	70.3
Memorandum items								
(In billions of Malagasy francs)								
Total assets	4,222.0	4,931.0	5,668.0	6,723.0	6,965.2	7,685.9	9,350.0	9,431.8
Total profits before tax	137.2	214.0	226.5	186.6	79.7	249.6	199.8	310.1
Highest foreign exchange exposure	..	..	..	17.2	19.6	58.3	141.0	109.4

Source: Banking and Financial Supervision Commission, Central Bank of Madagascar (BCM).

[8] Achievements in the tax and customs administration include (i) the informatization of customs controls and the introduction of pre-shipment inspections; (ii) the creation of a large taxpayers unit; and (iii) the reorganization of the tax department into regional offices.

Table 5. Madagascar: Indicators of Financial Deepening Broad Money (M2), 1985–2003
(In percent of GDP)

	1985	1990	1995	2000	2001	2002	2003
Botswana	16.9	16.1	18.2	27.3	31.7	28.4	32.7
Burundi	19.9	17.6	20.0	19.5	20.9	25.6	28.7
Cameroon	18.5	21.1	18.0	15.9	17.3	20.6	19.3
Congo, Dem. Rep. of	6.7	11.7	4.9	7.4	5.0	4.6	5.1
Ethiopia	28.8	40.2	42.5	42.2	45.4	53.2	53.4
Gambia, The	23.4	21.1	23.8	36.8	36.1	43.5	45.9
Ghana	12.9	12.6	21.3	26.7	26.9	31.4	32.0
Kenya	26.7	29.6	52.7	39.5	36.5	36.2	37.2
Madagascar	**19.1**	**17.9**	**18.0**	**19.3**	**22.1**	**23.3**	**23.0**
Malawi	19.8	20.3	19.0	16.7	15.1	15.8	17.2
Mauritius	46.8	61.0	73.0	78.9	78.2	80.5	82.8
Mozambique	47.4	21.2	24.9	30.0	31.4	31.9	31.4
Namibia	13.3	20.1	37.4	40.4	36.1	33.9	40.0
Nigeria	24.0	21.7	15.6	22.1	24.6	28.4	26.4
Tanzania	28.0	15.1	18.7	13.2	13.3	14.1	14.6
Uganda	6.4	4.4	9.6	13.5	15.4	16.2	18.0
SSA Average	27.6	25.5	27.6	31.2	32.4	34.6	35.6
Credit to Private Sector, 1985–2003 (In percent of M2)							
Botswana	73.4	66.5	73.7	61.2	56.8	69.6	55.9
Burundi		81.3	68.9	107.6	105.2	106.6	89.9
Cameroon	94.8	97.3	54.8	73.9	63.3	55.4	61.0
Congo, Dem. Rep. of	29.2	19.6	29.2	13.4	16.1	13.5	15.5
Ethiopia			36.7	50.6	49.7	41.1	34.3
Gambia, The	177.0	58.0	54.5	0.0	20.4	15.1	10.5
Ghana	63.7	49.2	38.0	61.7	59.9	48.1	48.9
Kenya	81.1	115.3	67.5	78.5	73.5	70.8	67.2
Madagascar			**64.3**	**47.6**	**43.0**	**40.6**	**40.0**
Mali			46.8	69.5	69.4	65.7	63.6
Mauritius	59.7	54.0	64.0	78.3	77.0	73.8	69.9
Namibia		96.5	103.4	93.9	102.9	115.2	120.5
Nigeria		52.5	63.3	56.3	62.4	58.3	59.7
Tanzania	54.1	116.1	43.9	32.8	34.4	36.1	42.2
Uganda			41.3	44.4	40.8	34.8	36.1
SSA Average	78.8	71.6	55.0	53.4	51.6	49.5	50.3

Source: World Economic Outlook, 2004.

Figure 9. Madagascar: Fiscal Deficit, 1988–2004
(In percent of GDP)

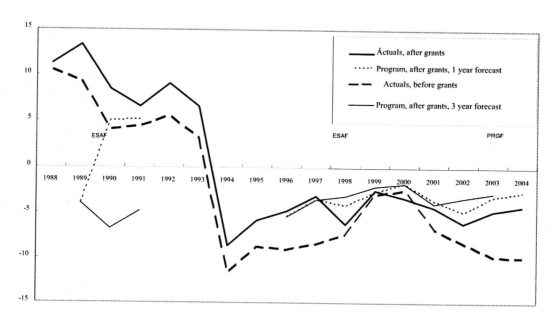

Figure 10. Madagascar: Tax Revenue, 1988–2004
(In percent of GDP)

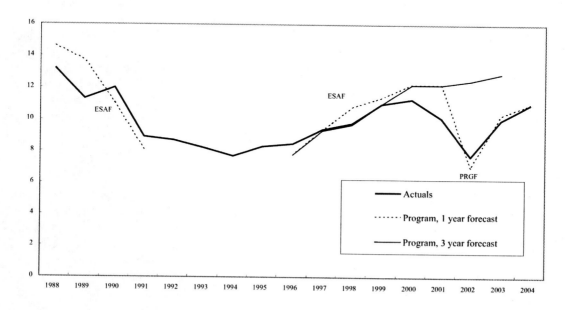

Figure 11. Madagascar: Tax Revenue in Selected Comparator Countries, 1989–2004
(In percent of GDP)

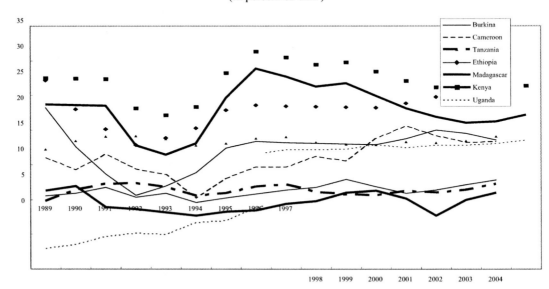

Budgetary process and public expenditure management (PEM)

31.   **Slow progress in PEM reform remains a bottleneck in the fight against poverty**.
Important achievements of the early 1990s were the inclusion of the public investment plan
into the budget; and the presentation of central government operations on a cash,
commitment, and payment-order basis. An ambitious reform agenda was developed under
the 1996 ESAF, but measures were often delayed. Progress was made in strengthening local
treasury offices and a new budgetary classification was introduced. The track record of
reforms in PEM improved recently, as conditionality in the PRGF on PEM was key to
reaching the HIPC completion point. Some progress was made in streamlining budgetary
procedures to accelerate the execution of spending in priority areas and in improving tracking
of this spending.

Monetary policy reform

32.   **Conditions for the use of indirect instruments have now been broadly met, but
policy effectiveness still needs improvement**. Attempts at reforming the monetary policy
framework through the adoption of indirect instruments started early on. However, the
conditions for indirect instruments to be effective were not met in those early years. The
gradual development of a treasury bill market and a money market in the mid-1990s, made
the use of open-market operations gradually feasible. Administered interest rates were
abolished and credit ceilings removed as these markets developed. Finally, financial sector
reform improved the transmission of monetary policy through indirect instruments. However,

markets remain shallow and the central bank's liquidity management capabilities weak, often contributing to inconsistent policy responses.

Privatization

33. **Privatization has been slow, but major enterprises have been taken out of public management in the past four to five years.** Even though privatization has been a policy objective since the late 1980s, only a handful of public enterprises has been effectively privatized. Progress began following the 1996 approval by parliament of a legal and institutional framework for privatization. Commercial banks were the first strategic companies to be fully privatized. In 1996, legal state monopolies were abolished in key sectors (power, petroleum, telecommunications, and air transport). Progress under the most recent PRGF program was mixed. The telecommunications company (TELMA) and the cotton company (HASYMA) were privatized, while the sugar company (SIRAMA), Air Madagascar, and the electricity and water company (JIRAMA) have been put under private management—but still majority owned by the government.

Civil service reform

34. **Progress in implementing civil service reform has been slow and proves to be a bottleneck for progress in other areas.** The need for reform was recognized early on. However, the wage bill—which was already not high by sub-Saharan standards (Table 6)—was cut repeatedly in the ensuing years, due to shortfalls in fiscal revenue, and salary reform and other reforms remained hampered by these shortfalls. Ambitious reforms were included in the ESAF in 1997, but implementation was delayed because of political resistance. The relevant statute introducing a mechanism for advancement and promotions based strictly on merit, and including a code of ethics and discipline, was approved by the National Assembly in 2001, but not implemented.

Private sector development

35. **Private sector development has been slow.**[9] Foreign and domestic investment started to pick up around the turn of the twenty-first century, benefiting from three to four years of macroeconomic stability and taking advantage of the legal provisions, which allowed foreigners to lease land for a period up to 99 years.

---

[9] Private sector development has been hampered by a number of factors, including, macroeconomic and political instability in the first half of the 1990s, low domestic savings, low quality of public services, lack of infrastructure, legal monopolies of public enterprises in several sectors, nontransparent and unpredictable application of government regulations affecting potential investors, and the prohibition for foreigners to own land in the country. Several of these issues have been addressed since the late 1990s.

Table 6. Madagascar: Civil Service Wages and Salaries in Selected African Countries 1998–2003
(In percent of GDP)

	1998	1999	2000	2001	2002	2003
Angola	8.9	4.1	5.6	7.5	10.9	12.1
Benin	4.7	4.5	4.7	4.6	4.8	5.1
Botswana	8.7	9.4	9.2	10.2	11.5	12.2
Burkina Faso	3.9	4.5	4.8	4.7	4.5	4.5
Burundi	6.8	6.6	6.6	7.3	7.9	8.3
Cameroon	4.9	5.1	5.0	5.3	5.9	5.8
Cape Verde	9.5	9.7	9.9	9.4	9.5	11.5
Central African Republic	4.4	4.1	4.2	4.1	4.6	5.0
Chad	3.4	3.6	3.9	3.6	3.5	3.7
Comoros	7.5	6.3	5.7	5.3	5.6	5.7
Congo	8.9	6.9	4.7	5.8	5.7	5.8
Côte d'Ivoire	5.5	5.5	5.9	6.2	6.4	7.2
Ethiopia	5.9	5.9	6.6	7.4	7.3	7.8
Gabon	7.7	7.5	6.0	6.4	6.4	6.5
Gambia, The	6.3	6.1	6.3	5.2	5.4	4.5
Ghana	5.5	5.6	5.2	6.1	8.5	8.4
Guinea	4.1	4.1	3.8	3.6	3.7	3.6
Guinea-Bissau	4.7	5.0	6.8	7.5	7.4	7.9
Kenya	9.0	8.7	8.4	8.1	8.4	8.3
Lesotho	16.5	14.7	15.1	14.5	14.0	13.2
Madagascar	**4.1**	**4.3**	**4.0**	**4.5**	**4.6**	**5.4**
Malawi	5.1	4.9	5.0	5.7	7.3	6.9
Mali	3.4	3.6	3.8	3.9	4.0	4.2
Mauritius	6.9	7.0	6.9	6.5	6.5	6.2
Mozambique	4.5	5.8	6.7	7.0	7.3	7.5
Namibia	16.4	16.9	15.6	15.1	14.6	15.7
Niger	3.7	4.1	4.0	3.5	3.7	3.6
Nigeria	2.0	4.0	6.0	5.3	6.5	4.9
Rwanda	4.7	5.3	5.2	5.2	4.9	4.9
São Tomé & Príncipe	4.6	6.2	6.7	7.7	7.3	9.1
Senegal	5.7	5.6	5.5	5.3	5.7	5.5
Seychelles	15.1	14.5	14.2	14.2	13.7	14.6
Sierra Leone	4.8	6.0	6.7	7.0	7.3	6.7
South Africa	11.0	10.6	10.2	10.0	9.6	9.8
Swaziland	11.1	12.1	11.1	10.5	10.9	13.0
Tanzania	3.9	3.4	3.9	3.7	3.6	3.7
Togo	6.3	6.1	5.9	5.7	5.0	4.9
Uganda	3.1	3.8	3.7	4.2	4.6	4.6
Zambia	5.4	5.4	5.3	6.8	8.0	8.4
Zimbabwe	11.6	12.3	18.1	11.4	10.3	9.1
Average for Sub-Saharan Africa	6.8	6.7	6.9	6.9	7.2	7.4

Source: World Economic Outlook, 2004.

36. **The contribution of the EPZ regime, created in 1989, to employment and exports has been growing steadily.**[10] The EPZs' success is attributable to a combination of factors including, a favorable and stable fiscal regime, the availability of labor with matching skills, relatively low wages and more recently, the relative political and economic stability and Madagascar's eligibility under AGOA. Nonetheless, worries remain that the spillover effects of the EPZs on growth of other sectors remain limited.

Social and sectoral policies

37. **Until the beginning of the PRSP process, social and sectoral policies did not yield significant results.** Broadly until the turn of the millennium, education and health policies only reached the urban population and, as such, increased the poverty wedge between urban and rural population.

38. **The most recent PRSP-JSA (Country Report No. 04/403, 12/10/04) notes significant progress in recent years in several critical areas,** including rural development, education, health, infrastructure, HIV/AIDS, nutrition, rural water and sanitation, and social protection. Madagascar is, at current trends, likely to meet a number of MDGs by 2015 (gender equality, complete enrollment in primary school, halting HIV/AIDS spread, malaria, and deforestation), but the likelihood of meeting other goals, such as halving extreme poverty and hunger, 100 percent primary school completion, reducing by 2/3 infant and maternal mortality) is slim on current trends.[11]

D. Compliance with Program Conditionality

39. **The record on meeting quantitative performance criteria is uneven.** The first ESAF (1988) had a promising start, with all quantitative performance criteria being met in the first two reviews (Appendix III). During some reviews in the last two programs, up to 50 percent of the PCs and indicative targets were not met. Compliance with the floor on tax revenue proved systematically problematic. Typical is that PCs were often just narrowly missed, which seems to be an indication of lack of implementation capacity more than of inconsistent policies.[12]

---

[10] "Zones" in Madagascar do not refer to a geographic concept. EPZ enterprises need to comply with certain criteria but can be established anywhere.

[11] The World Bank, "Country Note—Madagascar—Reaching the Millennium Development Goals." (July 11, 2003). See also Appendix I.

[12] Indicative ceilings on broad money and reserve money were often missed under the ESAF and PRGF, mainly because of this lack of implementation capacity.

40.   **The record on structural benchmarks is mixed, but has been improving** (Appendix IV). During the first program, a few, rather easy, benchmarks were met. The more challenging ones (e.g., privatization and a start with civil service reform) were not implemented. Structural conditionality intensified significantly during the last two programs. During the 1996–2000 ESAF, implementation of several structural conditions was delayed. The track record during the most recent PRGF is better, with progress in privatization, fiscal policy management and, to a lesser extent, in civil service reform.

41.   **The compliance rate under the latest PRGF is markedly better than under the previous Fund-supported programs.** Even though the number of PCs and SBs was higher under the PRGF than under the ESAF, the compliance rate was much higher. Under the ESAF, Madagascar implemented 40 percent of the conditionality, whereas under the PRGF, this share went up to 87.5 percent. This positive development is also clear from a comparison with African programs in general and mainly reflects increased ownership of the program: under the 1996 ESAF, Madagascar was far below the African average (61 percent) for the period 1995–2000, while under the PRGF, Madagascar was far above the average for the continent (65 percent).

IV. POLICY IMPLEMENTATION—EXPERIENCE AND LESSONS

42.   **A combination of factors explains the lack of more broad-based success.** First of all, political crises and external shocks frequently interrupted the authorities' reform efforts and the Fund's support. Secondly, ownership was extremely low until the mid-1990s. In the early years, political crises and lack of ownership were not totally separable. The 1991 political crisis was in part against the government's economic liberalization plans, and because the government's efforts were not whole-hearted, they stalled in the face of the protests. In that sense, the political crisis was not a completely exogenous shock. Since the mid-1990s, ownership has become increasingly stronger. However, at that point a third factor became even clearer than before: the limited absorption and implementation capacity of the country. Factors that influenced progress in implementation are reviewed in this section.

A. Program Objectives and Design

43.   **Macro-stabilization objectives were generally adequate.** One of the main achievements of the Fund's involvement has been to enhance the authorities' capacity in macroeconomic stabilization. "Erratic policy implementation" or "inconsistent policies" were often mentioned as major problems early on.[13] In more recent years, stabilization capacity has certainly improved—as was shown by the quick reaction to bring inflation under control in the wake of the 2002 political crisis.

---

[13] Examples of policy inconsistencies include the introduction of a floating exchange rate (1994), unaccompanied by tighter fiscal and monetary policies, leading to an exchange rate depreciation of 45 percent to 50 percent against the U.S. dollar.

44.   **Macroeconomic program design on exchange rate policy was generally adequate, but in monetary policy it was initially over-optimistic**. The advice on exchange rate policies was appropriate and has, in general, supported the government's macroeconomic policy. On monetary policy, the desire to rely on indirect instruments seemed premature (see above) in light of the fact that the markets and their infrastructure, as well as the authorities' implementation capacity, were for a long time not ready for this transition. This undermined policy effectiveness.

45.   **The design of fiscal policies was constrained by underperforming tax revenues**. Throughout the period, programs allowed for large fiscal deficits (before grants), which were justified, given the country's development needs. On the other hand, the room for maneuver to shrink the fiscal deficits over time and to make qualitative cuts in expenditure was limited, given the constraint imposed by low tax revenues.

46.   **Program design with respect to tax policies and tax and customs administration struggled systematically with the effects of the disappointing tax revenue record**. Revenue shortfalls compared to program targets mainly stemmed from the fact that the authorities did not implement promised policy measures, or reversed them afterwards—signs of lack of ownership.[14][15] Confronted with this underperformance and with the lack of policy consistency, program conditionality focused almost exclusively on weaknesses in tax and customs administration, in the hope that revenue would expand through these measures. Almost no tax policy measures were part of the conditionality since 1997. While strengthening the administration was necessary in its own right, programs seem to have put too much hope in short-term revenue gains from these improvements and tried to move too fast.[16] Limited implementation capacity and resistance from vested political interests prevented reform in this area.

47.   **Fund arrangements exhibited a certain degree of flexibility to accommodate shocks**. The floors on net foreign assets of the central bank, tax revenue, and bank credit to the government, were adjusted on several occasions to take into account the impact of natural disasters, and economic and political shocks, which allowed the country to comply with the (revised and adjusted) framework.

48.   **Implementation of the broad-based structural reform agenda since 1996 was constrained by the limited implementation capacity of the authorities**. The reform agenda became broad-based, addressing simultaneously several areas critical to generating

---

[14] Natural disasters and political crises also played a part in the lack of progress of tax revenue collection.

[15] Including the elimination and subsequent reintroduction of exemptions, granting of ad hoc exemption, reduction in excise taxes, liberalization of foreign trade without compensating domestic tax measures.

[16] For instance, the Policy Framework Paper (October 1996) listed 20 measures to improve tax policy and administration in 1997.

sustained growth. The broadening of the reform agenda was, on the one hand, a reflection of the greater attention that IFIs, in general, had started to pay to issues such as corruption and governance.[17] On the other hand, this shift in focus was in response to signs of a greater willingness by the authorities to tackle poverty at its roots. However, in response to this change in approach, programs did perhaps not fully appreciate the limited implementation capacity of the authorities as a major stumbling block (as well as lingering political resistance from vested interest groups against some parts of the programs).

B. Ownership and Implementation Capacity

49. **Until the mid-to-late 1990s, program implementation was hampered by lack of ownership**. Lack of ownership of, and political resistance to, reforms was obvious in the late 1980s and early 1990s. The authorities were willing to take those measures necessary to jumpstart the economy, but there was certainly no consensus around more far-reaching measures such as privatization and civil service reform.

50. **The turning point came in the second half of the 1990s.** Civil society, social and religious groups converged on the view that structural reform was the country's only way out of poverty and began to consider the IMF (and other IFIs) as vehicles to achieve this goal. The movement in favor of removing the president in 1996-97 was, among other reasons, inspired by the fact that he was seen as an obstruction to the government's reform efforts. Once the new president's, the government's and the civil society's interests were aligned, ownership of Fund-supported programs improved significantly. From 1997–98 onward, the structural reform agenda started to move forward. The support of civil society also brought corruption and governance to the forefront of the agenda, although initial results were weak.[18]

51. **Growing ownership became even more evident from the domestic consultative process that preceded the publication of the PRSP, and from the contents of this document**. The same sense of ownership was also felt in the negotiations on the most recent PRGF. The goals of the PFRG were fully consistent with the PRSP framework and were fully supported by the authorities. The high degree of compliance with the structural agenda under the PRGF (see above) is a reflection of the high sense of ownership of program and PRSP. The prospect of debt relief at the HIPC completion point was, of course, an additional incentive for the government to engage in the above initiative, but even without that, there has been a significant change in the climate surrounding Fund program negotiations.

52. **Cultural factors contributed to the authorities' cautious attitude toward Fund-supported programs**. The authorities—and Malagasy society as a whole—were for a long time cautious with respect to foreign investment in domestic, productive resources.

---

[17] See IMF, "Governance Note" August 1997.

[18] It was not until 2002 that the fight against fraud and corruption started in earnest.

Critical modifications to the legal framework, to facilitate the entry of foreigners and provide them security regarding their investment, were introduced slowly.

53.   **Program implementation continues to suffer from limited absorption capacity**. The civil service in general is weak and ministries lack adequate technical skills. While recognized early on by the Fund and the Bank as impediments to reform, success in addressing them has been limited. Weaknesses in public expenditure management have aggravated the problems. This has a number of consequences. First, a weak civil service makes implementation of specific policies difficult; in addition, the civil service cannot fulfill its role as advisor or institutional memory for the government; hence, the presence of ad hoc or inconsistent policies.

54.   **Madagascar has been a recipient of extensive technical assistance in the monetary, fiscal, and statistical areas, but implementation has generally been weak**. Thus far, the technical assistance input has only been able to make a small dent in Madagascar's capacity problems.[19] This limited success seems attributable to two factors. One is the limited absorption capacity. Several implementing agencies chronically suffer a lack of adequate funding, with repercussions on staffing and equipment. These constraints have impeded the implementation process. Secondly, technical assistance recommendations could have been better aligned with the authorities' priorities. In those cases, the authorities did not see a need for implementation, but Fund-supported programs were often based on the assumption that the advice would be implemented.

C. Collaboration with World Bank

55.   **The division of labor between both institutions has generally been satisfactory**. The World Bank has focused its advice on sectoral structural reforms, including privatization and private sector development, basic infrastructure, agriculture, education and health, civil service reform, legal reform, and poverty monitoring and evaluation. The Fund has relied to a great extent on the Bank's technical expertise in these areas. Cooperation was close on the PRSP and the Bank has become more active in some sectors, such as agriculture, since the publication of the PRSP.

56.   **A few episodes have caused frictions between both institutions**. First, the World Bank was reluctant to engage in a wide-ranging civil service reform, which, to some extent, delayed the Fund's work in that area. This reluctance stemmed from the Bank's (negative) experience in other parts of Africa with civil service reform. Hence, the Bank preferred to focus instead on pointed interventions to make specific public-sector units more effective. Secondly, during the 2002 political crisis, the Bank kept its presence in Antananarivo, unlike

---

[19] Fiscal Affairs Department (FAD) fielded 20 missions in the period under review and deployed one long-term advisor. Other donors were also involved, in particular, in revenue administration and public expenditure management. Statistics Department (STA) had 6 missions in the period under review and a total of 15 MFD missions visited the country since 1993, of which 12 have done so since 1998.

the Fund. In the absence of the Fund, the Bank was asked by the new president to provide advice on a wide range of policy issues. Advice on tax exemptions, inconsistent with the Fund's views, created tensions between both institutions for a while. Meanwhile, these issues have been resolved and coordination is smooth.

D. Donor Coordination

57.   **Donor coordination has gone through ups and downs, but generally could have been better**. At times, lack of coordination among donors led to competition among them. The 2002 crisis led to confusion among the donors, putting them in two camps. At other times, coordination was optimal. For instance, in 1997 the Fund managed to get all the donors behind its requirement that tax exemptions be revoked before understanding could be reached on a new Fund-supported program.

58.   **The lack of a solid public expenditure management framework has impaired the effectiveness of donor assistance**. The lack of a good tracking system in the government has impaired the smooth channeling of funds to the projects. The PRSP calls for improvements in public expenditure management and for better coordination among donors. Initiatives to that effect have already been taken.

59.   **Aid flows were not evenly distributed over time**. Aid flows dropped significantly during periods of political uncertainty (1992, 1998, and 2002) (Figure 12). Sharp increases were seen in 1997, 1999, and 2003, coinciding with a new program or the resumption of a program. Reductions, interruptions, and volatility in aid flows sometimes interfered with smooth program implementation.[20]

E. Summary: Lessons for the Future

60.   **The satisfactory outcome in terms of macro stabilization is the result of constant involvement to ensure that the authorities remained focused on stabilization**. More generally, as the following examples indicate, maintaining a constant dialogue—even in the absence of a Fund program—has proven beneficial in the long run. On the positive side, the exchange rate regime was established in 1994 outside the program, but with Fund assistance, and turned out to be a success. On the negative side, the absence of the resident representative during the 2002 political crisis damaged the Fund's reputation and required a great effort to (re)gain the new government's confidence.

61.   **Involvement of civil society (social and religious groups) in the policy dialogue has facilitated achieving the program objectives**. The start of a dialogue between Fund and civil society in the mid-1990s has helped in convincing important groups in the Malagasy

---

[20] Staff Reports contain some references that shortfalls in aid flows contributed to nonobservance of the ceiling of bank credit to the government.

society of the need for structural reform to address the country's poverty. This, in turn, strengthened government ownership of the reform agenda in the ensuing period.

Figure 12. Madagascar: Grants and External Borrowing, 1987–2003

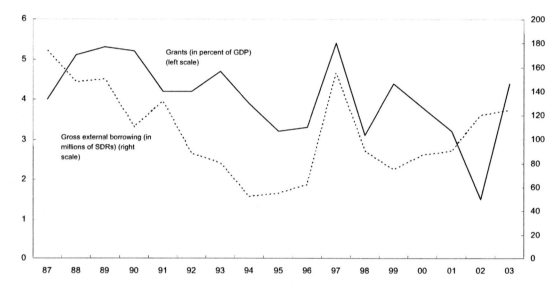

62.   **Weak governance and corruption hindered progress in key areas**. Various international governance and corruption watchdogs put Madagascar typically between 20 and 50 on a scale from 0 (worst) to 100 (best).[21] These sources also agree on improvements in the past three–four years. However, certain parts of the administration—in particular tax and customs administration—are still widely perceived as corrupt.

63.   **The lack of progress in tax policy and administration begs the question whether a stricter approach, with greater emphasis on tax policy, could have achieved better results**. During the last two programs, waivers were typically given when tax revenue did not meet the floor.[22] On some occasions, this was justified (impact of cyclones), but on other occasions, the shortfalls were due to policy reversals or to non-implementation of structural measures. The reviews justified the waivers because, in some cases, the authorities had taken additional measures in the run-up to the program review or had committed during the review to strengthening tax and customs administration. Although increasing tax revenue was

[21] Transparency International, International Country Risk Guide, and World Bank Country Policy and Institutional Assessment.

[22] This happened four times out of 10 reviews in the 1996 ESAF and seven times out of 11 reviews in the PRGF.

considered by all programs as an essential policy objective, it was apparently never considered important enough to trigger the noncompletion of a review, perhaps out of fear that the growing momentum in structural reform would have been lost.

64.   **Faced with this situation, program conditionality could have incorporated more tax policy measures**. The combination of failing to meet the quantitative performance criterion on tax revenue, and the PCs or SBs on tax policy could then have been used to take a much harder line during the respective program reviews.

65.   **A tougher approach once worked**. In one instance (1997), the Fund took a harder line by setting the removal of specific ad hoc customs exemptions as a condition for agreeing on a Fund program.[23] Coordinated donor support helped in bringing about the desired result. Therefore, the more general question remains whether the Fund should have taken a harder line, given that low tax revenue mortgaged several other aspects of the macroeconomic framework and of the structural reform agenda.

66.   **More insistence with respect to civil service reform in the mid-1990s could have been beneficial in the medium-to-long term**. When it became obvious in the mid-1990s that weaknesses in the civil service would be a bottleneck for reforms in other areas, the Fund should perhaps have insisted more with the World Bank to expedite its work and move to an all-encompassing reform. The inability of the civil service to attract sufficient numbers of skilled staff has impaired the country's capacity to mobilize revenue and deliver essential public services—justice, public security, education, and health—and ultimately, assist in laying the foundations for poverty reduction. The need to decompress the salary scale and to introduce performance contracts were cited as crucial objectives as early as 1995, but partial implementation only began after 2000.

67.   **Initially, the structural reform agenda could perhaps have benefited from a more parsimonious approach**. When the government began to demonstrate stronger ownership in the late 1990s, the reform agenda—and the program conditionality—was broadened significantly under the ESAF.[24] However, the country's limited absorptive capacity would probably have warranted a more parsimonious approach. While selectivity in terms of areas of reform was not a real option, in light of the country's wide-ranging needs, a

[23] The issue was that there was a suspicion that many EPZ applicants were not interested in setting up a business but just wanted to benefit from the duty-free import regime for EPZs. Fund staff wanted this loophole to be closed.

[24] Fund program conditionality was actually below the Fund average and the average for Africa (in the 1996 ESAF 23 PAs, PCs and SBs, compared with 33 Fund wide and 31 for Africa). On the other hand, a UN report shows that in the period 1999–2000, among Sub-Saharan countries, Madagascar had the highest number of IFI conditionality to meet (30, with the average for the group of countries at 23). See D. Kapur and R. Webb, "Governance-Related Conditionalities of the International Financial Institutions" G-24 Discussion Paper Series, No.6, August 2000.

more selective approach in terms of conditionality could have achieved better ownership and outcomes at that time.

V. POLICY CHALLENGES FOR THE MEDIUM TERM

68.   **Madagascar's overarching economic challenge is to achieve higher economic growth and to reduce poverty significantly.** Broadly consistent with the MDGs, the government's goal, as stated in the PRSP (June 2003), is to reduce the poverty rate by half in 10 years by working along three axes: improved governance, growth that benefits the poor, and improved social service delivery. The country's capacity to address these issues remains constrained by low domestic savings, external viability, limited availability of skilled workers, and a weak public administration network. Hence, in order to achieve the broader goals, it will be necessary to continue reforms in most of the areas discussed in this report.

69.   **Durable success in reducing poverty and achieving sustained economic development requires a further acceleration of growth.** Madagascar's economic growth rate is still not in the range required to achieve the goals stated in the PRSP and the MDGs. Future programs should contain ambitious measures to bring about this acceleration, including by fostering private sector-led growth—among others, through further privatization—further diversifying the economy, rebuilding the infrastructure, enhancing productivity in agriculture, and capacity building. Special attention needs to go to the post-AGOA period (the AGOA III "third-party" fabrics provision is set to expire in 2007), to ensure that the EPZs contribute more to economic development and are better linked to the domestic economy.

70.   **Further capacity building is the key to success in meeting these challenges.** Enhancing the authorities' absorption and implementation capacity is to be achieved through further technical assistance in the monetary, financial, fiscal, and statistical fields. Capacity building needs to be accompanied by further civil service reform to ensure capacity retention. To overcome the problems of the past, coordination with the authorities and among donors should be strengthened and the authorities should devote sufficient resources to ensure more effective absorption. Technical assistance should be aligned with the policy priorities. The authorities are currently finalizing a time-bound technical assistance plan in which they define and prioritize their needs. When finalized, it will be taken to the donors in order to arrive at a coordinated delivery process. This current initiative is an excellent starting point for addressing this challenge.

A. Macroeconomic Challenges

71.   **A key challenge for sustained growth is to maintain a stable macroeconomic environment and reduce external vulnerabilities.** To that end, further enhancements in policy formulation and implementation are essential, both in the fiscal and monetary areas. The 2002 crisis demonstrated, on the positive side, that macroeconomic stability can be regained more quickly than before with appropriate policies. However, on the downside, it also demonstrated the importance of a stable environment to reach the country's long-term

goals of poverty reduction. Even though the crisis only lasted a few months, it led to a significant increase in income poverty—thereby washing away many of the gains made in previous years—and in unemployment.

72.   **Making the fiscal position sustainable in the medium term should rank high on the policy agenda**. Given the pitfalls of the past, tax policy reform should be a priority. The authorities need to establish a tax code that is simple, stable, transparent, and eliminates loopholes. An important first step would be to eliminate any remaining ad hoc exemptions. Work should be geared toward broadening the tax base. The tax base is relatively narrow, excluding or only lightly taxing some important sectors (such as the EPZs and the mining sector). This issue needs to be handled with care and changes should be implemented over time. A balance needs to be found between maintaining the country's competitive edge and increasing domestic tax revenue.

73.   **Addressing the low level of domestic savings is a third challenge**. The authorities are to be commended for building a sound banking system. Further work is needed to enhance financial intermediation and access to credit, among other things through the development of other intermediation channels such as microfinance, to reach the rural population, and by removing other impediments to financial services.[25] Financial deepening will help boast domestic savings, could contribute to poverty reduction, and thus make the country less vulnerable to external shocks.

B. Structural Reforms

74.   **Madagascar's recent track record in reform is promising and the current momentum should be maintained**. Moreover, there is good correspondence between the outstanding elements of the structural reform agenda and the priority areas identified in the PRSP. [26] Within this broad agenda, the Fund should focus on the areas discussed below, while working in close collaboration with the World Bank, who is actively engaged in several other structural reform areas.

•   **Tax and customs administration**. An action plan to rehabilitate the tax and customs administration has been formulated recently with FAD's technical assistance, and its implementation began under the just-completed PRGF. Under a new program, the needs in the areas of management improvement, simplification of procedures, and improved IT should be a priority. Gains in efficiency and effectiveness of customs

---

[25] Structural impediments to lending include restrictions imposed by banks' headquarters on exposure to country risk and cumbersome procedures for the seizure of collateral in case of nonpayment.

[26] The agenda includes: reforms in the social sector, including education and health services; infrastructure; ensuring that growth becomes broad-based and diversified; enhancing productivity in the agricultural sector; civil service reform; tax policy; tax and customs administration reform; public expenditure management; strengthening the statistical base; finalization of the privatization agenda; legal reforms; and strengthening the judiciary system.

procedures should lead to better duty collection, which would to some extent offset the effects of tariff reductions. Finally, tax evasion and fraud should be tackled decisively.

- **Public expenditure management**. Strengthening the links between approved budgets and budget outturns, and between the PRSP and the annual budgets is needed to protect priority spending, safeguard spending discipline, prevent the accumulation of expenditure arrears, and ensure the efficient delivery of public services. In order to achieve this, it is necessary to (i) strengthen the budget preparation process; (ii) strengthen the link between the treasury and the budget; (iii) strengthen internal and external controls; and (iv) develop an expenditure tracking system.

- **Trade liberalization**. Notwithstanding the progress made, given Madagascar's dependency on external trade for economic growth, further liberalization would be welcome. The recommendation of the Diagnostic Trade Integration Study should be further implemented. A recent paper on regional trade initiatives in Africa argues that countries should engage more in nondiscriminatory liberalization (i.e., beyond the regional initiatives) and take additional measures to facilitate trade.[27][28] As such, the focus should be on continuing to simplify the tariff structure; improving export services; strengthening the domestic supply response to export opportunities; developing a strategy to maximize the benefits from joining SADC; preparing measures to adjust to the new market conditions in the textile sector in the near term; and fostering cross-border sector cooperation.

- **Corruption and governance**. An anti-corruption strategy has been developed. An independent anti-corruption bureau was established at the end of 2004. In the coming years, the government is urged to implement anti-corruption reforms, focusing on government services. Corruption is perceived to be still pervasive in the police force, medical centers, land-titling agencies, and customs and lower courts (Country Report No. 04/403, 12/10/04). Progress in this area is essential to improve the business climate. In that regard, special attention should be given to making the judicial system more efficient and effective (the World Bank is providing technical assistance) and recent improvements in customs should be consolidated.

---

[27] See Y. Yang and S. Gupta, "Regional Trade Arrangements in Africa: Past Performance and the Way Forward," (IMF WP/05/36).

[28] These reforms would need to be phased in carefully and coordinated with the strengthening of domestic tax collection to minimize possible revenue losses.

VI. FUTURE FUND RELATIONS

A. Rationale for a Successor Program

75.   **To assist in achieving Madagascar's poverty reduction goals, there is a strong case for continued Fund engagement, preferably through a successor-PRGF arrangement**. A PRGF would be justified on the grounds that Madagascar's economy remains vulnerable, domestically as well as externally. In addition, it is expected that the country will continue to have significant balance-of- payments needs in the medium term, given the very large investment needs and the low domestic saving rate. Continued Fund support would also facilitate the mobilization of donor support, in the form of grants and technical assistance. Donors themselves are keen on having further Fund involvement. Given the country's vulnerable position, external borrowing should be measured and remain at highly concessional rates. External assistance should preferably be in the form of grants. The structural reform agenda should build on the momentum achieved during the recently completed PRGF, and continue in the areas listed above. Fund involvement should assist in building up a diversified economy. Actions and benchmarks should be specific and selective.

76.   **Risks associated with this strategy mainly stem from the political side**. There is nowadays a broad consensus in Madagascar about the need for, and direction of, reforms. However, this stronger ownership, experienced during the most recent years, needs to be consolidated. Democracy is maturing, although political upheaval remains a risk. In this context, broader-based growth will help distribute the benefits of the reforms and contribute to political and economic stability. To minimize the risks of political resistance to Fund program conditionality, careful coordination and prioritization, in consultation with the authorities, will be necessary. Finally, Madagascar is in very good standing with respect to repaying the Fund, so this is not considered among the high-risk factors.

B. Exit Strategy

77.   **Fund involvement with Madagascar should be reevaluated after this successor program**. If the country continues on the current path of economic growth, stability, and structural reform, and lasting impact is made on poverty reduction, Madagascar could then perhaps move toward a low-access PRGF arrangement. If no progress is made, the Fund's position should be re-evaluated, in particular, with respect to the credibility of its involvement.

Madagascar: Millennium Development Goals

	1990	1995	2001	2002	2015 Target
Goal 1. Eradicate extreme poverty and hunger					
Target 1: Halve between 1990 and 2015, the proportion of people whose income is less than one dollar a day.					
1. Population below US$ 1 a day (percent)	...	...	49.1	...	...
2. Poverty gap ratio at US$ 1 a day (percent)	...	...	18.3	...	...
3. Share of income or consumption held by poorest 20 percent (percent)	...	...	6.4	...	...
Target 2: Halve, between 1990 and 2015, the proportion of people suffering hunger					
4. Prevalence of child malnutrition (percent of children under 5)	40.9	34.1	...	33.1	20.5
5. Population below minimum level of dietary energy consumption (percent)	35.0	40.0	36.0	...	17.5
Goal 2. Achieve universal primary education					
Target 3: Ensure that, by 2015, children will be able to complete a full course of primary schooling					
6. Net primary enrollment ratio (percent of relevant age group)	...	60.6	68.7	...	
7. Percentage of cohort reaching grade 5	21.5	39.7	33.6	...	
8. Youth literacy rate (percent age 15-24)	72.2	76.3	80.8	81.5	
Goal 3. Promote gender equality and empower women					
Target 4: Eliminate gender disparity in primary and secondary education preferably by 2005 and to all levels of education by 2015					
9. Ratio of girls to boys in primary and secondary education (percent)	98.9	99.2	...	...	100.0
10. Ratio of young literate females to males (percent ages 15-24)	85.6	88.8	92.1	92.5	
11. Share of women employed in the nonagricultural sector (percent)	26.0	...	...	...	
12. Proportion of seats held by women in the national parliament (percent)	7.0	4.0	8.0	8.0	

Madagascar: Millennium Development Goals (continued)

	1990	1995	2001	2002	2015 Target
Goal 4. Reduce child mortality					
Target 5: reduce by two-thirds between 1990 and 2015, the under-five mortality rate					
13. Under-five mortality rate (per 1,000)	168.0	156.0	139.0	135.0	54.0
14. Infant mortality rate (per 1,000 live births)	103.0	95.0	86.0	84.0	
15. Immunization against measles (percent of children under 12-months)	47.0	55.0	55.0	61.0	
Goal 5. Improve maternal health					
Target 6: Reduce by three-quarters, between 1990 and 2015, the maternal mortality ratio.					
16. Maternal mortality ratio (modeled estimate, per 100,000 live births)	...	580.0	550.0	...	127.0
17. Proportion of births attended by skilled health personnel	57.0	47.3	46.2	...	
Goal 6. Combat HIV/AIDS, malaria and other diseases					
Target 7: Halt by 2015, and begin to reverse, the spread of HIV/AIDS					
18. HIV prevalence among females (percent ages 15-24)			0.2	...	
19. Contraceptive prevalence rate (percent of women ages 15-49)	16.7	19.4	...	16.9	
20. Number of children orphaned by HIV/AIDS	...	...	6,300	...	
Target 8: Halt by 2015, and begin to reverse, the incidence of malaria and other major diseases					
21. Prevalence of death associated with malaria	...	...	...	...	
22. Share of population in malaria risk areas using effective prevention and treatment	...	...	...	...	
23. Incidence of tuberculosis (per 100,000 people)	...	...	254.5	...	
24. Tuberculosis cases detected under DOTS (percent)	...	65.0	60.0	61.6	

Madagascar: Millennium Development Goals

	1990	1995	2001	2002	2015 Target
Goal 7. Ensure environmental sustainability					
Target 9: Integrate the principles of sustainable development into policies and programs. Reverse the loss of environmental resources					
25. Forest area (percent of total land area)	22.2	...	20.2	...	
26. Nationally protected areas (percent of total land area)	...	1.9	1.9	2.1	
27. GDP per unit of energy use (PPP $ per kg oil equivalent)	...	...	...	...	
28. CO_2 emissions (metric tons per capita)	0.1	0.1	0.1	...	
29. Proportion of population using solid fuels					
Target 10: Halve by 2015 proportion of people without access to safe drinking water					
30. Access to improved water source (percent of population)	44.0	...	47.0	...	72.0
Target 11: Achieve by 2020 significant improvement for at least 100 million slum dwellers					
31. Access to improved sanitation (percent of population)	36.0	...	42.0	...	
32. Access to secure tenure (percent of population)	...	...	...	...	

Madagascar: Millennium Development Goals (concluded)

	1990	1995	2001	2002	2015 Target
Goal 8. Develop a Global Partnership for Development 1/					
Target 16: Develop and implement strategies for productive work for youth.					
45. Unemployment rate of population ages 15-24 (total)	...	...	...	...	
Female	...	...	...	...	
Male	...	...	...	...	
Target 17: Provide access to affordable essential drugs					
46. Proportion of population access with access to affordable essential drugs	...	...	...	...	
Target 18: Make available new technologies, especially information and communications					
47. Fixed line and mobile telephones (per 1,000 people)	2.8	3.0	13.3	14.0	...
48. Personal computers (per 1,000 people)		1.5	2.6	4.4	...

Sources: World Bank; and Fund staff estimates.

1/ Targets 12-15 and indicators 33-44 are excluded because they can not be measured on a country specific basis. These are related to official development assistance, market access, and the HIPC initiative.

Madagascar, Ethiopia, and Tanzania—A Comparison

	Madagascar	Ethiopia	Tanzania
1995 Real GDP per capita (in 1990 U.S. dollars)	228	164	177
Banking sector reform	As early as 1994, emphasis was on restoring a sound banking system. New banking legislation had been enacted in early 1996. Independent managers had been appointed for the two remaining state-owned banks in 1995, which were privatized in 1998. The legal framework for the divestiture program was approved in 1996.	Financial restructuring of the largest commercial bank (CBE) started in November 2003. The second largest commercial bank (CBB) to be privatized soon.	In November 2003, Parliament approved privatization plan for the rural development bank.
Privatization	Excluding commercial banks, only three strategic companies were privatized (e.g., the telecommunications company, cotton company, railway company).	Half of all SOEs were privatized. Many strategic corporations remain in state hands (including the largest commercial bank, the telecommunications corporation, Ethiopian Airlines, and a large number of industrial enterprises).	Two-thirds of all state-owned enterprises (SOEs) privatized, including some strategic corporations (e.g., The National Bank of Commerce, Port Container Terminal, Telecommunications, and Air Tanzania).
Land reform	Land Act revised to allow foreigners to own land under certain conditions (e.g. requirement of US$ 500,000 investment).	Some reforms have been implemented to improve security of tenure. Land, however, cannot be offered as collateral.	Land Act revised to allow land to be used as collateral, including the preparation of a land registry.

Madagascar, Ethiopia, and Tanzania—A Comparison (concluded)

	Madagascar	Ethiopia	Tanzania
Private sector credit growth (average 2001-03)	9.4 percent.	-2 percent.	35 percent
Credit to private sector in percent of GDP (average 2000-03)	9.2	22.9	5.8
Broad money in percent of GDP (average 2000-03)	22.8	46.3	20.8
Foreign direct investment (average 2001-03)	0.8 percent of GDP.	0.3 percent of GDP.	3.3 percent of GDP
Current account deficit excluding grants (average 2001-03)	5.6 percent of GDP (4.4 percent, including grants)	11.8 percent of GDP (4.7 percent, including grants).	8.5 percent of GDP (3.9 percent, including grants)
Fiscal deficit (average 2001-03)	8.9 percent of GDP (5.1 percent, including grants).	13.6 percent of GDP (7.7 percent, including grants)	6.4 percent of GDP (1.5 percent, including grants)
Domestic savings (average 2001-03)	11.1 percent of GDP	2.5 percent of GDP	9.6 percent of GDP
Private investment (average 2001-03)	10.2 percent of GDP	9.7 percent of GDP	13.5 percent of GDP
HIPC Completion point	October, 2004	April, 2004	November, 2001
2003 Real GDP per capita (in 1990 U.S. dollars)	220	202	217

1/ Madagascar, Ethiopia, and Tanzania emerged from decades of economic stagnation under a policy of state controls and planning in 1995. Since then, Tanzania has made greater progress in a number of areas than Ethiopia and Madagascar.

Madagascar: Quantitative Performance Criteria and Benchmarks Under Fund Programs, 1988–2004

Ceiling on external arrears	M	M	M
Ceiling on net claims of the banking system on government	M	M	M
Ceiling on total domestic credit	M	M	M
Ceiling on credit to public enterprises	M	M	M
Ceiling on contracting or guaranteeing of external debt on nonconcessional loans			
5-15 years	M	M	M
5-15 years	M	M	M
Total number of conditions	6	6	6
Share not met (in percent)	0	0	0

ESAF (1996-2000)

	Sep-96	Dec-96	Mar-97	Jun-97 1/	Sep-97 1/	Dec-97 1/	Dec-99 1/	Mar-00	Jun-00	Sep-00
			PC				PC		PC	
Quantitative performance criteria and benchmarks										
Ceiling on external arrears	NM	M	NM	...	...	NM	M	M	M	M
Floor on net foreign assets of the central bank	M	M	M	M	M	NM	NM	NM	M	M
Ceiling on net claims of the banking system on government	M	M	M	M	M	M	NM	NM	M	M
Ceiling on net domestic assets of the central bank	M	M	M	M	M	M	NM	M	NM	M
Ceiling on contracting or guaranteeing of external debt on nonconcessional loans more than 15 years	M	M	M	M	M	M	M	M	M	M
Floor on tax revenue	M	M	M	NM	NM	NM	M	M	M	NM
Ceiling on treasury loans and advances (discontinued from 2000)	M	M	M	M	M	M				
Floor on petroleum tax payments to the treasury	NM	NM	NM	M	M	M				
Indicative targets:										
Floor on petroleum tax payments to the treasury (became indicative target in 1999)				NM	NM	M	M	M	M	NM
Ceiling on reserve money	NM	NM	NM	NM	NM	NM	NM	M	NM	NM
Ceiling on broad money	NM	NM	NM	NM	NM	NM	NM	M	NM	NM
Total number of conditions	8	8	8	8	8	8	6	6	6	6
Share not met (in percent)	25	0	38	14	38	38	50	33	17	17

Madagascar: Quantitative Performance Criteria and Benchmarks Under Fund Programs, 1988-2004 (concluded)

	Mar-01	Jun-01	Sep-01	Dec-01	Mar-02	Dec-02	Mar-03	Jun-03	Mar-04 1/	Jun-04	Sep-04 2/
	PC		PC	PC		PC	PC	PC			PC
Number of waivers			2				4				0
of which: structural performance criteria			1				1				0
Quantitative performance criteria and benchmarks											
Ceiling on external arrears	M	M	M	M	NM	M	M	M	M	M	M
Floor on net foreign assets of the central bank	M	M	M	M	M	M	M	M	NM	NM	M
Ceiling on net domestic assets of the central bank	M	M	M	M	M	M	M	M	M	M	M
Ceiling on domestic financing of the government	M	M	M	M	M	M	M	M	NM	NM	M
Ceiling on contracting or guaranteeing of external debt on nonconcessional terms	M	M	M	M	M	M	M	M	M	M	M
Floor on tax revenue	NM	NM	NM	NM	NM	M	M	M	NM	NM	M
Ceiling on accumulation of domestic arrears (PC starting in 2004)										NM	M
Indicative targets											
Ceiling on reserve money	M	M	M	NM	M	M	M	M	M	M	M
Ceiling on broad money	NM	NM	NM	NM	M	M	M	NM	M	M	NM
Floor on arrears payment (introduced during the Third Review)							M	M			
Ceiling on accumulation of domestic arrears (introduced during the Third Review)								M			
Total number of conditions	6	6	6	6	6	6	6	6	6	7	7
Share not met (in percent)	17	33	20	50	33	0	0	0	0	57	29
Number of waivers	1			4						5	0
of which: structural performance criteria	0			1						1	0

1/ Revised targets.
2/ At the time of the 4th review several of the December 2003 PCs were predicted to have been missed, hence it was decided to assess compliance with the program based on March 2004 targets

Madagascar: Structural Conditionality Under Fund Program 1988-2004

	Target date	ESAF (1988-91) Met	ESAF (1988-91) Not met	ESAF (1996-2000) Met	ESAF (1996-2000) Not met	PRGF (2001-04) Met	PRGF (2001-04) Not met
I. Tax policy and administration							
Prior Actions							
Fully implement the new value-added tax (VAT) reimbursement system for free export zone producers.	June 1, 1999				Not met		
Modify and implement the new contract with the preshipment inspection company, BIVAC, in line with Fund staff recommendations, and instruct the customs administration to collect customs taxes in an amount that equals, as a minimum, the level assessed by BIVAC.	Mid-June 1999				Not met		
Adjust the prices for petroleum products, that is, increase super gasoline price by 10 percent and regular gasoline by 5 percent.	Mid-June 1999				Not met		
Implement an effective tax audit program within the large-taxpayer unit (SGE) that will be the basis of a program to combat tax evasion.	July 1, 1999				Not met		
Establish a bipartite committee (private-public) to monitor implementation of tax and customs administration reform.	End-May 2003					Met	
Performance Criteria							
Start operations of the Tax Bureau for Large Taxpayers	End-March 1997				Not met		
ASYCUDA 2.7 customs system to become operational at the 3 main customs offices.	June 30, 2001					Met	
Bill to revise upward the mining royalty and lower the excise tax.	End-2001					Met	
Adopt new regulations, in consultation with the Fiscal Affairs Department of the Fund, introducing a system authorizing the deferment of the VAT payment obligations on capital goods imports until the monthly declaration following the import.	End-June 2003						Not met
Issue a resolution approving the newly installed ASYCUDA ++ software and setting a date for the use of the software by customs.	End-December 2004					Met	
No tax or tariff exemptions will be granted beyond those specified in the 2004 budget law.	End-December 2004					Met	
Structural benchmarks							
Reduction of the number of prohibited customs nomenclatures.	End-June 1989	Met					
Install new version of SYDONIA software in the customs administration.	End-1999				Not met		
ASYCUDA 3 ++ installed in three most important offices.	End-September 2001						Not met
ASYCUDA 3 ++ installed in four more offices.	End-December 2001						Not met
II. Fiscal policy management (including expenditure policy)							
Prior actions							
Complete the harmonization of the budget and the public accounting nomenclature (in accordance with Fund technical assistance recommendations).	End-June 1999				Not met		
VAT reimbursement arrears will be settled.	End-May 2003					Met	
Performance criteria							
Treasury computer system, designed to centralize each month the accounts of the 22 main treasury offices, will be operational.	End-November 2001					Met	
Submission of draft budget execution laws for 2000 and 2001 to the Audit Court.	End-December 2003					Met	
Structural benchmarks							
Presentation of budget on three agreed bases.	End-June 1990	Met					
Apply the new nomenclature in the preparation of the budget law for 2000.	August 1, 1999			Met			
Integrate the administrative personnel database and pay systems.	End-June 2001					Met	
Separation of the functions of the Chairman of the Central Procurement Committee and the Director General of Expenditure Commitment Control.	End-June 2001					Met	
Study on the improvement in the operation of the State Inspector General.	End-June 2001					Met	
Treasury's monthly balance sheets up to end 2001 will be prepared.	End-June 2003						Not met

Madagascar: Structural Conditionality Under Fund Program 1988-2004 (continued)

	Target date	ESAF (1988-91) Met	ESAF (1988-91) Not met	ESAF (1996-2000) Met	ESAF (1996-2000) Not met	PRGF (2001-04) Met	PRGF (2001-04) Not met
III. Monetary and exchange rate policies							
Performance criteria							
Introduction of new money market.	End-October 1990	Met					
Structural benchmarks							
Replacement of the existing system of exchange rate determination by a continuous interbank system.	End-March 2004						Delayed (Jan. 2004)
Issue a resolution by the Board of Executive Directors of the Central Bank (BCM) establishing the operational guidelines for BCM intervention in the interbank foreign exchange market.	End-December 2004					Met	
IV. Financial sector reform							
Performance criteria							
Complete clearing of the BTM and BFV portfolios with private sector agreement to 25 percent participation in the equity capital of at least one of the two banks.	End-June 1989		Not met				
Complete the organizational, financial and actuarial audits of the pension systems for government workers.	End-May 2000			Met			
Structural benchmarks							
Privatization of BNI.	End-December 1989		Not met				
Finalize a scheme for the restructuring of the nonperforming assets of the two public banks (BTM and BFV).	End-September 1997				Not met		
Authorize legislation that orders debtors in default to one of the two banks being privatized to pay their debts.	End-September 1999			Met			
Draw up activity plan for the central bank's internal audit department, together with an organizational chart defining how the internal audit department will report to the various organs of the bank.	End-March 2003					Met	
Conduct an internal audit of the management of the central bank reserves.	End-June 2003					Met	
Publication of the BCM's 2001, 2002, and sub-present financial statements and attendant audit opinions in the *Journal Officiel*.	End-March 2004					Met	
Publish the BCM's complete audited financial statements for 2003.	End-December 2004					Met	
V. Civil service reform							
Performance Criteria							
Correct the budgetary wage bill for "ghost" workers identified in the civil service census of April 1999.	End-August 1999				Delayed (end-March 2000)		
Structural benchmarks							
Completion of census of central government personnel.	End-October 1989		Delayed (Jun-90)				
Finalization of strategy for civil service reform.	End-June 1997				Not met		
Implement a new code of conduct for the civil service.	End-February 2000				Not met		

NEW! WORLD OFFSHORE TAX GUIDES– 2006

Price: $99.95 each

1.	Andorra Offshore Tax Guide
2.	Anguilla Offshore Tax Guide
3.	Bahamas Offshore Tax Guide
4.	Barbados Offshore Tax Guide
5.	Belize Offshore Tax Guide
6.	Bermuda Offshore Tax Guide
7.	British Virgin Islands Offshore Tax Guide
8.	Cayman Islands Offshore Tax Guide
9.	Cook Islands Offshore Tax Guide
10.	Costa Rica Offshore Tax Guide
11.	Cyprus Offshore Tax Guide
12.	Dubai Offshore Tax Guide
13.	Gibraltar Offshore Tax Guide
14.	Grenada Offshore Tax Guide
15.	Guernsey Offshore Tax Guide
16.	Hong Kong Offshore Tax Guide
17.	Ireland Offshore Tax Guide
18.	Isle of Man Offshore Tax Guide
19.	Jersey Offshore Tax Guide
20.	Labuan Offshore Tax Guide
21.	Liechtenstein Offshore Tax Guide
22.	Luxembourg Offshore Tax Guide
23.	Madeira Offshore Tax Guide
24.	Malta Offshore Tax Guide
25.	Mauritius Offshore Business and Investment Opportunities Handbook
26.	Mauritius Offshore Tax Guide
27.	Monaco Offshore Tax Guide
28.	Nauru Offshore Tax Guide
29.	Netherlands Antilles Offshore Tax Guide
30.	Panama Offshore Tax Guide
31.	Seychelles Offshore Tax Guide
32.	Switzerland Offshore Tax Guide
33.	Turks & Caicos Islands Offshore Tax Guide
34.	Vanuatu Offshore Tax Guide

**To order and for additional analytical and marketing information, please contacrt
International Business Publications, USA at:**
**P.O. Box 15343, Washington, DC 20003, USA. Phone: (202) 546-2103. Fax: (202) 546-3275.
E-mail: rusric@erols.com**

Madagascar
Selective Justice

Introduction

The December 2001 presidential elections in Madagascar provoked a major political crisis between the incumbent President, Didier Ratsiraka and his main rival, Marc Ravalomanana. The official results of the election's first round gave no candidate an absolute majority, but these were challenged by Marc Ravalomanana who claimed he had won the election outright. On 22 February 2002, Marc Ravalomanana declared himself President after weeks of demonstrations in the capital, Antananarivo, in support of his claim. Didier Ratsiraka left the capital for Toamasina, an important port in the east of the country.

This led to increasing tension and violence between the supporters of the two candidates. Marc Ravalomanana's supporters erected barricades in the capital to "protect themselves" against possible action by the security forces or rival supporters. Didier Ratsiraka's supporters blocked roads linking the provincial ports to the capital in order to isolate the inland capital. This period was marked by increasing confusion, disrespect for the rule of law and a breakdown of security. Parts of the army and the security forces became divided in favour of one or other candidate. However, some army generals tried to remain neutral condemning both the economic blockade of the capital and Marc Ravalomanana's "self-declaration" as President.

Marc Ravalomanana was installed as President on 6 May 2002 after the votes had been recounted. He then sent troops to recapture four provinces where the governors had declared themselves "independent" from the Antananarivo government. Marc Ravalomanana called upon reservists and other recent recruits to boost his troops, known as the "pacifying army". This army regained control of the provinces after some fighting with supporters and the security forces which had remained loyal to Ratsiraka. Hundreds of people were arrested by Marc Ravalomanana's troops during and after the re-taking of the provinces. They remain held awaiting trial for crimes or offences allegedly committed during the political crisis.

This report presents Amnesty International's main concern and recommendations relating to impunity for human rights abuses committed in the context of the political crisis. It does not provide a complete overview of Amnesty International's concerns in Madagascar. Amnesty International is independent from any government, political group or religious belief. Amnesty International does not support or oppose any government or political system, nor does it support or oppose the views of the victims whose rights it seeks to protect. The organization is concerned solely with the impartial protection of human rights.

Once his troops arrived in the provinces, Marc Ravalomanana stated that a commission of inquiry would be established to investigate crimes or offences committed by the former government during the crisis and that his government would fight against the culture of impunity which had been pervasive before he came to power. However, no commission of inquiry has been set up and the government decided that those suspected of committing crimes or offences during the crisis will be tried by ordinary courts.

Amnesty International welcomes the government's stated willingness to fight against impunity. The organization is calling upon the Malagasy government to take concrete steps towards this commitment by investigating all human rights abuses and violations – past and present - committed in Madagascar, including cases of killings and torture, and to bring the suspected perpetrators to justice. Amnesty International is reiterating that it is essential there is no impunity for the perpetrators of human rights violations and abuses, not only so that justice can be done for the victims of these abuses, but also to avoid giving the perpetrators of such actions the impression that they are above the law. The organization believes there is a direct link between impunity and the fact that human rights abuses continue to be committed.

Amnesty International is concerned that almost all the current judicial proceedings are dealing with alleged crimes or offences committed by the former government. The organization urges that all alleged crimes or offences must be investigated, including those involving supporters of the new government. It is essential that all perpetrators of serious human rights abuse be brought to justice regardless of their political affiliation. If national reconciliation is to be possible, it is imperative that justice is not selective. Hundreds of people have been arrested in connection with the political crisis, most, if not all, of these being politicians, members of the security forces or civilians who are seen or appear to be seen as having supported former President Didier Ratsiraka during the political crisis. Recent reports suggested that some 90 people were arrested in Brickaville in the east, during October 2002, and approximately 120 people in Mahajanga in the west. Between June and August, some 200 people were arrested in the context of the new government's military activities in the coastal provinces and were transferred to detention centres in Antananarivo. The total number of people arrested is somewhere between 400 and 500. They have mostly been accused of participating in the "economic" barricades aimed against the capital, or forming "militias" in support of the former President. The pending charges are variously "threatening internal state security", "abuse of power", "insurrection", "destruction of public goods", "aggravated assault" or "criminal conspiracy"

Amnesty International is also concerned that the arrests have often been carried out in an arbitrary manner. Some of those arrested are prisoners of conscience[1], arrested solely for expressing their opinions in a non-violent manner or for making statements which were interpreted as critical of the current authorities. In recent months political opponents of the Didier Ratsiraka's AREMA party have also been arrested and interrogated on the pretext of corruption investigations. The organization fears that arresting and detaining numerous

---

[1] Amnesty International considers that any person detained for their political beliefs or because of their ethnic origin, sex, colour, language, national or social origin, economic status, birth or other status, and who have not used or advocated violence, are prisoners of conscience.

political opponents at the time when the new government is seeking to assert its authority in the country, may not only silence the new government's political opponents but also anyone who simply does not share the views of those in power. AREMA party representatives state the new government is using the pattern of arrests and detentions as a tactic to restrict and weaken the political opposition in preparation for legislative elections due on 15 December 2002. Others claim that the judicial proceedings pending against Ratsiraka supporters are designed to influence public opinion by showing them as responsible for the crisis prior to the next elections.

Amnesty International is not stating that all those awaiting trial or all those who have already been tried are innocent. However, it is vital that a distinction is made between those who are suspected of having committed crimes or offences and those who have been arbitrarily arrested. The organization is calling upon the Malagasy authorities to respect the basic human rights of all prisoners, including those accused of human rights abuses, at the time of their arrest, while in detention and during their trial and appeal. It is essential that all those suspected of having committed human rights abuses are brought to trial before fair, independent and impartial courts which are prepared to punish the abuses, regardless of the perpetrator. It is only by respecting human rights principles that the government can ensure the perpetrators of human rights abuse are brought to justice and the victims of these abuses gain redress.

General Background

Didier Ratsiraka, incumbent President and registered candidate for the December 2001 election, came to power in 1975. He was re-elected three times in succession after electoral processes which were generally considered to be unfair and so remained in power until 1991. During this period, numerous human rights violations were committed in Madagascar including repression of political opponents, long-term arbitrary detentions and alleged political killings. The activities of a popular political protest movement in 1991 resulted in a new constitution being adopted by referendum in 1992; it included human rights guarantees and increased powers for the National Assembly. Albert Zafy won the presidential elections in November 1991. He remained in power until 1996 when the National Assembly removed him from office. Didier Ratsiraka presented himself as a candidate in the November 1996 presidential elections and was re-elected. Amendments to the 1992 constitution increased presidential power at the expense of the National Assembly and accelerated the process of decentralising power to the provinces.

Presidential elections in December 2001 provoked a major political crisis in the country. Marc Ravalomanana, the capital's mayor and the incumbent President's main rival, contested the official results of the first round claiming that the electoral system had been tainted by fraud and that he would refuse a second round. Tens of thousands of Marc Ravalomanana supporters demonstrated in the streets of the capital. Although the strikes were generally peaceful, there were sporadic outbreaks of violence in the capital, where Ravalomanana supporters erected "protective" barricades, and in the rest of the country between the supporters and security forces of each of the two candidates.

Once Marc Ravalomanana declared himself President on 22 February 2002, Didier Ratsiraka declared a state of emergency (*état de nécessité*) in the capital. This was not respected: Marc Ravalomanana's supporters installed ministers he had named into government offices without any reaction from the army or the security forces. So, Didier Ratsiraka set up a rival government in Toamasina, which he called his "capital", with members of his government and the security forces who had remained loyal together with the support of some regional governors. Ratsiraka supporters erected barricades on the main routes between the capital and the provinces to stop merchandise reaching the ports and people from travelling freely. Strategic bridges were destroyed. In the province of Fianarantsoa there were violent clashes between two army factions when Marc Ravalomanana's supporters tried to replace a pro-Ratsiraka governor with their "President". Several people, civilians and members of the security forces from both sides, died in unclear circumstances. Dozens of people, predominantly Marc Ravalomanana supporters from the provinces, were also arrested, tortured or killed during this period. Fearing for their lives, many fled from the provinces and sought temporary refuge in the capital, Antananarivo.

After the Supreme Court annulled the first results, the Constitutional High Court of Madagascar recounted the votes and declared Marc Ravalomanana the winner on 29 April. Ratsiraka contested their decision for being "biased" arguing many members of the Constitutional High Court were sympathetic to Marc Ravalomanana. Then the governors of Antsiranana, Mahajanga, Toliara and Toamasina provinces declared their own "independence" from Marc Ravalomanana's government. On 6 May, Marc Ravalomanana was installed as President. In June, he took the decision to send the armed forces to regain control of the four provinces, to dismantle the barricades around the capital and to install his own "Special Delegation Presidents" in the place of the governors. This phase is called the period of "pacification". The confrontation – a period marked by an increase in violence and in human rights abuses - ended with localised fighting in Antsiranana and Mahajanga between the army, loyal to Marc Ravalomanana, and the armed forces and supporters of Didier Ratsiraka. Dozens of people including civilians were killed or injured in this fighting. However, in most cases Marc Ravalomanana's armed forces dismantled the barricades without much resistance from Ratsiraka supporters who often fled once the army's arrival was announced. On 7 July Didier Ratsiraka left Madagascar and sought refuge in France. Marc Ravalomanana's troops entered the final province of Toamasina on 9 July.

Amnesty International's concerns

Cases of human rights abused and violated during the political crisis

On a visit to Madagascar between 14 and 28 August, Amnesty International was able to meet victims of human rights violations and to obtain information about numerous human rights abuses which were committed during the crisis by Didier Ratsiraka supporters and security forces remaining loyal to him and also by those close to Marc Ravalomanana. Most were illegal killings and cases of torture. This document is not an exhaustive account of all abuses reported during the crisis period. The cases publicised below are however representative of the most serious human rights abuses and violations which were committed during the crisis.

Political killings

During the night of 2 March 2002, supporters of Didier Ratsiraka dressed in military uniforms, entered the home of Lalason Rajaobelina, a trader and member of the TIM[2] association, living on the island of Nosy-Be, Antsiranana province. They beat him and his wife with gun butts until he fainted. When he regained consciousness he found himself in the back of his car, being driven by the same men who had attacked him, together with Olivier Ratsimba, another member of TIM and branch manager of a bank who appeared unconscious. The car stopped and the men in military uniform threw Olivier Ratsimba, Lalason Rajaobelina and finally the car over the edge of a cliff. They kicked the men to ensure their bodies fell down the cliff and could not be seen from the road. Lalason Rajaobelina survived, but Olivier Ratsimba was killed. According to Amnesty International's information, an inquiry has been opened.

There are reports that on 16 April 2002 General Raymond Andrinaivo was killed by gun shots fired by three unidentified masked armed men, while he was receiving treatment in Fianarantsoa hospital, 400 kilometres from Antananarivo. The General had apparently been injured during a confrontation with other soldiers when he was defending the governor of Fianarantsoa against Marc Ravalomanana's supporters and security forces who wanted to install their own "governor" in the official building. It appears he was extrajudicially executed. According to information available to Amnesty International, there has been no inquiry into his death.

---

[2] *Tiako I Madasikara,* I love Madagascar, political support group for Marc Ravalomanana which is now his political party.

Evidence of torture and ill-treatment

Amnesty International received dozens of reports that people suspected of supporting Marc Ravalomanana in the provinces were tortured by either Didier Ratsiraka's security forces or his supporters. Those suspected of supporting Didier Ratsiraka were also victims of torture and ill-treatment by Marc Ravalomanana supporters, especially at the time of their arrest.

On 19 April 2002 Jonathon Odilon Vénor, aka "Veve", Vice-President of the *Leader Fanilo* political party in the town of Sambava and member of KMSB[3], was arrested in the same town in Antsiranana province by five armed supporters of Ratsiraka including two soldiers. He was beaten on the head with gun buts, then forced to get into a car and burned with cigarettes. He was taken to the VIP lounge at the local airport where the same men stabbed him. Veve was cut on his right leg below the knee; the knife was put into the wound several times before being withdrawn. Veve was then taken to the home of a local elected official where other men dressed in military uniforms beat him to the point of unconsciousness. They then transported him to the "Ambolomadinika Military Camp" in Sambava where soldiers again hit him on the head with gun buts. While pouring alcohol onto his wounds, they asked him "where he hid his weapons" and then locked him in a tiny cell half-naked. The next day, Veve was taken with another old man who was imprisoned with him back to the airport where the soldiers forced them to dance while being threatened with weapons. Veve was transferred by plane to the "Pardes Gendarmerie Camp" in Antsiranana, the main town in the province of the same name. He could be examined there by a doctor from the local military hospital who ordered his evacuation to Antananarivo. Veve was suffering from headaches, memory loss and from the wound in his leg. Amnesty International has learned that he died on 15 October 2002. Veve had lodged a complaint against his attackers. Reports suggest that an inquiry is underway.

On 9 April 2002, Gaby Roland Rajaonarivelo, Yves Ralison and Philippe Rakotomavo were arrested by the bodyguards of Jacques Sylla, who had been nominated Prime Minister by Marc Ravalomanana, on the terrace of Hotel Colbert in central Antananarivo. An arrest warrant had reportedly been issued against them because of allegations that they were planning to assassinate Jacques Sylla. The three men were taken into the offices of Marc Ravalomanana in Ambohitsorohitra by the bodyguards. The next day, Gaby Roland Rajaonarivelo was found dead at the DGIDIE[4] with injuries to his head, stomach and feet. The two others were taken to hospital. Philippe Rakotomavo is currently in detention in Tsiafahy, a detention centre for criminals situated 40 kilometres from Antananarivo. Gaby Roland Rajaonarivelo was buried without an autopsy despite visible wounds to his head and stomach. An inquiry was opened on the orders of the Antananarivo Court Prosecutor, who has received, to date, only the security forces' version of events that Gaby Roland Rajaonarivelo had to be subdued by the security forces after he tried to escape. Amnesty International is concerned that the inquiry is being carried out by the police without any guarantee of independence or

---

[3] *Komity Miaro ny Safidim-Bahoaka,* Defence Committee for Citizens Voting, which campaigned for a recount of votes following Marc Ravalomanana's request.
[4]

impartiality, that no member of the security forces has been suspended while the inquiry is underway and that no witness from the security forces seems to have been heard. According to reports, the inquiry is still open.

On 23 June, vehicles returning from the capital were stopped on the route towards Ambilobe (Antsiranana province) by Ratsiraka soldiers and supporters. At least 73 people, most of whom were travelling traders from the province of Antananarivo, were forced out of their vehicles with threats, beaten up and tied together using rope. Ratisraka's soldiers and supporters then took them by lorry to the "Second RFI camp[5]" in the town of Antsiranana. During the night of 23 to 24 June, these 73 people were kicked, hit with gun buts and their bodies burned with cigarettes. They were denied access to food and water and any jewellery, money and some of their clothes were stolen. Several dozen soldiers at the camp tortured or ill-treated these travelling traders. The next day, the 73 people were taken to the Governor of Antsiranana's Palace and attached to the entrance gate of the building. Ratsiraka's soldiers and supporters continued to beat them, sometimes using a block of cement. That evening they were taken back to the military camp and the following day they were released, after some paid money for the purpose. The 73 people were told they had been taken as hostages to thwart the advance of Marc Ravalomanana's troops towards the town of Antsiranana.

Reports suggest that between June and August 2002 dozens of people were tortured or ill-treated at the time of their arrest by Marc Ravalomanana's "reservist" or "pacifying" soldiers in the provinces of Mahajanga, Antsiranana, Toliara at Toamasina. Others were reportedly tortured when they were transferred to detention centres in Antananarivo. The methods of torture and ill-treatment used include being stabbed, hit with gun butts in the face and on the body, kicked and verbally or physically humiliated. One report states that someone was allegedly forced to drink his urine. There are several reports concerning personal effects being stolen and "pacifying" soldiers pillaging and burning homes.

On 14 June Venance Raharimanana, a 63-year old researcher and instructor, was arrested by "reservists" in Mahajanga while on his way home. He was forced out of his car and a rope was used to tie his feet to his head. He was taken to the local airport and transferred to Antananarivo by plane. When he arrived at Ivato, Antananarivo's airport, he was forced into a vehicle occupied by soldiers who hit him with gun buts and kicked him while hurling insults at him. They then put a firearm in his mouth and twisted it until Mr Raharimanana's teeth fell out. He was then held incommunicado. It was not until the next day that his family managed to find out where he was, despite their repeated efforts to find him. He was in a small cell at the "Fiadanana Gendarmerie" covered in blood and no longer able to open his mouth. On 17 June his house in Mahajanga was pillaged and burned, apparently by reservists; the homes of his two daughters were also raided. Despite various efforts, the authorities have still not agreed to register his torture complaint.

Four employees of SIRAMA, the state sugar company, were arrested on 27 June on Nosy-Be by some twenty soldiers, apparently because they were accused of providing logistical help to the local administration which remained loyal to the ex-President during the political crisis.

5

When they were arrested, they were beaten and ill-treated by soldiers who stole their personal belongings. They were held in a cell at the Nosy-Be police Commissariat until 1 July when they were transferred by plane to the capital Antananarivo. During the plane transfer they were again severely beaten. On 13 July, they were placed in detention at the *Brigade Spéciale de Betongolo,* Special Betongolo Brigade, in Antananarivo where they were interrogated and then on 17 July charged by the Antananarivo Court. Immediately afterwards they were placed in pre-trial detention at the *Maison de Force de Tsiafahy,* Tsiafahy detention centre.

President Marc Ravalomanana and Minister of Defence Jules Mamizara called upon the army not to commit abuses during their "pacification" operations in the provinces. When the Malagasy authorities met with representatives of Amnesty International they did acknowledge that reservists had committed "some mistakes" and that they would take measures to ensure that arrests in the provinces are carried out lawfully. On 28 September Jules Mamizara stated that 700 reservists who had committed abuses during military operations had been punished. However, Amnesty International has not been able to obtain any detailed information about these punishments. It is not known if the alleged perpetrators of acts of torture or ill-treatment have been suspended from their posts or if they have been brought to trial.

In accordance with international law, all allegations and reports of torture must be the subject of an independent and impartial inquiry and the alleged perpetrators must be brought to justice. Victims of torture must obtain redress and receive appropriate medical assistance. According to information available to Amnesty International, no allegation of torture of those arrested following the political crisis has been investigated.

Irregularities at time of arrest

Throughout the crisis Amnesty International received many reports that people opposed to Didier Ratsiraka had been arbitrarily arrested, especially in the provinces. Veve (see above) was held at the Pardes Camp in Antsiranana with 19 other people. All were suspected of supporting Marc Ravalomanana and most had been arrested in April by members of Didier Ratsiraka's security forces and his supporters. They were arrested without warrant, tortured or ill-treated and taken to Pardes Gendarmerie Camp in Antsiranana without being informed of the reasons for their arrest. They were held without charge for several weeks before their case was transferred to the courts in their home area. Regular judicial proceedings were not followed in any of these cases[6].

After Marc Ravalomanana's army regained control of the provinces dozens of people were arrested without warrant and without any preliminary investigation by soldiers who had no training in arrest procedures. The case of Venance Raharimanana and the four SIRAMA employees is typical of the way such arrests were carried out. There are reports that the

---

[6] See Amnesty International Urgent Action (UA 155/02): **Fear for safety/Medical concern, probable prisoner of conscience: Ali Sarety.**

KMMR[7] played a role in the Mahajanga arrests. These reports allege that KMMR members told the army to arrest certain people. It seems these people were then arbitrarily arrested without any preliminary investigation purely to settle personal scores.

In accordance with Malagasy law, criminal investigation officers have the right to arrest people in connection with the investigations they are pursuing. Public order officials from the Gendarmerie, the police and security forces can arrest people suspected of committing crimes or offences but they must hand them over to a criminal investigation officer without undue delay.

The criminal investigation officers can only retain someone in custody for 48 hours, the legal period of *garde-à-vue*[8], police custody. People held in *garde-à-vue* can have access to a medical examination at the request of the criminal investigation officer in charge of the inquiry[9]

Amnesty International deplores the fact that Malagasy legal standards regulating arrest procedures have not been respected.

Irregularities concerning detainees' contact with the outside world

Access to adequate medical assistance

Many people held after the crisis, including those who were injured as a result of torture or ill-treatment, have not had access to adequate medical assistance and care. Further obstacles to appropriate medical treatment for the detainees are their conditions of detention, the lack of adequate hygiene and nutrition standards, and the overcrowding in prisons. This situation requires urgent attention.

Amnesty International is aware of the death in custody of at least one person arrested during the political crisis. The death was probably a result of his conditions of detention. Bernardin Tsano, a SIRAMA employee from Nosy-Be, was arrested with others at the end of June. He was transferred to Tsiafahy on 17 July. On 22 July he died from an asthma attack brought on by the dust and damp conditions, but mostly by the overcrowding in his cell. His body was returned to his family. There has been no inquiry into his death, and the authorities have taken no steps to reduce overcrowding or improve hygiene standards in Tsiafahy. According to the prison authorities, a doctor comes to Tsiafahy to examine the detainees twice a week and recommends hospitalisation if required. The decision about whether to hospitalise a detainee is taken by the chief guard at the prison. If there is a medical emergency, the chief guard calls the central prison authorities in Antananarivo to send a doctor. Because of the

---

[7] *Komity Mpanohana ny filatsahan'Atoa Marc Ravalomanana ho Filoha*, Marc Ravalomanana Support Committee, composed mainly of Marc Ravalomanana supporters and members of the TIM Association.
[8] Code of Penal Procedure, Article 136 (Law No 97-036 of 30 October 1997) A criminal investigation officer cannot hold anyone at his disposal for the requirements of preliminary investigation for longer than 48 hours.
[9] Article 138 (a) (Law No 97-036 of 30 October 1997).

distance between Tsiafahy and the capital, it could take a doctor between 30 minutes and one hour to reach the prison. There is no medical equipment or supplies at Tsiafahy and no infirmary where sick people can be separated from other detainees. One detainee stated that the only person able to give him advice was a fellow detainee who was a doctor.

Venance Raharimanana (already mentioned above) was transferred to hospital once his family had traced him. He was diagnosed as having an injury to his skull with the incumbent risk of loss of consciousness. Despite his state of health, his case was handed over to the prosecuting authorities in Antananarivo which charged him with "spreading false news" and "inciting crimes and offences" and he was placed under a committal order in Antanimora, the central prison in Antananarivo. He was held despite the prison doctor's concerns for his state of health. The prison doctor and a lawyer wrote to the Antananarivo Court to request Venance Raharimanana's hospitalisation because of the lack of adequate medical facilities at the prison. There was no response to their demands. Amnesty International was told by the chief guard of Antanimora that for security reasons it is the Court alone which can permit the transfer of a detainee to hospital. The Procurator of the Lower Court in Antananarivo told Amnesty International representatives that orders had been given to the prison authorities to transfer sick prisoners to hospital but this had not been possible because they lacked the personnel to ensure the prisoners did not escape. Amnesty International deeply regrets that Venance Raharimanana did not get access to adequate medical care despite many attempts to make the authorities aware of his seriously worrying state of health.

Access to family

The families of numerous people held in pre-trial custody following the political crisis were denied access to detention centres while the alleged crimes were being investigated. Other detainees, like Venance Raharimanana, were not able to tell their families where they were held. Their families had to contact the competent court to seek permission to be able to visit them. Normally, people in pre-trial custody are allowed such visits twice a week. These visits are essential not only to provide moral support to the detainees, but also because the family can bring food to supplement the meagre rations provided in prison. At least 20 detainees confirmed they were denied access to their family during July and August. When they asked why they were refused the right to communicate, the families were told it was for "political" or "security" reasons. Recent reports suggest that the right to communicate is now respected, apparently because the investigations are near to conclusion.

A Supreme Court of Madagascar decision of 2 July 2002 has made detainees' access to their families more difficult. Supreme Court Decision 70 "removed responsibility for the above mentioned offences from the normally competent jurisdictions and placed it with the sole jurisdiction of Antananarivo". The offences referred to by the Supreme Court were those "resulting from the economic barricades, and offences connected to attacks on state security and public and private possessions, and attacks on the physical integrity or restrictions on the individual freedom of others". According to Article 31 of Madagascar's Code of Penal Procedure: "Representatives of the prosecuting authorities in the place the crime was committed, the place where one of those suspected of having committed the crime resides, or the place of arrest of one of these people even when the arrest was carried out for another reason, are also competent to effect and proceed with a prosecution".

Some 200 people arrested in the provinces and accused of crimes or offences committed in the provinces have been transferred to Antananarivo to be tried. Travelling to the capital and finding accommodation, without any guarantee that they would be able to talk with the detainees, has caused the families financial and practical difficulties. Given that the majority of the detainees are men who provide the family's regular income, many families have not been able to travel to Antananarivo.

Right to the assistance of a lawyer

Most of the detainees currently held awaiting trial have been able to receive visits from their lawyers in prison. Malagasy law stipulates that all charged prisoners have the right to the assistance of a lawyer. Law 97/036 which modifies and completes Code of Penal Procedure provisions concerning defence for suspects and charged individuals, stipulates that when someone suspected of having committed a crime or offence attends the first hearing, the criminal investigation officer must inform them of their right to choose their defence from among the lawyers of the Malagasy Bar or that they many choose any other person to defend them. The law also states that the chosen defence can attend any interrogation, cross-examination and searches carried out in the context of the investigation.

However, some people have been refused the right to legal assistance. Tantely Andrianarivo, Prime Minister of the previous Didier Ratsiraka government, was placed under "house arrest" on 27 May 2002 when security forces loyal to Marc Ravalomanana stormed and captured his home. Two people guarding his home were killed during the attack. He was held under house arrest for almost five months without charge even though the Malagasy press reported that he was suspected by the new authorities of embezzling public funds. He was only allowed to communicate with his lawyers on one occasion, 5 July. His lawyers were able to visit him a second time on 7 or 8 October, when some foreign lawyers interested in his case visited Madagascar in October 2002. Amnesty International believes Tantely Andrianarivo was arbitrarily detained throughout this period when he was held without access to lawyer and without being charged with any offence from the penal code. His case was finally handed over to the prosecuting authorities in Antananarivo on 21 October. His hearing lasted nine hours. According to information available to Amnesty International, only one of his lawyers could attend the interrogation because it was claimed he was being questioned as a witness. However, following the interrogation he was charged with "usurping his function" "embezzling public funds" "harbouring criminals" and "threatening state security". He was transferred to Antanimora prison that same day.

Other people suspected of committing crimes or offences during the crisis have been denied access to legal assistance during their interrogation by the police or a magistrate. Having a lawyer present during police interrogation is an important deterrent to the risks of torture or ill-treatment. It is during interrogation by the prosecutor or the examining magistrate that charges can be brought against the suspect. It is crucial that a lawyer is present at that moment.

On 9 July General Jean-Paul Bory, Secretary of the National Gendarmerie who was nominated "Minister of Defence" by Didier Ratsiraka in March after General Marcel Ranjeva resigned the same post in Didier Ratsiraka's government, was arrested. On 25 July his case was passed to the Antananarivo prosecution authorities. The Prosecutor who interrogated him reportedly told him that he did not need a lawyer because he was only being interrogated as a witness. However, as the interrogation unfolded, he realised he was being questioned as a suspect. It was not until he sought the right for legal assistance that his lawyer was able to enter the room. He was charged with "rebellion" and placed under a committal order at Antanimora prison. It seems the same tactic has been used against other people in order to prevent them having access to the services of a lawyer during interrogation.

Conditions of detention

For decades human rights organisations and bodies both local and international have criticised the inhuman conditions of detention in Madagascar. According to information received by Amnesty International, a government program, led by the Ministry of Justice to improve conditions of detention, was put in place a few years ago. However, conditions of detention remain seriously below the minimum standards necessary to ensure the physical and psychological well-being of the detainees.

Those arrested following the crisis have been held in custody awaiting trial in overcrowded prisons which contravene the minimum standards for detention. Most of the officials from Didier Ratsiraka's government and the members of the security forces who remained loyal to him are held in Antananarivo, in Antanimora prison, or at the Tsiafahy detention centre. Amnesty International's main concerns in these centres are overcrowding and the disregard for standards of hygiene and nutrition. When Amnesty International representatives visited Antanimora prison 2,300 people were held there in a prison with capacity for 800. Around 65% of the detainees were held in pre-trial custody. Each area of the prison is equipped with a basic shower and toilet, but each area contained between 60 and 300 detainees. The prisoners are entitled to a meal of manioc or maize twice a day. These rations are complemented by charities and by families who bring food when they visit the prison.

Reports suggest that in the Tsiafahy detention centre – a place normally reserved for "serious criminals" – 620 people were held at the end of August even though the prison can only accommodate 200. The standards of hygiene and nutrition are below the minimum standards necessary to ensure respect for human dignity. Detainees are held together in cells which are far too small: information received from detainees states that one of the two rooms in Zone 1 is 12 metres long, 5 metres wide and 5 metres high. This room is expected to accommodate 50 detainees, but in August it held 120. There is only one toilet in each room, no running water and no electricity. The water given to detainees is rationed. Two concrete shelves in each room serve as beds where the detainees sleep one piled on top of another. There is no permanent infirmary or medical facilities at Tsiafahy.

The Malagasy authorities have acknowledged that the arrests following the political crisis have increased the prison population and they told Amnesty International representatives that improving the conditions of detention was one of their priorities. Amnesty International has received no information which would suggest that the detainees have been tortured or ill-treated by the prison guards. However, the organization believes that the conditions of detention could constitute cruel, inhuman and degrading treatment. Conditions of detention at Tsiafahy are such that they put the life of detainees at risk.

Amnesty International also deplores the fact that in contravention of international standards those detained awaiting trial are not separated from those already found guilty and sentenced.

Presumption of innocence

According to Madagascar's laws, all persons have the right to be presumed innocent and to be treated as such until they may be tried and found guilty. International standards stipulate that guilt can only be established if the trial meets prescribed standards of fairness. Under Malagasy law and in conformity with the right to be presumed innocent, detention of those awaiting trial is an exceptional measure[10]. Yet all those charged with penal offences relating to the political crisis remain held awaiting trial. The only people freed are those who have been acquitted or were released after being given the benefit of doubt during the trial, or those who have had their charges dismissed.

According to Law 97/036, the person facing charges can seek bail at any moment. However, many detainees have stated they would not make that request because they think it would be refused "as a result of the prevailing political climate" Others have had their request for bail refused. Amnesty International believes that the systematic refusal to grant bail has further eroded the right of those held in relation to the political crisis to be presumed innocent.

Arbitrary arrests and violations of the fundamental right to freedom of expression

People have been arbitrarily arrested and charged in the context of this crisis simply for expressing opinions or transmitting information which is seen as critical of the new government. Amnesty International has also received information that other people have been arrested as a result of false allegations made against them.

Nestor Rasolofonjatovo, journalist with FMA (*Feo Mazava Atsinanana*, Clear Voice of the East) radio in Toamasina which apparently benefited from some financial support from Pierrot Rajaonarivelo, one of Didier Ratsiraka's AREMA party leaders, was arrested and placed in pre-trial detention on 7 August after being charged with "spreading false news" and "incitement to tribal hatred". The accusations referred to two pieces of information the journalist had broadcast. One, dating back to the period when Didier Ratsiraka declared he

---

[10] Code of Penal Procedure, Article 333: Pre-trial detention is an exceptional measure.

had established his government in Toamasina, spoke of *Zatovo*[11], a group of young people in Toamasina who had apparently been paid by the pro-Ratsiraka authorities during the crisis and who were terrorising the local population and committing acts of violence. This extract apparently lasted one and a half minutes and reportedly gave information about a *Zatovo* meeting in Toamasina. The other piece spoke of the new President and was reportedly interpreted as a criticism of Marc Ravalomanana. After a week in pre-trial custody in Toamasina, Nestor Rasolofonjatovo was granted bail. On 10 September 2002 the Toamasina court acquitted him.

Venance Raharimanana (see earlier references to his case) was first questioned by the examining magistrate about false allegations that he had reportedly been a pro-Ratsiraka "militia" leader in Mahajanga during the crisis. After the interrogation he was eventually charged with "spreading false news" and "inciting crimes and offences". The charges were based on the allegation that he reportedly stated on the local Mahajanga television channel *Feon' ny Boina* that Mahajanga province was "independent " which was taken as proof of his support for the barricades erected against the capital. Amnesty International believes Venance Raharimanana was arrested solely for expressing his non-violent opinion and that he has been detained and tried in violation of his fundamental right to freedom of expression and opinion.

Arrest of political opponents

Many people including political opponents were arbitrarily detained when Didier Ratsiraka was in power as well as in the provinces under his control during the recent crisis. Since the Marc Ravalomanana government has been in power, this practice seems to be continuing. Most of those arrested following the political crisis are people associated with the former government. Members of AREMA have also been arrested and interrogated even though they had no clear link with the alleged offences relating to the period of political crisis. According to official statements, these people were arrested in connection with investigations about corruption[12]. Amnesty International is not opposed to judicial proceedings against those suspected of corruption. However, the organization is urging that all judicial proceedings conform to international standards of fairness. Amnesty International is concerned by the almost systematic arrest of people associated with the former government just as Marc Ravalomanana's government is seeking to assert its authority in the country.

On 1 October Elire Rabemananjara, an AREMA party member was arrested, handed over to the prosecuting authorities and questioned about alleged embezzlement of funds when he was the former Head of Cabinet to Pierre Rajaonarivelo, former Vice-Prime Minister under Didier Ratsiraka. On 3 October Roland Ratsiraka, nephew of Didier Ratsiraka and mayor of Toamasina, was arrested and taken to the court in Antananarivo. His interrogation focused on

---

[11] "Youth of Toamasina at the ready"
[12] Madagascar is considered to be of the most corrupt countries according to the non-governmental organization Transparency International's classification (Corruption Perception *Index 2002, Transparency International*).

suspicions of his corrupt activities, but he has since been questioned about his activities in Toamasina during the crisis. He has been released, but it is not known whether he has in fact been charged with any criminal offence.

Pierrot Rajaonarivelo, national secretary of AREMA and possible candidate in future parliamentary elections is currently in France. There are allegations that he may be subject to an order to return to Madagascar to present himself to face charges of corruption or alleged criminal offences linked to the political crisis. Members of AREMA believe that if such an order exists, it is simply a government tactic to stop Pierrot Rajaonarivelo returning to Madagascar to participate in the parliamentary elections.

Crimes punishable by death

According to information received by Amnesty International at least ten people have been charged with "threatening state security" as defined by Article 91, paragraph 3 of the Malagasy Penal Code which carries a prison sentence. Amnesty International is concerned that crimes connected to inciting civil war and arming civilians are punishable by death as stipulated in paragraph 1 of the same article of the Penal Code. Crimes relating to "treason" and "destruction of public goods" are also punishable by death according to articles of the Malagasy Penal Code.

No-one sentenced to death has been executed in Madagascar since independence; their sentences have been commuted to life imprisonment. The Constitution gives the President the right to grant clemency. Amnesty International is nevertheless concerned that some of those detained since the political crisis face accusations for crimes which carry the death penalty. The organization is opposed to the death penalty in all cases on the basis that it constitutes the most cruel inhuman and degrading punishment and violates the right to life.

Unfair Trials

The right to defend oneself

Anyone accused of a criminal offence has the right to defend themselves against those accusations. A fundamental aspect of this right to defence is the right of the accused to summons witnesses. Those arrested at the end of the crisis are mostly suspected of crimes or offences committed in the provinces of Mahajanga, Toamasina, Antsiranana and Toliara. Some 200 people are waiting to be tried in Antananarivo following Supreme Court decision 70 (see section on access to family). This presents further obstacles for the lawyers preparing to defend the accused, for example, distance from the capital, lack of good communications and the additional costs. The same logistical obstacles could prevent an accused person from summoning potential defence witnesses.

Amnesty International is concerned by reports that lawyers defending the accused are in a difficult situation and feel intimidated and harassed. Even if there is no direct threat against

the lawyers, they are apparently seen as "pro-Ratsiraka" and have received scornful remarks from some colleagues. They have also had difficulties when trying to consult their clients' files at court; for example they are often made to wait, and some have only been allowed to take notes from the file on the spot.

Amnesty International fears that the current political climate in Madagascar could also affect the right to defence and dissuade potential defence witnesses from coming to testify.

The right to a fair trial

According to reports some 50 people have already been tried for offences which come under the jurisdiction of a minor offences court. Those found guilty have appealed. Those charged with more serious crimes, in particular leading figures in the former government, are still awaiting trial. There is still no definite date set for their trial but it is reported that they will take place before the next parliamentary elections.

Amnesty International representatives observed the trial of Venance Raharimanana on 23 August. He was given a suspended two-year prison sentence. The main concerns of the organization with regard to this trial are as follows:

-    Venance Raharimanana was not informed of the date of his trial until two days before;

-    He was clearly suffering from wounds caused by torture and he was unable to walk into the trial chamber without help. However, his torture has not been investigated nor was it raised during the trial;

-    He had to respond before the court about his "activities in Mahajanga between March and June 2002"and "inciting state security crimes and offences "even though he was charged with "spreading false news" and "inciting crimes and offences".

The only "proof" provided by the prosecution was a video-cassette which reportedly showed the accused declaring that Mahajanga province was "independent". The existence of this video cassette was not revealed before the trial. The prosecution used a 30-second extract from the video cassette which showed the accused reading something. The source of this video cassette was not revealed and the entire recording was never played despite statements by the accused and his lawyer that the extracts used had been taken out of context. The accused explained he had read a letter written to him and he had used it in a television debate and at the time of the debate had himself warned against the dangers of secession in the provinces. The television debate was about the declaration of "independence for the provinces" made by pro-Ratsiraka governors during the political crisis. Neither the prosecution nor the defence summoned witnesses.

The trial was summary. The judge asked three questions of the accused, the prosecution asked three questions and the defence addressed the court. After posing a final question to the accused, the judge passed his verdict from the bench.

The conduct of Venance Raharimanana's trial raises serious doubts about the independence and impartiality of the justice system in Madagascar and calls into question respect for the principle that all are equal before the law.

The independence of the judicial system

Under Ratsiraka's presidency, there were reports that magistrates were intimidated to force them to favour those in power, and that their lack of resources and difficult working conditions reportedly led to corrupt practices. Generally speaking the judicial system was not seen as impartial while Ratsiraka was in power. Amnesty International representatives raised this point when they met members of the new government. One of the new government's proposed solutions to alleviate this problem was the Supreme Court Decision (see preceding sections) which gives the Lower Court of Antananarivo jurisdiction over offences relating to the 2002 crisis, because of allegations that the provincial courts were favourable to the former government. However, Amnesty International believes that it would be far more important to introduce reforms which would guarantee the independence, impartiality and efficiency of the magistrates. This would considerably reinforce the independence of the judicial system and the legal profession. The government could guarantee judicial independence by nominating magistrates in accordance with clear criteria which conform to international standards.

According to recent information, now that the new government has nominated several magistrates, provincial courts have reportedly regained their competence to try some offences connected to the crisis. However, Amnesty International is concerned by reports that some magistrates nominated by the new government to the highest posts within the Procuracy, in particular the procurators themselves, reportedly participated in Marc Ravalomanana's first investiture on 22 February. Marc Ravalomanana declared himself President before a crowd of more than 100,000 people in Antananarivo. This raises questions about their independence, their impartiality and their objectivity and also about the fundamental principles connected to the separation of powers. While their participation in the first investiture does not in itself diminish the qualities of those magistrates, it could be interpreted as compromising their actual independence. Some of those magistrates now have responsibility for judicial proceedings against members of the former government. Amnesty International is urging the government to demonstrate that judicial independence is guaranteed not only in Malagasy laws and the country's constitution, but also in practice.

International standards

By ratifying the International Covenant on Civil and Political Rights (ICCPR) and the African Charter on Human and Peoples' Rights (African Charter), Madagascar has undertaken to respect international standards regulating fair trials, and notably to guarantee the rights of any accused person at every stage of the procedure, from the time of arrest, while in detention, throughout the trial and appeal up to final judgement. These include the right not to be subjected to torture or to cruel, inhuman or degrading treatment, the right to liberty, the right not to be arrested or detained arbitrarily and the right to be presumed innocent.

According to Article 5 of the African Charter:

> *"Every individual shall have the right to the respect for dignity inherent in a human being .... All forms of exploitation and degradation of man particularly.... torture, cruel, inhuman or degrading punishment and treatment shall be prohibited."*

The African Commission on Human and Peoples' Rights stated that to detain an individual without allowing them access to their family and refusing to inform their family of their detention and their place of detention constitutes inhuman treatment of the detainee and the family concerned and that it constitutes a violation of Article 5 of the African Charter.

According to Article 6 of the African Charter:

> *"Every individual shall have the right to liberty and to the security of his person. No one may be deprived of his freedom except for reasons and conditions previously laid down by law. In particular, no one may be arbitrarily arrested or detained."*

The international treaties mentioned above guarantee the right of all individuals to be presumed innocent and to be treated as such unless they are convicted according to law in the course of proceedings which meet at least the minimum prescribed requirements of fairness. The right to be presumed innocent applies not only to the treatment in court and the evaluation of the evidence, but also to the treatment before trial.

It also means that the prosecution has to prove the accused person's guilt. If there is a reasonable doubt, the accused must not be found guilty. According to the Human Rights Committee, which oversees the application of the ICCPR: "[b]y reason of the presumption of innocence, the burden of proof of the charge is on the prosecution and the accused has the benefit of the doubt."

According to Article 7.1 of the African Charter:

> *"Every individual shall have the right to have his case heard .This comprises:*
>
> - *the right to an appeal to competent national organs against acts violating his fundamental rights as recognized and guaranteed by conventions, laws, regulations and customs in force;*
>
> - *the right to be presumed innocent until proved guilty by a competent court or tribunal;*
>
> - *the right to defence, including the right to be defended by counsel of his choice;*
>
> - *the right to be tried within a reasonable time by an impartial court or tribunal."*

According to the African Commission, all these provisions are mutually dependent and when the right to be heard is violated, that can lead to other violations, for example detentions which become arbitrary. Moreover the Commission has reiterated that the right to a fair trial implies the establishment of certain objective criteria in order to guarantee a fair trial for all, such as the right to equality before the law, the right to self defence and to be assisted by a lawyer, and an undertaking by the courts and tribunals to conform to international standards. The right to a fair trial is essential to the protection of all rights and fundamental freedoms.

The African Commission's resolution on the right to a fair trial stated that this includes among others the right to be informed of the reasons for arrest, at the moment of arrest and in a language the individual understands as well as the right to be informed of any charges. Once charges are drawn up against an individual, that person has the right to sufficient time and the necessary means to prepare their defence and the right to communicate confidentially with a lawyer of their choosing.

Article 14(3) of the ICCPR and Article 7(1) of the African Charter stipulate that judicial proceedings must be started and concluded within a reasonable time. This implies that while respecting the right of the accused to have sufficient time and the necessary means to prepare their defence, the procedure must start and the final judgement must be reached after exhausting appeal possibilities without excessive delays. This right binds the authorities to ensure that all procedures, from the pre-trial phase right through the appeals, are completed within a reasonable period. Any individual accused of a criminal offence and placed in pre-trial custody has the right to have their case given priority and to have proceedings conducted with particular expedition.

Amnesty International's Recommendations

Recommendations to the Government of Madagascar

Amnesty International recognises the right of each society to bring the perpetrators of crimes or offences, in particular those who violate human rights, to justice. Amnesty International reiterates that the fight against impunity for human rights abuses and violations is indispensable. The organization acknowledges that the new government came to power in difficult circumstances and is conscious of the obstacles it may face when dealing with the political crisis. However, Amnesty International believes that through its commitment to national legislation and international law, the Malagasy authorities have undertaken to respect and protect the human rights of all citizens. Amnesty International calls upon the government of Madagascar to implement all of the recommendations detailed above.

Furthermore, Amnesty International urges the government of Madagascar to respect and protect the principles enshrined in the following international standards:

• Universal Declaration of Human Rights;

• Body of Principles for the Protection of All Persons under Any Form of Detention or Imprisonment;

• Standard Minimum Rules for the Treatment of Prisoners;

- Basic Principles on the Role of Lawyers;

- Guidelines on the Role of Prosecutors;

- Basic Principles on the Independence of the Judiciary;

- Code of Conduct for Law Enforcement Officials.

Fighting impunity

- The government of Madagascar must open independent and impartial inquiries into all reports and allegations of serious human rights abuses, such as killings and torture. The government could create a commission of inquiry with a mandate not only to look into crimes and offences allegedly committed by the former government during the crisis, but also to investigate crimes and offences allegedly committed by supporters of the new government.

- The results of the inquiry and the methods used in carrying out the investigation should be made public.

- The potential perpetrators should be tried in accordance with international standards of fairness and without recourse to the death penalty.

- Anyone who has been subjected to torture or ill-treatment has the right to receive adequate medical treatment and redress.

- A system must be set up to protect the victims, their families and the potential witnesses of human rights abuse. Many people will not agree to testify unless their protection is guaranteed.

Preventing torture

- All detainees must be examined by a doctor as soon as possible after their arrest. An independent and impartial inquiry must be made into any allegation of torture in custody.

- Public instructions must be issued to all members of the security forces that acts of torture or ill-treatment will not be tolerated and those suspected of carrying out such acts will be brought to trial.

- Anyone suspected of committing acts of torture must be suspended from duty while awaiting the results of an independent and impartial inquiry.

- The government must ratify the Convention against Torture and Other Cruel, Inhuman or Degrading Treatment or Punishment without delay.

Preventing arbitrary arrests and detentions:

- In every case the government must respect the fundamental human rights to freedom of opinion, expression and association enshrined in Madagascar's Constitution and in international law. No one should be detained or imprisoned for non-violently expressing their opinions or for exercising their right to freedom of expression or association.

- Anyone suspected of committing a crime or offence in the context of the political crisis and currently in detention must be charged with an offence listed in the penal code and tried in accordance with international standards of fairness, or released.

- The government must take steps to prevent arbitrary arrests by ensuring that any arrest follows preliminary investigations which provide a clear basis for the arrest. All arrests must respect international standards of fairness.

- Measures must be taken to ensure that all members of the security forces who carry out arrests receive training about human rights which are guaranteed in international law including the right not to be arbitrarily or illegally arrested and the right to be presumed innocent.

- Anyone arrested must be immediately informed of the reasons for their arrest or detention and of the right to be assisted by a lawyer.

- The government must ensure that any detainee has the right to challenge the lawfulness of their detention at any moment while detained. If there is insufficient evidence against a person, they should be provisionally released while the investigation is completed or until charges are dropped.

Guaranteeing fair trials

- Every detainee has the right to adequate and regular medical assistance. The Malagasy authorities must guarantee any detainee is transferred to hospital if their state of health requires specific treatment.

- Every detainee has the right to contact with their family. Detainees' families must have regular and unrestrained access to their relative at any moment while in detention, including at the time of investigation.

- Measures must be taken to ensure the accused has the right to access the services of a lawyer at every stage of judicial proceedings, including the interrogation phase.

- Every person detained must be informed without delay of any charges against them and of the facts behind the accusations.

- Those defending people suspected of committing crimes and offences during the political crisis must be allowed to carry out their professional duties without intimidation and without being identified with their clients' alleged crimes.

- Steps must be taken to ensure that Supreme Court Decision 70 does not violate the right of detainees to have access to their families and their right to defence, including their right to summons witnesses.

- Everyone is equal before the law. Anyone who is brought to justice for alleged criminal offences must be tried by an impartial and independent court and have a fair trial.

Improving conditions of detention

- Urgent steps must be taken to provide prisons with adequate medical and other material facilities. When the government incarcerates someone, it makes an undertaking to care for that person. In particular the Tsiafahy detention centre where conditions are extremely dangerous must be provided with an infirmary, competent medical staff and satisfactory facilities. In order to improve standards of hygiene, food and medical assistance, the reforms of conditions in all of Madagascar's prisons must be implemented.

- Those detained awaiting trial must be separated from those who have been found guilty and convicted.

Death penalty

- The government must ratify the Second Optional Protocol to the International Covenant on Civil and Political Rights, aiming at the abolition of the death penalty.

- Amnesty International calls upon Madagascar's courts to not hand down death sentences and upon the President to commute any death sentences which may be passed.

- Particular attention must be paid to the fate of those accused of crimes which carry the death penalty, to ensure that they have access to a lawyer at every stage of proceedings, that they have sufficient time to prepare their defence and to prepare their appeal or petition for reprieve if they were to be sentenced to death.

Recommendations to the International Community

Amnesty International urges the international community to:

- Support and facilitate the work of doctors, hospitals and non-governmental organizations in Madagascar trying to provide medical and psychological help to victims of torture and their families;

- Assist the Malagasy prison service to improve conditions of detention and to guarantee that all detainees have access at all times to necessary medical care;

- Work with Madagascar's judicial system with a view to improving the competence, independence and impartiality of magistrates;

- Ensure that those accused of serious human rights abuses in Madagascar, for example torture and killings, are brought to trial or extradited, in line with the principle of universal competence. Some alleged perpetrators of serious human rights abuse have fled to other countries. Judicial proceedings for alleged perpetrators of human rights violations must be fair and must not impose the death penalty or cruel, inhuman or degrading punishments.

- Use its influence on the Malagasy authorities and the country's security forces to ensure that they respect international standards of human rights and that they implement the recommendations made above.

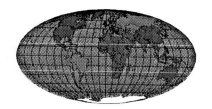

WORLD CLOTHING AND TTEXTILE INDUSTRY LIBRARY 2006

Price: $99.95 Each

1. Argentina Clothing & Textile Industry Handbook
2. Australia Clothing & Textile Industry Handbook
3. Austria Clothing & Textile Industry Handbook
4. Bangladesh Clothing & Textile Industry Handbook
5. Belgium Clothing & Textile Industry Handbook
6. Bolivia Clothing & Textile Industry Handbook
7. Brazil Clothing & Textile Industry Handbook
8. Bulgaria Clothing & Textile Industry Handbook
9. Canada Clothing & Textile Industry Handbook
10. China Clothing & Textile Industry Handbook
11. ChileClothing & Textile Industry Handbook
12. Colombia Clothing & Textile Industry Handbook
13. Costa Rica Clothing & Textile Industry Handbook
14. Cuba Clothing & Textile Industry Handbook
15. Czech Republic Clothing & Textile Industry Handbook
16. Denmark Clothing & Textile Industry Handbook
17. Dominican Republic Clothing & Textile Industry Handbook
18. Ecuador Clothing & Textile Industry Handbook
19. Egypt Clothing & Textile Industry Handbook
20. El Salvador Clothing & Textile Industry Handbook
21. Estonia Clothing & Textile Industry Handbook
22. European Union (EU) Clothing & Textile Industry Handbook
23. Fiji Clothing & Textile Industry Handbook
24. Finland Clothing & Textile Industry Handbook
25. France Clothing & Textile Industry Handbook
26. Germany Clothing & Textile Industry Handbook
27. Greece Clothing & Textile Industry Handbook
28. Hong Kong Clothing & Textile Industry Handbook
29. Hungary Clothing & Textile Industry Handbook
30. India Clothing & Textile Industry Handbook
31. Indonesia Clothing & Textile Industry Handbook
32. Israel Clothing & Textile Industry Handbook

For additional analytical, business and investment opportunities information,
please contact Global Investment & Business Center, USA
at (202) 546-2103. Fax: (202) 546-3275. E-mail: rusric@erols.com

33. **Italy Clothing & Textile Industry Handbook**
34. **Japan Clothing & Textile Industry Handbook**
35. **Jordan Clothing & Textile Industry Handbook**
36. **Kenya Clothing & Textile Industry Handbook**
37. **Korea, South Clothing & Textile Industry Handbook**
38. **Kuwait Clothing & Textile Industry Handbook**
39. **Laos Clothing & Textile Industry Handbook**
40. **Latvia Clothing & Textile Industry Handbook**
41. **Lithuania Clothing & Textile Industry Handbook**
42. **Malaysia Clothing & Textile Industry Handbook**
43. **Mauritius Clothing & Textile Industry Handbook**
44. **Mexico Clothing & Textile Industry Handbook**
45. **Myanmar Clothing & Textile Industry Handbook**
46. **Nepal Clothing & Textile Industry Handbook**
47. **New Zealand Clothing & Textile Industry Handbook**
48. **Norway Clothing & Textile Industry Handbook**
49. **Pakistan Clothing & Textile Industry Handbook**
50. **Paraguay Clothing & Textile Industry Handbook**
51. **Peru Clothing & Textile Industry Handbook**
52. **Philippines Clothing & Textile Industry Handbook**
53. **Portugal Clothing & Textile Industry Handbook**
54. **Romania Clothing & Textile Industry Handbook**
55. **Russia Clothing & Textile Industry Handbook**
56. **Samoa Clothing & Textile Industry Handbook**
57. **Singapore Clothing & Textile Industry Handbook**
58. **South Africa Clothing & Textile Industry Handbook**
59. **Spain Clothing & Textile Industry Handbook**
60. **Sri Lanka Clothing & Textile Industry Handbook**
61. **Swaziland Clothing & Textile Industry Handbook**
62. **Sweden Clothing & Textile Industry Handbook**
63. **Switzerland Clothing & Textile Industry Handbook**
64. **Taiwan Clothing & Textile Industry Handbook**
65. **Thailand Clothing & Textile Industry Handbook**
66. **Tunisia Clothing & Textile Industry Handbook**
67. **Turkey Clothing & Textile Industry Handbook**
68. **Ukraine Clothing & Textile Industry Handbook**
69. **United Kingdom Clothing & Textile Industry Handbook**
70. **United States Clothing & Textile Industry Handbook**
71. **Uruguay Clothing & Textile Industry Handbook**
72. **Vietnam Clothing & Textile Industry Handbook**
73. **Zambia Clothing & Textile Industry Handbook**

For additional analytical, business and investment opportunities information,
please contact Global Investment & Business Center, USA
at (202) 546-2103. Fax: (202) 546-3275. E-mail: rusric@erols.com

2006
WORLD INTERNATIONAL ORGANIZATIONS
BUSINESS AND DEVELOPMENT LIBRARY

1. Abu Dhabi Fund for Development Handbook
2. African Development Bank Group(AfDB) Handbook
3. African Development Fund (AfDF) Handbook
4. Nigeria Trust Fund (NTF) Handbook
5. African Export-Import Bank (AFREXIMBANK) Handbook
6. Andean Community General Secretariat Handbook
7. Andean Development Corporation (CAF) Handbook
8. Arab Authority for Agricultural Investment and Development (AAAID) Handbook
9. Arab Bank for Economic Development in Africa (BADEA) Handbook
10. Arab Fund for Economic and Social Development (AFESD) Handbook
11. Arab Gulf Programme for United Nations Development Organizations (AGFUND) Handbook
12. Arab Maghreb Union (AMU) Handbook
13. Arab Monetary Fund (AMF) Handbook
14. Arab Organization for Agricultural Development (AOAD)   Handbook
15. Arab Planning Institute - Kuwait Handbook
16. Arab Trade Financing Program (ATFP) Handbook
17. Asia-Pacific Economic Cooperation (APEC) Handbook
18. Asian and Pacific Coconut Community (APCC) Handbook
19. Asian Clearing Union (ACU) Handbook
20. Asian Development Bank (AsDB) Handbook
21. Association of Natural Rubber Producing Countries (ANRPC) Handbook
22. Association of South East Asian Nations (ASEAN) Handbook
23. Baltic Council of Ministers Handbook
24. Bank for International Settlements (BIS) Handbook
25. Bank of Central African States (BEAC) Handbook
26. Black Sea Trade and Development Bank (BSTDB) Handbook
27. Caribbean Centre for Monetary Studies (CCMS) Handbook
28. Caribbean Community (CARICOM) Handbook
29. Caribbean Development Bank (CDB) Handbook
30. Caribbean Regional Technical Assistance Centre (CARTAC) Handbook
31. Center for Latin American Monetary Studies (CEMLA) Handbook
32. Center for Marketing Information and Advisory Services for Fishery Products in Latin America and the Caribbean (INFOPESCA) Handbook
33. Central American Bank for Economic Integration (CABEI) Handbook
34. Central American Monetary Council (CAMC) Handbook
35. Central Bank of West African States (BCEAO) Handbook
36. Colombo Plan for Co-operative Economic and Social Development in Asia and the Pacific Handbook
37. Colombo Plan Staff College for Technician Education Handbook

38. **Common Fund for Commodities Handbook**
39. **Common Market for Eastern and Southern Africa (COMESA) Handbook**
40. **Cooperation Council for the Arab States of the Gulf (GCC) Handbook**
41. **Council of the Baltic Sea States (CBSS) Handbook**
42. **Council of Europe Development Bank (CEB) Handbook**
43. **East African Development Bank (EADB) Handbook**
44. **Eastern Caribbean Central Bank (ECCB) Handbook**
45. **Economic Community of West African States (ECOWAS) Handbook**
46. **Economic Cooperation Organization (ECO) Handbook**
47. **European Bank for Reconstruction and Development (EBRD) Handbook**
48. **European Central Bank (ECB) Handbook**
49. **European Free Trade Association (EFTA) Handbook**
50. **European Investment Bank (EIB) Handbook**
51. **European Investment Fund (EIF) Handbook**
52. **European Union, The (EC) Handbook**
53. **Financial Fund for the Development of the River Plate Basin (FONPLATA) Handbook**
54. **Food and Agriculture Organization of the United Nations (FAO) Handbook**
55. **Fund for Co-operation, Compensation and Development (ECOWAS Fund) Handbook**
56. **Inter-American Development Bank (IDB) Handbook**
57. **Inter-American Institute for Cooperation on Agriculture (IICA) Handbook**
58. **Inter-Arab Investment Guarantee Corporation (IAIGC) Handbook**
59. **International Atomic Energy Agency (IAEA) Handbook**
60. **International Civil Aviation Organization (ICAO) Handbook**
61. **International Cocoa Organization (ICCO) Handbook**
62. **International Coffee Organization (ICO) Handbook**
63. **International Confederation of Free Trade Unions (ICFTU) Handbook**
64. **International Cotton Advisory Committee (ICAC) Handbook**
65. **International Fund for Agricultural Development (IFAD) Handbook**
66. **International Grains Council Handbook**
67. **International Labour Organization (ILO) Handbook**
68. **International Lead and Zinc Study Group Handbook**
69. **International Monetary Fund (IMF) Handbook**
70. **International Olive Oil Council (IOOC) Handbook**
71. **International Rubber Study Group Handbook**
72. **International Sugar Organization (ISO) Handbook**
73. **International Telecommunications Union (ITU) Handbook**
74. **International Tropical Timber Organization (ITTO) Handbook**
75. **Islamic Development Bank Group (IsDB) Handbook**
76. **Islamic Research and Training Institute (IRTI) Handbook**
77. **Joint Vienna Institute (JVI)   Handbook**
78. **Kuwait Fund for Arab Economic Development Handbook**
79. **Lake Chad Basin Commission (LCBC) Handbook**
80. **Latin American Association of Development Financing Institutions (ALIDE) Handbook**
81. **Latin American Economic System (SELA) Handbook**
82. **Latin American Energy Organization (OLADE) Handbook**
83. **Latin American Export Bank (BLADEX) Handbook**
84. **Latin American Integration Association (ALADI) Handbook**
85. **Latin American Reserve Fund (LARF) Handbook**
86. **League of Arab States   Handbook**
87. **Mekong River Commission (MRC) Handbook**
88. **Nordic Development Fund (NDF) Handbook**

89. Nordic Investment Bank (NIB) Handbook
90. OPEC Fund for International Development Handbook
91. Organisation for Economic Co-operation and Development (OECD) Handbook
92. Organisation of Eastern Caribbean States (OECS) Handbook
93. Organization of American States (OAS) Handbook
94. Organization of Arab Petroleum Exporting Countries (OAPEC) Handbook
95. Organization of the Petroleum Exporting Countries (OPEC) Handbook
96. Pacific Financial Technical Assistance Centre Handbook
97. Pacific Islands Forum Secretariat Handbook
98. Pan American Health Organization (PAHO) Handbook
99. Regional Association of Oil and Natural Gas Companies in Latin America and the Caribbean (ARPEL) Handbook
100.   Regional Electrical Integration Commission (CIER) Handbook
101.   Saudi Fund for Development (SFD) Handbook
102.   Secretariat for Central American Economic Integration (SIECA) Handbook
103.   Secretariat of the Pacific Community Handbook
104.   Sectorial Commission for the Common Market of the South (MERCOSUR) - Uruguay Handbook
105.   South Asian Association for Regional Cooperation (SAARC) Handbook
106.   South-East Asian Central Banks (SEACEN) Research and Training Centre Handbook
107.   Training Centre for Regional Integration (CEFIR) Handbook
108.   United Nations African Institute for Economic Development and Planning (IDEP) Handbook
109.   United Nations Conference on Trade and Development (UNCTAD) Handbook
110.   United Nations Development Program (UNDP) Handbook
111.   United Nations Economic and Social Commission for Asia and the Pacific (ESCAP) Handbook
112.   Asian and Pacific Centre for Transfer of Technology (APCTT) Handbook
113.   Regional Coordination Centre for Research and Development of Coarse Grains, Pulses, Roots and Tuber Crops in the Humid Tropics of Asia and the Pacific (ESCAP CGPRT Centre) Handbook
114.   Statistical Institute for Asia and the Pacific (SIAP) Handbook
115.   United Nations Economic and Social Commission for Western Asia (ESCWA) Handbook
116.   United Nations Economic Commission for Africa (UNECA) Handbook
117.   United Nations Economic Commission for Europe (UN/ECE) Handbook
118.   United Nations Economic Commission for Latin America and the Caribbean (ECLAC) Handbook
119.   United Nations Educational, Scientific and Cultural Organization (UNESCO) Handbook
120.   United Nations Industrial Development Organization (UNIDO) Handbook
121.   United Nations Latin American and Caribbean Institute for Economic and Social Planning (ILPES) Handbook
122.   Universal Postal Union (UPU) Handbook
123.   West African Development Bank (BOAD) Handbook
124.   West Africa Economic and Monetary Union Handbook
125.   World Bank Group Handbook
126.   World Food Program (WFP) Handbook
127.   World Health Organization (WHO) Handbook
128.   World Trade Organization (WTO) Handbook

To order our publications as well as for additional analytical, business and investment opportunities information, please contact International Business Publications, USA at (202) 546-2103. Fax: (202) 546-3275. E-mail: rusric@erols.com

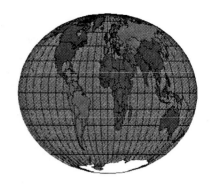

WORLD MINERAL & MINING SECTOR INVESTMENT & BUSINESS GUIDE LIBRARY
Price: $99.95 Each

1.	Afghanistan Mineral & Mining Sector Investment and Business Guide
2.	Albania Mineral & Mining Sector Investment and Business Guide
3.	Algeria Mineral & Mining Sector Investment and Business Guide
4.	Angola Mineral & Mining Sector Investment and Business Guide
5.	Argentina Mineral & Mining Sector Investment and Business Guide
6.	Armenia Mineral & Mining Sector Investment and Business Guide
7.	Australia Mineral & Mining Sector Investment and Business Guide
8.	Austria Mineral & Mining Sector Investment and Business Guide
9.	Azerbaijan Mineral & Mining Sector Investment and Business Guide
10.	Bahrain Mineral & Mining Sector Investment and Business Guide
11.	Bangladesh Mineral & Mining Sector Investment and Business Guide
12.	Belarus Mineral & Mining Sector Investment and Business Guide
13.	Belgium Mineral & Mining Sector Investment and Business Guide
14.	Benin Mineral & Mining Sector Investment and Business Guide
15.	Bolivia Mineral & Mining Sector Investment and Business Guide
16.	Bosnia and Herzegovina Mineral & Mining Sector Investment and Business Guide
17.	Botswana Mineral & Mining Sector Investment and Business Guide
18.	Brazil Mineral & Mining Sector Investment and Business Guide
19.	Brunei Mineral & Mining Sector Investment and Business Guide
20.	Bulgaria Mineral & Mining Sector Investment and Business Guide
21.	Burkina Faso Mineral & Mining Sector Investment and Business Guide
22.	Burundi Mineral & Mining Sector Investment and Business Guide
23.	Cambodia Mineral & Mining Sector Investment and Business Guide
24.	Cameroon Mineral & Mining Sector Investment and Business Guide
25.	Canada Mineral & Mining Sector Investment and Business Guide
26.	Cape Verde Mineral & Mining Sector Investment and Business Guide
27.	Cayman Islands Investment & Business Guide
28.	Central African Republic Mineral & Mining Sector Investment and Business Guide

For additional analytical, business and investment opportunities information,
please contact Global Investment & Business Center, USA
at (202) 546-2103. Fax: (202) 546-3275. E-mail: rusric@erols.com

29.	Chad Mineral & Mining Sector Investment and Business Guide
30.	Chile Mineral & Mining Sector Investment and Business Guide
31.	China Mineral & Mining Sector Investment and Business Guide
32.	Colombia Mineral & Mining Sector Investment and Business Guide
33.	Comoros Mineral & Mining Sector Investment and Business Guide
34.	Congo Mineral & Mining Sector Investment and Business Guide
35.	Congo, Dem. Republic Mineral & Mining Sector Investment and Business Guide
36.	Cook Islands Mineral & Mining Sector Investment and Business Guide
37.	Costa Rica Mineral & Mining Sector Investment and Business Guide
38.	Cote d'Ivoire Mineral & Mining Sector Investment and Business Guide
39.	Croatia Mineral & Mining Sector Investment and Business Guide
40.	Cuba Mineral & Mining Sector Investment and Business Guide
41.	Czech Republic Mineral & Mining Sector Investment and Business Guide
42.	Denmark Mineral & Mining Sector Investment and Business Guide
43.	Djibouti Mineral & Mining Sector Investment and Business Guide
44.	Dominican Republic Mineral & Mining Sector Investment and Business Guide
45.	Dubai Mineral & Mining Sector Investment and Business Guide
46.	Ecuador Mineral & Mining Sector Investment and Business Guide
47.	Egypt Mineral & Mining Sector Investment and Business Guide
48.	El Salvador Mineral & Mining Sector Investment and Business Guide
49.	Equatorial Guinea Mineral & Mining Sector Investment and Business Guide
50.	Eritrea Mineral & Mining Sector Investment and Business Guide
51.	Estonia Mineral & Mining Sector Investment and Business Guide
52.	Ethiopia Mineral & Mining Sector Investment and Business Guide
53.	Fiji Mineral & Mining Sector Investment and Business Guide
54.	Finland Mineral & Mining Sector Investment and Business Guide
55.	France Mineral & Mining Sector Investment and Business Guide
56.	Gabon Mineral & Mining Sector Investment and Business Guide
57.	Gambia Mineral & Mining Sector Investment and Business Guide
58.	Georgia Mineral & Mining Sector Investment and Business Guide
59.	Germany Mineral & Mining Sector Investment and Business Guide
60.	Ghana Mineral & Mining Sector Investment and Business Guide
61.	Greece Mineral & Mining Sector Investment and Business Guide
62.	Guatemala Mineral & Mining Sector Investment and Business Guide
63.	Guinea Mineral & Mining Sector Investment and Business Guide
64.	Guinea-Bissau Mineral & Mining Sector Investment and Business Guide
65.	Guyana Mineral & Mining Sector Investment and Business Guide
66.	Haiti Mineral & Mining Sector Investment and Business Guide
67.	Honduras Mineral & Mining Sector Investment and Business Guide
68.	Hungary Mineral & Mining Sector Investment and Business Guide
69.	Iceland Mineral & Mining Sector Investment and Business Guide
70.	India Mineral & Mining Sector Investment and Business Guide
71.	Indonesia Mineral & Mining Sector Investment and Business Guide

For additional analytical, business and investment opportunities information,
please contact Global Investment & Business Center, USA
at (202) 546-2103. Fax: (202) 546-3275. E-mail: rusric@erols.com

72.	Iran Mineral & Mining Sector Investment and Business Guide
73.	Iraq Mineral & Mining Sector Investment and Business Guide
74.	Ireland Mineral & Mining Sector Investment and Business Guide
75.	Israel Mineral & Mining Sector Investment and Business Guide
76.	Italy Mineral & Mining Sector Investment and Business Guide
77.	Jamaica Mineral & Mining Sector Investment and Business Guide
78.	Japan Mineral & Mining Sector Investment and Business Guide
79.	Jordan Mineral & Mining Sector Investment and Business Guide
80.	Kazakhstan Mineral & Mining Sector Investment and Business Guide
81.	Kenya Mineral & Mining Sector Investment and Business Guide
82.	Korea, North Mineral & Mining Sector Investment and Business Guide
83.	Korea, South Mineral & Mining Sector Investment and Business Guide
84.	Kuwait Mineral & Mining Sector Investment and Business Guide
85.	Kyrgyzstan Mineral & Mining Sector Investment and Business Guide
86.	Laos Mineral & Mining Sector Investment and Business Guide
87.	Latvia Mineral & Mining Sector Investment and Business Guide
88.	Lesotho Mineral & Mining Sector Investment and Business Guide
89.	Liberia Mineral & Mining Sector Investment and Business Guide
90.	Libya Mineral & Mining Sector Investment and Business Guide
91.	Lithuania Mineral & Mining Sector Investment and Business Guide
92.	Macedonia Republic Mineral & Mining Sector Investment and Business Guide
93.	Madagascar Mineral & Mining Sector Investment and Business Guide
94.	Malawi Mineral & Mining Sector Investment and Business Guide
95.	Malaysia Mineral & Mining Sector Investment and Business Guide
96.	Mali Mineral & Mining Sector Investment and Business Guide
97.	Mauritania Mineral & Mining Sector Investment and Business Guide
98.	Mauritius Mineral & Mining Sector Investment and Business Guide
99.	Mayotte Investment & Business Guide
100.	Mexico Mineral & Mining Sector Investment and Business Guide
101.	Micronesia Mineral & Mining Sector Investment and Business Guide
102.	Moldova Mineral & Mining Sector Investment and Business Guide
103.	Mongolia Mineral & Mining Sector Investment and Business Guide
104.	Morocco Mineral & Mining Sector Investment and Business Guide
105.	Mozambique Mineral & Mining Sector Investment and Business Guide
106.	Myanmar Mineral & Mining Sector Investment and Business Guide
107.	Namibia Mineral & Mining Sector Investment and Business Guide
108.	Nepal Mineral & Mining Sector Investment and Business Guide
109.	Netherlands Mineral & Mining Sector Investment and Business Guide
110.	New Zealand Mineral & Mining Sector Investment and Business Guide
111.	Nicaragua Mineral & Mining Sector Investment and Business Guide
112.	Niger Mineral & Mining Sector Investment and Business Guide
113.	Nigeria Mineral & Mining Sector Investment and Business Guide
114.	Norway Mineral & Mining Sector Investment and Business Guide

**For additional analytical, business and investment opportunities information,
please contact Global Investment & Business Center, USA
at (202) 546-2103. Fax: (202) 546-3275. E-mail: rusric@erols.com**

115. Oman Mineral & Mining Sector Investment and Business Guide
116. Pakistan Mineral & Mining Sector Investment and Business Guide
117. Papua New Guinea Mineral & Mining Sector Investment and Business Guide
118. Paraguay Mineral & Mining Sector Investment and Business Guide
119. Peru Mineral & Mining Sector Investment and Business Guide
120. Philippines Mineral & Mining Sector Investment and Business Guide
121. Poland Mineral & Mining Sector Investment and Business Guide
122. Portugal Mineral & Mining Sector Investment and Business Guide
123. Qatar Mineral & Mining Sector Investment and Business Guide
124. Romania Mineral & Mining Sector Investment and Business Guide
125. Russia Mineral & Mining Sector Investment and Business Guide
126. Rwanda Mineral & Mining Sector Investment and Business Guide
127. Sao Tome and Principe Mineral & Mining Sector Investment and Business Guide
128. Saudi Arabia Mineral & Mining Sector Investment and Business Guide
129. Scotland Mineral & Mining Sector Investment and Business Guide
130. Senegal Mineral & Mining Sector Investment and Business Guide
131. Sierra Leone Mineral & Mining Sector Investment and Business Guide
132. Slovakia Mineral & Mining Sector Investment and Business Guide
133. Slovenia Mineral & Mining Sector Investment and Business Guide
134. Somalia Mineral & Mining Sector Investment and Business Guide
135. South Africa Mineral & Mining Sector Investment and Business Guide
136. Spain Mineral & Mining Sector Investment and Business Guide
137. Sri Lanka Mineral & Mining Sector Investment and Business Guide
138. Sudan Mineral & Mining Sector Investment and Business Guide
139. Suriname Mineral & Mining Sector Investment and Business Guide
140. Swaziland Mineral & Mining Sector Investment and Business Guide
141. Sweden Mineral & Mining Sector Investment and Business Guide
142. Syria Mineral & Mining Sector Investment and Business Guide
143. Taiwan Mineral & Mining Sector Investment and Business Guide
144. Tajikistan Mineral & Mining Sector Investment and Business Guide
145. Tanzania Mineral & Mining Sector Investment and Business Guide
146. Thailand Mineral & Mining Sector Investment and Business Guide
147. Togo Mineral & Mining Sector Investment and Business Guide
148. Trinidad and Tobago Mineral & Mining Sector Investment and Business Guide
149. Tunisia Mineral & Mining Sector Investment and Business Guide
150. Turkey Mineral & Mining Sector Investment and Business Guide
151. Turkmenistan Mineral & Mining Sector Investment and Business Guide
152. Uganda Mineral & Mining Sector Investment and Business Guide
153. Ukraine Mineral & Mining Sector Investment and Business Guide
154. United Arab Emirates Mineral & Mining Sector Investment and Business Guide
155. United Kingdom Mineral & Mining Sector Investment and Business Guide
156. United States Mineral & Mining Sector Investment and Business Guide
157. Uruguay Mineral & Mining Sector Investment and Business Guide

For additional analytical, business and investment opportunities information,
please contact Global Investment & Business Center, USA
at (202) 546-2103. Fax: (202) 546-3275. E-mail: rusric@erols.com

158.	Uzbekistan Mineral & Mining Sector Investment and Business Guide
159.	Venezuela Mineral & Mining Sector Investment and Business Guide
160.	Vietnam Mineral & Mining Sector Investment and Business Guide
161.	Yemen Mineral & Mining Sector Investment and Business Guide
162.	Yugoslavia Mineral & Mining Sector Investment and Business Guide
163.	Zambia Mineral & Mining Sector Investment and Business Guide
164.	Zimbabwe Mineral & Mining Sector Investment and Business Guide
165.	Baltic Countries Mining and Mineral Industry Handbook
166.	North America Mining and Mineral Industry Handbook
167.	Pacific Countries Mining and Mineral Industry Handbook
168.	Russia and NIS Mining and Mineral Industry Handbook
169.	Africa – West Mining and Mineral Industry Handbook
170.	Caribbean Countries Mining and Mineral Industry Handbook
171.	Central Europe Mining and Mineral Industry Handbook
172.	Middle East Mining and Mineral Industry Handbook
173.	South America Mining and Mineral Industry Handbook
174.	EU Mining and Mineral Policy Handbook

For additional analytical, business and investment opportunities information,
please contact Global Investment & Business Center, USA
at (202) 546-2103. Fax: (202) 546-3275. E-mail: rusric@erols.com

GLOBAL ARMY, DEFENSE, INTELLIGENCE, COUNTERINTELLIGENCE, NATIONAL SECURITY HANDBOOK LIBRARY
(PRICE $99.95)

Ultimate handbooks on army, defense policy, intelligence, counterintelligence, national security and related operation, conducted by specific countries. National security and intelligence agencies operations and structure

TITLE
1. Albania Army, National Security and Defense Policy Handbook
2. Argentina Intelligence & Security Activities & Operations Handbook
3. Australia Army, National Security and Defense Policy Handbook
4. Australia Intelligence & Security Activities & Operations Handbook
5. Bangladesh Army, National Security and Defense Policy Handbook
6. Bulgaria and NATO Handbook
7. Bulgaria Department of Defense Handbook
8. Canada Intelligence & Security Activities & Operations Handbook
9. Canadian Security Intelligence Service (CSIS) Handbook
10. China Army, National Security and Defense Policy Handbook
11. Cuba Army, National Security and Defense Policy Handbook
12. Czech Repuiblic Army, National Security and Defense Policy Handbook
13. Estonia Army, National Security and Defense Policy Handbook
14. Estonia Intelligence & Security Activities & Operations Handbook
15. EUROPOL – EUROPEAN POLICE OFFICE Handbook
16. Finland Army, National Security and Defense Policy Handbook
17. Finland Intelligence & Security Activities & Operations Handbook
18. France Army, National Security and Defense Policy Handbook
19. German Intelligence & Security Activities & Operations Handbook
20. Germany Army, National Security and Defense Policy Handbook
21. Global Counter-Terrorism Handbook
22. Global National Intelligence and Security Agencies Handbook
23. Global Terrorism Attacks Encyclopedic Handbook
24. Greece Intelligence & Security Activities & Operations Handbook

To order and for additional analytical and marketing information, please contacrt
International Business Publications, USA at:
P.O. Box 15343, Washington, DC 20003, USA. Phone: (202) 546-2103. Fax: (202) 546-3275.
E-mail: rusric@erols.com

TITLE
25. **Hungary Army, National Security and Defense Policy Handbook**
26. Hungary Intelligence & Security Activities & Operations Handbook
27. **India Army, National Security and Defense Policy Handbook**
28. India Intelligence & Security Activities & Operations Handbook
29. India Textime Industry Investment and Business Guide
30. **Iraq Economic Sanctions, Customs, Trade Regulations and Procedures Handbook**
31. **Ireland Army, National Security and Defense Policy Handbook**
32. Ireland Intelligence & Security Activities & Operations Handbook
33. **Israel Army, National Security and Defense Policy Handbook**
34. Israel Intelligence & Security Activities & Operations Handbook
35. Italy Intelligence & Security Activities & Operations Handbook
36. **Japan Army, National Security and Defense Policy Handbook**
37. Japan Intelligence & Security Activities & Operations Handbook
38. Jordan Intelligence & Security Activities & Operations Handbook
39. **Korea North Army, National Security and Defense Policy Handbook**
40. **Korea South Army, National Security and Defense Policy Handbook**
41. Korea South Intelligence & Security Activities & Operations Handbook
42. **Latvia Army, National Security and Defense Policy Handbook**
43. **Lebanon Army, National Security and Defense Policy Handbook**
44. Lesotho Telecommunication Industry Investment Guide
45. **Lithuania Army, National Security and Defense Policy Handbook**
46. **Macedonia National Security, Army and Defence Policy Handbook**
47. **Malaysia Army, National Security and Defense Policy Handbook**
48. **Myanmar Army, National Security and Defense Policy Handbook**
49. **New Zealand Army, National Security and Defense Policy Handbook**
50. New Zealand Intelligence & Security Activities & Operations Handbook
51. **Norway Army, National Security and Defense Policy Handbook**
52. **Pakistan Army, National Security and Defense Policy Handbook**
53. Pakistan Intelligence & Security Activities & Operations Handbook
54. **Philippines Army, National Security and Defense Policy Handbook**
55. **Poland Army, National Security and Defense Policy Handbook**
56. Portugal Intelligence & Security Activities & Operations Handbook
57. **Romania Army, National Security and Defense Policy Handbook**
58. Romania Intelligence & Security Activities & Operations Handbook
59. **Russia Army, National Security and Defense Policy Handbook**
60. Russia Intelligence & Security Activities & Operations Handbook

To order and for additional analytical and marketing information, please contacrt
International Business Publications, USA at:
P.O. Box 15343, Washington, DC 20003, USA. Phone: (202) 546-2103. Fax: (202) 546-3275.
E-mail: rusric@erols.com

TITLE
61. **Russian KGB Handbook: Past and Present**
62. **Russian Navy Handbook: History and Modern Situation**
63. **Russia-NATO Cooperatiion Handbook**
64. **Singapore Army, National Security and Defense Policy Handbook**
65. **Slovak Republic Army, National Security and Defense Policy Handbook**
66. **South Africa Army, National Security and Defense Policy Handbook**
67. **South Africa Intelligence & Security Activities & Operations Handbook**
68. **Sri Lanka Army, National Security and Defense Policy Handbook**
69. **Starting Business (Incorporating) in India Encyclopedic Guide**
70. **Sweden Intelligence & Security Activities & Operations Handbook**
71. **Switzerland Army, National Security and Defense Policy Handbook**
72. **Switzerland Intelligence & Security Activities & Operations Handbook**
73. **Taiwan Army, National Security and Defense Policy Handbook**
74. **Taiwan Intelligence & Security Activities & Operations Handbook**
75. **Thailand Royal Army, National Security and Defense Policy Handbook**
76. **The French Foreign Legion Handbook**
77. **The INTERPOL Handbook**
78. **The United Stated Ambassadors Yearbook**
79. **Turkey Army, National Security and Defense Policy Handbook**
80. **Turkey Intelligence & Security Activities & Operations Handbook**
81. **UK Department of Trade and Industry (DTI) Handbook**
82. **UK Intelligence & Counterintelligence Handbook**
83. **UK Intelligence & Security Activities & Operations Handbook**
84. **UK Intelligence and Security Policy Handbook**
85. **UK MI5 Security Service Handbook**
86. **UK Military Intelligence Handbook**
87. **UK National Intelligence Service Handbook**
88. **UK National Police Handbook**
89. **UK Royal Airforce Handbook**
90. **UK Royal Army Handbook**
91. **UK Royal Navy Handbook**
92. **Ukraine Army, National Security and Defense Policy Handbook**
93. **Ukraine Intelligence & Security Activities & Operations Handbook**
94. **United Kingdom Army, National Security and Defense Policy Handbook**
95. **US Arms Sales to Foreign Countries Handbook**
96. **US Business Intelligence Handbook**

**To order and for additional analytical and marketing information, please contacrt
International Business Publications, USA at:
P.O. Box 15343, Washington, DC 20003, USA. Phone: (202) 546-2103. Fax: (202) 546-3275.
E-mail: rusric@erols.com**

TITLE
97. US Counterintelligence Operations against Cuba Handbook
98. US Defense Policy Handbook
99. US Federal Depository Libraries Directory
100. US Federal Government Directory
101. US Federal Grant Management Handbook
102. US Immingration Policy and Programs Handbook
103. US Military Intelligence Handbook
104. US Ocean Transportation Companies Directory
105. US Political Intelligence Handbook
106. US War Against International Terrorism Handbook
107. US War Against Iraq Handbook: Political Strategy and Operations
108. US-Russia Cooperation Against Terrorism Handbook
109. US-Russia Economic & Financial Cooperation Handbook
110. US-Russia Military Cooperation Handbook
111. US-Russia Political Cooperation Handbook
112. US-Russia Scientific & Techological Cooperation Handbook
113. US-Russia Space Cooperation Handbook

To order and for additional analytical and marketing information, please contacrt
International Business Publications, USA at:
P.O. Box 15343, Washington, DC 20003, USA. Phone: (202) 546-2103. Fax: (202) 546-3275.
E-mail: rusric@erols.com

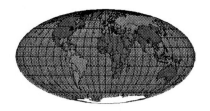

WORLD MEDICAL & PHARMACEUTICAL INDUSTRY LIBRARY 2006
Price: $99.95 Each

Title *
1. Australia Medical & Pharmaceutical Industry Handbook
2. Austria Medical & Pharmaceutical Industry Handbook
3. Bangladesh Medical & Pharmaceutical Industry Handbook
4. Belgium Medical & Pharmaceutical Industry Handbook
5. Canada Medical & Pharmaceutical Industry Handbook
6. China Medical & Pharmaceutical Industry Handbook
7. Costa Rica Medical & Pharmaceutical Industry Handbook
8. Cuba Medical & Pharmaceutical Industry Handbook
9. Czech Republic Medical & Pharmaceutical Industry Handbook
10. Egypt Medical & Pharmaceutical Industry Handbook
11. Estonia Medical & Pharmaceutical Industry Handbook
12. Finland Medical & Pharmaceutical Industry Handbook
13. France Medical & Pharmaceutical Industry Handbook
14. Germany Medical & Pharmaceutical Industry Handbook
15. Greece Medical & Pharmaceutical Industry Handbook
16. Hungary Medical & Pharmaceutical Industry Handbook
17. India Medical & Pharmaceutical Industry Handbook
18. Indonesia Medical & Pharmaceutical Industry Handbook
19. Israel Medical & Pharmaceutical Industry Handbook
20. Italy Medical & Pharmaceutical Industry Handbook
21. Japan Medical & Pharmaceutical Industry Handbook
22. Korea, South Medical & Pharmaceutical Industry Handbook
23. Kuwait Medical & Pharmaceutical Industry Handbook
24. Laos Medical & Pharmaceutical Industry Handbook
25. Latvia Medical & Pharmaceutical Industry Handbook

For additional analytical, business and investment opportunities information,
please contact Global Investment & Business Center, USA
at (202) 546-2103. Fax: (202) 546-3275. E-mail: rusric@erols.com

Title *
26. Lithuania Medical & Pharmaceutical Industry Handbook
27. Malaysia Medical & Pharmaceutical Industry Handbook
28. Mexico Medical & Pharmaceutical Industry Handbook
29. Myanmar Medical & Pharmaceutical Industry Handbook
30. Pakistan Medical & Pharmaceutical Industry Handbook
31. Palau Medical & Pharmaceutical Industry Handbook
32. Palestine Medical & Pharmaceutical Industry Handbook
33. Philippines Medical & Pharmaceutical Industry Handbook
34. Russia Medical & Pharmaceutical Industry Handbook
35. Singapore Medical & Pharmaceutical Industry Handbook
36. South Africa Medical & Pharmaceutical Industry Handbook
37. Sri Lanka Medical & Pharmaceutical Industry Handbook
38. Sweden Medical & Pharmaceutical Industry Handbook
39. Taiwan Medical & Pharmaceutical Industry Handbook
40. Thailand Medical & Pharmaceutical Industry Handbook
41. Turkey Medical & Pharmaceutical Industry Handbook
42. Ukraine Medical & Pharmaceutical Industry Handbook
43. United Kingdom Medical & Pharmaceutical Industry Handbook
44. United States Medical & Pharmaceutical Industry Handbook

For additional analytical, business and investment opportunities information,
please contact Global Investment & Business Center, USA
at (202) 546-2103. Fax: (202) 546-3275. E-mail: rusric@erols.com

NEW! WORLD OFFSHORE, LAW, INVESTMENT & BUSINESS LIBRARY

**Detailed Information on conducting business and investment activity in the countries
with special offshore status
Price: $99.95 each**

Andorra Offshore Investment and Business Guide
Anguilla Offshore Investment and Business Guide
Bahamas Offshore Investment and Business Guide
Barbados Offshore Investment and Business Guide
Belize Offshore Investment and Business Guide
Bermuda Offshore Investment and Business Guide
British Virgin Islands Offshore Investment and Business Guide
Cayman Islands Offshore Investment and Business Guide
Cook Islands Offshore Investment and Business Guide
Costa Rica Offshore Investment and Business Guide
Cyprus Offshore Investment and Business Guide
Dubai Offshore Investment and Business Guide
Gibraltar Offshore Investment and Business Guide
Grenada Offshore Investment and Business Guide
Guernsey Offshore Investment and Business Guide
Hong Kong Offshore Investment and Business Guide
Ireland Offshore Investment and Business Guide
Isle of Man Offshore Investment and Business Guide
Jersey Offshore Investment and Business Guide
Labuan Offshore Investment and Business Guide
Liechtenstein Offshore Investment and Business Guide
Luxembourg Offshore Investment and Business Guide
Madeira Offshore Investment and Business Guide
Malta Offshore Investment and Business Guide
Mauritius Offshore Business and Investment Opportunities Handbook
Mauritius Offshore Investment and Business Guide
Monaco Offshore Investment and Business Guide
Nauru Offshore Investment and Business Guide
Netherlands Antilles Offshore Investment and Business Guide
Panama Offshore Investment and Business Guide
Seychelles Offshore Investment and Business Guide
Switzerland Offshore Investment and Business Guide
Turks & Caicos Islands Offshore Investment and Business Guide
Vanuatu Offshore Investment and Business Guide

**To order and for additional analytical and marketing information, please contacrt
International Business Publications, USA at:
P.O. Box 15343, Washington, DC 20003, USA. Phone: (202) 546-2103. Fax: (202) 546-3275.
E-mail: rusric@erols.com**

Basic Laws and Regulations for conducting business and investment activity in the countries with special offshore status

Andorra Offshore Business Law Handbook
Anguilla Offshore Business Law Handbook
Bahamas Offshore Business Law Handbook
Barbados Offshore Business Law Handbook
Belize Offshore Business Law Handbook
Bermuda Offshore Business Law Handbook
British Virgin Islands Offshore Business Law Handbook
Cayman Islands Offshore Business Law Handbook
Cook Islands Offshore Business Law Handbook
Costa Rica Offshore Business Law Handbook
Cyprus Offshore Business Law Handbook
Dubai Offshore Business Law Handbook
Gibraltar Offshore Business Law Handbook
Grenada Offshore Business Law Handbook
Guernsey Offshore Business Law Handbook
Hong Kong Offshore Business Law Handbook
Ireland Offshore Business Law Handbook
Isle of Man Offshore Business Law Handbook
Jersey Offshore Business Law Handbook
Labuan Offshore Business Law Handbook
Liechtenstein Offshore Business Law Handbook
Luxembourg Offshore Business Law Handbook
Madeira Offshore Business Law Handbook
Malta Offshore Business Law Handbook
Mauritius Offshore Business and Investment Opportunities Handbook
Mauritius Offshore Business Law Handbook
Monaco Offshore Business Law Handbook
Nauru Offshore Business Law Handbook
Netherlands Antilles Offshore Business Law Handbook
Panama Offshore Business Law Handbook
Seychelles Offshore Business Law Handbook
Switzerland Offshore Business Law Handbook
Turks & Caicos Islands Offshore Business Law Handbook
Vanuatu Offshore Business Law Handbook

To order and for additional analytical and marketing information, please contacrt
International Business Publications, USA at:
P.O. Box 15343, Washington, DC 20003, USA. Phone: (202) 546-2103. Fax: (202) 546-3275.
E-mail: rusric@erols.com

Printed in the United States
49184LVS00001B/167-168